5TH EDITION

BASIC ALLIED HEALTH
STATISTICS & ANALYSIS

Lorie Darche, RN, MBA, MS | Gerda Koch, MA, RHIA

CENGAGE

Australia • Brazil • Mexico • Singapore • United Kingdom • United States

Basic Allied Health Statistics and Analysis
Fifth Edition-Lorie Darche, RN, MBA, MS \ Gerda Koch, MR, RHIA

SVP, GM Skills & Global Product Management: Jonathan Lau

Product Director: Matthew Seeley

Executive Director, Content Design: Marah Bellegarde

Learning Designer Director: Juliet Steiner

Associate Product Manager: Lauren Whalen

Learning Designer: Deborah Bordeaux

Product Assistant: Jessica Molesky

Vice President, Strategic Marketing Service: Jennifer Baker

Market Manager: Jonathan Sheehan

Senior Director, Content Delivery: Wendy Troeger

Manager, Content Delivery: Stacey Lamodi

Content Manager: Mark Peplowski

Art Designer: Angela Sheehan

Cover image(s): © Zffoto/ Shutterstock.com

For product information and technology assistance, contact us at
Cengage Customer & Sales Support, 1-800-354-9706
For permission to use material from this text or product,
submit all requests online at **www.cengage.com/permissions.**
Further permissions questions can be e-mailed to
permissionrequest@cengage.com

Library of Congress Control Number: 2018962211

ISBN-13: 978-1-337-79696-5

Cengage
20 Channel Center Street
Boston, MA 02210
USA

Cengage is a leading provider of customized learning solutions with employees residing in nearly 40 different countries and sales in more than 125 countries around the world. Find your local representative at: **www.cengage.com**.

Cengage products are represented in Canada by Nelson Education, Ltd.

Printed in the United States of America
Print Number: 02   Print Year: 2020

TABLE OF CONTENTS

PREFACE

This book was designed and developed to provide students in health care programs, such as health information management/technology, health informatics technology, medical assisting and surgical technology, with a beginning understanding of the terms, definitions, and formulas used in computing health care statistics and to provide self-testing opportunities and applications of the statistical formulas. Although the book was developed with the health information student in mind, the material is applicable to all health care professionals and students enrolled in allied health statistics and analysis. The primary emphasis is on inpatient health care data and statistical computations, but most applications can be transferred to the outpatient or alternative health care setting as well. Written at a level that even the novice can read and comprehend, this book should be useful for students who have been afraid of or who have not understood statistical concepts.

Definitions, formulas, and terms are available in other books, but very few computational problems are included in these books. The major weakness an instructor encounters when teaching students is not so much that they cannot manipulate a formula but that they have difficulties in selecting the appropriate number to be used in the formula. Statistical skills are best acquired and developed through actual use and analysis of data. This book provides many opportunities for computing various health care rates.

Most data are no longer captured manually; the data are entered instead into a computer and are available electronically. Many organizations have also installed software packages that can assist in the collection and calculation of many statistics deemed important for the organization and its key stakeholders. The electronic patient record has become the norm in most health care settings. Even with the computerization of statistical data, it is still imperative that health information professionals understand the meaning of statistical data and how it was derived.

Although "statistics" is a term that creates a phobic state in some students due to its association with mathematics, the problems throughout this book can be accomplished with basic arithmetic skills (addition, subtraction, multiplication, and division) and computation is aided with the use of a calculator and/or computer. Overall this book provides a step-by-step approach to assist students in building a vocabulary of key terms associated with health care statistics, as well as practice in developing skills in computing specific statistics.

CHAPTER FEATURES

- Each chapter is organized into a chapter outline, learning objectives, presentation of the topic, examples, self-tests, chapter summary, and chapter exam.

- Self-tests are generally included following the topic presented to ensure better comprehension.

- The chapter exams may include review questions relating to a previous chapter. The review questions are identified by an asterisk (*) followed by an R and the chapter in which the topic was presented. For example, an *R7 indicates a review question based on Chapter 7.

- Review questions are provided to reinforce knowledge previously acquired.

- The appendix includes a section on definitions, formulas, abbreviations, and quick reference sheets. The quick reference sheets are designed to be torn out and used for handy reference and computation aids.

NEW TO THIS EDITION

- Chapters have been realigned, based primarily on user-faculty input, to better scaffold learning concepts for the student.

- A new chapter on Nonclinical Statistics has been added.

- Additional end of chapter review questions have been added to enhance student content comprehension.

- Answer rationales are provided in the *Instructor's Manual* answer keys for quick instructor reference.

ABOUT THE AUTHOR

Lorie Darche, RN, MBA, MS is a faculty member at Lake Erie College of Osteopathic Medicine in the Masters of Health Services Administration program.

Her work history includes clinical and administrative nursing work, work in hospital finance, decision support and strategic planning and healthcare consulting. In addition, she has fourteen years of undergraduate and graduate faculty and administration experience. Her teaching experience covers the domains of health care, business and accounting. She holds a bachlor's degree in nursing and graduate degrees in business administration and accounting. This book is a revision of the prior work compiled by Gerda Koch, MA, RHIA.

Health Statistics: *Why Are They Important?*

CHAPTER OUTLINE

A. Introduction
  1. Scope of the Book and the Role of the HIM Department
  2. Why Study Statistics?
  3. What Is Statistics?
  4. Types of Statistics
  5. Data/Data Terms
B. Health Care Data Collection
  1. Sources of Health Care Data
  2. Requestors of Health Care Data
  3. Uses of Health Care Data
  4. Management Decisions
  5. Patient Care Decisions
  6. Users of Health Care Data
  7. Major Health Care Collection Entities
C. Abbreviations
D. Summary
E. Chapter 1 Test

LEARNING OBJECTIVES

After studying this chapter, the learner should be able to:

✓ Define statistics and data.

✓ Identify requestors of health care data.

✓ Identify uses of health care data.

✓ Identify users of health care data.

✓ Interpret abbreviations used in health care statistics.

✓ Distinguish between key statistical terms such as primary and secondary data, qualitative and quantitative data, and population and samples.

PRELIMINARY QUESTIONS

1. Distinguish between:
   a. Data and information
   b. Population and sample
   c. Primary and secondary data
   d. Constant and variable
   e. Representative sample and random sample
   f. Morbidity and mortality
2. Define demography/demographic variables.
3. Define vital statistics.
4. Name three users of health care data.
5. Name three uses of health care data.
6. Name a U.S. government public health agency or department.
7. Identify the following abbreviations:
   a. IP   c. DOA   e. Σ
   b. OP   d. NB

A. INTRODUCTION

1. Scope of the Book and the Role of the Health Information Management Department

The purpose of this book is to introduce the reader to the terms, formulas, and computations applicable to health care statistics, with the major emphasis on inpatient hospital statistics. Much of what applies in the inpatient hospital setting can be equally applied in other health care settings such as ambulatory care, nursing home care, cancer care, and other care facilities. In the past two decades, hospital lengths of stay have decreased, and outpatient facilities are handling more of patient care. The major focus of this book is the statistical treatment of inpatient hospital statistics, and it is assumed that the data referred to are inpatient hospital data unless otherwise specified. The general principles that will be applied to the inpatient setting can also be used for settings across the health care continuum.

It is anticipated that the book's content and problems will be useful to health care personnel whose function is the collection and interpretation of numerical data, especially health information personnel. The Health Information Management (HIM) and the Decision Support Departments are frequently responsible for compiling, collecting, and organizing data. This book provides material and problems to facilitate the processing and interpretation of these numerical data by the responsible personnel.

The health care industry is challenged by the fact that it has access to tremendous amounts of information. Those responsible for collecting information within a health care facility need to determine which data to collect to effectively report performance and to support decision making. The goal is to collect the right amount of information that is useful, value-added, and cost-effective for the organization. Since HIM professionals are often in the forefront of collecting and presenting much of the data necessary in the operation of a health care facility, HIM practitioners need a basic understanding of statistics as applied to health care information, both in the collection of the appropriate data elements and in their appropriate use. Results are only as reliable as the accuracy of the data input, which should then be appropriately analyzed, reported, and understood by all key stakeholders.

2. Why Study Statistics?

Statistical data collection has increased over the last several decades with the growing availability of computers and statistical software packages. Media reports these days often contain statistical data and graphics when reporting on disasters; for example, the number of casualties resulting from a tornado, hurricane, earthquake, or deaths due to auto accidents, new cases of a disease, number of workers losing jobs, or the percentage of the population who are cigarette smokers. Statistics even come in simple forms such as the miles per gallon that cars have depending on whether they use gasoline, diesel, hybrid fuels, or electricity.

The health care industry is a major collector of data. Patient care data and patient care statistics are compiled daily; and these data are then compiled into daily, weekly, monthly, and yearly reports. To collect, calculate, and interpret health care data appropriately, the user needs an understanding of the basic concepts, terms, and formulas relating to health care statistics. Most of health care personnel collect and report some type of statistical data. This includes patient care data (such as lab test results, operative procedures, or number of babies born on a specific day) and administrative data (such as number of hospital beds occupied or vacant on any specified day and on each clinical unit, number of discharges, or number of staff required to adequately staff and provided optimal care). To accurately assess and manage data, the user needs an understanding of how data is collected, why specific data is meaningful, how to use appropriate formulas, and how to properly evaluate and report data and statistics.

3. What Is Statistics?

Statistics has two meanings:

(1) *Statistics* is a numerical fact. Numerical facts include the number representing:

    (a) A family's income

    (b) The age of a patient

    (c) Touchdowns thrown by a quarterback in a season

    (d) The amount spent on flu shots in the United States in a given year according to the Centers for Disease Control and Prevention (CDC)

    (e) The number of pregnancies a woman has had

(2) *Statistics* is a field or discipline of study. A basic definition of *statistics* is the method of collecting, organizing, analyzing, presenting, and interpreting numerical data. Statistical methods help us make scientific and intelligent decisions based on the data collected. Decisions made based on scientific methods are called *educated guesses*, whereas those made without such methods are *pure guesses* and may prove to be unreliable. Reasonable decisions and valid conclusions may be drawn based on the analysis of statistical data. *Statistics* therefore involves both numbers and the techniques and procedures to be followed in collecting, organizing, analyzing, interpreting, and presenting information in a numerical form. Although the term *statistics* is a broad term, it is narrowed and defined by its representative group data—such as accident statistics, hospital statistics, employment statistics, vital statistics, and several other descriptors.

4. Types of Statistics

Statistics has two main aspects: theoretical and applied. *Theoretical statistics* deals with the development, derivation, and proof of statistical theorems, formulas, rules, and laws. *Applied statistics* involves the application of those theorems, formulas, rules, and laws to solve real-world problems. **This text is concerned only with *applied statistics* and more specifically *health care statistics*.**

Applied statistics can be divided into two areas: *descriptive statistics* and *inferential statistics*.

(1) *Descriptive Statistics.* Descriptive statistics describe and analyze a given group without drawing any conclusions or inferences about a larger group; they describe a population. Once data have been assembled and tabulated according to some useful categories, they then need to be summarized to determine the general trend of the data. Descriptive statistics deal with data that are enumerated, organized, and possibly graphically represented. The decennial census carried out by the U.S. government is an example of descriptive statistics. Data gathered and obtained can then be compiled into some type of table or graph. All the statistics in this text are descriptive statistics.

(2) *Inferential Statistics.* Inferential statistics give information regarding kinds of claims or statements that can be reasonably made about the population based on data from a sample. Inferential statistics are concerned with reaching conclusions. At times, the information

available is incomplete, and generalizations are reached based on the data available. When generalizations about a population are made based on information obtained from a sample, inferential statistics are utilized. A common example includes making inferences about a population based on opinion polls. This type of statistical treatment is most frequently found in more advanced statistical texts. Inferential statistics consists of methods that use sample results to help make decisions or predictions about a population.

5. **Data/Data Terms**

   (a) **Data versus Information**

   Data is roughly defined as facts—measured or otherwise determined facts or propositions, basic facts, or observations; information organized for analysis or used as the basis for a decision; or numerical information. Data are those facts that any situation provides to an observer. Some sources define data as raw facts and figures that are meaningless in and of themselves and refer to information as meaningful data—knowledge resulting from processing data. The term *data* is generally and preferably the plural of the singular datum, although it has become increasingly accepted in the singular construction as well.

   Information is data selected, organized, and processed to be useful.

   (b) **Data Set**

   Data, as described, are the dates, numbers, symbols, words, and values that represent an observation or measurement about people, processes, and conditions. A *data set* is a collection of observations on one or more variables.

   Suppose a class is given a statistics exam. The scores of all the students in the class comprise a *data set*. The name of each student is called an *element*, and the score of each individual student is called an *observation*. A data set in its original form may contain a very large number of observations. It is easier to draw conclusions or make decisions when the data are summarized into a more manageable form and size through statistical formulas and presented in a more understandable format that may or may not include tables or graphs.

   (c) **Data Collection:** The process by which data are gathered.

   (d) **Data Processing:** According to *Merriam-Webster's Dictionary*, the definition of data processing is "the converting of raw data to machine-readable form and its subsequent processing (such as storing, updating, rearranging, or printing out) by a computer." https://www.merriam-webster.com/dictionary/data%20processing July 15, 2018

   (e) **Data Accuracy:** Data free of identifiable errors.

   (f) **Aggregate Data:** Data extracted from individual (health) records and combined to form de-identified information about the (patient) group that can be compared and analyzed.

   (g) **Research Data:** Data used for the purpose of testing a hypothesis or answering a proposed question.

(h) Qualitative versus Quantitative Variables

    (1) *Qualitative Variables*: Qualitative variables yield observations that can be categorized according to some characteristic or quality. Examples include a person's occupation, marital status, education level, and race.

    (2) *Quantitative Variables*: Quantitative variables yield observations that can be measured. Examples include height, weight, blood pressure, serum cholesterol, heart rate, etc. Quantitative data are subdivided into discrete and continuous data.

(i) Discrete Data versus Continuous Data

    (1) *Discrete Data*: Data always expressed as a whole number or integer (a number without a fractional or decimal subdivision). Discrete data are most commonly obtained by counting, for example, the number of teeth in the mouth, the number of admissions in a hospital, number of children in a family, or the number of pregnancies. (In other words, it would be inaccurate to report 2.5 teeth or 3.5 pregnancies.)

    (2) *Continuous Data*: Measurable quantities not restricted to a whole number; data that fall into the category of "measured to the nearest." Continuous data can be measured in fractions or decimals, as in a runner ran 3.5 miles or a person is 5 feet 8 inches tall. Measurements can be recorded dependent on the specificity required. For instance, distance can be measured to the nearest mile, to the nearest half mile, quarter mile, eighth of a mile, or whatever specificity is designated. Data measured in decimal fractions but recorded to the nearest whole number are still continuous data. Height, weight, and age are all continuous variables. A person who is two months away from his or her 22nd birthday is closer to age 22 than to age 21; but in most instances, that person would be considered to be age 21 until his or her actual birthday. An individual whose height measures 5 feet 4¾ inches is closer to 5 feet 5 inches than 5 feet 4 inches.

✔ SELF-TEST 1-1

1. Indicate whether the following represent quantitative or qualitative data:

    a. Eye color _____

    b. Heart rate per minute _____

    c. Number of hospital admissions in the past year _____

2. Indicate whether the following represents discrete or continuous data:

    a. Number of incomplete medical records for the past week _____

    b. Patient's age recorded on preadmission _____

    c. Time taken to complete an examination _____

    d. Class ranking a graduating class _____

(j) Categorical Data: Four types of data (nominal, ordinal, interval, and ratio) that represent values or observations that can be sorted into a category; also referred to as scales of measurement.

(1) *Nominal Data*:
Nominal data are qualitative data in which a number is assigned to elements within a category. The data are often coded information. For instance, distinguishing a person's eye color with a code number such as 1 for blue eyes or #2 for brown eyes is an example of nominal data. Race is similarly (such as White, #1; African American, #2; Asian, #3; American Indian, #4; etc.). Other examples may include employment status (unemployed, #1; employed, #2; disabled, #3; etc.), sex (male, #1; female, #2), insurance carriers, and payment categories. It is *inappropriate* to perform arithmetic operations on nominal data.

(2) *Ordinal Data/Ranked Data*:
Ordinal data: Data of values or observations that can be ranked or ordered; ordinal refers to the order or rank. An ordinal number represents a specified (or ordered) position in a numbered series, such as an ordinal rank of seven. If it is stated that cancer is the third leading cause of death in the United States, three is the ordinal number. Grouping into low, middle, or high scores involves the ordinal scale. The principal weakness of an ordinal scale is that the number separating each score may not be equal. For example, if 10 students are ranked from high to low, the difference between each may not be equal. Ordinal data in which the data are ranked from "high to low" or "worst to best" is referred to as *ranked data*. Surveys in which respondents are asked to rate a characteristic on a scale (1 to 5 or 1 to 10) are examples of ordinal data. Other examples include intelligence quotient (IQ) scores or test scores ranked in some manner.

(3) *Interval Data*:
Interval data represent values or observations that can be measured on an evenly distributed scale beginning at a point other than true zero. Interval data include units of equal size, such as IQ results. There is no zero point. Other examples include temperature measured in Fahrenheit degrees and time. The most important characteristic is that the intervals between values are equal. The time between each hour is always 60 minutes whether between 2:00 A.M. and 3:00 A.M. or between 7:00 P.M. and 8:00 P.M.

(4) *Ratio Data or Ratio Scale*:
Ratio data are similar to interval data in that the intervals between successive units are of equal size; however, there is a zero starting point and can thus be manipulated mathematically, such a 0, 5, 10, 15, and 20. Age distribution is an example of a ratio scale. The difference between age 18 and age 20 is the same number of years as between age 65 and age 67 (two years). There is also a zero point, in that zero means unborn. Also, 75-year old person is three times as old as a 25-year-old person.

SELF-TEST 1-2

1. Indicate whether the following are nominal or ordinal data or neither:

   a. Ethnic groups _____

   b. Hair color _____

   c. Age _____

   d. Order of students by GPA in graduating class _____

(k) Ungrouped versus Grouped Data

Ungrouped Data/Raw Data: Ungrouped data (raw data) are the recorded scores as they are obtained. Ungrouped data also refer to a distribution in which scores are ranked from highest to lowest, or lowest to highest, but each score has its own place in the array.

Grouped Data (Aggregate Data): Grouped data involve some type of grouping or combining of scores. The most common method of grouping is by counting or tallying like scores. In this method, all identical scores are tallied, and the number recorded after the score. If 50 students took the same exam and eight received the same score of 92, then a tally of eight would be placed after the score of 92. With a broad range of scores, it often becomes necessary to combine several scores together and reduce the spread. If ages were recorded and ranged between a low of 1 and a high of 100, it may be necessary to group ages by decade and include all those from 1–9 together, 10–19, 20–29, and so forth, and thus narrow the range.

EXAMPLE: A class of 30 students took a statistics exam. The scores ranged from a high of 99 to 55. The scores in descending order are: 99, 98, 95, 91, 90, 89, 87, 86, 83, 82, 81, 81, 80, 79, 78, 76, 74, 73, 73, 73, 72, 70, 70, 68, 66, 65, 62, 61, 57, 55. The listing of each score individually is ungrouped data. However, when the scores are combined into various categories—for example, 95–99, 90–94, 85–89, 80–84, 75–79, 70–74, 65–69, 60–64, 55–59, the data are referred to as grouped or aggregate data.

(l) Population versus Sample

Population: Population refers to an entire group. A population is a set of persons (or objects) having a common observable characteristic. Every 10 years, the U.S. Census Bureau conducts a population census. Each house and residence in the United States is sent a questionnaire to be completed and returned, indicating the number of inhabitants residing at that site. Sites failing to respond are visited by census takers to get as accurate a count as possible. A hospital is also an example of a specific population—a group of patients admitted to receive medical treatment and care. A population may be composed of all patients suffering from a specific disease or undergoing a specific form of treatment such as chemotherapy.

Sample: A sample is a subset or small part of a population. Information obtained from a sample is often used to generalize from it to the

NOTES

entire population. A transcription supervisor lacks the time to check the accuracy of every report transcribed by each transcriptionist. It is virtually unfeasible to check every word on every report transcribed by all transcriptionists; therefore, a sample is taken from the transcribed reports, and the accuracy and quality of the transcriptionist's work is based on this sample. Most of the data in this book focuses on population statistics. When handling information such as mortality (death) statistics, census data, and pregnancy data, all cases will be included. Sampling technique employs only every fifth case or another designated number. When sampling is used, it is common to *infer* that the sample is representative of a given population and *deductions* are made relative to this sample. *Probability analyses* and *deductive statistics* are not included in this book.

 SELF-TEST 1-3

1. Indicate whether the following are based on a population or a sample.

   a. The percentage of all mammograms resulting in a cancer diagnosis. _____

   b. Number of car accident cases seen in the Emergency Department in the past month. _____

   c. Weekly salary of all coders in a health information department. _____

   d. Amount spent on prescription drugs by 200 citizens in a large city. _____

   e. Outcomes of 25 patients selected to test a new drug. _____

(m) Cross-Sectional Data versus Time-Series Data

Cross-Sectional Data contain information on different elements of a population or a sample for the *same* period of time. The incomes of 200 patients recorded for 2010 is an example of cross-sectional data.

Time-Series Data contain information on the same element for *different* periods of time. Information on U.S. exports in the past 10 years is an example of time-series data.

(n) Primary Data Sources versus Secondary Data Sources

Data sources are often referred to as either primary or secondary sources. A more detailed listing is included in Chapter 5.

(1) *Primary Data*: The major primary patient data source is found in the patient health record. All the facts and data regarding a patient's care are entered at the point of care. Information entered relative to this care is a primary data source.

(2) *Secondary Data*: A secondary source is abstracted information—that is, information taken from the health record and generally recorded into another document, such as a list, a register, or an index. Cancer abstracts and indexes (such as the master patient index) are prime examples of secondary data sources. Registers, indexes, lists, and abstracts are detailed in Chapter 5. Secondary sources include data extracted from websites.

(o) Representative Sample versus Random Sample

(1) A *representative sample* is a sample that represents the characteristics of the population as closely as possible. As an example, to find the average income of families living in Las Vegas, the sample must contain families who belong to different income groups in almost the same proportion as they exist in that population.

(2) A *random sample* is a sample drawn in such a way that each element of the population has a chance of being selected. One way to select a random sample is by lottery or draw (for instance, every fifth person or tenth person, or putting all the names in a box and randomly drawing 50 names).

(p) Constant versus Variable

(1) A *constant* is something that assumes only one value; it is a value that is replaceable by one and only one number; a fixed value. A constant is that which does not change and has one and only one value. A constant is one's date of birth or any value or specific that applies to everyone in the distribution. When constants are expressed as symbols, they are generally represented by the letters at the beginning of the alphabet.

(2) A *variable* is something that can change, in contrast to a constant, which remains the same. Variables are often represented by the letters at the end of the alphabet (X, x, Y, y). N is commonly used to represent the number of cases in a distribution. It often becomes desirable to compare variables and determine the relationship between them. For example, it may be useful to compare one variable (such as age) with another variable (such as occupation, severity of illness, or a specific diagnosis).

(q) Demography/Demographic Variables

Demography is the study of characteristics of human populations. *Demographic variables* include the size of a population and how it changes over time; the composition of the population, such as the age, sex, ethnicity, income, and health status of its members; and geographic density. As inner-city residents became more affluent, families fled the inner city and moved to the suburbs, leaving the less affluent behind. This emigration to the suburbs changed the demographics of the city. Demographic data are invaluable to hospital administrators in their attempt to provide the services most needed in their communities and the areas they serve.

(r) Vital Statistics

Vital Statistics refers to data that record significant events and dates in human life. These data include births, deaths, marriages, and divorces. Measures of illness and disease (morbidity) also fall under this umbrella term. A more detailed analysis and reporting of vital statistics information is provided in Chapter 13.

(s) Morbidity versus Mortality

(1) *Morbidity* data refer to disease statistics and are gathered to provide data on the prevalence of disease. Morbidity data are far more difficult to gather than mortality (death) data due to the lack of an adequate universal state and national reporting

system. Additional information regarding morbidity data gathering is provided in the chapter on vital statistics (Chapter 13).

(2) *Mortality* refers to death statistics. The death certificate identifies the state in which the death occurred and the date of death. An entire chapter is devoted to computation of death rates, and additional information on death certificates is provided in the section on vital statistics in a future chapter.

B. HEALTH CARE DATA COLLECTION

1. Sources of Health Care Data

Data sources are often referred to as either *primary* or *secondary* sources. A more detailed listing is included in Chapter 5.

(a) *Primary Data*: The major primary data source is the patient health care record. All the facts and data regarding a patient's care are entered at the point of care. Information entered relative to this care is a *primary data source*.

(b) *Secondary Data*: A secondary data source is abstracted information— that is, information taken from the patient record and recorded in another document, such as a list, register, or index. Cancer abstracts and indexes (such as the master patient index) are prime examples of *secondary data sources*. Registers, indexes, lists, and abstracts are detailed in Chapter 5.

2. Requestors of Health Care Data

Data are requested by a variety of users for multiple reasons. These will be discussed in the next section. The major requestors of data include the following:

(a) **Administration and Governing Board:** A health care facility must operate efficiently to continue serving the needs of its public. The governing board, administrators, and management staff are highly dependent on statistical reports. They not only compare current data with past data but also use the data to make future plans. In addition to patient care, their main concern is financial, utilization, and personnel data. Data are invaluable in determining if additional services can be provided or if a service is no longer viable. The effectiveness of an organization often rests on decisions made by the administrative staff. Administration may request information regarding the cost of disease entities, cost per physician, cost per clinical care staff unit, percent of occupancy, or the average length of stay of obstetric patients. Administration relies heavily on statistical reports. The statistical data contained in these reports are the basis on which management and financial decisions are made.

(b) **Medical Staff:** The physicians on the hospital's medical staff use statistical data to assess and appraise their own or their colleagues' performance. The medical staff request data on the services they provide. If infection rates tend to be high, an assessment of possible causes can be investigated. If data indicate a medical staff member has a high rate of complications following a surgical procedure, steps can be taken to assess the cause.

(c) **Other Treatment Facilities:** A patient may be transferred to another care facility (nursing home, trauma center, rehabilitation center) or scheduled for additional care on an outpatient basis (physical therapy, home health care or hospice care, mental health treatment) for continuing care. The record of care provided at the current facility is extremely helpful in providing the appropriate continuum of care.

(d) **Outside Agencies and Organizations:** State and federal licensing, accrediting, and regulatory organizations have data requirements. Local, state, and national agencies request statistical information. Data are also supplied to meet accreditation and licensure standards. In addition, certain funds (grants, for instance) may be disbursed based on statistical data. Some of the agencies requesting data include the Joint Commission, the American Hospital Association (AHA), and the Internal Revenue Service (IRS). In addition, health departments at all levels are dependent on data provided.

(e) **Insurers:** Reimbursement by third-party payers is highly dependent on data provided by a health care facility. Reimbursement is often dependent on the accurate and timely coding of patient care records, primarily performed in the HIM department. Accurate diagnosis and procedure codes are vital to reimbursement. The timelier the coding is completed, the sooner the facility is reimbursed for its services. Third-party payers also want to be assured the service billed was necessary, delivered, appropriate, and accurate. Third-party payers include Medicare, Medicaid, and private insurance companies.

(f) **Researchers:** Research studies provide important information and assist in determining factors that may contribute to an illness. Other studies assess the quality of care delivered. Research studies may be conducted on almost any aspect of disease in hopes of determining the cause and to provide more effective treatment.

3. Uses of Health Care Data

Just as there are myriad different requestors of data, there are also innumerable different uses. Within any inpatient, outpatient or long-term care facility decisions need to be made daily in terms of facility management and planning, as well as in making patient care decision. Statistics enable health care providers to assess utilization of services and assure quality of care is being delivered. Data are useful to justify the need for new equipment, facilities, and staff. Data are invaluable to physicians in diagnosing and treating their patients. Statistics provide an invaluable resource for evaluating and analyzing all aspects of a health care organization.

4. Management Decisions

Effective operation of any service provider entails the use of feedback based on accurate, appropriate data. Financial decisions are the primary responsibility of management. Many organizations have developed "dashboards" that contain high-level key data that are critical for the success of the organization, which are then tracked and reported on a monthly and an annual basis. This data may also be compared with external benchmarks. Listed below are several types of decisions that impact the well-being or vitality of a health care organization.

(a) **Services:** Organizations must decide what type of services will be provided. Is mental health care an option? Will the facility operate a trauma center? Will open-heart surgery services be available? Can a service currently not available, such as neurosurgery, become available?

(b) **Facilities and Equipment:** Are the facilities adequate? Is new equipment needed? Should equipment be purchased or leased? Should a new wing be added to the facility, or should a unit or wing be eliminated or converted to another use? What is the projected return on investment for a proposed new service, such as pain management, to a facility?

(c) **Staffing:** Are additional personnel needed to provide quality service? Are additional care providers needed, or coders, or support staff? Is there a need to retrain existing personnel? What is the rate of overtime that is being used for a certain time period? What is the mix of personnel that we are staffing a unit with in terms of registered nurses, licensed practical nurses, aides, etc.?

(d) **Quality Assessment/Improvement:** Quality assessment and improvement are hospital-wide functions—from patient care to patient accounts to housekeeping and food service. As health care costs keep rising and patients are faced with higher co-payments and higher deductibles, patients will demand better quality for their health care dollars. As the crisis in health care continues, quality data will be necessary to justify expenditures and assess quality and efficiency of care provided. Patients seek a provider (physician or other health care provider) that delivers top-rated care.

(e) **Setting Efficiency Standards:** A manager needs to set standards and goals for efficient management of his or her department, both in terms of the quantity and quality/accuracy of work. The HIM manager, for example, should set standards as to the number of records to be coded, or how many lines of dictation a transcriptionist should transcribe daily, or determine the most efficient release of information procedure. Productivity standards and timeliness of service, employee workload, and quality and quantity of work to be accomplished are all aided by a thorough analysis of data. All employees undergo a performance appraisal most often on an annual or semiannual basis or occasionally more frequently. Fair evaluations are based on appropriate data and on established standards. This is referred to as *benchmarking*.

Benchmarking is the process of comparing the performance of an organization to a standard (either the performance of a peer group or another similar organization). Quality data assists in quality assessment. In the absence of data, it is impossible for a manager to truly "manage a process" in his or her department.

5. **Patient Care Decisions**

Quality care is dependent on expert care by each care provider. Physicians are the primary overseers of care, but physicians' orders are carried out by staff (nurses, therapists, laboratory, or radiologic technicians and pharmacists.) The patient health care record is the primary source for care evaluations. Frequent evaluation assessments are made on reducing hospital-acquired infections, reducing medication errors (improper medication or improper dose), or evaluating length of stay for a specified diagnosis.

(a) **Accountability and Statistical Reports:** A health care facility needs statistical data to complete statistical reports. These reports include the number of patients treated daily, weekly, monthly, and yearly. Such reports show the amount of care rendered. The percentage of beds utilized on a regular basis is another indicator of care, as are the birth rate, death rate, and other rates. A health care facility must be accountable to state and federal licensing and regulatory agencies as well as third-party payers, and the data collected serve this purpose. Local, state, and national organizations collect and aggregate this data for monthly and annual reports.

EXAMPLES: Data collected on newly reported cases of a disease (AIDS, cancer, TB, Zika virus); reporting births and deaths; reporting the number of children born to mothers with drug addictions or the number of gunshot wounds treated in a facility.

(b) **Research:** As previously mentioned, the major purpose of research studies is to improve treatment protocol and, in so doing, improve patient care.

(c) **Determining Trends:** Determining trends in the incidence of disease is another data collection function. If a study indicates an increase in cases of a disease (such as breast cancer), additional research may provide answers in hopes of reversing the trend. Health care providers are increasingly rated by outside agencies—news outlets and online rating companies such as Health Grades, Inc. report the best providers of care in America or the best facilities for treatment. More and more information is available to the consumer based on statistical data and analysis. Governmental agencies use data to estimate population growth, either nationally or regionally. Data assist in planning and evaluating social welfare and public health programs, including maternal and child health care programs.

6. Users of Health Care Data

The major users of health care data are often referred to as internal and external users.

(a) **Internal Users**

(1) Health care facilities and caregivers—hospitals, long-term care facilities, home health agencies, mental health centers, drug and alcohol rehabilitation facilities, outpatient care centers, and managed care organizations. Caregivers include physicians, nursing staff, case managers, therapists, pharmacists, and radiologists.

(2) Management—hospital administrators and departmental managers.

(3) Researchers.

(4) Board of Directors.

(b) External Users
   (1) Licensing, regulatory and accrediting agencies—state and national.
   (2) Government—local, state, and national departments of health and vital statistics.
   (3) Insurers/third-party payers—including Medicare and Medicaid.

7. **Major Health Care Collection Entities**

   (a) Governmental Data Collection (Public Health)

   Public health data are collected at the local or county level with transmission forwarded on to the state. The government is primarily concerned with public health, especially communicable disease. A major public health goal is preventing the spread of communicable diseases, including developing vaccines and aiding in detection of the cause of the disease. A variety of governmental publications are related to public health reports.

   (1) *National Public Health Data Collection*: The U.S. government collects and reports a myriad of public health statistics. The decennial census (carried out every 10 years) gathers demographic data on all U.S. residents. Vital statistics data (number of births, deaths, marriages, and divorces) are also a governmental function. Disease data of all types are collected as well as death statistics such as the number of deaths due to motor vehicle accidents, drowning, or suicide. The government is also concerned with the number of residents without health insurance and the percentage of children without prescribed childhood vaccinations. There are many departments and agencies concerned with public health at the national level. These departments and agencies collect and analyze data and issue reports. Listed are the major health-related agencies/departments.

   (a) *National Center for Health Statistics (NCHS)*: This department is the repository for vital statistics. Although each state issues its own certificates or licenses (birth, marriage, divorce, and death), the statistical data are transmitted on to the national level for compilation. The data are compiled and published in *National Vital Statistics*.

   (b) *Department of Health and Human Services (DHHS)*: This branch of government holds a cabinet-level position and shares information with the president of the United States. The department has many components, one of which is the Food and Drug Administration (FDA), concerned with the safety of foods, drugs, and medical equipment. Another component of DHHS is the Center for Medicare and Medicaid Services (CMS). This department administers the Medicare program and the federal aspect of the Medicaid program.

   (c) *Centers for Disease Control and Prevention (CDC)*: The CDC is concerned with health promotion and prevention of diseases (such as AIDS, tuberculosis, influenza, cholera, Ebola virus, and Zika virus).

(2) *State Data Collection*: Each state has an array of departments and agencies that serve many of the same functions as those on the national level. In most cases, as stated, the states collect the data and forward that information to the appropriate national agency.

(3) *Local Data Collection*: Much of the data assembled at the state and national levels originates at the local or county level. Diseases are diagnosed by local physicians, and the appropriate data are abstracted and relayed to the appropriate health department or agency.

(b) Patient Data Collection

Computerization in health care facilities has increased greatly during the past several decades, introducing both the electronic health record (EHR) and the electronic medical record (EMR). The EHR creates a digital record of a person's health that is both portable and streamlined—able to move with patients to provide seamless care. The EMR is a digital version of the traditional paper patient chart, used primarily for the internal purposes of diagnosing and treating. The EMR collects and maintains information starting with a history, diagnosis, plan of care, medications, allergies, and other pertinent information required by the provider.

(1) *Demographic and Nonmedical Information*
Demographics include a patient's name, social security number, date of birth, occupation, and so forth. Additional nonmedical information includes dates—date of admission, date of discharge, date of a surgical procedure, date of delivery (giving birth)—and consents and authorizations (as in release of information, consent for an operation or procedure, and third-party payer consents).

(2) *Counts*
Examples of counts include the number of patients admitted on a certain date or discharged on a certain date; the number of complete blood counts (CBCs), electrocardiograms (EKGs), or other tests performed; the number of patients seen in physical therapy or receiving chemotherapy; the number of babies delivered (live or aborted), the number of patients who expired; or the number of patients treated in the emergency room.

(3) *Test Results*
Laboratory tests are a major data collection component in both inpatient and outpatient treatments. Tests include hematology tests including CBC, white blood cell (WBC) differential, and red blood cell (RBC) morphology; blood chemistries, such as blood glucose, blood urea nitrogen (BUN), and alkaline phosphatase; urinalysis (UA); cerebrospinal fluid (CFS) analysis; bone marrow tests; blood typing, serology, toxicology; and many more.

(4) *Diagnoses/Procedures*
Upon admission, patients are assigned an admitting diagnosis (also called provisional or tentative diagnosis). Discharge diagnoses are assigned at the time of discharge and include the principal diagnosis and other diagnoses and complications. In addition, consultants assign diagnoses in their specialty area, and surgeons assign preoperative and postoperative diagnoses. Diagnoses are assigned code numbers used for billing purposes and to generate disease and procedure indexes. If a patient undergoes a surgical procedure or operation, it is recorded and assigned a code number. Totals can be generated for specific procedures (gastroscopies, mammographies, colonoscopies, and hysterectomies) in a manner similar to that used for diagnoses.

(5) *Treatment Outcomes and Assessments*
Upon discharge, a notation is made in the health record regarding the condition of the patient at the time of discharge. The disposition of the care is indicated as well to include discharged home in good condition, transferred to another facility (nursing home, another hospital), or expired. Assessments can be compared with other similar care facilities and can serve as a basis for a research study.

C. ABBREVIATIONS

Abbreviations (acronyms) are routinely used by health care facilities for efficiency. Mastery of these acronyms is a critical success factor for beginning health care professionals. Listed below are some common abbreviations used throughout this text.

a. **Patient Care**

AMA	against medical advice (patient left without a discharge order)
DOA	dead on arrival
ER/ED	emergency room/emergency department
IP	inpatient
NB	newborn
OP	outpatient
OB	obstetrics/obstetrical

b. **Statistical**

ADM	admission
DIS/DC	discharge
A&D	admitted and discharged on the same day
	Also called I&O (in-and-out); or "come-and-go" or same-day patients. In this text, they will be designated A&D.
A&C	adults and children
	This designation is used to refer to all patients other than newborns. Many formulas require separate computations for the two groups as the two populations have unique characteristics and need to be treated separately.

TRF-in	transferred in (patient transferred into a clinical unit)
TRF-out	transferred out (patient transferred out of a clinical unit)
>	greater than
<	less than
Σ	summation (the uppercase Greek letter sigma means summation—it indicates that whatever follows the sign is to be added).

c. **Clinical Units (Some of the More Common Designations)**

CCU	coronary care unit
ICU	intensive care unit
ENT	ear-nose-throat for otorhinolaryngology
GYN	gynecology
OB	obstetrics
PED	pediatrics
NICU	neonatal intensive care unit
NEURO	neurology
OPHTH	ophthalmology
ORTHO	orthopedics
PSYCH	psychiatry
REHAB	rehabilitation
SURG	surgery
MED	medical/medical care unit
ONCO	oncology
URO	urology

d. **Nonofficial/Non-Universal Abbreviations—abbreviations used throughout this text:**

Cor	coroner/medical examiner case
CTT	census-taking time
DD	discharge days
DIPC	daily inpatient census
HPath	hospital pathologist
IPSD	inpatient service day
LOS	length of stay

D. SUMMARY

1. Statistics is both a numerical fact and a field of study.
2. Data are facts; a data set is a collection of observations on one or more variables; a set includes all scores in a distribution; the name of each individual is called an *element*; each individual score is called an *observation*. Data can be ungrouped or grouped.
3. A quantitative variable can be measured numerically; a qualitative variable *cannot* assume a numerical value.

4. Numerical data or quantitative data include both discrete and continuous data. Discrete data are always expressed as a whole number; continuous data are *not* restricted to a whole number and may have fractional or decimal values.

5. Categorical data include nominal, ordinal, interval, and ratio data. Nominal data are identifying data, but *no arithmetic* operations can be performed on nominal data; ordinal data are data that can be ranked; interval data include a scale without a true zero point but have units of equal size; ratio data also include a scale with units of equal size but with a zero starting point.

6. A population includes an entire group. A sample is a subset of a population.

7. Cross-sectional data are reported for the same time period; time-series data report data for different periods of time.

8. A representative sample represents the population as closely as possible; a random sample includes choosing the sample at random from the population.

9. A constant assumes only one value; a variable is something that can change.

10. Data that report disease statistics are referred to as morbidity data; mortality data report death statistics.

11. Demographic data are data on human populations and incorporate factors such as age, sex, ethnicity, income, and health status of its members.

12. Vital statistics references data on human events—birth, death, marriage, divorce, and disease.

13. Abbreviations are used for the sake of brevity and are especially numerous in health care.

14. Data have many uses, and the proper collection and interpretation is increasingly important with efforts to reduce health care costs and maintain quality care.

15. Data are invaluable to management and patient care decision making, accountability, statistical reports to outside agencies, research, and determining trends.

16. The major users of health care data are both internal and external to an organization.

17. In health care, the primary source of data is the patient health record; secondary sources include abstracted data.

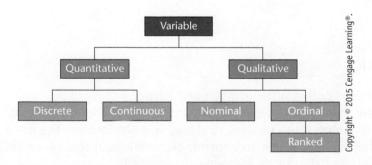

Name _____ Date _____

E. CHAPTER 1 TEST

1. Indicate if the following are part of a population or sample:

   a. Fifty cases of Zika virus have been reported in the past year, and a comprehensive care _____
   study is to be carried out using data from all 50 cases.

   b. Two hundred fifty total hip replacement surgeries have been performed in the past year; _____
   a clinical performance improvement study is to be carried out on 35 of these cases.

   c. A total of 180 open-heart surgeries were performed during the past six months. The Quality _____
   Assurance department will review 10% of the group.

2. Indicate if the following are part of a population or a sample:

   a. Two thousand patients were admitted in the past year for chest pain; case managers plan to review 20% of these
   cases to develop a best-practice care plan for this type of patient.

   b. Fifty patients in the United States were diagnosed with Tuberculosis (TB) in the past five years; these cases will
   be examined at a national case conference.

   c. Two hundred fifty students graduated from the HIM program last year. The dean plans to review 10% of these
   transcripts to look for trends in performance.

3. Indicate if the following represent qualitative or quantitative variables and, if quantitative, are the data discrete or
   continuous?

a. Total number of ER visits reported in March.	Qual	Quan	Disc	Cont
b. Patient's gender.	Qual	Quan	Disc	Cont
c. Patient's age.	Qual	Quan	Disc	Cont
d. A car's gas mileage.	Qual	Quan	Disc	Cont
e. Marital status.	Qual	Quan	Disc	Cont
f. Number of children in a family.	Qual	Quan	Disc	Cont
g. Favorite food.	Qual	Quan	Disc	Cont
h. Type of insurance.	Qual	Quan	Disc	Cont
i. Smoker, former smoker, or nonsmoker.	Qual	Quan	Disc	Cont
j. Number of hospital admissions in the past month.	Qual	Quan	Disc	Cont
k. Number of outpatient visits.	Qual	Quan	Disc	Cont
l. Type of exercise engaged in for fitness.	Qual	Quan	Disc	Cont

4. Indicate if the following represent nominal or ordinal data.

a. Placement on an entrance exam.	Nominal	Ordinal
b. Listing of the top 10 scores on a final exam.	Nominal	Ordinal
c. Type of long-term care facility.	Nominal	Ordinal
d. Designation of payer group.	Nominal	Ordinal
e. Finished in a marathon.	Nominal	Ordinal

5. Indicate the term for:

   a. A value that can change. _____

   b. Type of data reported by mortality statistics. _____

   c. Type of data that records births, deaths, and marriages. _____

   d. Type of statistics based on generalizations about a population based on a sample. _____

   e. Sample drawn in such a way that each element of the population has a chance of being selected. _____

6. Define benchmarking.

7. Differentiate between:

   a. Primary and secondary data.

   b. Representative sample and random sample.

8. Identify several:

   a. Requestors of health care data.

   b. Uses of health care data.

   c. Users of health care data.

9. Identify:

   a. What CMS administers.
   b. Department in which CMS is located.
   c. Government department holding a cabinet-level position.

10. True or False.

a. Statistics is a numerical fact.	T	F
b. Descriptive statistics analyzes a specific group.	T	F
c. Decisions made based on scientific methods are pure guesses.	T	F
d. Information is data organized and processed to be useful.	T	F
e. The name of each participant in a study is called an element.	T	F
f. Interval data have intervals starting at zero.	T	F
g. Ratio data have units of unequal size.	T	F
h. Ungrouped data is raw data.	T	F
i. A population in which every fifth person is selected is a representative sample.	T	F
j. Time-series data contain information for the same period of time.	T	F
k. Indexes serve as a secondary source of data.	T	F
l. NCHS is the repository of vital statistics.	T	F
m. The CDC is an agency of DHHS.	T	F

11. Identify the following abbreviations:

   a. NB   g. Σ
   b. ICU   h. IP
   c. LOS   i. >
   d. A&D   j. NCHS
   e. CDC   k. NICU
   f. A&C

12. Five counties in Florida reported shark bites in the past year:

    Volusia, 15 bites   Brevard, 6 bites   Duval, 4 bites
    St. Johns, 3 bites   Indian River, 2 bites

   a. What is the variable in the data set?   _____
   b. How many elements are in the data set?   _____
   c. What is the total number of bites (observations) reported in these five counties?   _____
   d. Are these qualitative or quantitative variables?   _____
   e. Are the data discrete, continuous, or neither?   _____
   f. Are the data cross-sectional or time-series?   _____

13. Fifty students completed a medical terminology course at Hillside Community College. The final exam scores are listed below:

70	90	55	97	72	74	84	55	49	100
71	88	44	38	92	67	75	82	81	66
84	50	66	81	68	95	90	91	60	72
86	63	72	77	70	44	66	73	48	82
93	75	98	74	77	54	78	57	72	99

   a. Rank the individual scores from best to worst.
   b. List each individual score only once. Indicate the number of individuals receiving each individual score.
   c. Using the grouping below, indicate after each interval, the number of scores that fall within the interval.

98–100	82–85	66–69	50–53
94–97	78–81	62–65	46–49
90–93	74–77	58–61	42–45
86–89	70–73	54–57	38–41

14. Fifty students completed a health care midterm exam at Upstate College. The final exam grades are listed below:

```
93   87   82   71   68   65   86   82   64   83
88   100  71   69   85   100  78   99   72   90
56   82   92   59   82   45   80   85   95   82
91   76   81   85   75   80   72   56   91   77
77   48   100  86   90   74   86   90   83   88
```

a. Rank the individual scores from best to worst.
b. List each individual score only once. Indicate the number of individuals receiving each individual score.
c. Using the grouping below, indicate, after each interval, the number of scores that fall within the interval.

```
98–100   82–85   66–69   50–53
94–97    78–81   62–65   46–49
90–93    74–77   58–61   42–45
86–89    70–73   54–57   38–41
```

Mathematics: *Reviewing the Basics*

2

LEARNING OBJECTIVES

After studying this chapter, the learner should be able to:

✔ Calculate fractions, decimals, percentages, and rates.

✔ Distinguish between a numerator, a denominator, and a quotient.

✔ Average a set of numbers.

✔ Round data to a specified number.

✔ Convert data from one set of measures to another.

✔ Convert data to another unit of measure.

✔ Determine resource needs.

✔ Interpret variances.

PRELIMINARY QUESTIONS

1. Reduce the following fractions:
   a. 12/60
   b. 27/162
   c. 40/520
   d. 7/42
2. Calculate the quotient, correct to two decimal places:
   a. 70/13
   b. 9,246/27
   c. 3/11
3. Compute the following percentages, correct to two decimal places:
   a. 36/92
   b. 54/358
   c. 612/1,348
   d. 72/54
4. Calculate the decimal equivalent, correct to two decimal places:
   a. 6/200
   b. 7/510
   c. 4/450
   d. 32/75
5. Determine the average for the following set of numbers:
   a. 700 681 213 36
   b. 0.12 3.15 0.003 10.85
   c. 1,185 8.85 348 93 750.6
6. Round to the designated place:
   a. Whole number 96.3
   b. Two decimal places 125.876
   c. Hundred 349
7. Convert the following fractions to percentages:
   a. 2/40
   b. 3/67
   c. 762/1,045
8. Convert the following decimals to percentages:
   a. 0.000998
   b. 7.61546
   c. 60.72

9. Carry out the following computations:
    a. 8(60) + 2/3 (9) − 64/6
    b. 32.946 (2) + 6.75 − 3/5 (70)
    c. 60% (420) − 2/3 (75) − 45% (380)
10. a. Add: 1/2 + 3/5 + 7/10
    b. Multiply: 3/5 × 15/60
    c. Divide 3/10 by 6/24.

A. REVIEW OF MATHEMATICAL FUNCTIONS

Data is used within health care organizations for many purposes, such as monitoring internal operations, for comparison with internal and external benchmarks, and for regulatory reporting. Data must be collected and interpreted using standard methods to make it both valid and comparable. This chapter focuses on helping students feel more comfortable in performing basic mathematical functions to make accurate calculations.

Data are often recorded as numerical information. These data also need to be organized in some manner to become meaningful, not only to the gatherer of the information but also to those with whom the information is shared. As previously stated, data serve as a basis for decision making and reporting. Health care institutions routinely gather a large amount of data on their patients and myriad other types of information as well. To be useful, statistical formulas have been formulated, and only through standardized data gathering and analysis can legitimate comparisons be made. Basic mathematical terms, functions, and computations are reviewed in this chapter to facilitate computation in subsequent chapters.

1. Fraction

A fraction is a fragment or part of a whole; small part; bit. A fraction is designated by placing one number over another number, such as 6/7 or 2/3. The top number (number above the line) is referred to as the *numerator*; the bottom number is the *denominator*. In the fraction 2/3, 2 is the numerator and 3 is the denominator. If one is asked to convert the fraction to a decimal, the numerator is divided by the denominator, and the result is referred to as a *quotient*. The division is more correctly referred to as the dividend (numerator) divided by the divisor (denominator). (Dividing 2 by 3, the quotient is 0.667 or 0.67.) There are two ways to increase the value of a fraction—increase the numerator or decrease the denominator. Conversely, to decrease the value of a fraction, the numerator must be decreased, or the denominator increased.

EXAMPLES:

EX 1. A pizza is divided into six equal slices, and an individual eats one slice or one-sixth of the pie. If two slices are eaten, one-third of the pie was consumed (2/6 = 1/3). Once three slices are eaten, the pie is one-half eaten (3/6 = 1/2).

EX 2. There are 12 beds set up and available on a medical unit but only eight of the beds are occupied by patients. Therefore, two-thirds of the beds on the unit (8/12 = 2/3) are occupied, and one-third (4/12 = 1/3) is still available.

EX 3. Twenty cookies are to be equally divided among 15 people. Therefore, each person receives 1 1/3 cookies (20/15 = 15/15 + 5/15 = 1 1/3).

     SELF-TEST 2-1

1. Eighty-five babies are delivered during May. Of these babies, 43 were Caucasian, 25 were African American, 12 were Hispanic, and 5 were Asian. Calculate the fraction of these 85 babies born to each race in May:
   a. Caucasian
   b. African American
   c. Hispanic
   d. Asian

2. a. Circle the numerator for the following fractions:

      (1) 3/13
      (2) 10/18
      (3) 6/5
      (4) 35/60

   b. Circle the denominator for the following fractions:

      (1) 7/17
      (2) 3/10
      (3) 9/8
      (4) 45/80

   c. Calculate the quotient for each of the following fractions:

      (1) 325/25
      (2) 49/7
      (3) 1,800/9
      (4) 72/8

Reducing Fractions: Multiplying or dividing both the numerator and the denominator of a fraction by the same number (except 0) does *not* change the value of the fraction (1/2 is the same as 3/6 or 100/200). Fractions are more easily handled when reduced to their lowest form and should be reported in this simplest form. The reduction is achieved by dividing both the numerator and the denominator by the largest common number that is divisible by both the numerator and the denominator.

EXAMPLES:

EX 1. The fraction 5/10 can be reduced to 1/2 by dividing both the numerator and the denominator by 5; 8/60 can be reduced to 2/15 by using 4 as the dividing number. Reducing 15/20 = 3/4 (using 5 as the divisor); 8/32 = 1/4; 45/135 = 1/3.

EX 2. 25 out of 60 picnic attendees came down with food poisoning. Written as a fraction, there are 25/60 who got sick; and to reduce the result, both the numerator and the denominator are divided by 5, resulting in a fraction of 5/12.

EX 3. Forty-eight patients were seen in the ER following an explosion at a chemical plant. Of these, 4 were treated for cuts, lacerations, and contusions; 8 were treated for respiratory problems; 32 were treated for chemical burns. Converting the data to reduced fractions:

Cuts, lacerations, contusions: 4/48 = 1/12 (divisor is 4)

Respiratory problems: 8/48 = 1/6 (divisor is 8)

Chemical burns: 32/48 = 2/3 (divisor is 16)

 SELF-TEST 2-2

Reduce each of the following fractions:
  a. 32/100   b. 6/36   c. 4/80   d. 7/56   e. 15/75

2. Decimals

A decimal is an amount less than 1. A decimal is a fraction based on divisions that are powers to the negative base 10 (10 to the −1 power is 1/10). (1/10 = 0.10; 1/100 = 0.01; 1/1,000 = 0.001; etc.)

EXAMPLES:

EX 1. A pan of brownies is divided into ten pieces and eight are eaten; therefore, 0.8 is the decimal equivalent of the number eaten (8/10 = 0.8).

EX 2. Ten residents of a city with a population of 100,000 are diagnosed with pertussis. Therefore, the decimal equivalent is 0.0001.

EX 3. A pie is cut into eight pieces, and six of the eight are still available. The amount of pie uneaten is 0.75 (6/8 = 0.75); the amount eaten is 0.25 (2/8 = 1/4).

 SELF-TEST 2-3

Determine the decimal equivalent for each of the following fractions:
  a. 6/60   b. 4/1,000   c. 9/200   d. 10/77

3. Percentages

A percentage is the number of times something happens out of every 100 times. A percentage is a specific rate followed by a percent sign; it is a proportion of a whole. To convert a decimal to a percentage, multiply the decimal by 100.

EXAMPLES:

EX 1. If 40 out of every 100 hospital employees have attained a four-year college degree, then it can be said that 40% of all employees at that hospital have been awarded a bachelor's degree.

EX 2. A total of 125 mammograms were performed in February, of which 15 were reported to show some type of abnormality. Therefore, a total of 12% were abnormal (15/125 = 0.12; 0.12 multiplied by 100 = 12%).

 SELF-TEST 2-4

Compute the percentage for each of the following fractions:
  a. 12/50   b. 4/10   c. 3/1,000   d. 45/8,640

4. Rate/Ratio/Proportion

a. Rate

A rate has many meanings. It can mean a value or price (as in 50 cents per pound); it can be a unit of something (as in the rate of speed is 30 mph, or the birth rate is 20 births per every 100 teenagers, gas mileage is 25 miles per gallon, or the interest rate is 8.6%). A rate is also a ratio, proportion, or rank. Most commonly, a rate is expressed as a percentage.

EXAMPLE: A bank advertises the interest rate for a savings account as 2%. A hospital reports an 85% occupancy rate. Statistics might indicate the infection rate at Hospital ABC was 8% during the previous year.

 SELF-TEST 2-5

The newborn nursery reports 160 infants were born at the hospital in May. Four of these infants died shortly after birth, and the remainder were discharged alive. Calculate the newborn death rate.

b. Ratio

A ratio is a relationship between things or one number to another number. Ratios are generally reported by a fraction, or numbers side by side separated by a colon (8:10, read 8 out of 10). As with fractions, the ratio can be reduced to its lowest equivalent so that 8 out of 10 is equivalent to 4 out of 5.

EXAMPLE: If 7 out of 10 people admitted to the hospital are found to be over 50 years of age, this ratio can be written as 7/10 or 7:10.

c. Proportion

A proportion is a relationship of one portion to another or to the whole, or of one thing to another. A proportion is a ratio in which the elements in the numerator must also be included in the denominator.

EXAMPLE: A class of 30 students has 12 boys and 18 girls. It would be incorrect in this case to state that the proportion is 12 boys/18 girls. The proportion, stated correctly, is a class where 12/30 are boys and 18/30 are girls.

 SELF-TEST 2-6

One hundred operations were performed during the past month. Of these, 20 were orthopedic operations, 12 gynecological, 18 ophthalmological, 22 urological, and the remainder were general surgeries. Calculate the ratio for each surgical category.

5. Averaging

An *average* is a number that typifies a set of numbers of which it is a function. Statistically speaking, an average is referred to as a *mean*, or *arithmetic mean*, to distinguish it from the *median* and *mode*, which

NOTES

are also used statistically as measures of central tendency. Chapter 14 includes the computation of the measures of central tendency.

Formula for Average: To compute an average, add all scores in the distribution and divide by the number of scores (N) in the distribution.

$$\text{Average} = \frac{\Sigma \text{ (Sum) of all scores}}{N}$$

N = number of scores in the distribution

EXAMPLES:

EX 1. A student has taken 10 math tests. The scores for these 10 tests are 100, 95, 85, 90, 78, 92, 87, 81, 72, 94. Summing the 10 scores yields a total 874. This total is then divided by 10 (N = number of tests taken); and the resultant average math test score is 87.4 or 87.

EX 2. A hospital's 10-day admission figures are reported as 10, 15, 12, 8, 6, 18, 16, 5, 9, 13. To calculate the average number of patients admitted during this 10-day period, add all the admission figures (112) and divide by the number of days (10). The average calculates to 11.2 or 11 admissions per day during the designated 10-day period.

 SELF-TEST 2-7

1. The surgical center lists the number of operations performed each day during the week as 6, 10, 8, 9, 5, 12, 7.
    Determine the average number of operations carried out during that week.

2. A hospital's yearly death records reveal the following monthly figures: 3, 4, 1, 2, 6, 2, 5, 8, 1, 4, 6, 3.
    Determine the average number of deaths reported each month.

3. A total of 575 stress electrocardiograms were performed in May. Determine the average number performed daily in May.

4. A total of 1,050 patients were seen in the ER during the first six months of a non-leap year.
    Determine the average number of patients seen in the ER during that period.

5. The following numbers of newborn babies were reported for the week: 2, 2, 4, 1, 3, 1, 3.
    Determine the average number of babies born each day.

6. Rounding Data

Rounding is a process that approximates a total or final number. Often, this is done when the final quotient results in a decimal, although it is also used when large numbers of cases are included in a study or a report. The primary reason for rounding data is to arrive at a usable number.

EXAMPLE: When averaging, the scores were totaled and divided by the number of scores in the distribution. To find the average of the numbers 6, 9, and 7, the total is determined (22) and divided by 3 (N). The quotient is 7.33333, with three extending indefinitely. A more usable quotient is 7.33, 7.3, or even 7.

Carried To: This term is used to indicate to what decimal place or whole number the quotient is to be determined, to round the data to the specified number. Handheld calculators carry out the division well beyond the place needed for most calculations. The quotient should always be carried out at least *one* place beyond the specified (corrected) place. In this way, the final answer can be rounded correctly. If it is stated that the answer is to be correct to two decimal places, the quotient should be carried out to at least three places. If the answer is to be correct to the nearest whole number, the answer must be carried to one decimal place.

Corrected To: This term is used to indicate the degree to which the answer should be specified. Seldom will data be specified beyond one or two decimal places.

When to Increase When Rounding: If the last digit is 5 or greater, the preceding number should be increased by one digit. If the last digit is less than 5, the number remains the same. It should always be noted to what place the computation should be "correct to." Carry the quotient one additional place beyond this and round the answer based on this additional digit.

EXAMPLES:

EX 1. A city with a population of 40,216 may be rounded to 40,200 should the total be requested to the nearest hundred. However, if the total requested is "to the nearest thousand," the reported answer is 40,000. In this case, 40,000 is also the correct answer should the request have read "to the nearest ten thousand."

EX 2. A group of individuals are on a diet to lose weight. Each individual's weight is recorded prior to the start of the program and at the end, and the amount of weight lost or gained is determined. At the end of the scheduled 10-week period, it was determined that the average individual lost 8.2 pounds. If the result was to be stated correct to the nearest pound, then the average weight loss per individual in the group for the 10 weeks was 8 pounds.

EX 3. Rounding the following scores to

   a. one decimal place:
      $7.35 = 7.4; 7.84 = 7.8; 17.6555 = 17.7; 1.725 = 1.7; 7.65 = 7.7$

   b. two decimal places:
      $17.655 = 17.66; 45.653 = 45.65; 103.005 = 103.01;$
      $313.004 = 313.00$

   c. the nearest whole number:
      $365.6 = 366; 455.91 = 456; 35.49 = 35; 33.55 = 34; 18.51 = 19$

 SELF-TEST 2-8

1. Round correct to the nearest whole number:

a. 65.4	d. 70.5	g. 38.499	j. 10.05
b. 65.5	e. 7,051.4	h. 595.85	k. 15.555
c. 65.6	f. 0.6	i. 148.475	l. 55.505

2. Round correct to one decimal place:

a. 12.35	d. 0.005	g. 83.95	i. 6.555
b. 27.625	e. 456.955	h. 1.05	j. 76.049
c. 31.6511	f. 698.99		

3. Round correct to two decimal places:
   a. 65.699   d. 953.799   g. 17.999   i. 100.055
   b. 68.636   e. 125.9995   h. 79.995   j. 1.1548
   c. 0.005   f. 65.666

4. Round correct to the nearest:
   a. hundred   3,256   e. million   3,502,378
   b. tenth   5.781   f. ten   2,184.73
   c. thousandth 0.0045   g. hundredth   43.87500
   d. hundredth   46.7385

7. Converting to Another Form

a. Fraction to Percentage

To convert a fraction to a percentage, divide the numerator by the denominator, multiply by 100, and add a percent sign.

> **EXAMPLES:**
>
> **EX 1.** To convert 60/80 to a percentage, divide 60 by 80, then multiply the quotient by 100 which equals 75% (60/80 = 0.75 multiplied by 100 = 75%).
>
> **EX 2.** A test has five questions. A student answers two of the five correctly or 40% (2/5 = 0.40 multiplied by 100 = 40%).

 SELF-TEST 2-9

Convert the following fractions to percentages—correct to one decimal place.
   a. 5/8   b. 65/83   c. 1/7   d. 7/8   e. 70/200

b. Ratio to Percentage

To convert a ratio to a percentage, write the ratio as a fraction and proceed as in "a" above.

> **EXAMPLE:** One out of eight nurses indicated working a double shift the previous month. The ratio is 1/8, which converts to a percentage of 12.5% or 13% (1/8 = 0.125 multiplied by 100 = 12.5%).

 SELF-TEST 2-10

Convert the following ratios to a percent—correct to the nearest whole number.
   a. 1:3   b. 7:11   c. 5:6   d. 11:17   e. 15:60

c. Decimal to Percentage

To convert a decimal to a percentage, simply multiply by 100 (which moves the decimal point two places to the right) and add a percent sign.

> **EXAMPLES:**
>
> **EX 1.** To convert 0.50 to a percentage, 0.50 is multiplied by 100 resulting in 50%.
>
> **EX 2.** To convert 0.001 to a percent, multiply by 100 (0.001 × 100 = 0.1%. It is common practice to use a zero in front of a

decimal point if the answer is less than 1; also, zeros are eliminated to the right of the decimal point if they are not followed by another number (50.100 is correctly reported as 50.1 or 50.1%).

 SELF-TEST 2-11

1. Convert the following decimals into percentages without rounding:

a.	1.25	d.	0.03	g.	0.0162
b.	0.635	e.	0.006	h.	0.55
c.	0.3	f.	0.8235		

2. Convert the following decimals into percentages—correct to the nearest whole number:

a.	3.25	c.	0.005	e.	0.0166
b.	0.4567	d.	0.5555	f.	0.0449

   d. Percentage to Decimal

   To convert from a percentage to a decimal, cross out the percent sign and move the decimal point two places to the left of the decimal point or divide by 100. (To convert 65% to a decimal, eliminate the percent sign and divide by 100: 65/100 = 0.65).

 SELF-TEST 2-12

Convert the following percentages to a decimal:

a. 5%	b. 11.4%	c. 0.5%	d. 125%

   e. Percentage to Fraction

   The conversion is achieved by eliminating the percent sign, placing the percentage number in the numerator and 100 in the denominator, and converting to the lowest fraction. (To change 55% to a fraction, 55 becomes the numerator with 100 in the denominator—55/100; dividing each number by 5 results in a fraction of 11/20.)

 SELF-TEST 2-13

Convert the following percentages to the lowest fraction:

a.	75%	c.	30%	e.	20%	g.	50%
b.	85%	d.	110%	f.	84%	h.	98%

8. Computing with a Percentage

When computing with a percentage, convert the percent to a decimal and proceed from there (40% of 100 scores = 0.40 × 100 = 40).

EXAMPLES:

EX 1. It was reported that 20% of all patients admitted to the hospital in the past year had a blood glucose test. Out of a total of 6,000 admissions, 1,200 patients had a blood glucose test (0.20 × 6,000 = 1,200 patients).

EX 2. A hospital has 80% of its 120 beds filled. To find how many beds are available (not filled):

METHOD 1: Calculate the number occupied and subtract from the total. 80% = 0.80 × 120 (number of beds) = 96 beds occupied; subtract 96 from 120 to determine the number of beds available—or 24 beds available.

METHOD 2: The same result can be attained directly; if 80% are occupied, then 20% are available (0.20 × 120 = 24).

 SELF-TEST 2-14

1. Convert the following:
   a. 25% to the lowest fraction
   b. 62.5% to the lowest fraction
   c. 60% to the lowest ratio
   d. 0.5% to a decimal
   e. 3% to a decimal
   f. 12% to a decimal

2. A hospital report indicates 25% of its patients had an MRI in January. If 1,060 patients were hospitalized in January, how many had a MRI?

3. A report indicated that two-thirds of all patients on a given day had a CBC blood test done. How many out of every 100 patients had a CBC? Report the answer—correct to the nearest whole number.

4. A health information management department has 28 full-time employees. If 18% are home with the flu, how many employees are working?

5. A salmonella outbreak occurs in a hospital and 8% of the patients and staff are diagnosed with the illness. The hospital has 350 employees and the present patient count is 225. How many people (patients and staff) have been diagnosed with the illness, correct to the nearest whole number?

9. Converting to Other Units of Measure

Occasionally, it may be necessary to convert data from U.S. standards of measure to metric units or vice versa. More and more data are being recorded in metric units. Most weigh scales in medical facilities now display weight in metric units (kilograms) and, with conversion tables, the patient can be informed of his or her weight in U.S. pounds. In addition, distances (linear measures) may also employ metric units (centimeters, meters, kilometers). In analyzing data, it is important to remember that all data must be in the same units. It is inadmissible to have some data measures in pounds and others in kilograms without converting to one scale or the other.

The following data are equivalents:

(kilo means 1,000; kilogram [kg] = 1,000 grams [gm]; kilometer [km] = 1,000 meters)

Linear measures: 1 centimeter (cm) = 0.0328 foot; 0.3937 inch

1 inch = 2.54 cm

1 foot = 0.3048 meter

1 meter = 1.0936 yards (yd); 3.2808 feet; 39.37 inches

1 mile = 1.6094 km

1 km = 0.6214 mile

Weight measures: 1 gm = 0.0022 pound (lb); 0.0353 ounce (oz)

1 kg = 2.2046 lb

1 lb = 0.4536 kg; 45.36 gm

1 oz = 28.3495 gm

Liquid weight measures: 1 quart = 0.94633 liter

1 liter = 0.2642 gallon; 1.0567 quarts

EXAMPLES:

EX 1. To convert the weight of a 125 lb person to kilograms, multiply 125 by the conversion factor (0.4536) for an equivalent weight of 56.7 kg.

EX 2. To convert 62 kg into pounds, multiply 62 by the factor, 2.2046, which results in a weight of 136.69 pounds, or 137 pounds.

EX 3. A newborn's weight is recorded as 8 lb 8 oz. To complete a conversion, the data must first be converted either to pounds (8 lb 8 oz = 8.5 pounds since there are 16 oz in 1 pound) or completely to ounces (8 × 16 = 128 + 8 = 136 oz). To convert to kilograms, use the pound conversion factor in the first case and the ounces conversion in the second case: (8.5 × 0.4536 = 3.86 kg); (136 × 28.3495 = 3,855.53 gm divided by 1,000 = 3.86 kg).

EX 4. A runner competing in a 5-km race is running 3.11 miles (5 × 0.6214 = 3.107 or 3.11 miles).

 SELF-TEST 2-15

1. a. Choose the greater amount.　　　　1 liter/1 quart
   b. Choose the greater distance.　　　　10 km/6 miles
   c. Who weighs more?　　　　　　　　　90 kg/200 lb
   d. Choose the greater distance.　　　　100 meters/100 yards

2. a. Convert 63 kg into pounds.
   b. Convert 150 lb into kg.
   c. Convert 30 km to miles.

B. APPLYING THE NUMBERS

Health Information Management (HIM) managers apply basic mathematics when determining labor costs, deciding on equipment purchases or leases, computing productivity, and making staffing decisions. These are all factors relevant to the budgeting process. Budgeting and management are generally presented in a separate course in the HIM program, but some basic mathematical calculations are included in this chapter.

1. Salary and Staffing Calculations

Full-time employee (FTE): Generally, a 40-hour work week is considered standard for full-time employment. With 52 weeks in a year, a full-time employee will be paid for a total of 2,080 hours a year (52 multiplied by 40). The employee is also granted benefits such as paid holiday, vacation, and sick days, so actual hours at work do not total 2,080. But the employee is paid at their standard hourly wage during these days, and therefore all 2,080 hours are counted.

Part-time employee (PTE): A part-time employee is paid in accordance to the equivalent hours and days worked and often accrues fewer benefits.

EXAMPLE: A full-time employee, paid $15 per hour, receives a yearly salary of $31,200 (2,080 multiplied by 15 = $31,200). However, the total cost to the department is greater than this amount since the employee often receives additional benefits (health insurance, retirement benefits, life insurance, training days, etc.) provided by the health care facility. These costs need to be included when budgeting but will be excluded in the computations to follow.

 SELF-TEST 2-16

In addition to salary, managers need to determine the number of staff necessary to accomplish the various tasks performed in the department and the workload for each staff member. If additional care units are added, or if the workload increases by 20%, due to a sharp increase in outpatient services, a staffing reevaluation becomes necessary and additional staff may be needed. Also, it may be imperative to reduce staff hours or lay-off staff, should there be a decrease in outpatient services.

1. a. Determine the annual salary of a full-time employee earning $18 an hour.
    b. Determine the annual salary paid to a part-time employee who works 15 hours a week for the entire year at a base rate of $20 an hour.

EXAMPLE: A new pulmonary medicine clinic has been added to the local health care facility. The HIM department has found an increase of 18% (60 charts per day) to be processed in the department. Coders are spending an average of 10 minutes per chart. How many additional coders are required to handle the additional coding volume? At 10 minutes per chart, an average of 6 charts can be coded each hour. Assuming a traditional 8-hour shift, a total of 48 charts could be coded each day per coder. However, 60 additional charts need to be coded, which requires 1.25 FTEs to handle the additional workload (60 divided by 48 = 1.25).

 SELF-TEST 2-17

A health care facility has an average of 220 inpatient discharges each week. Assuming it takes an average of 20 minutes to code each chart, how many full-time coders are needed to code 220 charts?

2. Filing Space

Most large medical centers have converted to the electronic medical record (EMR) and no longer have the need for additional storage space for paper records. However, smaller clinics and health centers may still employ shelf space for filing charts, and filing and storage space must be calculated.

EXAMPLES:

EX 1. A health clinic currently has open-shelf filing units. Each unit has a total of five shelves, and each shelf holds 35 inches of filed charts. There is a total of four 5-shelf units available. The total filing space is 700 inches ($5 \times 35 = 175$; $175 \times 4 = 700$). If the shelf space were to be converted to feet, the 700 inches would be divided by 12 (12 inches in one foot) for a total of 581/3 feet.

EX 2. If the average chart is 1/2 inch thick, the total number of charts that can be filed on the existing units is 1,400 (700 inches available, but each chart is only 1/2 inch thick, therefore two charts can be filed per inch or $700 \times 2 = 1,400$ charts can be filed in the available space).

 SELF-TEST 2-18

It is estimated that a five-year expansion will require an additional 350 inches of filing space. Using the dimensions above (5-shelf unit, 35 inches per shelf), how many additional units will need to be purchased?

3. Equipment

Equipment is either purchased or leased. It is often the manager's responsibility to determine the annual cost of each option for budgeting purposes. Lease amounts can be stated in monthly, quarterly, semiannual, or annual terms.

EXAMPLES:

EX 1. The HIM department has leased a scanner for converting their paper records into electronic form. The terms of the lease are $6,000 semiannually. What is the monthly cost of this lease? $6,000 for six months would be converted to a monthly rate by dividing $6,000 by 6 = $1,000 per month.

EX 2. The HIM Department has a proposal to lease equipment with the following terms: $4,800 annually with a 5% discount. What is the net cost of the proposed leased equipment? $4,800 \times .05 = $240 discount; $4,800 - $240 = $4,560 net cost.

 SELF-TEST 2-19

A department has leased three pieces of equipment at the following rates:

Scanner @ $1,600 per quarter
Two copiers @ $120 per month each.

a. What is the quarterly cost of leasing the equipment?
b. What is the amount to be budgeted annually for this equipment?

4. Productivity

Standards of productivity are often set for each job performed in a department. This is especially true when employees are paid on an incentive-pay basis. A baseline scale is established, and employees who exceed the baseline are compensated for the additional work, generally at a higher rate. However, quantity alone should not be the determining factor, as a quality standard should also be met. An example of a quality measure could be number of errors in coding a chart.

EXAMPLE: An HIM department has 50,000 active records on file. The record supervisor has established a maximum 15-minute time period for retrieval of a record. During the past month, 750 charts were requested. Of this number, 688 were retrieved within the 15-minute period. What percentage of the records fell below the established standard?

Subtracting 688 from 750 indicates that 62 charts did not meet the required standard. Thus, 62 out of 750 retrievals were not in compliance for an 8.27% non-compliance rate (62/750).

 SELF-TEST 2-20

Referring to the example above, if a compliance rate of 95% is expected, how many of the 750 charts requested could fall below the standard and still be within the 95% goal?

5. Budget Variance

Each department in a health care facility prepares an annual budget that includes all expected operating costs for the fiscal year. The budget includes salaries and wages as well as expenses for equipment, supplies, contracts, and all foreseeable expenses. A monthly review is carried out to determine if the department operated within the budget, or if the expenses exceeded or fell below the budgetary amount. The difference between the actual operating expenses and the budgeted amount is referred to as the variance. Line items in budgets can also be expressed as a percentage of total expenses.

EXAMPLE:

EX 1. If $100,000 was budgeted for salaries and the department paid out $105,000 instead, the department was $5,000 over budget for a variance of 5% (5,000 divided by 100,000 = 0.05 = 5%).

 SELF-TEST 2-21

A total of $6,000 was budgeted for supplies last year, and the department used $5,520 of supplies.

    a. Is the amount under or over budget?
    b. What is the variance?
    c. What is the percentage of variance?

C. SUMMARY

1. A fraction is a part of a whole written as one number over another number. The numerator is the top number; the denominator is the bottom number. The quotient is obtained by dividing the top number by the bottom number.
2. A decimal is an amount less than one and is preceded by a decimal point.
3. A percentage is a decimal multiplied by 100 followed by a percent sign.

4. A rate is a quantity measured with respect to another measured quantity; it is often defined as the number of times something happens divided by the number of times it could happen.

5. A ratio (also known as a proportion) is the relationship between items or to other items.

6. An average is determined by totaling all scores in a distribution and dividing by the total number of scores in that distribution.

7. Rounding numbers makes them more manageable. When rounding, computations should always be carried out at least one place beyond the specified answer—that is, a number specified as correct to two places should be carried out to at least 3. If the third-place number is 5 or more, the second-place number is increased by 1.

8. Computations can be converted from one form to another.

9. When computing with percentages, the percent is converted to a fraction or decimal before proceeding with the computation.

10. Basic mathematics is the basis for most of the calculations necessary for budgeting, staffing, equipment purchases or leases, and developing productivity standards.

Name _____ Date _____

Part 1: Mathematical Functions

1. Reduce the following fractions:

   a. 35/40   c. 25/125
   b. 8/64   d. 18/27

2. Calculate the quotient correct to two decimal places:

   a. 32/167   d. 250/40
   b. 88/17   e. 3/8
   c. 7,435/313   f. 36/50

3. Compute the following percentages:

   a. 6/100   c. 8/1,000
   b. 5/10   d. 73/400

4. Calculate the decimal equivalent (to two decimal places) of:

   a. 10/200   c. 6/600
   b. 14/1,000   d. 20/480

5. Round to two decimal places:

   a. 40.636   d. 10.999
   b. 40.666   e. 18.555
   c. 40.699   f. 0.095

6. Round to the nearest whole number:

   a. 62.499   d. 10,551.51
   b. 56.503   e. 10.5
   c. 88.8   f. 67.4

7. Round to the nearest:

   a. hundred 4,455
   b. tenth 4.657
   c. thousandth 0.0055
   d. million 4,500,000
   e. hundredth 63.895
   f. ten 77.499
   g. thousand 87,485.7

8. Convert to a percentage—correct to one decimal place:

   a. 4/5   e. 2.1535
   b. 8/10   f. 6/7
   c. 0.06   g. 50/200
   d. 0.84

9. Convert to the lowest fraction:

   a. 60/100   d. 33/99
   b. 80%   e. 10%
   c. 35/65   f. 5:100

10. Convert to a decimal—correct to two decimal places:

   a. 2/17   d. 52%
   b. 3/11   e. 10/90
   c. 25/85   f. 11/11

11. Convert each ratio or proportion to a decimal equivalent and the corresponding percentage:

Ratio or Proportion   Decimal Equivalent   Percentage

a. 2/100

b. 6/25

c. 16:84

d. 360/900

12. For each percentage, determine the corresponding decimal equivalent and ratio:

Percentage   Decimal Equivalent   Ratio

a. 83.33%

b. 87.5%

c. 66.67%

d. 40%

e. 0.50%

f. 0.025%

13. Compute the following—correct to the nearest whole number:

a. If 7 out of 10 patients admitted to the hospital are discharged in 3 days or less, how many out of 13,554 recorded admissions exceeded a stay of 3 days?

b. A hospital discharged 3,520 patients in January. If 5% developed a hospital-based infection, how many were affected?

c. A hospital reported 126,778 discharges during the past year. If 35% of these patients were seen in consultation, how many of the discharged patients were seen by a consultant?

14. Compute the following averages:

a. Ten patients were discharged yesterday. Two of these patients were hospitalized 3 days, two were hospitalized 4 days, and the rest were inpatients for 5, 7, 8, 1, 9, and 2 days, respectively. What was the average number of hospitalized days for this group—correct to one decimal place?

b. During the past week, the following number of cases of measles was reported statewide each day: 11, 8, 13, 15, 5, 9, 12. What was the average daily number of reported cases—correct to one decimal place?

c. A hospital reports the following number of trauma cases seen each month during the past year: 28, 35, 21, 26, 38, 42, 29, 31, 22, 36, 25, 21. Determine the average number of trauma cases seen monthly—correct to the nearest whole number.

15. Convert the weight of a 160 lb female patient to kilograms, correct to two decimal places.

Part 2: HIM Applications

16. A new employee is paid $22.50 an hour. A performance evaluation is completed at the end of the year, and it is determined that the employee should receive a 2.5% raise. What will be the new hourly rate?

17. If the average record is 1/2 inch thick:

a. How many records will a shelf-filing system accommodate if each unit of a four-unit system has five shelves and holds 35 inches of filed charts?

b. If two additional units are purchased, how many charts can be filed?

c. If the average record is 3/4 inch thick, how many charts will the original four units hold?

18. A file room contains 1,720 charts. The department decides to purge 300 charts for digitizing. There are five units of five shelves each, with each shelf holding 35 inches of records. The average chart is 1/2 inch thick.

a. How many inches of shelf space are still available prior to purging?

b. How much shelf space (in inches) will be available after the purging?

c. Approximately how many 1/2-inch charts will fit in the open shelf space after the purge?

19. A department needs new equipment. The manager receives the following bids from four different vendors. The bids are as follows:

Vendor	Cost	Discount
A	$5,000	5%
B	$2,800	10%
C	$3,800	4%
D	$2,700	8%

   a. What would be the final cost for each proposal?
   b. Which vendor offers the best deal?

20. A department leases a scanner at a cost of $1,700 per quarter and three copy machines for $60 per month each. How much must be budgeted for this equipment on an annual basis?

21. The annual budget includes:

Office supplies and postage	$ 2,800
Outsourced staffing	$15,350
Travel and conference fees	$ 3,660
Maintenance contracts	$ 1,990

   Determine the percentage of the total cost budgeted for each expense.

22. During the first half of the year, 686 patients were admitted to the cardiovascular care unit. Of these, 79 were readmissions. What percentage were readmitted?

23. The HIM department has two experienced coders and two coders with training but without experience. The hourly pay for experienced coders is $15 an hour; and, for the inexperienced coders, the hourly pay rate is $12. What is the annual salary for each level of coding?

24. A health clinic has 10,000 paper-based charts on file. In the past six months, 1,200 charts were requested. What was the six-month chart request rate?

25. A medical center, with 75,000 charts on file, has established that a chart should be located within a 15-minute time frame. At the end of one month, it was determined that out of a total of 675 chart requests, 650 were located within the quality standard of 15 minutes. What is the compliance rate?

26. A department has budgeted $163,317.00 for salaries and wages. The actual expenses, over the same period of time, were $171,633.00. Determine the variance.

27. An hourly wage earner in the department earns $13.10. In the past four weeks, the employee worked full time and, in addition, worked a 4-hour shift one Saturday (paid at time-and-a-half). How much is the computed four-week salary?

28. A full-time employee has a base salary of $14.25 per hour. During the employee's yearly evaluation, a 1.5% cost of living increase plus a 2% merit pay increase was granted, both to be added to the base salary. What will be the new hourly wage?

29. The present budget for supplies ($16,300) is to be increased by 7% in the coming year. What amount should be included for supplies in the new budget?

30. A coding supervisor has two full-time coders who average 35 productive hours per week. A standard of 20 minutes per chart has been established as the departmental coding standard. The facility anticipates an increase in the number of discharges since a new wing to the facility is nearing completion. It is anticipated that the number of discharges will increase to a total of 300 discharges to be coded per week. Will new staff be required; and, if so, how many additional coders will be needed?

31. It has been estimated that a full-time employee at the medical center costs an average of $3.00 per hour in fringe benefits.

Employee	Hourly Wage	Hours Worked per Week
A	$12.00	40
B	$11.00	40
C	$14.00	20 (no fringe benefits)

   a. What is the regular weekly salary of each employee?
   b. What is the total cost to the employer for each employee?
   c. What is the total amount to be budgeted to cover all three employees for a year?

32. A department reports the following (for the past year):

	Budgeted	Actual	Difference	%Variance
Salaries	250,000	260,000		
Supplies	1,500	1,640		
Contract Obligations	1,400	1,400		
Continuing Education	2,000	1,960		

   a. Indicate the amount of difference for each category and include the use of a plus sign (+) if over the budgeted amount and a minus sign (−) if under budget.
   b. Calculate the percent of variance for each.

33. An inpatient coder in the HIM department is expected to code 400 charts each month. A total of three inpatient coders are employed full time, and a total of 1,250 charts were coded in September. Of these, 20 failed to pass quality screening.

   a. What percentage of charts was accurately coded?
   b. How many charts could fail the screening if a 99% accuracy rate was required?

34. An HIM coder for a local group internal medicine practice has been given a target of coding 380 charts per month with a 98% accuracy rate. During the past month, the coder achieved his target and coded 380 charts; of the charts coded, six charts were found to have errors.

   a. What percentage of charts was accurately coded?
   b. How many charts could fail the screening if a 99% accuracy rate was required?

Health Data Across the Continuum

CHAPTER OUTLINE

LEARNING OBJECTIVES

After studying this chapter, the learner should be able to:

✓ Discuss various health care provider types across the continuum.

✓ Explain how facility beds are classified by age.

✓ Describe how services are classified within a health care organization.

✓ Differentiate between various types of patient transfers.

✓ Correlate data collection methods with sources of health care data.

PRELIMINARY QUESTIONS

1. Describe how care administered in a hospital differs from a nursing facility.
2. Define: encounter; occasion of service; visit; and MCO.
3. Describe the difference between Medicare and Medicaid.
4. Define: hospice care; respite care.
5. Describe the type of care provided by a primary care center.
6. What is the most common upper age limit for a "child"?
7. Describe the difference between concurrent and retrospective collection of data.
8. What is an abstract? Give an example of an abstract used in health care.
9. What is an index? Give an example of an index used in health care.
10. What is the difference between an index and a register?
11. Name a type of registry other than a cancer registry.
12. What are incident reports?

Many changes have occurred in the health care industry in the past decade, and all indications point to this trend continuing in the years ahead. Previously, patients received most of their medical care that could not be provided in a physician's office in the hospital setting. Today, more and more care is being provided in the outpatient (OP) setting, including surgical and diagnostic procedures performed in outpatient surgery centers and physician offices. Although the primary focus of this book is the computation of the most commonly used statistical rates used in inpatient settings, many of the rates can be adapted to meet the needs of alternative care facilities. Each health care facility needs to assess its data needs in evaluating its mission. Hopefully, the knowledge and skills developed in the coming chapters will aid in this task.

It is important that statistical terms and data be uniformly applied and that the data collected are accurate. Statistics are only as accurate as the original data collected, and the uses made of the data vary from one health care institution to another. Data compiled and analyzed must be based on uniform collection and reporting methods to make it comparable to benchmarks used to determine operational efficiency and effectiveness.

A. HEALTH CARE OVERVIEW

As mentioned previously, health care services are provided in a wide variety of settings—some residential and others ambulatory. A sampling of both types follows.

1. Facilities and Health Care Providers

a. Hospital (Acute Care/Short-Term Care)

A hospital is defined as a health care institution with an organized medical and professional staff and with inpatient beds available on a 24/7 basis, whose primary function is to provide inpatient medical, nursing, diagnostic, and other health-related services to patients for both surgical and nonsurgical conditions. These facilities usually provide some amount of outpatient services, particularly emergency care. For licensure purposes, each state has its own definition of "hospital." Hospitals come in all shapes and sizes and provide a wide variety of services.

b. Long-Term Care Facility; Extended Care Facility; Nursing Home

The primary difference between a long-term care (LTC) facility and a hospital is the level of care. Long-term care patients are not considered to be in an acute phase of illness but require extended inpatient care. Patients are assigned a LTC bed and receive round-the-clock care by professional staff.

1) Skilled Nursing Facility

A skilled nursing facility (SNF) provides the highest level of LTC. SNFs are no longer just nursing homes (NH) for elderly patients but also provide additional care for discharged hospital inpatients who continue to need skilled nursing care. Therefore, they serve a dual population—those with long stays (possibly years) and those who may remain for days or weeks as they continue their convalescence from an acute episode. Many of these patients previously remained in the hospital until they made a complete recovery. In the present health care environment, a patient recovering from a stroke or hip replacement surgery may continue care in a skilled nursing facility prior to being discharged home.

2) Intermediate Care Facility

An intermediate care facility (ICF) also provides long-term care but provides a more limited degree of support and nursing services than are provided in the SNF. Persons with a variety of physical or emotional conditions may still need institutional care; however, they need less skilled nursing care. An example of this would be an assisted living facility.

3) **Residential Care Facility/Life Care Center**
A residential care facility (RCF) provides custodial care to those unable to live independently. The residents may suffer from physical, mental, or emotional conditions. Examples of these include nursing homes and continuing care retirement communities (CCRCs).

2. Specialized Facilities

A specialized facility treats a unique population. As with hospitals, the treatment can be on an inpatient or outpatient basis. Some examples of specialized facilities include:

(1) Rehabilitation Facilities

(2) Psychiatric Facilities

(3) Substance Abuse Treatment Facilities

(4) Children's Hospitals

(5) Burn Facilities

(6) Dialysis Centers

(7) Cancer Treatment Centers

(8) Alzheimer's Facilities

a. Ambulatory Care; Outpatient Care

Increasingly, more and more patient care is being carried out on an outpatient or ambulatory care basis, in part to help contain health care costs. Outpatient care can be delivered in many locations such as physician offices, clinics, outpatient centers, and even in the home.

3. Terms

(a) *Encounter*. An encounter is direct, professional, personal contact between a patient and a physician or health care provider to order or deliver health care services for the diagnosis or treatment of a patient. Encounters do *not* include ancillary service visits or telephone contact. However, social services are included.

(b) *Occasion of Service*. An occasion of service is a specified, identifiable service involved in the care of a patient that is *not* an encounter (for example, a lab test ordered during an encounter). Occasions of service may be the result of an encounter.

(c) *Visit*. A visit is a single encounter with a health care professional that includes all the services supplied during the encounter. A visit may involve one occasion of service or a number of related or unrelated services. A patient scheduled and undergoing blood tests, an electrocardiogram (EKG), and an x-ray (all performed during the same scheduled appearance) is credited with one outpatient visit and three occasions of service. A health care facility needs to maintain data on each encounter and on the number and types of these encounters. Ambulatory care facilities must have appropriate procedures to record data on outpatient visits, encounters, and occasions of service so that accurate patterns of care are appropriately documented and readily available for analysis. A variety of outpatient care alternatives are listed below.

4. **Ambulatory Care Settings**

Ambulatory care can be provided in a hospital (on-site) or at a satellite (off-site) facility or at a stand-alone care center. Ambulatory care includes diagnostic tests or treatment. Tests include laboratory tests (blood work), radiology (x-rays, MRIs, CT scan, or therapeutic services (physical therapy, chemotherapy, mental health treatments).

(a) **Types of Ancillary Treatment Facilities**

(1) *Primary Care Center.* Care provided by a primary care center is like care provided in physicians' offices. Many hospitals have set up and staffed such facilities either on their premises or as a satellite (off-site) operation. Basic health care is provided by a primary care physician (family practice, internist, or pediatrician).

(2) *Emergency Department/Room.* Most hospitals have some type of emergency department/room (ED/ER). Certain hospitals are also designated as trauma centers (Level I and Level II) that are equipped to handle the most threatening emergencies. Care in a hospital ER is very costly and therefore increased restrictions have been placed on the use of these facilities by employee-sponsored benefit plans. Patients are therefore encouraged to use freestanding primary care centers for general, immediate care (colds, cuts, sore throats, coughs). In addition, physician group practices often have expanded physician office hours to provide walk-in care.

(3) *Ambulatory Surgery Facilities/Surgery Centers.* More and more surgical procedures are performed on an ambulatory basis. In ambulatory surgery facilities, surgical services are provided by professional staff to patients who do not require an inpatient bed. The facilities may be located at the hospital or in a satellite or stand-alone facility.

4. **Additional Care Providers**

(a) **Home Care/Home Health Care**

Many hospitals have established home health care departments that provide professional services in a patient's home. Independent home care organizations also provide care, and a hospital may contract with a home health provider for these services. Home health care is a means of providing continuity of care in a cost-effective environment.

(b) **Hospice Care**

Hospice care is care for the terminally ill and their families. Many hospitals provide OP hospice care and some also maintain an inpatient hospice unit, should inpatient care be required.

(c) **Respite Care**

Respite means a short interval of rest or relief. Respite care provides relief to a caregiver by providing care to the person in need of care. For example, a family caring for an ailing parent at home may require care for the parent during the interval of time when they will be away to attend a wedding. The care provided by the relief provider is known as *respite care*. Another example would be someone providing care to a child with a debilitating condition like cerebral palsy so the rest of the family can have a break from the constant care needed by their child.

6. Payment Providers

Hospitals often track their financial data by payer or payer class. Many hospitals keep statistics on Medicare and Medicaid patients. Medicare is national health insurance for seniors, age 65 or older, or disabled Americans. Medicaid is a national program, administered on the state level, provided to those who qualify—usually welfare recipients. Each state sets eligibility and payment standards for Medicaid recipients.

Insurance carriers (both private and governmental) are major health care payment providers. Some insurance plans are called "managed care organizations" (MCOs). The MCO manages all aspects of a patient's care; it is an integrated reimbursement and delivery system. Patients without insurance are billed directly and are often called "self-pay" patients.

7. Bed/Bassinet Classification

Hospitals provide inpatient services to those who have been assigned a bed or bassinet (isolette, incubator). Separate statistics are often computed for each of these categories.

a. Beds

Adults and children (A&C) are included in inpatient bed statistics. The majority of hospitals combine adults and children into one group, although some hospitals separate the two groups for statistical purposes. Occasionally three age classifications are made—adults, children, and adolescents.

1) Beds by Age Classification

(a) Adult—those above the age of children.

(b) Children. No age standard has been universally accepted as the age limit for classifying a patient as a child. The terms *child* and *pediatric patient* are *not* synonymous terms. Technically pediatric patients are those cared for by a physician from the pediatric medical staff. However, a child treated for leukemia by an oncologist on the oncology medical staff unit would be included in "children" data. Whenever adult and children data are to be reported separately the hospital must state the upper age limit for a "child." No universal age limit separating adults and children have been established in the United States. Most often, the dividing line is the 14th birthday; that is, a child who is age 13 or younger (under the age of 14) is assumed to be a child. Some facilities include 14-year-olds as children. Standards should be established by the facility that keeps separate statistics on children.

(c) Adolescent. Again, no universal age limit applies to adolescents, but most facilities use 13 or 14 as the lower age limit and the late teens or early 20s as the upper age limit. In most instances, adolescents are included in adult statistics.

2) Additional Beds

(a) Temporary Beds. Beds used on a temporary basis for treatment are *not* included in bed statistics. Temporary beds include:

(1) Treatment beds temporarily occupied during treatment.

(2) Disaster beds are beds set up in lounges, hallways, and rooms not normally equipped with beds during times of disaster (such as an earthquake or a plane crash).

(3) Delivery room beds.

(4) Recovery room beds.

(5) Observation beds are temporary beds used on an outpatient basis. A patient assigned as an observation may remain under observation for a scheduled period of time (generally 24 hours), during which time the patient is classified as an outpatient. Should the patient require additional care, the patient is admitted and no longer remains an outpatient.

(b) Swing Beds. Swing beds are hospital beds (for adults and children) that may be used flexibly to serve either acute or long-term care beds. Swing beds are most common in rural hospitals with less than 50 beds (staffed and operating with 49 or fewer beds).

b. Bassinets

Bassinets are the beds or Isolettes in the newborn nursery. Newborn statistics are generated from bassinet data. Since a newborn is a patient born in the hospital at the beginning of his or her current inpatient hospitalization, it excludes other babies, even though they occupy a similar bassinet. Also, only babies with signs of life at birth are newborns. A stillborn infant or dead fetus is *not* a newborn and is *not* included in bassinet data. Also, a stillborn is *not* considered a hospital admission.

8. Service Classification

There are several terms used to indicate where hospital care is provided, which medical specialties provide the care, and which medical services were administered during a patient's hospitalization. The terms *medical care unit, medical staff unit, medical service unit,* and *patient care unit* (PCU) are often used to indicate where and by whom care or service was provided. Since the major emphasis of this text is to prepare students for statistical computation of standardized formulas that apply to health care settings, these terms will not be explained in detail. Mention is made of these terms since each patient is assigned or classified by service designation during their hospitalization, and statistics are generated based on the classification.

a. Patient Care Unit

A patient care unit (PCU) refers to an assemblage of beds or bassinets where care for a particular type of condition is provided. Patients are assigned to a unit best equipped to provide optimal medical care. Patient care units may be further designated by the type of care provided (pediatric unit or psychiatric unit) or by the unit's location within a facility (3 South for third floor, south wing).

b. Medical Staff Unit

A medical staff is formally organized into medical staff units. These designations vary greatly from hospital to hospital. Among the factors affecting medical staff assignments are the following:

(1) Size of the facility. The larger the facility (300 beds vs. 50 beds), the more services are likely to be provided.

(2) Number of physicians on the medical staff and the degree of specialization of these physicians.

(3) Type of treatment rendered to patients.

(4) Type of medical staff organization. The organization of each medical staff into medical staff units is stated in its bylaws and the rules and regulations of the medical staff.

c. Basic Service Classifications

A hospital lacking formal organization into medical staff/service units is to assign patients into one of four basic units or service classifications.

1) Medical

All patients not classified in any of the following categories are classified as medical patients.

2) Surgical

An assignment is made to surgical if the surgical operation was performed in the operating room. The primary exception to this rule is obstetrical surgery. A patient delivering by C-section is counted and classified as an obstetrical patient, although the surgery is included as a surgical operation in operating room statistics.

3) Obstetrics

Any patient being treated for a pregnancy condition, whether or not the delivery occurred during the current hospitalization, is an obstetric patient. A patient undergoing treatment for a pregnancy-related condition (labor and the puerperium), whether normal or pathological, is an obstetric (OB) patient. Obstetric patients may be subdivided into:

(a) Delivered in the hospital, whether liveborn or fetal death, or

(b) Admitted after delivery, or

(c) Not delivered.

4) Newborn

A liveborn delivered in the hospital is a newborn (NB). As stated previously, a newborn must be alive at birth and be born in the hospital.

d. Expanded Service Classifications

A major teaching hospital or other large city hospital may have a large number of medical care/staff/service unit classifications. In addition to the four basic medical staff units, as many as 60 "standard" staff units are used. The term "special care unit" is also used to designate a specialized type of treatment provided by that unit. Special care units may include burn, cardiac care, cardiovascular surgery, neonatal intensive care, renal dialysis, and intensive care units. Special care units are patient care units. Medical staff units can include dermatology, otorhinolaryngology, physical medicine and rehabilitation, neurology, orthopedic surgery, urology, and psychiatry, to name a few.

e. Assigning Service Classifications

Patient care units do not ordinarily correspond to medical staff units. For example, medical care units are often classified into medical, obstetrical, newborn, pediatrics, intensive care, and surgery. However, the medical staff may be organized into medical, surgical, obstetrics/gynecology, and otorhinolaryngology.

A service classification is generally assigned upon discharge based on the major care received by the patient during hospitalization. Statistics are generally based on service classification. Service classifications assist in comparing patients with similar conditions. Comparing a urology patient with another urology patient is more appropriate than comparing a urology patient with a neurology patient diagnosed with a cerebrovascular accident (CVA) or a pediatric patient. Although patients may be assigned a service classification upon admission, the classification may change when a more definitive diagnosis is determined. Service classifications are useful to health care administrators in assessing utilization of services and planning future patient care needs of the community being served.

EXAMPLES:

EX 1. A physician admits a patient complaining of chest pain, and the patient is admitted to the cardiology unit. However, subsequent studies (lab test, EKG, etc.) rule out heart problems, and the physician orders additional tests that indicate digestive problems. A diagnosis of severe gastroesophageal reflux disease (GERD) is suggested. The patient is discharged with this latter final diagnosis. The service classification entered is gastroenterology.

EX 2. Statistical data revealed the number of OB patients has been increasing over an extended period of time. The health care facility wants to make sure enough OB beds, staff, and services will be available to meet the needs of the health care providers and their patients. Physicians prefer to send their patients to the facility offering the best care and services, and a health care facility needs to stay competitive in providing services.

When assigning a service classification, there are several factors that aid in the assignment:

(1) Final, principal diagnosis and procedure
(2) Physician specialty (cardiologist, neurologist)
(3) Treatment received (physical therapy following a stroke; dialysis)
(4) Medical staff unit providing treatment (orthopedic unit; cardiology)

NOTE: Only those units into which the medical staff is formally organized should be used in assigning service classification. Many physicians (family practice, internists, pediatricians) treat a variety of conditions. Assignments should be made based on the principal diagnosis and procedures. For statistical considerations throughout this text, it will be assumed the medical staff units and service classifications are identical to the medical staff units. Each health care facility determines the number and type of service classifications. In one facility, a diagnosis of severe gastroesophageal bleeding may be classified to gastroenterology, whereas in another facility, the same diagnosis may be classified to internal medicine. In large teaching hospitals, a classification may be subdivided by specialty area; for example, orthopedics may be subdivided into hand surgery, spinal surgery, and knee and hip surgery. No universal classification system exists, and assignments serve to assist in managing the utilization of services.

EX 3. Listed are some diagnoses and their service classification:

Disorder	Service Classification
Acne rosacea	Dermatology
Adenomatous goiter	Endocrinology
Cataract	Ophthalmology
Anaphylactic reaction from bee sting	Allergy
Iron-deficiency anemia	Hematology
Klebsiella pneumonia	Pulmonary medicine
Prolapsed uterus	Gynecology
Schizophrenia	Psychiatry
Syphilis	Infectious disease

TABLE 3-1 Diagnosis Classification

Abbrev.	Category	Disorders Treated
A&I	Allergy/immunology	Hypersensitivity and autoimmune disorders
CV	Cardiovascular	Heart and blood vessel disorders
Derm	Dermatology	Skin disorders
Endo	Endocrine	Endocrine gland disorders
GI	Gastrointestinal	GI tract disorders
Gyn	Gynecology	Female reproductive system/breast disorders
GU	Genitourinary	Urinary tract/male reproductive disorders
Hem	Hematology	Blood disorders
Neuro	Neurology	Brain and nerve disorders
NB	Neonatology	Newborn and infant disorders
OB	Obstetrics	Pregnancy and delivery complications
Onco	Oncology	Tumor disorders
Ophth	Ophthalmology	Eye disorders
Ortho	Orthopedics	Bone and muscle disorders
ENT	Otorhinolaryngology	Ear, nose, and throat disorders
Peds	Pediatrics	Healthy newborn/infant and children disorders
Psych	Psychiatric	Mind and behavior disorders
Pulm	Pulmonary	Respiratory tract disorders

Additional service classifications (not included in assignments) include anesthesiology; dentistry; genetics; gerontology/geriatrics; hepatic and biliary diseases; infectious and parasitic diseases; internal medicine; podiatry; radiology/nuclear medicine; and rheumatology.

TABLE 3-2 Surgical Classification

Code	Type of Surgery	Code	Type of Surgery
C	Cardiac/cardiovascular	Or	Orthopedic
Ge	General (often abdominal)	Ot	Otorhinolaryngologic
Gy	Gynecological	P	Plastic and reconstructive
N	Neurosurgery	T	Thoracic
Op	Ophthalmologic	U	Urologic

Copyright© 2015 Cengage Learning®

Additional possibilities (not included in assignments) include abdominal surgery; colorectal; gastrointestinal; maxillofacial; obstetrical; oral; and trauma surgery.

 SELF-TEST 3-1

Classify the following diagnoses based on the choices from Table 3-1 above.

a. _____ Esophageal varices due to chronic alcoholism
b. _____ Pneumothorax due to accidental puncture
c. _____ Skull fracture with concussion
d. _____ Diverticulitis of the right colon
e. _____ Thrombophlebitis, postop
f. _____ Epilepsy, grand mal type
g. _____ Otitis media
h. _____ Angina pectoris
i. _____ Osteosarcoma
j. _____ Hemophilia
k. _____ Viral meningitis
l. _____ Deep vein thrombosis
m. _____ Tear of the medial meniscus
n. _____ Acute cervicitis
o. _____ Psoriasis
p. _____ Endometriosis
q. _____ Pyelonephritis
r. _____ Multiple myeloma
s. _____ Colles' fracture
t. _____ Acute cystitis, due to *E. coli*
u. _____ Ventricular tachycardia
v. _____ Left maxillary sinusitis
w. _____ Diabetic retinitis
x. _____ Hyperparathyroidism

SELF-TEST 3-2

Classify the following procedures using the choices from Table 3-2.

a. _____ Face lift

b. _____ Splenectomy

c. _____ Closure of colostomy

d. _____ Myringotomy with tubes

e. _____ Culdocentesis

f. _____ Scleral buckling, OS

g. _____ Cholecystectomy

h. _____ Craniotomy

i. _____ Laminectomy

j. _____ Excision of neuroma, left foot

k. _____ Thyroidectomy

l. _____ Intravenous pyelogram

m. _____ Left radical mastoidectomy

n. _____ Anterior vitrectomy, OD

o. _____ Meniscectomy

p. _____ Left orchiectomy

q. _____ Herniorrhaphy

r. _____ Insertion of cardiac pacemaker

s. _____ Nephrectomy

t. _____ Right hemicolectomy

9. Transfers

Patients are occasionally transferred after their initial admission to either another medical care unit or occasionally to another health care facility. A patient transferred within the admitting facility is referred to as an intrahospital transfer, and the latter is a discharge transfer.

a. Intrahospital Transfer

An intrahospital transfer is a change in medical care/staff unit, or responsible physician, of an inpatient during hospitalization. In larger hospitals, care on a specific medical care unit may be restricted to patients with the appropriate diagnosis. Also, levels of care change and a seriously ill patient assigned to the intensive care unit will likely be transferred to a lesser level of care prior to discharge.

Records are kept on the number of days on each unit. Reports should clearly indicate whenever patient transfers occur during hospitalization and to which unit the patient was transferred. All units are expected to keep track of all patient transfers. A patient transferred into a unit (TRF-in) was admitted to the unit, and a patient transferred out (TRF-out) was reassigned to another unit. The days of care on each unit can be tabulated from these data.

b. Discharge Transfer

A discharge transfer is the disposition of an inpatient to another health care facility at the time of discharge. The patient may be transferred for many reasons, including the need for more specialized care than can be provided at the current facility or to continue convalescence at a lower level of care. Pertinent medical record data are sent with the patient to the new facility to aid in continuity of care.

c. **Additional Discharge Options**

At the time of discharge, a notation is included in the patient's medical record as to the disposition of the patient. A patient not transferred to another facility is most likely a routine discharge (discharged home). Other discharges include patients who leave the hospital prior to a formal discharge and are reported as leaving AMA (against medical advice) and those who died (expired during hospitalization).

Some facilities use some form of code to indicate the discharge status of a patient. This might include:

1—alive to home

2—alive to another acute care facility

3—alive to nursing facility

4—alive to IP rehab

5—alive to hospice

6—alive to home health

7—alive to mental health

8—expired

9—against medical advice

B. DATA ENTRY/COLLECTION

1. Collection Terms

a. **Concurrent versus Retrospective Collection**

Concurrent data collection refers to entering data at the same time or as the care of the patient is taking place. Some facilities send coders to the nursing station to code the information in the patient chart while the patient is still hospitalized (concurrent). A nurse who records a patient's temperature directly into the chart is doing so concurrently. *Retrospective* refers to looking back or happening later. A coder who receives the chart after the patient is discharged is performing retrospective coding.

b. **Manual versus Direct Electronic Collection**

The electronic medical record is becoming more and more a reality. Health care facilities are incorporating electronic data entry as they transition to a completely computerized medical record. Direct electronic entry is much more efficient than initially entering data onto a worksheet and later transferring the data into a computer. A hybrid medical record is one in which part of the record is paper based and the remainder resides electronically.

c. **Amount of Data Collection**

Computers not only aid data entry but also serve to store and retrieve increasing amounts of data. An annual review should be carried out to determine what statistical reports are needed. When undertaking the review, the following should be considered.

(1) What reports are needed routinely in-house by the administration and medical staff?

(2) What reports are required by outside agencies?

(3) What ad hoc data requests are made?

(4) Are there data needs not being met; in other words, are there data that could prove valuable to or aid the organization?

2. Sources of Statistical Data

In a previous chapter, patient data sources were listed as primary or secondary data sources.

a. Primary Source

The primary source for health care data is the patient's medical record. The data include notations by the physicians, nurses, and ancillary services (radiology, lab, pharmacy, physical therapy); operative reports; delivery room reports; and ER records and ambulatory surgery reports. The patient record also provides information such as admission and discharge dates, demographic information, diagnoses, operations and procedures, attending and consulting physicians, expected payer, and more.

b. Secondary Source

Secondary data sources are primarily data abstracted from the primary source. A cancer registrar abstracts data from a host of similar diagnoses into a cancer registry abstract. In addition to abstracts of various types, lists, indexes, registers, and registries are secondary data sources; they are compiled data. An example would be a surgical index that lists all surgeries that are performed at a facility and are broken down by the type of surgery, the day it was performed, and the surgeon(s) that performed the surgery. Indexes and registers are kept and maintained to more easily retrieve information. Retrieval of information is as vital to an organization as the original accurate recording and reporting of data. Indexes and registers contain much valuable information. Indexes serve as retrieval tools in evaluating patient care. Quality assurance or quality resource management (QRM) is a major health care function. Physicians and departments determine the focus of the study to be performed. The surgical staff may choose to study all head trauma patients, the physical therapy staff may elect to review stroke rehabilitation patients, and so forth. The retrieval of patient care charts is generally facilitated by accessing the appropriate index.

1) Abstract

An abstract is a concentrated essence of a larger whole. It is concise information and a compilation of pertinent information. A case abstract is data condensed into a more concise form. A cancer registrar completes an abstract on all cancer patients. In abstracting, information from the patient record is condensed based on previously established criteria. Abstracts may also be completed on patients upon discharge. Reports can be generated from abstracted data entered into a database. Many states have a centralized cancer registry, and the abstracted data from throughout the state are used to generate cancer statistics.

2) List

A list is undoubtedly the easiest to generate. A daily admission list provides census information. Additional lists may include a transfer list—a list of patients transferred from one unit to another—as well as a discharge list, which includes all patients transferred out of the facility as well as those who expired on a specified date.

3) Index

An index is a tool used as a guide to locate information. Everyone is familiar with a book index. When searching for a site or topic in a book, an individual uses the index to find the appropriate location in the book where the topic was presented. An index is anything that serves to guide, point out, or otherwise facilitate reference. Health care facilities maintain a variety of indexes. Most importantly, these include the master patient index (MPI), number index, disease and operation/procedure index, and physician index.

a) MPI

The MPI maintains the name of every patient receiving service at a facility. Identification and demographic information is retained in the MPI. Most often, this includes the patient's name, address, sex, birth date, hospital number (patient identification number), admission and discharge dates, and the attending physician.

b) Number Index

The number index is maintained as a source for patient identification number control. Correct use of this index prevents two different patients from being admitted with the same hospital identification number.

c) Disease Index

The disease index is a listing of patients discharged with a specific diagnosis code. Upon discharge, a coder codes the final diagnoses on a patient's chart using a coding system. In the United States, the most common coding system in use is ICD-9-CM, which may soon be replaced by ICD-10-CM. If the diagnosis is "congestive heart failure," the appropriate code is assigned. All patients assigned this diagnosis code are then listed in the disease index for this code. Patients are listed by hospital identification number or by both the hospital number and name. Should members of the medical staff choose to evaluate the care of congestive heart failure patients, the index facilitates the retrieval of patient care charts.

d) Procedure/Operation Index

The procedure/operation index is like the disease index in that it is a listing of all patients with the same procedure code. Current Procedural Terminology (CPT) is a coding system for procedures and operations, especially outpatient procedures. The amount of information in indexes varies. A large facility, such as a teaching or research center, will undoubtedly benefit from more than just basic information (patient name and identification number). Some indexes may include the sex, age, attending physician/surgeon, dates of admission and discharge, end results (died, discharged, autopsied), and associated diseases and operations. The greater the amount of information abstracted, the greater the cost to the facility in terms of personnel time. However, if a study were to be carried out on all female patients who underwent coronary bypass surgery, it would be extremely helpful to have the sex of the patient included in an index. Consideration should be given to the uses of the index and the amount of information requested.

e) Physicians' Index

Each physician on staff has a listing in the physicians' index. Most commonly, the patient's name and hospital identification number are recorded. Other data, such as hospital service, length of stay, or patients for whom the physician served as a surgeon or consultant, may also be included. Since the information in the physicians' index is confidential, many facilities use a code number rather than the physician's name to identify the physician. However, the code number should not be reassigned should the physician die or resign from the medical staff.

4) **Register**

A register is a chronological list of data in a health care facility. Registers serve as a reference for a department. The radiology department may keep a chronological register of all patients treated in their department each day. If they want to check if Mary Jones, for example, had a mammogram on June 6, the register for June 6 can be referenced. Each department determines the amount and type of information and data to be maintained based on legal requirements.

a) Admission and Discharge Register

As stated, a daily log of each day's admissions and discharges is prepared. These lists serve as the basis of the admission and discharge register. Daily, each patient is entered chronologically into the appropriate (admission or discharge) register by name and hospital identification number. In the discharge register, a notation is included to indicate whether the patient died or was discharged alive. Generally, it is also noted if the patient was transferred to another facility (another hospital, nursing home, rehab center, etc.). Prior to computerization, these registers were often the responsibility of the medical record department, whereas they are now generally maintained in the admitting department. In addition, many departments keep some type of register. Two of the most common are the operating room (OR) register and the ER register.

b) Birth and Death Registers

As with admissions and discharges, a chronological register is kept of the daily births (in the obstetric department) and a chronological death register (all patients who expired each day).

5) Registry

Registries have been established for a variety of conditions. The oldest and most recognized registry is the cancer/tumor registry. A registry contains abstracts that are then shared to form a larger database. The amount of information generally exceeds that found in a register or an index. In addition to the cancer/tumor registry, registries have been established for AIDS, birth defects, organ transplants, trauma, and others.

6) Incident Reports

The primary means to assess risk in a facility is the incident report. Medical treatment errors have the potential to end in a lawsuit against the institution. A health care facility hopes to eliminate potentially compensable events (PCEs) through investigation of untoward incidents. Medication errors and falls are examples of potential problems, and these risks or incidents are investigated and identified through completion of an incident report. Data collected from these reports can identify trends and promote necessary corrective action.

C. SUMMARY

1. Health care is offered in a wide variety of both inpatient (IP) and outpatient (OP) settings.
2. Hospitals provide care to acutely ill patients, whereas a long-term care facility extends a lesser level of care.
3. Long-term care facilities are classified as SNF, ICF, or RCF.
4. Many facilities offer specialized care, including rehabilitative, substance dependency, cancer, and burn care, to name a few.
5. Outpatient treatment includes ambulatory care, ambulatory surgery, home care, and hospice care.
6. Primary care centers have relieved hospital emergency rooms from caring for non-emergencies, such as colds, upset stomachs, minor cuts, and abrasions.
7. Adults and children are assigned beds; newborns are assigned bassinets. Some statistical formulas combine the two groups in the same formula; others have separate formulas for the two groups.
8. A patient is generally considered a child below the age of 14; no universal age has been established as the dividing line between adults and children.
9. Temporary beds are not counted in bed statistics.
10. The four basic service classifications include medical, surgical, obstetric, and newborn.
11. Medical staff units provide care on medical care units.
12. Patients are assigned a service classification at the time of discharge, based on the final diagnoses and treatment. Service classification aids in determining utilization of facilities and services.
13. An intrahospital transfer occurs when patients are transferred from one care unit to another care unit within the same facility; discharge transfers involve transfer to another health care facility.
14. Accurate and adequate data collection is extremely important, but a facility should avoid collecting unnecessary data.
15. Incident reports assess untoward risks.

16. The patient's medical record is the primary source for health care data.

17. Secondary health care data sources include abstracts, lists, indexes, registers, and registries.
18. An abstract is data condensed into a more concise form.
19. An index serves as a guide to locate information. Hospitals maintain an MPI, number index, disease index, procedure/operation index, and physicians' index.
20. A register is a chronological list.
21. A registry maintains information; it is a repository of abstracted data.
22. An encounter is a direct, personal contact between a patient and a health care provider to order or provide health care services.
23. An occasion of service is a specified service, often the result of an encounter.
24. A visit is a single encounter that includes all the services supplied during the encounter.

Name _____ Date _____

D. CHAPTER 3 TEST

1. Distinguish the care provided in a/an:

    a. Hospital (acute care facility) versus SNF.
    b. SNF versus ICF.
    c. ICF versus RCF.
    d. Emergency room versus trauma center.

2. Distinguish between:

    a. Medicare and Medicaid insurance.
    b. Retrospective and concurrent data collection.

3. Describe the type of care provided by a primary care center.

4. Name:

    a. An ancillary service.
    b. A primary care physician.
    c. The four basic service classifications.
    d. A discharge option other than a routine discharge or discharge transfer.
    e. The age most often used as the dividing line between adults and children.

5. Identify and explain the initials:

    a. AMA as related to discharge.
    b. MCO.

6. State the term for:

    a. A facility associated with the hospital but often located off-site rather than on campus.
    b. Care provided to the terminally ill.
    c. Hospital beds that may be assigned as LTC beds.
    d. Temporary beds in which the maximum occupancy period is generally 24 hours.
    e. Care administered to provide relief to a caregiver.
    f. A transfer between medical care units within the same facility.
    g. A report filed regarding the investigation of treatment errors and inappropriate care.

7. Is an adolescent included in adult or children statistics?

8. Name a list compiled daily in a hospital.

9. Name three indexes maintained in a hospital.

10. Name a register maintained in a hospital.

11. Explain the difference between the terms encounter, occasion of service, and visit.

12. Name three types of temporary beds. Are temporary beds included in bed statistics?

13. Using the service classification list (Table 3-1) classify the following diagnoses:

    a. _____Dissecting aneurysm
    b. _____Lupus erythematosus
    c. _____Diabetic ketoacidosis
    d. _____Acute myocardial infarction
    e. _____Peritonitis
    f. _____Emphysema
    g. _____Erythroblastosis fetalis
    h. _____Phimosis
    i. _____Parkinson's disease
    j. _____Laryngitis
    k. _____Hemorrhoids
    l. _____Heroin overdose
    m. _____Slipped capital femoral epiphysis

n. _____Lymphedema, postmastectomy

o. _____Glioma multiforme

p. _____SIDS

q. _____Muscular dystrophy

r. _____Sickle cell anemia

s. _____Epididymitis

t. _____Strabismus, divergent

u. _____Mitral stenosis

v. _____Urticaria

w. _____Tic douloureux

x. _____CVA (cerebrovascular accident)

y. _____Uterine bleeding, two-weeks postpartum

14. Using the surgical procedure classification list (Table 3-2), classify the following surgical procedures:

a. _____Excision of uterine leiomyoma

b. _____Insertion of arteriovenous shunt for dialysis

c. _____Arthroplasty

d. _____Osteotomy

e. _____Tympanectomy

f. _____Excision of astrocytoma

g. _____Jejunojejunostomy

h. _____Trephination

i. _____Cochlear implantation

j. _____Repair of esotropia

k. _____Vesiculectomy

l. _____Blepharoplasty

m. _____Arteriorrhaphy

n. _____Thoracentesis

o. _____Patellectomy

p. _____Mediastinoscopy

Hospital Census

CHAPTER OUTLINE

LEARNING OBJECTIVES

After studying this chapter, the learner should be able to:

☑ Distinguish between census, inpatient census, and daily inpatient census.

☑ Distinguish between methods for bed and bassinet counts.

☑ Compute daily census.

☑ Compute period census.

☑ Compute average census.

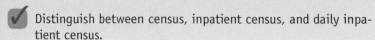

PRELIMINARY QUESTIONS

1. What is a census?
2. When does a health care facility conduct a census?
3. What distinguishes an inpatient from an outpatient?
4. Name two types of patient transfers that occur in health care.
5. Define DOA.
6. If a health care facility has 100 beds and during the past week, the number occupied each day were 60, 70, 75, 80, 65, 70, and 55, what is the average number of beds occupied during that week? Describe the value used in the denominator.
7. Name the number of days in a non-leap year; name the four months that have only 30 days.
8. Was 1988 a leap year? How does one determine if a designated year is a leap year?

The term *census* is a familiar term, as the U.S. Census Bureau conducts a population census every 10 years. Questionnaires are sent to all households in the United States regarding the number of people living at a specified residence—including the age, sex, race, and marital status of each individual. Questionnaires not returned are followed up by census takers who go house to house to gather the same information. The United States has been conducting a population census every decade since 1790. More than four-fifths of the world's population is counted in the census. Facilities of all types, including hospitals, nursing facilities, homeless shelters, and day care centers, to name a few, enumerate census data. Census data are kept daily, weekly, monthly, yearly, and at other specified intervals.

A. CENSUS COLLECTION AND TERMS

1. Census

The *American Heritage Dictionary* defines census as "an official, usually periodic, enumeration of population." A census is a count—a count of people. This count can be of the population as a whole or a subgroup—a count of every patient currently hospitalized or just those on a specified clinical unit, such as the surgical unit.

2. Inpatient Census

The *Glossary of Health Care Terms* defines inpatient census as "the number of inpatients present at any one time."

3. Hospital Patients

Two major designations apply to hospital patients—inpatients and out-patients also referred to as *ambulatory care patients*. Statistics are compiled separately on patients in these two categories.

a. Inpatients

A hospital inpatient is a patient who has been formally admitted to the hospital and to whom room, board, and continuous nursing service is provided. Inpatients (IPs) are admitted to the hospital and assigned a hospital bed on a clinical unit. Other health care facilities that provide inpatient care, such as extended care facilities, also compile statistics on their patients (or residents, as they are often referred to in long-term care facilities).

b. Outpatients

Outpatients (OPs) receive service on a more limited basis and are not assigned an inpatient hospital bed. A hospital outpatient is defined as a hospital patient who receives services in one or more facilities of the hospital when not currently an inpatient or a home care patient. Outpatient admissions are primarily for some type of test (laboratory tests—complete blood count [CBC], chemistry profile, lipid profile; x-rays; physical therapy) or in some instances, outpatient surgery. These data are recorded apart from inpatient data to evaluate services received by patients and services rendered by the health care facility.

4. Hospital Departments

A hospital consists of many departments that provide a wide range of services to patients. A few of the typical hospital departments are health information, patient accounts, clinical laboratory, radiology, physical medicine and rehabilitation (PM&R), housekeeping, and outpatient surgery.

5. Hospital Units and Services

The terms *medical care, staff,* and *service unit* were discussed in the previous chapter. As previously mentioned, smaller hospitals generally have fewer administrative units than larger hospitals. The most common services or units are medical, surgical, obstetrics, newborn, and pediatrics. Age may also be a factor in designating medical care units, with separate units designated for newborns and pediatric patients.

6. Census Taking

Census taking is the process of counting patients. Each day, a hospital keeps track of the number of patients treated—both inpatients and outpatients—and the services administered to patients. Throughout this book, the census applications will apply to inpatients, but most of the statistics are applicable to outpatient data as well.

a. Census-Taking Time

The most important factor in taking a census is consistency. A health care facility needs to establish the time of day when *all* nursing units take and report the census. This must be consistent every day and on all units. Midnight is most often chosen as census-taking time (CTT), as it is a less busy time for the nursing staff. However, if another time is selected, the time should be adhered to every day and on all nursing units.

b. Reporting the Census

Today, most hospitals are computerized in almost all aspects of their operation, and the census is automatically generated by a software program based on admission, discharge, and transfer data entered into the computer system throughout the day. What the software program does is to compile a real-time listing of all patients admitted since the last census; all patients discharged from a unit, including those who died, since the previous census; and all patients transferred—either transferred into the unit (TRF-in) or those transferred to another nursing unit (TRF-out).

EXAMPLE: Mary Jones is a patient on the medical unit and is taken to surgery at 8 A.M. Following surgery, Mary is transferred to the surgical unit. Mary would be listed as a TRF-out on the medical unit census and as a TRF-in on the surgical unit census.

c. Central Collection

Data collected throughout the hospital are combined so that upper level management can determine overall facility occupancy and related staffing needs. It is imperative that software programs are checked to insure the validity of patient data that are collected. The data must correspond to the total daily admissions and discharges and the number of patients transferred from one nursing unit to another nursing unit must balance out—the total number of TRF-ins must equal the number of TRF-outs—within the facility. Remember a transfer out is *not* a discharge.

d. Transfers

Patients transferred from one clinical unit in a health care facility to another clinical unit in the same facility are called intrahospital transfers. If Sue Smith were transferred out of one unit, she would have to be transferred into another unit, unless she was discharged. The clinical unit transfer total (in and out) need not be equal but the total within the facility must be equal. A patient may transfer out of the intensive care unit (ICU) without another patient being transferred in. A "discharge transfer" is a patient who is discharged and, upon discharge, is transferred to another health care facility—a skilled nursing facility, another acute care facility, or rehabilitation center.

EXAMPLE: On March 1, Sally Smith was admitted to the medical unit. It was determined that emergency surgery was necessary. After surgery, Sally was admitted to the surgical unit. While there, her condition worsened, and Sally was transferred to the ICU. There her condition stabilized and she was transferred back to the surgical unit. At CTT, Sally is listed as a TRF-out on the medical unit; she is a TRF-in and TRF-out on the surgical unit; a TRF-in and TRF-out of ICU; and again, listed as TRF-in on the surgical unit, where she is counted as an inpatient on the March 1 census report at CTT.

NOTE: A patient may only be counted as an inpatient on *one* unit at CTT but may be listed as a transfer on several units.

7. **Admitted and Discharged the Same Day**

A patient who is admitted and discharged the same day is an A&D. These patients are not to be confused with outpatients. Outpatients were not admitted—they were not assigned an inpatient hospital identification number and were not assigned an inpatient bed (called a bed count bed). Outpatient surgery patients are treated as outpatients unless they are formally admitted as an inpatient. Many conditions, formerly treated on an inpatient basis, are now being effectively treated on an outpatient basis. The number of A&Ds is generally small, but some patients may expire on the first day of hospitalization, others may be transferred to another facility for care not available at the current facility, and others may leave against medical advice. Since care and service was rendered, they need to be included in certain statistical reports and are included in some census statistics.

EXAMPLE: Sally Smith was admitted at 4:30 A.M. At 2:00 P.M. on the same day, she chooses to leave against medical advice. For statistical purposes she would be classified as an A&D.

8. **Census/Inpatient Census**

The term *hospital census* or *inpatient hospital census* refers only to patients present at the census-taking time. The term excludes any additional patients that may have received service on a unit during that day but who are no longer present at CTT.

9. **Daily Inpatient Census**

The *daily inpatient census* (DIPC) refers to all patients present at CTT *plus* any inpatients admitted and discharged before CTT (in other words, between the last CTT and the present CTT).

EXAMPLE: A patient admitted after the census (say, midnight of May 2) and discharged before the census was taken the following day (May 3) is not counted in the May 3 census as the patient is not present at CTT. However, the patient had received service in the hospital as an inpatient on May 3. The patient is an A&D and is included in the DIPC. If Jane Doe is admitted at 8 A.M. on May 2 and discharged at 10 P.M. the same day (May 2), Jane will no longer be hospitalized at CTT and thus will not be counted in the regular census. However, Jane received services on May 2, service for which the hospital should be credited. Thus, the DIPC includes the census total taken at CTT (May 2 in the example) *plus* any A&Ds for that date (such as Jane Doe).

10. Inpatient Service Day

An inpatient service day (IPSD) is a unit of measure denoting the services received by one inpatient for one 24-hour period. The 24-hour period is the 24 hours between census-taking times. Other terms occasionally used for inpatient service day are *patient day, inpatient day, census day, or bed occupancy day*. The preferred term is *inpatient service day*. An IPSD includes not only a patient present at CTT but also any patient admitted and discharged the same day.

An IPSD total is the sum of all inpatients who received service on a specific day. Each inpatient receiving service on a specific date is recorded as one IPSD; adding all the patients receiving service on the specified date is the IPSD total for that date. Based on these definitions, it is noted that the DIPC and the IPSD total compilations are identical. The totals represent all inpatients receiving service on one specific day.

a. Unit of Measure versus Totals

1) Unit of Measure

A unit is the smallest amount to be measured. In the statistical reporting to follow, a *unit* is represented by the singular term *day* as opposed to the plural *days*, which is a total of all the individual units. Each individual receiving inpatient service on a certain date is credited with an IPSD, and this includes a patient present at CTT and any A&D the same day.

2) Totals

Units of measure get combined into totals used for statistical purposes. Each patient is one *unit,* but it is important to determine the total amount of service rendered on a particular day or for a specified period of time.

(a) *Daily totals*. If each inpatient is one unit and 150 patients received service on a specific date (say, June 1), there would be a total of 150 IPSDs for June 1. The plural, days, indicates a total.

(b) *Period totals*. More than one day comprises a period. A period may be two days; it may be one, two, or more weeks; it may be a month, half-month, two months; it may be a year, half-year, or five years. Generally, period designations are in weeks, months, or years. It may be necessary to compare one year's totals with those of the previous year or compare last month's data with the current month, and so on. The period to be totaled is specified, and all IPSDs are added together to obtain the total for the period.

EXAMPLE: If 150 inpatients received care on Sunday, 152 on Monday, 145 on Tuesday, 155 on Wednesday, 152 on Thursday, 148 on Friday, and 149 on Saturday, then a total of 1,051 IPSDs of care were provided for the week—the total for the seven-day period.

As noted above, the DIPC and the IPSD values will be identical. Both terms add in any A&Ds to the CTT total. Whenever hospital statistics are computed, these totals are used rather than straight census totals, as they are more representative of service rendered by the health care facility. Do not confuse the terms *census* or *inpatient census* with IPSDs and DIPC. The terms *census* and *inpatient census* are strictly counted at CTT. The terms *IPSD* and *DIPC* include the services rendered to A&Ds.

11. Total Inpatient Service Days

Total IPSDs refers to the sum of all IPSDs for each of the days in the period under consideration. The beginning census is the census taken at CTT the previous day. One patient day is then added for each new admission, and one patient day is subtracted for each discharge during the 24 hours following the previous census. Transferred-ins (TRF-ins) are added and transferred-outs (TRF-outs) are subtracted on individual clinical units. Hospital-wide, the TRF-ins should equal the TRF-outs as those patients were just transferred within the same facility; they are only receiving care on another clinical unit within the same facility. Then, to this subtotal, one inpatient day must be added for each patient A&D between the two consecutive census-taking hours. This final total, then, is the most representative of the amount of service rendered by the health care facility on that specific day.

EXAMPLE: If 155 inpatients were present at CTT on June 1 and 15 patients were admitted on June 2, five were transferred between units, eight patients were discharged on June 2 (before CTT), and two patients were admitted and discharged on June 2. The total inpatient service days for June 2 is 164 ($155 + 15$ [admitted] $- 8$ [discharges] $+ 2$ [A&Ds] $= 164$ [inpatient service days]).

12. Deaths/Discharges

Deaths are considered discharges; and, although they are recorded separately, they are included in the total discharges, unless the term *live discharges* are used. In this latter instance, the deaths must be added to the live discharges to obtain the total number of inpatient discharges. The term *discharges* include deaths and live discharges.

In discharge totals there are several deaths that are *never* included. These are as follows:

(a) *Fetal deaths.* A fetus that was not alive at the time of delivery cannot be deemed an inpatient and is not included in inpatient hospital statistics, *except* in formulas related to fetal deaths (fetal death rate and fetal autopsy rate). The term *stillborn* is still in use, although the term *fetal death* is preferred. A stillborn is classified as a fetal death.

(b) *DOA.* The abbreviation DOA refers to *dead on arrival.* A patient brought to the hospital without any sign of life and for whom all recovery efforts are ineffective is included in outpatient statistics but never in inpatient census data.

(c) *OP death*. Only inpatients are included in inpatient hospital statistics. Outpatient data are maintained separately. An outpatient death is included in outpatient statistics but not inpatient statistics. An outpatient is not assigned an inpatient bed for statistical purposes.

13. Census Calculation Tips

In figuring census data, it is often helpful to use plus (+) signs and minus (−) signs in front of data to indicate whether a number should be added or subtracted in the calculation. Also, crossing out (drawing a line through) irrelevant data may be helpful.

EXAMPLE: Clinical unit:

May 31	Midnight census	43	(+43)
June 1	Admissions	8	(+8)
	Discharges	2	(−2)
	TRF-in	1	(+1)
	TRF-out	0	
	A&D	2	(Inclusion depends on the statistic; excluded in census calculation; included in DIPC and IPSD)

a. What is the census for June 1?

Lightly crossing out the A&D total; the result is 50 $(43 + 8 − 2 + 1 = 50)$.

b. What is the daily inpatient census for June 1?

The DIPC includes A&Ds, and therefore they are included in the total, 52; $(43 + 8 − 2 + 1 + 2 = 52)$.

c. What is the Inpatient Service Day total for June 1?

Again, A&Ds are included for a total of 52 (same as b).

14. Beds/Bassinets

Inpatients are classified, primarily, into two categories: Adults and children (A&C) and newborn (NB). Hospital patients are assigned either a *bed* or a *bassinet*.

These designations are for statistical purposes. Counts are recorded daily regarding the number of beds and bassinets occupied. Hospitals are set up and staffed for a certain number of beds and bassinets. Census data and percent of occupancy are determined using these counts.

a. **Beds**

Bed statistics include all patients *not* born in the hospital during that hospitalization. Inpatients admitted to an inpatient hospital bed are included in the category designated as "Adults and Children" (A&C). Most of the A&Cs are exactly what the term describes, and they occupy an inpatient hospital bed. However, babies born on the way to the hospital or at home and then admitted are assigned one of these so-called beds even though they are placed in a bassinet or an isolette. This is done to evaluate services between the two levels of care.

b. **Bassinets**

Only babies born in the hospital are included in the category referred to as *Newborns*. These are the babies included in bassinet statistics. It is important to remember that babies born at home or en route to the hospital are not included in newborn bassinet census data even though they are admitted shortly after birth. The infants in this latter category are assigned a so-called bed and are included in bed statistics and not bassinet census statistics.

EXAMPLE: A baby is born in a taxicab on the way to the hospital. The baby is admitted to the hospital but is not included in the bassinet statistics.

c. **Adults and Children**

Adults and children (A&C) includes any inpatient admitted to the hospital other than a newborn born in the hospital. When census data are recorded, the data for adults and children are kept separate from newborn data. Whenever the words "inpatient census" or "inpatient service days" are used, they refer to the adults and children census data.

d. **Newborns**

Any live infant born in the hospital is considered a newborn (NB) and is included in the bassinet count and the newborn data statistics. Since the care required by these patients is quite different from that required by A&C, the two groups are kept separate for statistical reporting and comparisons. Thus, a newborn must be (1) alive at birth and (2) born in the hospital. Newborns born elsewhere are considered hospital inpatients other than newborns and included in A&C statistics.

EXAMPLE: A newborn that is born in the hospital, discharged, and then readmitted to the hospital is no longer a newborn patient and is classified under adult and children statistics.

 SELF-TEST 4-1

1. The hospital census on May 3 is 456.

   On May 4:   Admissions   58
                Discharges   45
                A&D   6
                DOA   2

   Calculate:
   a. Census for May 4.
   b. Daily inpatient census (DIPC) for May 4.
   c. Inpatient service day (IPSD) total for May 4.

2. The newborn nursery census for May 1 is 22.

On May 2:	Births (Admissions)	4
	Discharges	2
	Fetal deaths	2

   Calculate the census for May 2.

3. A hospital has a total of 100 patients at midnight (CTT) on July 1. On July 2, two patients are admitted in the morning and discharged in the afternoon. Another patient is admitted at noon but expires at 4:30 P.M. the same day. A patient, admitted two days ago, is transferred to another hospital on July 2. No other patients are admitted or discharged on July 2.

   Calculate:
   a. Inpatient census for July 2.
   b. Daily inpatient census for July 2.
   c. Inpatient service day total for July 2.

4. Inpatient census at midnight (CTT) on August 1: 150.

August 2:	A Adams	admitted	8:00 A.M.	discharged 6:00 P.M.
	B Barnes	admitted	9:00 A.M.	
	C Carlson	admitted	10:00 A.M.	
	D Doran	discharged	3:30 P.M.	
	E Edwards	expired	11:15 A.M.	
	F Foster	admitted	1:00 P.M.	

   Calculate:
   a. Inpatient A&C census for August 2.
   b. Daily inpatient census (A&C) for August 2.
   c. Inpatient service day total (A&C) for August 2.

5. Listed are the IPSD Totals for April at Holy Family Hospital, a 50-Bed Hospital.

Date	IPSD	Date	IPSD	Date	IPSD
1	45	11	35	21	44
2	30	12	41	22	48
3	35	13	47	23	35
4	25	14	48	24	36
5	47	15	49	25	38
6	48	16	50	26	42
7	38	17	40	27	44
8	42	18	41	28	40
9	43	19	43	29	52
10	36	20	47	30	41

   Calculate:
   a. Inpatient service day total for April.
   b. Inpatient service day total for April 20.
   c. Inpatient service day total for April 7 through April 15.
   d. Average daily inpatient census for April, to the nearest whole number.
      (See formula listed under B. Average Census, question 1.)

B. AVERAGE CENSUS

1. Average Daily Inpatient Census (Average Daily Census)

An average census represents the average number of inpatients present each day for a specified period of time.

Formula for Average Census:

$$\frac{\text{Total inpatient services days (for a period)}}{\text{Total number of days (in the period)}}$$

Average figures are often more representative than totals for a given period of time. There may be periods when many patients receive service, and there may also be periods when admissions are down and inpatient count is low. Evaluating census data is easier when comparing the average DIPC rather than comparing daily census totals.

a. Separate A&C and NB Data

Since census data for adults and children and census data for newborns are recorded separately, the averages are also calculated on their respective individual databases rather than a combined average. Since calculating an average involves dividing by the number of days in a period, the period needs to be specified (one week, three months, six months, one year).

b. Days in Month

For computing averages, one needs to know the number of days in each month. There are several methods for remembering the number of days, including: *Jingle*. Thirty days hath September, April, June, and November. All the rest have 31, save February, which has 28 in line and leap year makes it 29. *Knuckles*. Make a fist with both hands, keeping the thumbs hidden. Start at the little finger side of either hand and begin with January, pointing first to the top knuckle (MCP joint), then the depression between knuckles. If the month lands on a knuckle, the month has 31 days. If it falls in a depression, it has either 28 or 30 days (only February has 28; all the others have 30 days).

c. Leap Year

To determine whether the indicated year is a leap year, divide the year by 4. If the quotient is a whole number (no remainder), the year is a leap year, which indicates that February has 29 days. For instance, 2000 is divisible by 4 (2000 divided by 4 = 500). However, 2010 divided by 4 equals 502 with a remainder of 2. The year 2000 is a leap year and 2010 is not.

d. Rounding

When dividing numbers, the quotient does not always calculate to a whole number; and, therefore, the rules for rounding need to be followed. When the figures are large, it is usually adequate to carry out the answer to two decimal places and round the answer correct to one decimal place. On occasion, the results are recorded to the nearest whole number.

e. Logical Answers

Whenever decimal points or percentages are involved, it is very important to watch the placement of a decimal point. Obviously, there is a great difference between 2.10, 21.0, and 210. Many errors can be averted by asking if the answer makes sense. If the hospital is a 210-bed hospital and the average IPSDs for January are reported as 20.1, the answer is most probably incorrect, because an average this low would probably jeopardize the existence of the health care facility and lead to its demise. A result of 2,010 is also absurd and impossible. Thus, it is extremely important to watch the placement of decimal points and to ask oneself if the answer is logical.

2. Additional Formulas for Census Averages

a. A&C (Average Daily Inpatient Census for A&C [excluding newborns])

Additional Formula for Census Averages:

$$\frac{\text{Total inpatient service days (excluding newborns) for a period}}{\text{Total number of days in the period}}$$

b. NB (Average Daily Newborn Inpatient Census)

Formula for Average NB Census:

$$\frac{\text{Total newborn inpatient service days for a period}}{\text{Total number of days in the period}}$$

c. Patient Care Unit (Average Daily Inpatient Census for a Patient Care Unit)

Formula for Average Census for a Patient Care Unit:

$$\frac{\text{Total inpatient service days for a patient care unit for a period}}{\text{Total number of days in the period}}$$

EXAMPLE: In question 5 of Self-Test 5-1 (Holy Family Hospital with 50 beds), a total of 1,250 IPSDs were recorded for April. To compute the average DIPC for April, the IPSD total (1,250) is divided by 30 (April has 30 days), which results in an average DIPC of 41.7 inpatients (corrected to one decimal place) for April for the 50-bed hospital.

 SELF-TEST 4-2

Assume a non-leap year for the following calculations.

1. St. Mark's Hospital data:

Months	IP Service Days	Bed Count
January through April	45,515	400
May through August	54,624	500
September through December	62,890	550

Calculate the average daily inpatient census for each of the three periods.

2. A 260-bed hospital with 20 newborn bassinets records the following IPSD for March.

A&C: 7,240

NB: 540

Calculate:

a. Average daily adults and children census.
b. Average daily newborn census.

3. Mercy Hospital statistics for September: A&C NB

Counts	Beds = 150	Bassinets = 15	Other
Census (midnight August 31)	140	11	
September admissions	310	90	
September discharges	315	94	
September deaths	15	2	
September fetal deaths			5
September inpatient service days	4,236	410	

Calculate:

a. Inpatient A&C census and NB census for midnight September 30.
b. Average daily inpatient A&C census for September.
c. Average daily newborn census for September.

4. Three clinical units at Holy Redeemer Medical Center reported the following data for November:

	Pediatrics	Orthopedics	Psychiatry
Bed count	12	15	10
Beginning census	10	12	6
Admissions	85	122	54
Discharges	87	123	53
Deaths	1	3	0
Inpatient service days	344	433	284

Calculate:

a. Average daily inpatient census for each clinical unit.
b. Ending census (November 30) for each clinical unit.
c. Total inpatient service days for the three combined clinical units for November.

C. SUMMARY

1. Census data on adults and children (A&C) are kept separate from census data on newborns (NB). Census counts are occasionally combined, but IPSD totals for adults and children and the totals for newborns are recorded separately to facilitate statistical computations.
2. The terms *census* and *inpatient census* refer only to the counts at census-taking time (CTT). A census needs to be taken at the same designated time each day on all clinical units. Transferred-ins (TRF-ins) and transferred-outs (TRF-outs) of a clinical unit are also recorded. Patients admitted and discharged the same day (A&D) are not counted in census reports.

3. The terms *daily inpatient census (DIPC)* and *inpatient service day(s) (IPSD)* include the census totals plus patients admitted and discharged (A&D) the same day.

4. The *total inpatient service days for a period* are determined by adding all daily IPSD totals for the designated period.

5. The *average daily inpatient census for a period* is determined by dividing the total IPSD for the period by the number of days in that period.

6. The same rules apply to a patient care unit as to the aggregate of all units.

7. Only inpatient data is used in DIPC and IPSD statistics.

8. Deaths are considered discharges. Unless the term *live discharges* is used, the deaths are included in the discharge numbers. However, death statistics are recorded separately.

9. Adults and children generate bed statistics.

10. Only newborns born in the hospital are included in newborn statistics and generate bassinet statistics. Fetal deaths are never included in NB statistics, only in fetal death statistics.

NOTES

Name _____   Date _____

D. CHAPTER 4 TEST

1. Distinguish between *daily inpatient census and inpatient census.*

2. When must a census be taken?

3. Should adults/children and newborn data be combined in calculating the average daily inpatient census?

4. What is needed to calculate the average daily inpatient census in addition to inpatient service days?

5. Must TRF-ins equal TRF-outs on a daily census report:
   a. On individual clinical units?
   b. Hospital-wide (aggregate from all clinical units)?

6. A patient admitted to the medical unit is transferred the same day to the surgical unit. On which unit is the patient counted at census-taking time?

7. When would a newborn be considered and A&D?

8. St. Luke's Hospital Data:

		A&C	NB	Other
May 31:	Census	141	10	
June 1:	Admissions	8	3	
	Live discharges	3	2	
	Deaths	1	0	
	Fetal deaths			2
	DOAs			2
	A&D	2	0	

Calculate:

a. Census for June 1.
b. Inpatient census for June 1.
c. DIPC for June 1.
d. IPSD for June 1.

9. Three patient care units reported the following data for April: Urology, ENT, and Orthopedics.

Clinical Unit	Bed Count	Beg Census	Admissions	Discharges	Deaths	IPSD
Urology	18	15	62	60	1	501
ENT	16	12	51	48	0	418
Orthopedics	24	20	89	87	1	607

Calculate:

a. Census for each clinical unit for April 30.
b. Total IPSD total for April.
c. Average DIPC for each patient care unit for April.

10. A 65-bed hospital recorded the following data for August:

Date	IPSD
May 1	52
2	50
3	47
4	54
5	52
6	56
7	50
8	45
9	44
10	48
11	48
12	59
13	58
14	57
15	59
16	60
17	59
18	58
19	57
20	52
21	52
22	58
23	66
24	65
25	63
26	62
27	67
28	60
29	62
30	63
31	50

Calculate:

a. IPSD total for August 20.
b. IPSD total for August 21 through August 31.
c. Average DIPC for August 21 through August 31.
d. Total IPSD for August.
e. Average IPSD for August.

11. Census/Admissions/Discharges/A&D/DOA

	Census	Admissions	Discharges	A&D	DOA
January 31:	456				
February 1:		58	45	6	3

Calculate:

a. Census for February 1.
b. IPSD total for February 1.
c. DIPC for February 1.

12. Newborn Unit:

Bassinet Count	Last Census	Births Discharges	Fetal Deaths	TRF-In	TRF-Out
21	15	53	2	0	1

Calculate: Census at census-taking time.

13. St. Peter's Hospital adults/children data for the year:

Admissions: 998

Discharges: 989

IPSD: 36,440

Calculate: Average A&C daily inpatient census for the year.

14. An 18-bed surgical unit data: Beginning census = 12

Admissions	Discharges	TRF-In	TRF-Out	A&D
4	3	2	0	2

Calculate:

a. Census at CTT.
b. IPSD total.

15.

Day 1:	Census 125			
Day 2	**Admissions**	**Live Discharges**	**Deaths**	**A&D**
	8	6	2	2

Calculate:

a. Ending census on day 2.
b. DIPC for day 2.
c. IPSD total for day 2.

16.

Day 1:	Census 285			
Day 2	**Admissions**	**Live Discharges**	**Deaths**	**A&D**
	15	10	2	2

Calculate:

a. Ending census on day 2.
b. DIPC for day 2.
c. IPSD total for day 2.

17.

May 31:	Census	150	
June 1	**Patient**	**Admissions**	**Discharges**
	A Adams	8:00 A.M.	4:50 P.M.
	B Brown	9:00 A.M.	
	C Carson	10:18 A.M.	

May 31:	Census	150	
June 1	Patient	Admissions	Discharges
	D Davis		11:55 A.M.
	E Edwards	2:40 P.M.	7:00 P.M. (TRF—another hospital)
	F Fulk		7:30 P.M.
	G Grant	7:50 P.M.	11:39 P.M. (expired)
	H Hughes	8:19 P.M.	
	I Ingals		9:15 P.M.
	J Jones	11:45 P.M.	
	K Kohl	4:22 P.M.	
	L Lamb		8:33 P.M.

Calculate:

a. IP census on June 1.
b. DIPC on June 1.
c. IPSD on June 1.

18. Sunny Care Hospital: Daily Census Report. 150 beds and 18 bassinets. Beginning Census: A&C <u>120</u> NB <u>14</u>

Unit	Beds/Bass	Beg Census	Adm.	TRF-In	Disch	Deaths	TRF-Out	Census	A&D	IPSD
Medical	40	35	1	1	3	1	1	___	1	___
Surgical	28	23	2	1	3	0	1	___	1	___
Pediatrics	20	15	3	0	2	1	1	___	1	___
Orthopedics	20	16	1	0	2	0	0	___	1	___
Urology	18	15	0	1	1	0	0	___	0	___
Obstetrics	18	13	3	0	2	0	0	___	0	___
Newborn	18	14	4	0	3	0	0	___	0	___
ICU	6	3	2	1	1	1	1	___	0	___
TOTALS										
A&C	150	___	___	___	___	___	___	___	___	___
NB	18	___	___	___	___	___	___	___	___	___

Final Census

A&C _____ NB _____

Complete the blanks above.

5

Hospital Occupancy

LEARNING OBJECTIVES

After studying this chapter, the learner should be able to:

✓ Carry out the general formula for computing a rate.

✓ Identify beds included and excluded in bed counts.

✓ Compute bed occupancy percentage for adults and children (A&C).

✓ Compute bassinet occupancy for newborns (NB).

✓ Compute bed/bassinet turnover rate.

PRELIMINARY QUESTIONS

1. If a health care facility has 100 beds and 60 are occupied, what is the occupancy percentage?
2. Does a health care facility hope to have a high or low occupancy percentage? Explain your answer.
3. Are the services provided to A&C and NBs similar or dissimilar? Explain your answer.
4. Should the two groups (A&C and NBs) be combined in the same statistical formula or be calculated separately? Explain your answer.
5. Why do health care facilities increase or decrease their number of beds/bassinets available? Explain your answer.

The census data in the previous chapter provided information regarding the number of inpatients (IPs) receiving services in a health care facility on any one day or any specified number of days (referred to as a period). The percentage of occupancy provides a health care facility with a ratio or percentage of utilization, or the percentage of the available beds and bassinets that are in use. If a facility has 100 beds available and the staff to provide the services, they most likely will lose revenue if only half the beds are occupied. A facility hopes to have enough beds and services available to their constituency to provide excellent care and operate "in the black." Changes in levels of occupancy explain why facilities "flex" staffing levels up or down to most efficiently meet patient care demands.

Typically, a health care facility is licensed by the state to operate with a specific number of beds (referred to as a 200-bed or 150-bed facility). When a city or region wants to establish a health care facility, or if an existing facility wants to expand and add beds or services, it must apply to the state for a *certificate of need* to prove that the beds or services are needed in the area. The number of beds available is the bed count or, more appropriately, the inpatient bed count. As previously mentioned, a hospital is equipped and staffed for a designated number of beds and bassinets. Statistical analysis is carried out to assess and ascertain how well these beds and bassinets are being utilized—referred to as the percentage *of occupancy*. Hospitals can also "deactivate" beds or an entire unit that are not in use in which case these beds would not be used in occupancy calculations.

A. BED/BASSINET COUNT TERMS

An *inpatient bed count* is the number of available inpatient beds, both occupied and vacant, on any given day. The *newborn bassinet count* is the number of newborn bassinets, both occupied and vacant, on any given day. Hospital staffing (nursing staff, housekeeping staff, laboratory personnel, etc.) is based on beds/bassinets available. It is not cost-effective to staff empty beds. Therefore, the number of beds set up and staffed for use may be less than the number of beds the facility is licensed to operate. Hospitals often open and close nursing units based on need. During a period of diminished demand, a clinical nursing unit may be closed; and, during periods of peak demand, another unit may be opened. The opening of an additional unit adds to the bed count, whereas, closing a clinical nursing unit decreases the bed count. Since staffing expense is, generally, the biggest factor in a facility's budget, the health care administrator is interested in percentage of occupancy. The term *bed capacity* generally refers to the number of beds a facility has been designed, constructed, and licensed to operate. For statistical purposes, bed/bassinet counts are the more appropriate terms.

A medical unit may close in December and be reopened in January or February, if a need exists. Many hospital administrative decisions are based on occupancy percentages. A health care facility that is overstaffed will lose revenue, but an inadequate number of beds and services may not meet the medical needs of the community it purports to serve.

Again, as mentioned earlier, the use of the singular "day" indicates a unit of measure. An *inpatient bed count day* indicates the number of beds that are set up, staffed, and equipped for patient care on a particular day. *Inpatient bed count days* indicate a total for a specified number of days in a period—week, month, and so on.

1. Temporary Beds

Some hospital beds are considered temporary beds and are not included in a bed count. Temporary beds include beds occupied while the patient is examined or treated in another area of the hospital. The patient is assigned an inpatient bed on a clinical nursing unit but may temporarily occupy a bed elsewhere. Temporary, or excluded, beds include beds in examining rooms, physical therapy beds, recovery room beds (following surgery), and beds in the emergency room (ER). The majority of ER beds are occupied by outpatients during the time of treatment, after which most outpatients are released. However, should a patient be admitted, the patient becomes an inpatient, receiving an inpatient hospital identification number, and is assigned a bed on a patient care unit. For example, a patient was admitted to room 205 (surgical unit) on April 1. On April 2, the patient is taken to surgery. Following surgery, the patient is taken to the recovery room before being returned to his or her room (205). The patient is considered to be a patient in 205 throughout this time, even though a temporary bed was occupied. If, however, the patient is taken to ICU following surgery, the patient is TRF-out of 205 and TRF-in to ICU on April 2, as discussed in Chapter 4 regarding census data.

2. Disaster Beds

Occasionally, at the time of a disaster (earthquake, train derailment, tornado, nuclear disaster) or during an epidemic (such as a flu epidemic), all the regular hospital beds are occupied. Most hospitals have extra beds available for set up during these peak periods. In some instances, these beds are set up in lounges, hallways, and other rooms not normally patient rooms. These extra beds are *not* counted as part of a bed count, but the patients occupying the beds are counted in census statistics that include inpatient service days.

3. Observation Days

A new trend for treating patients is to hold them in a facility under the status of "observation." A patient with this status is considered to be an outpatient even though they may occupy a bed. These "observation" patients would be excluded from inpatient calculations.

B. RATE FORMULA

A *rate* is defined as one quantity measured with respect to another quantity. Whenever a rate is computed, and for all computations carried out in this book, the general rule is that a rate is the ratio of the number of times something happens to the number of times it could happen.

EXAMPLES:

EX 1. A person shooting baskets takes 25 shots, and the ball goes through the basketball hoop 15 times. The percentage of baskets made by this individual is 15/25, or 60% of the attempted shots were successfully completed—the number of successful shots (numerator) divided by the number of attempted shots (denominator).

EX 2. There is a total of 50 questions on an exam. A student answers 40 of the 50 questions correctly; therefore, the student scored an 80% on the exam (40/50 = 80%).

EX 3. A school offers free flu shots to all its students. There is a total of 180 students in the school, and 90 sign up for the free flu shot. Therefore, 50% of the students will receive free flu shots (90/180 = 50%).

As in all these examples, the rate is a ratio of what was possible.

Rate Formula:

$$\frac{\text{Number of times something happens}}{\text{Number of times it } could \text{ happen}}$$

All formulas in this book are based on this rate formula.

C. BED/BASSINET COUNT DAY

A *bed count day* shares similarity with the concept of an inpatient service day (IPSD), since it refers to one patient occupying one bed for one day. The term *bed count* applies to all beds available for inpatient use that are set up and staffed, whether occupied or vacant.

An *inpatient bed count day* is a unit of measure denoting the presence of one inpatient bed, set up and staffed for use and either occupied or vacant, for one 24-hour period.

An *inpatient bassinet count day* is a unit of measure denoting the presence of one inpatient bassinet, set up and staffed for use and either occupied or vacant, for one 24-hour period.

Inpatient bed/bassinet count days are a total. It is the sum of inpatient bed/bassinet count days during the period under consideration.

D. OCCUPANCY RATIO/PERCENTAGE

Occupancy percentages (also called rates or ratios) state the percentage of available beds or bassinets that are being utilized (occupied) on a specific day or for a designated period of time—that is, the percentage of use or utilization of available beds. The term *occupancy ratio* is synonymous with percentage of occupancy and occupancy percentage.

1. Adults and Children (A&C)

The proportion of inpatient IP beds occupied is defined as the ratio of service days to inpatient bed count days (for the period under consideration).

Percentage *of Occupancy: Daily IP Bed Occupancy Percentage:*

$$\frac{\text{Daily IPSD}}{\text{Inpatient bed count for that day}} \times 100$$

EXAMPLE: On July 1, the bed count was 200, and the bassinet count was 20. The IPSD total for the day was A&C = 160, NB = 15. To determine the daily inpatient bed occupancy percentage, 160 (IPSD) is divided by 200 (bed count) = 0.80 and multiplied by 100 to convert the result to a percentage = 80%. Therefore, the daily inpatient bed occupancy percentage for July 1 was 80%, indicating that 80% of the available beds were occupied on that date.

If every available hospital bed is occupied on a specific day, the bed occupancy percentage for that day would be 100%. If every available hospital bed is occupied during a certain period of time (say, one week), the bed occupancy percentage for that (one week) period would be 100%. However, this is not generally the case, nor would it constitute good management. Hospitals plan to have some beds available for emergency and unforeseen situations. However, too many empty beds result in a low occupancy percentage, which is costly to a health care facility; therefore, the facility hopes for a high bed occupancy percentage.

In the event a disaster occurs and disaster beds are utilized, as previously mentioned, this does not add to the established bed count. However, the patient is counted as occupying a bed, and therefore the inpatient bed occupancy percentage could be greater than 100%.

EXAMPLE: The local hospital has a bed count of 200. A tornado hits a town generally served by the hospital. As patients are admitted, all 200 beds are assigned and occupied, and five additional beds are set up to accommodate five additional patients who are admitted. The bed occupancy rate on that day would be 102.5% (20 [IPSD] divided by 200 [bed count] = 1.025 × 100 = 102.5%). However, it is rare to have a bed occupancy rate above 100%. It is also quite likely that another hospital in the area has available beds and patients could be admitted at the other area hospital. However, should a major cataclysmic disaster occur, a hospital may need to utilize disaster beds. Epidemics might also put a strain on available beds.

In most cases, a hospital's inpatient bed occupancy percentage is less than 100%. A 200-bed facility with 180 beds assigned on a certain day has a bed occupancy percentage of 90% (180/200 = 90%). If the IPSD total drops to 175 the following day, the bed occupancy percentage decreases to 87.5% (175/200 = 87.5%).

2. Newborn (NB)

The same principle, applied to A&C, applies to newborns except the bassinet count is utilized rather than the bed count.

Formula for Daily Newborn Bassinet Occupancy Percentage:

$$\frac{\text{Daily NB IPSD}}{\text{NB bassinet count}} \times 100$$

EXAMPLE: A newborn nursery has 10 bassinets available. On a specific day, the daily NB census is eight newborns. The daily newborn bassinet occupancy percentage for that day is 80% (8/10 × 100 = 80%).

 SELF-TEST 5-1

Compute answers correct to one decimal place.

1. A 300-bed hospital has 210 of its beds occupied on February 20. What is the daily inpatient bed occupancy percentage for February 20?

2. On May 5, a hospital with 85 beds has an inpatient service day total of 72 patients. What is the inpatient bed occupancy percentage for May 5?

3. On September 10, an explosion occurs in a chemical plant, and a daily inpatient service day total at the local 150-bed hospital is 155. What is the inpatient bed occupancy percentage for September 10?

4. On January 8, the midnight bed census is 120. However, five patients were admitted and discharged that same day. The hospital has a bed complement of 130 beds. What is the inpatient bed occupancy percentage for January 8?

5. On March 6, a total of 12 bassinets are occupied, out of a bassinet count of 15. On March 7, three babies are born live, and one is stillborn. That same day, two babies are discharged home with their mothers. What is the bassinet occupancy percentage for March 7?

NOTES

6. The following statistics are recorded in the neonatal unit on June 8:

Bassinet count	12
Beginning census (midnight, June 7)	9
Births	3
NB discharges (live)	4
NB death	1
Fetal death	1

Calculate:

a. Inpatient service day total for the neonatal unit on June 8.
b. Bassinet occupancy percentage for the neonatal unit on June 8.

---

3. **Occupancy Percentage for a Period**

Generally, for long-term planning, it is necessary to know the percentage of occupancy for more than just one day. Individual day rates can vary greatly; and it is more advantageous to ascertain the percentage of occupancy over a longer period of time, as a month, quarter year, or year. Daily rates seem to vary more than those computed over a longer time frame.

a. **Beds**

Formula for Inpatient Bed Occupancy Percentage for a Period:

$$\frac{\text{Total inpatient service days (IPSD) for a period}}{\text{Total IP bed count} \times \text{number of days in the period}} \times 100$$

EXAMPLES:

EX 1. Suppose Pleasantville Hospital is a 50-bed hospital. In June, a total of 1,410 inpatient service days were documented. To calculate the inpatient bed occupancy percentage for June, the total IPSD (1,410) is divided by the product of bed count (50) times the number of days in June (30). The result is a bed occupancy percentage of 94% (1,410 divided by $1,500 = 0.94$; $0.94 \times 100 = 94\%$) for the month of June.

EX 2. In September, a hospital had a bed count of 200 and a bassinet count of 24. The IPSD total for A&C for the month was 4,520. To calculate the inpatient bed occupancy percentage, 4,520 is divided by 200×30 (30 days in September) and calculates to 4,520 divided by 6,000 multiplied by 100, for an inpatient bed occupancy percentage of 75.3% for the month of September.

EX 3. A 100-bed hospital reports the following IPSD totals for the first six months of a non-leap year. January, 2,460; February, 2,390; March, 2,555; April, 2,610; May, 2,635; and June, 2,570. From the reported data, the inpatient bed occupancy percentage can be determined. In addition, if the first or second quarter's bed occupancy percentage were requested, the IPSD totals for those months would be totaled and divided by the bed count multiplied by the days in the period and converted to a percentage. To calculate the percentage for the first six months 15,220 (2,460 + 2,390 + 2,555 + 2,610 + 2,635 + 2,570) is divided by 18,100 (100 beds multiplied by 181 days—January through June—equals 0.841) for an 84.1% bed occupancy percentage for the first six months of the year.

b. **Bassinets**

Formula for Newborn Bassinet Occupancy Percentage for a Period:

$$\frac{\text{Total NB IPSD for a period}}{\text{Total NB bassinet count} \times \text{number of days in the period}} \times 100$$

EXAMPLE: Caring Hospital has a bassinet count of 30. During July, a total of 825 NB inpatient service days of care were provided. Therefore, the newborn bassinet occupancy percentage for July is 88.7% (825 divided by 30 bassinets multiplied by 31 days in July or 825/930 = 0.887 or 88.7%).

c. **Clinical Unit**

Formula for Clinical Unit Occupancy Percentage for a Period:

$$\frac{\text{Total IPSD for a clinical unit for a period}}{\text{IP bed count total for that unit} \times \text{number of days in the period}} \times 100$$

EXAMPLE: The pediatric unit of a hospital has 15 beds. During the first week of October, the IPSD totals were 12, 11, 13, 9, 10, 13, 7. Therefore, the pediatric unit occupancy percentage for the first week of October was 71.4% (IPSD total = 75; bed count [15] multiplied by 7 [days] = 105; 75/105 = 0.714 = 71.4%).

 SELF-TEST 5-2

Answers should be correct to two decimal places. *Note*: All questions indicated by *R [as in *(R4)*] indicate the question is a review question. The number after the R indicates the chapter in which the topic was discussed. (R4 indicates the question relates to census data, presented in Chapter 4, should a reference be needed.) Future tests may include review questions so that information previously learned is not forgotten.

1. A clinical unit has a bed count of 18 beds. Inpatient service days totals are:

    December 1 through December 10 165

    December 11 through December 20 162

    December 21 through December 31 180

Calculate:
a. Period with the highest bed occupancy percentage.
b. Inpatient bed occupancy percentage for December.

2. St. Teresa Hospital Records indicate the following:

	IPSD	Bed Count
January through April	18,850	175
May through July	17,340	200
August through October	13,220	150
November through December	8,880	165

Calculate: The period with the highest inpatient bed occupancy percentage.

3. The daily inpatient service day totals in February for a 50-bed hospital are listed:

Date	IPSD	Date	IPSD	Date	IPSD	Date	IPSD
1	40	8	37	15	38	22	41
2	41	9	48	16	48	23	45
3	43	10	46	17	44	24	46
4	50	11	43	18	49	25	37
5	47	12	49	19	50	26	39
6	46	13	39	20	47	27	43
7	38	14	48	21	40	28	48

Calculate:

a. Inpatient bed occupancy percentage for February 14.
b. Day with the highest inpatient occupancy percentage in February, without calculating the individual percentages.
c. Inpatient bed occupancy percentage for February.
d. Divide the month into four equal periods (seven days each), and indicate the inpatient bed occupancy percentage for each of the four periods.

4. A newborn unit of 14 bassinets records the following data for April:

IP service day total	388 discharges (live)	88
Beginning census	12 newborn deaths	1
Admissions	88 fetal deaths	3

Calculate:

a. Bassinet occupancy percentage for April.
b. *(R4)* Census at the end of April.

5. November data for St. John Hospital:

Clinical Unit	IP Service Days	Bed/Bassinet Count
Medical	2,850	100
Surgical	988	34
Pediatric	422	15
Orthopedic	502	18
Obstetric	544	20
Neonatal	524	18

Calculate:

a. Bed and bassinet occupancy percentage for each clinical unit. Indicate the clinical unit with the highest percentage.
b. A&C inpatient bed occupancy percentage for November.

E. CHANGE IN BED/BASSINET COUNT

Occasionally, a change in bed count occurs in a health care facility. A new unit may open, a renovation may occur and a new wing may be added to the facility, or a unit may close due to any number of reasons. An expansion or elimination of beds will result in a change in bed count. The change is not temporary, as is the case with disaster beds, but is a fairly permanent change for a specified period of time. At times, hospital rooms no longer needed for patient care are converted to other uses (office space or laboratory space, for example). Patient care needs and administrative decisions dictate changes to the bed/bassinet count.

Formula for Occupancy Percentage with a Change in Bed Count for a Period:

$$\frac{\text{Total IP service days a period}}{\begin{array}{c}(\text{Bed count} \times \text{number of days in the period})\\ + (\text{Bed count} \times \text{number of days in the period})\end{array}} \times 100$$

EXAMPLES:

EX 1. Jubilee Hospital has decided to expand its facilities and add additional beds. The January through June bed count was 200 beds. On July 1, an additional 20 beds were added. The total number of inpatient service days for the first half of the year totaled 36,006. The second half of the year (with 20 additional beds) totaled 40,004. The IPSD total for the year was 76,010 (36,006 + 40,004). The denominator in the formula multiplies the bed count for each period by the number of days in the period; therefore, 200 × 181 = 36,200 (first half of the year) added to 220 × 184 = 40,480 (second half of the year) with a combined total of 76,680 (76,010 divided by 76,680 = 0.991 × 100 = 99.1% inpatient bed occupancy percentage for the year).

EX 2. Sunshine Hospital begins the year with an official bed count of 60 beds. On January 15, 10 beds are officially eliminated, and the bed count drops to 50 beds. The inpatient service day total for January was 1,575. Therefore, the bed occupancy percentage is determined by dividing 1,575 (IPSD) by 1,690 (60 beds multiplied by 14 days = 840 and 50 beds multiplied by 17 days = 850 resulting in a combined total of 1,690. 1,575/1,690 = 0.932 × 100 = 93.2% inpatient bed occupancy percentage for January).

 SELF-TEST 5-3

Calculate answers correct to two decimal places.

1. Expansion Hospital begins the year with a total of 150 beds and 10 bassinets. On March 1, 15 additional beds are added to the bed count, for a total of 165 beds.

    On April 1, five additional bassinets are added to the newborn nursery, for a total of 15 bassinets.

    On July 1, the hospital expands again, adding another 15 beds and five bassinets, bringing the total counts to 180 beds and 20 bassinets.

    On October 1, another expansion occurs and 20 additional beds are added.

The inpatient service day totals for the various periods are as follows:

Period	IP Service Days		Counts	
	Bed	Bassinet	Bed	Bassinet
January through February	8,550	555	150	10
March	4,775	288	165	10
April through June	14,425	1,242	165	15
July through September	16,005	1,666	180	20
October through December	17,704	1,744	200	20

Calculate:

a. IP bed occupancy percentage for each quarter (January through March; April through June; July through September; October through December).
b. Newborn occupancy percentage for each quarter.
c. IP bed occupancy percentage for the year.
d. Newborn occupancy percentage for the year.
e. Quarter with the highest IP bed occupancy percentage.

2. Prairie Hospital, with a bed complement of 250 beds, decides to close a section of the hospital and reduce the bed count to 200 beds. The administrative closure is implemented on July 17. During July, 5,710 inpatient service days of care were provided.

Calculate: percentage of inpatient bed occupancy for July.

3. A total of 76,006 inpatient service days of care were provided at Blessing Hospital during a non-leap year. The bed counts changed from a count of 200 at the beginning of the year to 220 on March 15. On July 1, the bed count went up to 230. However, on November 15, the count was reduced to 210, where it remained through the end of the year.

Calculate: Inpatient bed occupancy percentage for the year.

4. The neonatal nursery rendered a total of 676 patient days of care during January. The bassinet count was 25 on January 1 but dropped to 18 on January 22.

Calculate: Bassinet occupancy percentage for January.

5. General Hospital's statistics reveal the following for a non-leap year.

Period	IPSD		Count	
	A&C	NB	Bed	Bassinet
January	4,880	601	160	20
February through March	10,115	1,110	180	20
April through June	16,662	2,190	200	25
July through September	15,558	2,069	175	25
October through December	15,612	1,722	175	20

Calculate:

a. IP bed occupancy percentage for January.
b. Bassinet occupancy percentage for February through March.
c. IP bed occupancy percentage for January through June.
d. Bassinet occupancy percentage for July through December.
e. IP bed occupancy percentage for the entire year.
f. Bassinet occupancy percentage for the entire year.

g. Quarter with the highest inpatient bed occupancy percentage.

h. Quarter with the highest bassinet occupancy percentage.

6. On January 11, a 50-bed hospital added 10 beds (total bed count of 60). On January 21, another 10 beds were added (total bed count of 70). The inpatient service days for January were 1,800.

Calculate:

a. Inpatient bed occupancy percentage for January.

b. If the hospital reduced the beds from 70 to 60 on February 1 and maintained that bed count through February with a February IPSD total of 1,250, calculate the inpatient bed occupancy percentage for the entire period (January through February) in a non-leap year.

F. BED/BASSINET TURNOVER RATE

Another measure of hospital utilization of beds is the bed turnover rate. This rate indicates the number of times each of the hospital's beds changed occupants. Several formulas are in use for determining this rate, and there is no universal agreement on the most accurate representation or formula. However, administrators of acute care hospitals are increasingly interested in bed turnover rates because they are considered a measure of bed utilization, especially in conjunction with percentage of occupancy and length of stay. When occupancy increases and length of stay (days from admission to discharge for each individual patient) decreases, or vice versa, the bed turnover rate makes it easier to see the net effect of these changes.

The following two formulas (which are among several that can be used) are used most frequently in the United States. They are referred to as the *direct formula* and the *indirect formula*.

1. Direct Bed Turnover Rate

Direct Bed Turnover Rate:

$$\frac{\text{Total number of discharges (including deaths) for a period}}{\text{Average bed count during the period}}$$

2. Indirect Bed Turnover Rate

Indirect Bed Turnover Rate:

$$\frac{\text{Occupancy rate (in decimal format)} \times \text{number of days in a period}}{\text{Average length of stay}}$$

3. Bassinet Direct and Indirect Turnover Rate

The same procedure is followed to determine the bassinet turnover rates.

EXAMPLE: A 200-bed hospital reports 7,000 discharges in the past year. The average A&C length of stay was 8.5 days and the bed occupancy rate was 82%.

Using the *direct formula*, the bed turnover rate is 35 times (7,000 discharges divided by 200 beds = 35 turnovers).

Using the *indirect formula*, the bed turnover rate is 35.21 (0.82 occupancy rate × 365 days = 299.3 divided by 8.5 [average length of stay] = 35.21 turnovers).

Therefore, during the year, each of the hospital's 200 beds changed occupants about 35 times. Remember, with an 82% occupancy rate, there were times a bed was unoccupied.

Turnover rates can be useful in comparing one hospital with another. Turnover rates may also be useful in comparing rates within the same hospital in terms of utilization for different time periods or the utilization rate for different clinical units. Even though two time periods have identical occupancy percentages, the turnover rates may differ—a lower rate may be due to a longer length of stay during one of these periods. If a unit has a high turnover rate, even though it has a low occupancy rate (such as might occur in the obstetrics unit), this may indicate a greater number of patients are being cared for on that unit compared to a unit with a higher occupancy percentage (for example, the surgical unit) but a longer length of stay. The bed turnover rate is generally regarded as a measure of the degree of bed utilization.

 SELF-TEST 5-4

Answers should be correct to two decimal places.

Shoreline Hospital reported the following during the past non-leap year:

	A&C	NB
Bed/bassinet count	250	15
Admissions	9,205	1,256
Discharges	9,180	1,245
Deaths	103	5
IPSD	69,608	4,846
Average length of stay	7.64 days	3.93 days

Calculate:
a. Percentage of bed occupancy for the year.
b. Bed turnover rate: (1) Direct (2) Indirect
c. Percentage of bassinet occupancy for the year.
d. Bassinet turnover rate: (1) Direct (2) Indirect

G. SUMMARY

1. An inpatient bed count/bed complement is the number of beds, both occupied and vacant, on any given day.
2. An inpatient bassinet count/complement is the number of newborn bassinets, both occupied and vacant, on any given day.
3. Bed count beds exclude beds in examining rooms, labor beds, recovery room beds, observation beds, physical therapy beds, and any bed used only for treatment or examination. Bed count beds are the beds assigned on a clinical unit of the hospital.
4. Bed count beds are assigned to all patients except those born in the hospital. Any newborn admitted to a health care facility, even minutes after birth, is included in bed count statistics, even though newborn occupy a bassinet or an isolette in newborn intensive care.

5. Bassinet statistics include only newborns born in the health care facility during that admission.

6. Disaster beds may be added during emergency situations and are not included in a bed count.

7. A rate is the number of times something happens divided by the number of times it could happen.

8. To determine the occupancy percentage:
   a. A&C and NB are computed separately; they are generally not combined.
   b. Use IPSD totals, not census, in the numerator.
   c. Daily percentage is the IPSD divided by the bed/bassinet count.
   d. Period percentage is the IPSD divided by the bed/bassinet count multiplied by number of days in the period.
   e. For a change in bed count, the percentage is determined by dividing the IPSD total by the (bed count $\times$ days) + (bed count $\times$ days)—one for each period with a different bed count.

9. Disaster beds are temporary beds set up when all regular beds are occupied (as in a disaster). The percent of occupancy will exceed 100% in such instances.

10. Clinical unit percentages are computed in the same manner as bed/bassinet count rates.

11. A direct bed/bassinet turnover rate is the total discharges divided by the bed count.

12. An indirect bed/bassinet turnover rate is determined by dividing the [occupancy rate (in decimals) multiplied by the days in the period] by the average length of stay.

NOTES

Name _____ Date _____

H. CHAPTER 5 TEST

NOTE: Compute all answers correct to two decimal places.

1. Data from a 72-bed hospital in October:

Date	IPSD	Date	IPSD	Date	IPSD	Date	IPSD
1	50	9	44	17	59	25	63
2	50	10	46	18	58	26	62
3	49	11	48	19	54	27	60
4	54	12	56	20	55	28	60
5	52	13	58	21	55	29	62
6	51	14	56	22	58	30	63
7	50	15	59	23	62	31	50
8	43	16	60	24	65		

Calculate:

a. Percentage of occupancy for October.
b. Percentage of occupancy for October 25.
c. Percentage of occupancy for October 1 through October 10.
d. Percentage of occupancy for October 11 through October 20.
e. Percentage of occupancy for October 21 through October 31.

2. St. Catherine Hospital

	A&C	NB	Surgical
Bed/bassinet count	100	10	25
March 9: Census	95	8	18
March 10: Admissions	8	2	4
Discharges	6	1	3
Deaths	1	0	1
A&D	2	0	0

Calculate:

a. A&C bed occupancy percentage for March 10.
b. NB bassinet occupancy percentage for March 10.
c. Surgical unit bed occupancy percentage for March 10.
d. *(R4)* Census for March 10.

3. Mountain Medical Neonatal Unit (16 bassinets)

January 1:	Census	13
January 2:	Births	4
	Discharges	3
	NB deaths	1
	Fetal deaths	1
	A&D	1

Calculate:

a. *(R4)* Census for January 2; IPSD total for January 2.
b. Bassinet occupancy percentage for January 2.

4. St. Luke's Hospital

Period	Bed Count	Bed IPSD	Bassinet Count	Bassinet IPSD	Surgical Count	Surgical IPSD
January through March	160	12,405	18	1,378	25	2,180
April through June	180	14,621	15	1,247	30	2,516
July through September	200	15,777	20	1,615	30	2,601
October through December	175	14,813	25	2,084	35	2,913

Calculate:

a. Percentage of bed occupancy for each period.
b. Percentage of bassinet occupancy for each period.
c. Percentage of surgical unit occupancy for each period.
d. Name the category (bed, bassinet, or surgical unit) with the highest occupancy percentage for the entire year.

5. Golden Valley Hospital

	A&C	NB	Orthopedic Unit (Included in A&C)
Bed/bassinet Count:	80	10	12
March: Admissions	105	57	47
Discharges	104	55	46
Deaths	5	1	2
IPSD	1,998	268	278

Calculate:

a. Bed occupancy percentage for March.
b. Bassinet occupancy percentage for March.
c. Orthopedic unit occupancy percentage for March.

6. Highlands Regional Medical Center (for November)

	Count		
Unit	Bed	Bassinet	IPSD
Medical	58		1,660
Surgical	32		886
Pediatrics	10		215
Orthopedics	18		498
Obstetrics	15		405
Newborn		12	324
Totals:	133	12	

Calculate:

a. Percent of occupancy for each unit for November.
b. A&C percent of occupancy for November.

7. St. Frances Hospital

		Counts		I PSD	
Period	Dates	Beds	Bassinets	A&C	NB
A	January 1 through February 15	90	12	3,815	463
B	February 16 through March 31	100	8	4,079	314
C	April 1 through April 30	110	10	2,986	272
D	May 1 through June 30	85	14	4,021	708

Calculate:
a. Percent of bed occupancy for each period.
b. Percent of bassinet occupancy for each period.
c. Percent of bed occupancy for January through June.
d. Percent of bassinet occupancy for January through June.
e. Period with the highest IP bed occupancy percentage.

8. Pacific Regional Hospital

Period	Bed Count	IPSD
January	250	6,250
February	225	5,984
March	200	5,888
April through June	210	17,920
July through September	200	17,561
October through December	180	16,007

Calculate:
a. Bed occupancy percentage for January.
b. Bed occupancy percentage for February through March.
c. Bed occupancy percentage for the first half of the year.
d. Bed occupancy percentage for the second half of the year.
e. Bed occupancy percentage for the entire year.
f. Quarter with the highest bed occupancy percentage for the year.

9. Holy Cross Hospital (for June) Bed count: 50

Date	IPSD	Date	IPSD	Date	IPSD	Date	IPSD	Date	IPSD
1	45	7	38	13	47	19	43	25	38
2	30	8	42	14	48	20	47	26	42
3	35	9	43	15	49	21	44	27	44
4	25	10	36	16	50	22	48	28	40
5	47	11	35	17	40	23	35	29	52
6	48	12	41	18	41	24	36	30	41

Calculate:
a. *(R4)* Total IPSD for June.
b. *(R4)* IPSD for June 7 through June 15.
c. *(R4)* Average DIPC for June 1 through June 10.
d. *(R4)* Average IPSD for June.
e. Percent of bed occupancy for June.
f. If the bed count had increased to 55 beds on June 15, calculate the percent of bed occupancy for June.

10. Coastal Health Medical Center (September)
NOTE: ALOS—average length of stay.

Unit	Bed/Bassinet Count	Discharges	IPSD	% Occup	ALOS
Medical	70	298	1,503		5 days
Surgical	40	172	808		
Obstetrics	30	119	382		
Pediatrics	10	43	129		
Psychiatric	25	103	398		
ICU	13	60	277		
NB	10	85	171		
Totals:					
A&C					4.5 days
NB					2.0 days

Calculate:

a. Percentage of occupancy for each unit.
b. Direct bed turnover rate for A&C.
c. Direct bed turnover rate for the medical unit.
d. Indirect bed turnover rate for A&C.
e. Indirect bed turnover rate for the medical unit.
f. Direct bassinet turnover rate.
g. Indirect bassinet turnover rate.

11. Pine Ridge Hospital—100 beds; 15 bassinets, Census Report for February
NOTE: Cens—census; Dis—discharged; Exp—expired (deaths)

| | A&C | | | | | | | | | NB | | | | |
| | Beg | TRF- | | Dis | | TRF- | | | | Beg | | Dis | | |
Day	Cens	Adm	In	Live	Exp	Out	Cens	A&D	IPSD	Cens	Births	Live	Exp	IPSD
20	77	12	3	7	0	3	___	0	___	11	3	7	0	___
21	___	14	2	9	1	2	___	1	___	___	6	3	0	___
22	___	8	2	12	0	2	___	0	___	___	5	2	0	___
23	___	16	6	8	0	6	___	0	___	___	3	2	0	___
24	___	7	3	4	0	3	___	4	___	___	1	4	0	___
25	___	6	4	13	1	4	___	2	___	___	2	5	0	___
26	___	11	2	7	0	2	___	0	___	___	2	3	0	___
27	___	9	3	11	0	3	___	0	___	___	4	2	1	___
28	___	12	5	5	1	5	___	3	___	___	5	1	0	___

a. Complete the totals below for the remainder of the month:

A&C: Admissions	___	Transfer-outs	___	NB: Births	___
Transfer-ins	___	Ending census	___	Live disch	___
Live discharges	___	IPSD total	___	Deaths	___
Deaths	___	NB: Occupancy %	___	IPSD	___
A&C occupancy %	___				___

12. City General Hospital (for April) Bed count: 56

Date	IPSD	Date	IPSD	Date	IPSD	Date	IPSD	Date	IPSD
1	45	7	35	13	47	19	45	25	38
2	37	8	48	14	48	20	47	26	42
3	42	9	43	15	49	21	47	27	49
4	25	10	36	16	50	22	48	28	44
5	49	11	38	17	42	23	35	29	52
6	48	12	41	18	46	24	38	30	48

Calculate:

a. *(R4)* Total IPSD for April.
b. *(R4)* IPSD for April 7 through April 15.
c. *(R4)* Average DIPC for April 1 through April 10, correct to one decimal point.
d. Percent of bed occupancy for April, correct to one decimal point.
e. If the bed count had increased to 60 beds on June 15, calculate the percent of bed occupancy for June, correct to one decimal point.

Hospital Length of Stay

CHAPTER OUTLINE

A. Terms
   1. Discharge
   2. Length of Stay
   3. Total Length of Stay
   4. Discharge Days
   5. Average Length of Stay
   6. Leave of Absence Day
B. Length of Stay Calculation
   1. General Rule
   2. Admitted and Discharged (A&D) the Same Day
   3. Longer Stays
C. Total Combined Lengths of Stay
   1. Importance of Discharge Days
   2. Totaling
D. Average Length of Stay
   1. Adults and Children (A&C)
   2. Newborn (NB)
E. Summary
F. Chapter 6 Test

LEARNING OBJECTIVES

After studying this chapter, the learner should be able to:

✔ Define discharge/discharge days.

✔ Define length of stay (LOS).

✔ Identify the days counted and excluded in length of stay determinations.

✔ Describe when discharge days are acquired.

✔ Define *leave of absence day* and when it is included or excluded.

✔ Compute the following for A&C and NB:
   (1) Individual lengths of stay.
   (2) Total lengths of stay for a designated period.
   (3) Average length of stay.

PRELIMINARY QUESTIONS

1. Are all days of hospitalization counted in a patient's length of stay?

2. If a patient is only hospitalized four hours before the patient expires, does the patient get credit for a full day of hospitalization?

3. If a patient is admitted at 11 P.M., does the patient get credit for a full day of stay (hospitalization)?

4. Have lengths of stays been increasing or decreasing?

5. Which health care facility is most likely to have patients with stays longer than one or two months?

6. If seven patients are discharged on June 1 and their individual lengths of stay were 5, 7, 3, 4, 2, 4, and 3, what is the average length of stay for these seven patients? Describe the value used in the denominator.

7. Should adults/children and newborns be combined in statistical formulas for lengths of stay?

Census data and service days along with occupancy percentage data are based on admissions. To determine a patient's length of stay, the discharge date comes into play. Discharge days are compiled only after discharge from the health care facility. As long as a patient is still occupying an inpatient bed, the patient has not acquired any "discharge days." Upon discharge (or death), a length of stay (LOS) is determined for each inpatient. The LOS represents the number of days the patient was an inpatient—that is, occupying a bed or bassinet, and receiving inpatient care. Synonymous terms include (inpatient) days of stay, duration of hospitalization, and discharged days. Although the total inpatient service days (IPSDs) and discharge days (DDs) values can be similar, it is important to use the correct data in any computation.

A. TERMS

1. Discharge

A *discharge* is a termination of hospitalization. It is up to the attending physician to determine when it is appropriate for the patient to be released from the health care facility and write a discharge order in the patient's chart. The absence of a discharge order may indicate the patient left the health care facility against medical advice (AMA). However, these patients are included in discharge statistics in the same manner as any other discharged patient. Some patients are transferred to another health care facility to continue their recuperation, and this is indicated on the discharge order as well.

EXAMPLE: St Mary's Hospital for the month of May recorded 15 live discharges and five deaths. The total number of discharges would be $15 + 5 = 20$ total discharges.

There are many discharge options. A patient may be discharged home, to another health care facility (another hospital, rehabilitation facility, or nursing home), or to a variety of outpatient services such as home care, hospice care, drug or mental health treatment programs, to name a few.

Another type of discharge is a death. It is always assumed that the discharge includes all discharged patients and all patients who expired during their hospitalization. However, if the term *live discharges* is used, deaths need to be added to the live discharges to arrive at the total discharges for that date or period of time. In either case, deaths must also be recorded apart from discharges so that death rates and autopsy rates can be calculated.

2. Length of Stay

Length of stay refers to the number of calendar days from admission to discharge for an individual patient. Length of stay is calculated by subtracting the day of admission from the day of discharge.

EXAMPLE: Mary Smith is admitted on June 4 and discharged on June 10. Adding each day starting at the 4th and ending at the 10th is a total of six days. Her length of stay is 6 for this hospital stay.

3. Total Length of Stay

The total length of stay is the sum of all individual lengths of stay for all inpatients discharged during a specified period of time. The period may be for a certain date, a week, a month, a year, or any combination of days.

4. **Discharge Days**

   Discharge days are identical to length of stay or total length of stay.

5. **Average Length of Stay**

   The *average length of stay* (ALOS) refers to the average number of days a group of inpatients was hospitalized, during the specified period under consideration. It may be important to determine how long the average individual was hospitalized following hip replacement surgery or congestive heart failure to understand trends in treatment or in developing best practice care plans for patients with similar diagnoses.

6. **Leave of Absence Day**

   A *leave of absence day* is a day occurring after admission and prior to discharge of a hospital inpatient. The patient, in this instance, would be absent at the normal census-taking time and would not be counted on the clinical unit. A leave of absence day seldom exists in most hospitals, in part, due to shorter stays. The majority of longer-stay patients are now cared for at another skilled or intermediate nursing facility. Therefore, facilities that admit patients for longer stays (such as rehabilitation facilities, mental hospitals, and long-term substance abuse treatment centers) are more likely to grant a leave of absence day. Most leaves of absence days are granted to ascertain if a patient is capable of being cared for on a less intensive basis or is capable of caring for themselves at home with more minimal care. Leaves are generally granted on weekends prior to final discharge. The leave of absence should be authorized by the patient's attending physician. The leave may include an overnight pass or a weekend pass, and the period is specified prior to the leave. Only leaves that involve at least 24 hours of absence are considered in compiling statistical data.

   Leave of absence days differ from discharge and readmission. A leave is a segment of an uninterrupted hospitalization. Some patients, however, are discharged one day only to be readmitted the following day for the same or a different diagnosis. This latter scenario is not considered a leave of absence day. There is no uniform policy regarding the use of leave of absence days, and the final decision is up to the patient's attending physician.

   The use of leave of absence days affects the compilation of statistical data. The formulas in which a leave of absence day is *included* for statistical purposes are as follows:

   (1) Discharge Days. A patient accumulates a discharge day during the time the patient is away on a leave of absence (one discharge day for each day absent on leave).
   (2) Average Length of Stay. Since the average length of stay is based on discharge days, the leave of absence is included in computing the average length of stay.

   Leave of absence days are *excluded* for the following statistics:

   (1) Inpatient Service Days (IPSDs). No service is being rendered to the patient during the patient's absence from the health care facility.
   (2) Inpatient Census. The patient is not included at CTT.
   (3) Bed Occupancy Percentage. Since IPSD data are used to calculate occupancy percentages, the patient is not included as occupying a bed while he or she is on a leave of absence.

B. LENGTH OF STAY CALCULATION

1. General Rule

In figuring out the length of stay for a patient, each day counts as a discharge day, *except* the day of discharge. In general, the patient's day of admission is counted as one day, as are all intervening days between admission and discharge, but *not* the day of discharge. As stated previously, the day of admission is subtracted from the day of discharge.

EXAMPLES:

EX 1. A patient is admitted on June 3 and discharged on June 10. The patient has a length of stay of seven days (June 3, 4, 5, 6, 7, 8, and 9 but not June 10). Notice that the length of stay can be determined by subtracting the date of admission from the date of discharge when the patient has been admitted and discharged during the same month (in this case $10 - 3 = 7$ days of stay).

EX 2. If the patient is admitted one month and discharged the following month, the principle is the same, but the computation involves knowing the number of days in each month. A patient admitted May 28 and discharged June 4, also has a seven-day length of stay $(31 - 28 + 4 = 7)$. Keep in mind, however, that although the subtracting method helps in the calculation, the true days that are counted in this latter case are May 28, 29, 30, and 31 and June 1, 2, and $3 = 7$ days. Even though the answers are identical, it is important to remember which days are accurately included in the computation.

2. Admitted and Discharged the Same Day

Any patient admitted and discharged (A&D) on the same day accumulates a length of stay of *one* day. No patient admitted to the hospital ever has 0 (zero) days or negative days credited as a length of stay. Therefore, every patient admitted is credited with at least a length of stay of one day. A patient admitted at 6 A.M. and discharged (possibly with a transfer to another hospital) at 8 A.M. is credited with a length of stay of one day—as is the patient admitted at 10 A.M. April 2 and discharged 4 P.M. the next day, April 3. All A&D inpatients are credited with a one-day length of stay.

3. Longer Stays

The same principle that applies to short stays is applicable to longer stays—counting the day of admission and all subsequent days except the day of discharge. Longer stays primarily are applicable to long-term care facilities, such as nursing homes, where patients (residents) may have stays longer than a year.

EXAMPLES:

EX 1. Adjacent months. A patient admitted on March 30 and discharged on May 5 has a total length of stay of 36 days [calculated by counting March 30, 31, all of April (30 days) plus May 1, 2, 3, and $4 = 36$ days]. Alternately, the same total can be arrived at by subtracting 30 from 31, adding 30 days for April plus 5 days for May (36 days).

EX 2. A patient admitted November 11, 2010, and discharged (or expired) January 10, 2012, has a length of stay of 425 days. (November 11, 12, 13, 14, 15, 16, 17, 18, 19, 20, 21, 22, 23, 24, 25, 26, 27, 28, 29, 30 [20 days]+ 31 for December + 365 for 2011 (non-leap year) + 9 days for January 2012 = 20 + 31 + 365 + 9 equals a total of 425 days [length of stay or discharge days].)

 SELF-TEST 6-1

Compute the length of stay for the following patients. Assume the dates are in the same year (non-leap year) unless a year is indicated.

Admission/Discharge

	Adm	Disch
1.	5-25	5-25
2.	5-15	5-18
3.	5-11	5-20
4.	5-27	6-05
5.	5-31	6-10
6.	5-29	7-09
7.	12-26-10	1-15-11
8.	12-22-10	3-10-11

C. TOTAL COMBINED LENGTHS OF STAY

The total length of stay for a combination of patients during a specified time period is commonly referred to as *discharge days*. In computing census days, the total is stated in terms of service days. Combining individual lengths of stay is most commonly referred to as discharge days. Discharge days are acquired upon discharge from the health care facility. Service days (inpatient service days) are acquired daily as care (service) is being rendered. Service days are credited daily; discharge days are acquired upon discharge. A patient hospitalized for more than a year will have all the discharge days credited on the day of discharge. Therefore, it should be noted that service days and discharge days, while they may seem similar in number, are *not* interchangeable.

1. Importance of Discharge Days

Lengths of stay and discharge days are important because they serve as means of managing utilization of health care resources. Most payers only reimburse based on a diagnosis code, irrespective of how long a patient is hospitalized. This creates an incentive to reduce length of stay while still maintaining quality outcomes. A few payers of hospital services cover costs for a limited number of days of service, depending on the diagnosis. Longer stays can be extremely costly, and hospitals remain challenged to control costs to maintain some level of profitability.

Discharge days assist in analyzing and comparing patient subgroups in terms of disease, treatment, age, and so on. If the average length of stay for patients undergoing coronary bypass surgery computes to four days and Doctor X's patients are staying an average of six days, an evaluation is in order. When a physician's patients are exceeding the norm based on the diagnosis, the medical staff may choose to take this under advisement and evaluate the circumstances. It may be that the physician has patients with a greater severity of illness or more complications are occurring under the physician's care—both of which may be reviewed by the medical staff. Discharge days, used to compute average length of stay, serve as a basis for comparison among various subgroups.

2. Totaling

Whenever data are compared, it is important to compare similar data. Everyone has heard the expression "don't compare apples to oranges." Although both are fruits, they do not display the same characteristics. In making comparisons with patients, it is more appropriate to compare two patients with the same illness than it is to compare a person with a heart condition with a patient with a brain tumor. Again, average lengths of stay can be determined on all patients or a selected group of patients. Totaling is always necessary prior to calculating an average.

EXAMPLE: Suppose 10 patients were discharged on March 1 (LOS is in days).

Name	Age	Clinical Service	LOS
AA	50	Medical	6
BB	23	Surgical	5
CC	68	Medical	4
DD	22	Obstetrics	3
EE	8	Pediatrics	2
FF	35	Surgical	4
GG	80	Medical	7
HH	73	Medical	5
II	13	Pediatrics	3
JJ	59	Medical	2

The total of all the lengths of stay on March 1 is 41 days.

If, however, the request was for the total days on each clinical service, the results would be Medical, 24 days (6 + 4 + 7 + 5 + 2); Surgical, 9 days (5 + 4); Obstetrics, 3 days; and Pediatrics, 5 days (2 + 3).

The patients could also be grouped by age classification in which case the results would be as follows:

Ages: 61–80	3 patients	total LOS = 16 (4 + 7 + 5)
41–60	2 patients	total LOS = 8 (6 + 2)
21–40	3 patients	total LOS = 12 (3 + 5 + 4)
0–20	2 patients	total LOS = 5 (2 + 3)

D. AVERAGE LENGTH OF STAY

Since totals alone do not give much useful information, the most common use of discharge days is calculating the average length of stay. An average is generally much more easily interpreted—both for statistical purposes and for comparisons. The average length of stay is a representation of the average duration of hospitalization for the group under consideration.

> **NOTE:** Average length of stay calculations do not combine A&C and NB data for the same reason that average daily census and occupancy percentages are computed on two unique populations.

1. Adults and Children (A&C)

When a question asks for average length of stay, it is assumed that the A&C average is to be determined. As previously mentioned, it would be rare to want to combine A&C and newborns in the same average length of stay.

Formula: Average LOS (A&C)

$$\frac{\text{Total length of stay (discharge days)}}{\text{Total discharges}}$$

EXAMPLES:

EX 1. Data indicates a hospital had a total of 700 discharges during March, with a total of 3,500 discharge days. The data becomes more significant when the average length of stay is calculated for the 700 discharges, for an average stay of five days. The average discharged patient in March had a stay of five days of hospitalization (3,500/700 = 5 days).

EX 2. The discharges for the first quarter of the year, for obstetrical patients, total 275. The total discharge days, for the same quarter, were 825. The average length of stay, during the first quarter of the year, for OB patients was three days (825/275 = 3 days).

EX 3. In the previous section under totaling, the patients were listed by age and clinical service. The total lengths of stay were determined and, from the total, the average length of stay was calculated. Using the various clinical services, the average medical patient, discharged March 1, had an average stay of 4.8 days (24/5 = 4.8 days); surgical average stay was 4.5 days (9/2 = 4.5 days); since there was only one OB discharge, the average was 3 days; and pediatrics had two discharges for an average stay of 2.5 days (5/2 = 2.5 days).

Using the age categories, the average stay for a patient 20 years old or younger was 2.5 days (5/2 = 2.5 days); the 21–40 age group had an average length of stay of 4 days (12/3 = 4 days); the 41–60 age group also had an average length of stay of 4 days (8/2 = 4 days) and the 61–80 age group had an average length of stay of 5.3 days (16/3 = 5.3 days).

NOTES

 SELF-TEST 6-2

1. A&C Data for January

    Bed count: 50   Admissions: 300

                       Discharges: 313

                       Inpatient service days: 1,260

                       Discharge days: 1,252

    Calculate:

    a. Average length of stay for A&C in January.
    b. *(R5)* A&C occupancy percentage for January.

2. A&C Data for November

    Bed count: 100   Admissions: 675

                       Discharges: 683

                       Inpatient service days: 2,653

                       Discharge days: 2,685

    Calculate:

    a. Average length of stay for A&C in November.
    b. *(R5)* A&C occupancy percentage for November.

3. The following patients are discharged on June 5:
    (Adm—date of admission; Dis—date of discharge; Service—clinical service)

Name	Adm	Dis	Service
Abbott, A.	5-31	6-05	Medical
Black, B.	6-01	6-05	Surgical
Canfield, C.	6-03	6-05	Medical
Draper, D.	6-02	6-05	Medical
Eckhart, E.	5-31	6-05	Surgical
Franke, F.	6-03	6-05	Obstetrics
Graber, G.	6-03	6-05	Medical
Huber, H.	6-02	6-05	Surgical
Ibsen, I.	5-30	6-05	Medical
James, J.	6-03	6-05	Obstetrics

Calculate:

a. Average length of stay for all patients discharged June 5.
b. Average length of stay for medical patients discharged June 5.
c. Average length of stay for surgical patients discharged June 5.
d. Average length of stay for obstetrical patients discharged June 5.

4. February Data (non-leap year)
    Bed Count: 125

Clinical Service	Admissions	Discharges	Deaths	IPSDs	DDs
Medical	300	309	6	1,500	1,516
Surgical	120	127	3	960	972
Obstetrics	72	69	1	195	202
Pediatrics	63	66	1	188	194

Calculate:
a. A&C average length of stay in February.
b. Medical service average length of stay in February.
c. Surgical service average length of stay in February.
d. Obstetrical service average length of stay in February.
e. Pediatric service average length of stay in February.
f. *(R5)* A&C bed occupancy percentage for February.

5. Quarterly Statistics

	First Quarter	Second Quarter	Third Quarter	Fourth Quarter
Admissions	1,800	1,715	1,913	1,888
Discharges	1,785	1,717	1,902	1,885
IP Service Days	9,013	8,621	9,589	9,461
Discharge Days	8,955	8,581	9,502	9,470

Calculate:
a. Average length of stay for the year.
b. Quarter with the lowest average length of stay.
c. Quarter with the highest average length of stay.

6. A 40-bed surgical unit records the following data for the year:

Type of Surgery	Admissions	Discharges	Deaths	IPSDs	DDs
EENT	228	226	1	483	490
Neurosurgery	112	120	5	1,123	1,133
Thoracic	202	208	3	1,676	1,682
Abdominal	1,010	1,010	4	8,012	7,095
GU	276	277	1	1,659	1,654
Other	128	127	1	557	537

Calculate:
a. Average length of stay for patients on the surgical unit for the year.
b. The type of surgery with the highest average length of stay for the year.
c. The type of surgery with the lowest average length of stay for the year.
d. Average length of stay for patients on each surgical unit.

2. Newborn (NB)

NOTE: Newborn length of stay data, as mentioned, is not combined with adults and children. It would be unfair to compare the length of stay for the two unique populations. Mothers' length of stay data, however, is included in A&C statistics.

Formula for Newborn Average Length of Stay

$$\frac{\text{Total newborn length of stay (discharge days)}}{\text{Total newborn discharges}}$$

Remember that newborns who expired after birth are included but not fetal deaths (those with no signs of life at the time of birth).

EXAMPLE: A newborn unit recorded 135 births in February, 140 discharges, 270 newborn inpatient service days, and 280 newborn discharge days. (The computation is identical to that of A&C patients.) The discharge days (280) are divided by the total discharges (140) for an average newborn stay of two days.

 SELF-TEST 6-3

1. A newborn nursery records the following data for July:

   Bassinet count: 15

Admissions	204	IPSDs	408
Discharges	201	DDs	420

   Calculate:
   a. Average length of stay for newborns in July.
   b. *(R5)* Percentage of occupancy for the neonatal unit in July.

2. A neonatal unit has 10 bassinets. The data for October 1 through October 10 are as follows:

	10-01	10-02	10-03	10-04	10-05	10-06	10-07	10-08	10-09	10-10
Births	3	2	4	1	1	2	3	3	1	2
Discharges	2	3	5	2	1	1	2	3	2	0
IPSDs	8	6	6	5	6	7	5	4	6	5
DDs	7	8	10	6	4	5	4	5	6	0

   Calculate:
   a. Average newborn length of stay for October 1 through October 10.
   b. Average newborn length of stay for October 1 through October 5.
   c. Average newborn length of stay for October 6 through October 10.
   d. *(R6)* Average newborn occupancy percentage for the entire period (October 1 through October 10).

3. A newborn nursery records the following data for January 15:

Admissions			Discharges 1-15		
Girl	7 lb	6 oz	Girl	Admitted	1-13
Girl	6 lb	10 oz	Boy	Admitted	1-12
Boy	9 lb	1 oz	Girl	Admitted	1-14
Boy	8 lb	3 oz	Girl	Admitted	1-10
Girl	5 lb	11 oz	Boy	Admitted	1-13
Girl	8 lb	1 oz			

   Calculate:
   a. Average length of stay for newborns discharged January 15.
   b. Average length of stay for boys discharged January 15.
   c. Average length of stay for girls discharged January 15.
   d. Average birth weight of newborns born January 15.
   e. Average birth weight of boys born January 15.
   f. Average birth weight of girls born January 15.

E. SUMMARY

1. Length of stay (LOS) or discharge days (DD) refer to the number of days the patient was hospitalized (from admission to discharge).
2. LOS or DD accumulate only upon discharge from the hospital.
3. Length of stay or discharge days include all days of hospitalization except the day of discharge, except for patients admitted and discharged (A&D) the same day, in which case the patient is credited with a length of stay of one day (one discharge day).
4. Discharge day totals are the sum of all days of stay for all patients for a specific date or a specified period.
5. Average LOS is the total length of stays of all patients discharged during a specified period divided by the total number of discharges during that specified period.
6. A&C and NB data are computed separately. Generally, the two populations are not combined, especially when calculating average length of stay.
7. A leave of absence day is granted prior to discharge. The leave of absence day is included (counted) in computing discharge days and average length of stay. However, the leave of absence day is excluded in computing IPSDs, IP census, and bed occupancy percentage.

Name _____   **Date** _____

F. CHAPTER 7 TEST

Compute all answers correct to two decimal places.

1. Is it possible for an individual patient to have over 365 discharge days? If so, when?

2. In figuring length of stay for stays over one day:

    a. Is the day of admission counted?
    b. Is the day of discharge counted?

3. How does a patient acquire a leave of absence day?

4. In which formulas is a leave of absence day?

    a. Included in the computation?
    b. Excluded in the computation?

5. Are A&C and NB length of stay data computed separately or combined?

6. Determine the lengths of stay for each of the following, assuming a non-leap year.

	Admission	Discharge	LOS
a.	8-03	8-07	_____
b.	8-15	8-15	_____
c.	12-01	2-15	_____
d.	8-02	8-17	_____
e.	3-24	4-09	_____
f.	5-12	12-2	_____
g.	2-28	3-15	_____
h.	3-29	4-01	_____
i.	1-27	2-11	_____
j.	4-30	5-01	_____
k.	12-29	2-03	_____
l.	11-30	12-01	_____

7. Seneca Community Hospital (April data)

	A&C	NB
Bed/Bassinet count	180	15
Admissions	905	88
Discharges	895	86
IPSDs	4,820	339
DDs	4,785	330

Calculate:

a. Average length of stay for A&C.
b. Average length of stay for NB.
c. *(R5)* Occupancy percentage for A&C.
d. *(R5)* Occupancy percentage for NB.

8. Hillside Medical Center (October data)

    Bed count: 100; Bassinet count: 15

Clinical Service	Admissions	Discharges	Deaths	IPSDs	DDs
Medical	166	173	10	859	845
Surgical	101	99	2	754	751
OB	92	94	1	365	369
Gynecology	81	81	1	313	325
NB	90	94	1	349	352

Calculate:

a. Average length of stay for A&C.
b. Average length of stay for NB.
c. Average length of stay for each service:
    1. Medical
    2. Surgical
    3. Obstetrics
    4. Gynecology
d. *(R5)* Bed occupancy percentage for October.
e. *(R5)* Bassinet occupancy percentage for October.

9. Grandview Medical Center—Discharge List for June 3 (M—male; F—female)

Dis (live)	Service	Adm Date	ALOS	Dis (live)	Service	Adm Date	ALOS
(M)	Surgical	5-31	3	F	ENT	6-02	1
(F)	Medical	5-19	15	F	Gynecology	6-03	1
(F)	Surgical	5-23	11	M	Medical	5-29	5
(M)	Psychiatric	5-03	31	M	Urology	5-30	4
(F)	OB	5-28	10	F	Gynecology	5-27	7
(M)	Orthopedic	5-24	12	F	Orthopedic	5-28	6
(M)	Urology	5-28	4	M	Surgical	5-26	8
Death							
(M)	Medical	5-29	5				

Calculate:

a. Length of stay for each of the above discharges.
b. Average length of stay for all A&C patients.
c. Average length of stay for all male patients.
d. Average length of stay for all female patients.
e. Average length of stay for all surgical patients.
f. Average length of stay for all medical patients.
g. Average length of stay for all orthopedic patients.

10. Oceanside Hospital

Clinical service unit: Medical bed count: 50

Month	Adm	Disch	IPSDs	DDs
Jan.	250	248	1,250	1,270
Feb.	223	231	1,275	1,266
Mar.	266	264	1,266	1,295
Apr.	245	251	1,281	1,254
May	248	244	1,279	1,287
June	212	213	1,260	1,310
July	218	217	1,225	1,263
Aug.	227	225	1,248	1,240
Sept.	259	260	1,290	1,233
Oct.	271	266	1,313	1,322
Nov.	275	272	1,326	1,333
Dec.	244	246	1,288	1,301
Total:	2,938	2,937	15,301	15,374

Calculate:

a. Average length of stay for the year.
b. Month with the shortest average length of stay.
c. Month with the longest average length of stay.
d. Average length of stay for the first six months.
e. Average length of stay for the last six months.
f. *(R5)* Bed occupancy percentage for the year.

Hospital *Obstetric and Neonatal Statistics*

7

CHAPTER OUTLINE

A. Terms
1. Pregnancy Terms
2. Maternal Death/Obstetrical Death Terms
3. Newborn/Fetal Terms

B. Natality Classifications
1. Newborn Classification
2. Neonatal Periods
3. Fetal Death Classification

C. Hospital OB Mortality Rates
1. Direct Maternal Death Rate
2. Newborn/Neonatal/Infant Death Rates
3. Fetal Death Rate (Stillborn Rate)

D. Cesarean Section Rates
1. Cesarean Section Rate
2. VBAC (Vaginal Birth after C-section) Rate

E. Summary

F. Chapter 7 Test

LEARNING OBJECTIVES

After studying this chapter, the learner should be able to:

 Define and explain the following terms:
a. Delivered/undelivered
b. Puerperium
c. Neonate/infant
d. Neonatal, perinatal, and postnatal periods

 Classify neonates according to the American College of Obstetricians and Gynecologists (ACOG) classification system.

 When doing calculations, distinguish clearly between:
a. Direct and indirect maternal death
b. Abortion, stillbirth, and fetal death

 Classify fetal deaths by gram weight and gestational age.

Compute the following rates:
a. Maternal death rate
b. Newborn death rate
c. Fetal death rate
d. Cesarean section rates

Pregnancy is generally associated with a period of great expectation in a woman's life. Although most pregnancies result in what is termed a "normal pregnancy" and "normal birth," this is not always the case. Studies and statistics on reproductive health can often be facilitated with the use of statistical data accumulated on maternal and obstetrical data. Data accumulate from the onset of the pregnancy until the fetus or infant is expelled from the mother's womb. The rates in this chapter are designed to study and report maternal, obstetric, and neonatal data. From this information, interventions can be made to improve the overall health of mothers and babies.

A. TERMS

1. Pregnancy Terms

a. Delivery/Delivered

Delivery is the act of giving birth, either of a live infant or a dead fetus (and placenta) by manual, instrumental, or surgical means. A female may deliver a single infant or multiple infants. A delivery refers to expelling a product of conception or having it removed from the body, along with the expulsion of the placenta. Multiple births are considered a single delivery; and a woman who gives birth to twins, triplets, or other multiple births is credited with a single delivery, although each fetus delivered live is a newborn and each conceptus (fertilized ovum at any stage of development from fertilization until birth) delivered without signs of life is a fetal death. Consequently, a woman who delivers quintuplets is credited with one delivery, just as a woman who gives birth to a single infant is credited with a single delivery. However, the number of births (newborn admissions) will be increased by five when live quintuplets are born, in contrast to the delivery of a single newborn.

b. **Not Delivered/Undelivered**

Occasionally, a pregnant woman is admitted to the hospital because of complications of the pregnancy such as preeclampsia. If the female is discharged without having delivered, the patient's condition is noted to be "undelivered" upon discharge. A woman may also be admitted following delivery, possibly due to complications, or being admitted after giving birth en route. Undelivered refers to a pregnant female admitted to a hospital for a condition of pregnancy but who did not deliver either a live born, stillborn, or conceptus during that hospitalization. This category includes threatened abortions and false labor or the treatment of a pregnancy-related condition.

c. **Partum**

Partum means childbirth. *Antepartum* is the period before giving birth, and *postpartum* is the period after giving birth.

d. **Puerperium**

The puerperal period is the 42-day period following delivery and is included as part of the pregnancy period. It is approximately six-week period following childbirth during which the uterus returns to its normal size. A female who has delivered a baby (live or stillborn) and who dies within this period due to a pregnancy-related cause is also considered a maternal or obstetrical death.

e. **Pregnancy Termination**

Pregnancy termination is the expulsion or extraction of a dead fetus or other products of conception from the mother, or the birth of a live born or stillborn infant.

f. **Induced Termination of Pregnancy**

Induced termination of pregnancy is the purposeful interruption of an intrauterine pregnancy with the intention of not giving birth to a live born infant and which does not result in a live birth. This definition excludes management of prolonged retention of products of conception following fetal death.

2. **Maternal Death/Obstetrical Death Terms**

Maternal Death/Obstetrical Death. A maternal death is the death of any woman from any cause, either while pregnant or within 42 days of termination of pregnancy, irrespective of the duration and site of the pregnancy. Two terms are associated with maternal deaths—*direct maternal death* and *indirect maternal death*.

a. **Direct Maternal Death**

In computing hospital OB statistics, primarily only direct maternal deaths are included; that is, deaths directly related to pregnancy. Direct maternal deaths include the following:

(1) Abortion death—during or following an abortion.

(2) Antepartum death (death prior to delivery) due to the pregnancy.

(3) Postpartum death (death after delivery) due to the pregnancy.

(4) Deaths at the time of delivery due to the pregnancy.

Direct maternal deaths do *not* include the following:

(1) Death of a pregnant woman in a car accident.

(2) Death of a pregnant woman due to suicide.

(3) Death of a pregnant woman not directly related to her pregnant condition. (This death is a hospital death but *not* a direct maternal death.) A pregnant woman who dies as the result of an illness (such as cancer) is not a direct maternal death.

b. **Indirect Maternal Death**

An indirect maternal death is the death of a pregnant female that is not directly due to obstetric causes but is aggravated by the pregnant condition. A pregnant woman with diabetes mellitus who dies as the result of complications from diabetes, aggravated by being pregnant, is an example of an indirect maternal death. Any death of a pregnant woman resulting from a previously existing disease or a disease developing during the pregnancy (including labor or the puerperium) and aggravated by the pregnancy is an indirect maternal/obstetric death.

3. **Newborn/Fetal Terms**

A pregnancy may result in the delivery of either a live or dead product of conception. The presence of any sign of life (a heartbeat, respirations, pulsation of the umbilical cord, or some definite movement of voluntary muscles) indicates a live birth, and the infant is classified a newborn. Even if death occurs shortly after birth, the infant is a newborn, and the death is a newborn death. However, for statistical purposes, only those born in the hospital (during their current inpatient hospitalization) are included in hospital newborn/bassinet statistics. A baby delivered at home or en route to the hospital is *not* included in newborn statistics but rather in the adult and children (A&C) category. In addition, a newborn delivered in the hospital and discharged, only to develop a complication or an illness necessitating a readmission, is no longer included in newborn statistics during the readmission. If no signs of life are present at birth, the preferred term is *fetal death*. The terms *abortion, aborted fetus,* and *stillborn* are still in common usage, but the term *fetal death* is preferred. Fetal deaths are recorded and separate statistics compiled, but fetal deaths are never combined with live births or newborn deaths.

a. **Live Born Terms**

(1) *Newborn.* A newborn is a patient born in the hospital at the beginning of his or her current inpatient hospitalization.

(2) *Neonate/Neonatal.* A newborn is referred to as a neonate up to 28 days of age. The neonatal period extends from birth through the first 27 days, 23 hours, and 59 minutes. There are three

neonatal periods. These categories are listed in the upcoming section (Neonatal Periods). A newborn that dies prior to reaching 28 days of age is ruled a neonatal death.

(3) *Infant.* A newborn is considered an infant until one year of age. If the infant dies during its first year of life, it is an infant death.

b. Additional Terms

(1) *Perinatal Period/Perinatal Death.* The perinatal period is the period surrounding birth. A perinatal death includes both still-born infants and neonatal deaths.

(2) *Postnatal/Postneonatal.* The term *postnatal* or *postneonatal* (after the neonatal period) refers to the period from the end of the neonatal period up to one year of age.

(3) *Hospital Fetal Death.* A hospital fetal death is death prior to the complete expulsion or extraction from its mother, in a hospital facility, of a product of human conception (fetus and placenta), irrespective of the duration of the pregnancy and without any sign of life (no heartbeat, no respirations, no pulsation of the umbilical cord, or no definite movement of voluntary muscles). A fetal death never results in a hospital inpatient admission and does not generate a medical record. However, circumstances of the birth should be documented in the mother's medical record.

There are three fetal death categories, based on the stage in the pregnancy in which the fetal death occurred. The categories are defined either by the gram weight of the fetus or the estimated length of gestation calculated from the first day of the last normal menstrual period. Fetal deaths are referred to as *early, intermediate,* and *late fetal deaths.* These categories are further defined in the following section (Natality Classifications).

B. NATALITY CLASSIFICATIONS

1. Newborn Classification

Newborns or neonates are classified by two sets of criteria—one is birth weight (to the nearest gram), and the other is gestational age (dating from the woman's last normal menstrual period). Birth weight is determined immediately after delivery or as soon as feasible. Birth weight is more easily determined than gestational age. Grams can be converted to pounds by multiplying the gram weight by 0.0022046. Round the answer to the nearest hundredth decimal place, and add the unit of pounds to the amount to arrive at the converted weight. For example, 1,000 grams equals 2.2 pounds: $(1,000 \times 0.0022046 = 2.2046; 2.2046$ rounded $= 2.20$ pounds).

The term *premature birth* applies to a newborn born before the 37th week of pregnancy.

In addition, two methods of classification are routinely used in classifying newborns. One method was established by the American College of Obstetricians and Gynecologists (ACOG). The standards are found in *Standard Terminology for Reproductive Health Statistics in the United States.* The second classification system is that used in ICD-9-CM. (LMP stands for last menstrual period.)

a. **ACOG Classification by Gestational Age** *(November 2013)*

    (1) Early term: 37 0/7 weeks through 38 6/7 weeks

    (2) Full term: 39 0/7 weeks through 40 6/7 weeks

    (3) Late term: 41 0/7 weeks through 41 6/7 weeks

    (4) Post term: 42 0/7 weeks and beyond

b.

ICD-10-CM Classification	Gram Weight	Gestational Age
(1) Extreme Immaturity	1,000 grams	28 weeks
(2) Other Preterm Infants	1,000–2,499 grams	29–37 weeks
(3) Post-Term Infant		42 or more weeks
(4) Exceptionally Large Baby	4,500+ grams	
(5) Other Heavy for GA	4,000–4,499 grams	n/a

2. Neonatal Periods

a. Period I   Hour of birth through 23 hours and 59 minutes

b. Period II   Beginning of 24th hour of life through 6 days, 23 hours and 59 minutes (just under 7 days)

c. Period III   Beginning of the seventh day through 27 days, 23 hours and 59 minutes (just under 28 days)

3. Fetal Death Classification

a. **ACOG Classification by Gestational Age**

    (1) Early fetal death   Less than 20 weeks gestation

    (2) Intermediate fetal death   20 weeks to less than 28 weeks gestation

    (3) Late fetal death   28 or more weeks gestation

b. **ACOG Classification by Gram Weight**

    (1) Early fetal death   500 grams or less

    (2) Intermediate fetal death   501 grams to 1,000 grams

    (3) Late fetal death   1,001 grams or more

c. **ICD-10-CM**

    (1) Early fetal death   Before 22 weeks gestation

    (2) Late fetal death   After 22 weeks gestation

C. HOSPITAL OB MORTALITY RATES

1. Direct Maternal Death Rate

Formula for Maternal Death Rate:

$$\frac{\text{Total direct maternal deaths for a period}}{\text{Total maternal (obstetrical) discharges (including deaths) for the period}} \times 100$$

Direct maternal death rates should be low. Therefore, the rate is most commonly computed only on an annual basis rather than monthly. Low rates should generally be carried to three decimal places. Data are most often submitted to state or regional health departments where they are compiled into aggregate data. If all direct maternal deaths result from abortion, it is preferable to attach a note to the death rate stating this fact. This avoids confusing deaths resulting from abortions with deaths in the delivery room.

EXAMPLE: The year-end report from the obstetrical unit lists the following data:

Admissions:	1,550
Discharges:	1,554
Deliveries:	1,488
Undelivered:	38
Deaths:	3 (2 due to abortion; 1 following C-section)

Applying the formula, there were a total of three direct maternal deaths and a total of 1,554 discharges. Dividing 3 by 1,554 and converting to a percentage, results in a maternal death rate of 0.19% ($3 \div 1,554 = 0.00193 \times 100 = 0.19\%$) for the year.

 SELF-TEST 7-1

Compute answers correct to two decimal places.

1. The obstetrical unit reported five deaths of pregnant females for the year. The causes of death were:

    Puerperal septicemia

    Toxemia of pregnancy

    Ruptured ectopic (tubal) pregnancy

    Leukemia aggravated by pregnancy

    Placental hemorrhaging due to a fall down the basement steps.

Admissions:	1,222	Discharges:	1,225
Deliveries:	1,203	Undelivered:	38
Fetal deaths:	21	(15 early; 5 intermediate; 1 late)	

    Calculate: Maternal death rate for the year.

2. Year-end discharge data for OB unit at City Women's and Children's Hospital:

Admissions:		1,353
Discharges (live):	Delivered (live infant):	1,241
	Delivered (aborted):	38
	Undelivered (antepartum):	19
	Undelivered (postpartum):	2
Deaths (due to pregnancy):		2

    Calculate: Maternal death rate for the year.

3. Year-end OB statistics:

Admissions:	1,039
Discharges:	1,033
Deliveries:	Live, 975; Dead fetus, 37; Undelivered, 18
Maternal deaths:	Direct, 2; Indirect, 1

Calculate: Maternal death rate for the year.

2. Newborn/Neonatal/Infant Death Rates

a. Newborn Death Rate

Formula for Newborn Death Rate:

$$\frac{\text{Total number of newborn deaths for a period}}{\text{Total number of NB discharges (including deaths) for the period}} \times 100$$

b. Neonatal Death Rate

Formula for Neonatal Death Rate:

$$\frac{\text{Total number of neonatal deaths for a period}}{\text{Total number of neonatal discharges (including deaths) for the period}} \times 100$$

As mentioned, the neonatal period extends from birth up to, but not including, 28 days. During this period the infant is referred to as a *newborn*.

c. Infant Death Rate/Infant Mortality Rate

Formula for Infant Death Rate:

$$\frac{\text{Total number of infant deaths for a period}}{\text{Total number of infant discharges (including deaths) for the period}} \times 100$$

A newborn is an infant up to one year of age.
Additional rates (vital statistics death rates) are included in Chapter 13.

SELF-TEST 7-2

1. Neonatal Nursery Data for September:

Admissions:	233
Discharges:	240
Deaths (newborn):	2
Deaths (fetal):	2 early; 2 intermediate; 2 late

Calculate: Newborn death rate for September.

2. Yearly delivery room data:

Deliveries (live):	351
Deliveries (fetus/stillborn):	28 (13 early; 8 intermediate; 7 late)
Deaths (newborn):	3
Discharges (neonatal):	348

Calculate: Newborn death rate for the year.

3. Yearly Neonatal Intensive Care Unit:
   Admissions: 133

	Discharges	Deaths
Neonatal Period I	0	2
Neonatal Period II	33	2
Neonatal Period II	51	1
Postneonatal Period	44	0

Calculate:

a. Newborn death rate for the neonatal intensive care unit for the year.
b. Neonatal death rate for the neonatal intensive care unit for the year.
c. Postneonatal death rate for the unit for the year.

3. Fetal Death Rate (Stillborn Rate)

Although fetal deaths have been mentioned previously, they have not been included in any of the computations carried out to this point. Fetal deaths are only included in formulas specifically designated for them and that include the word *fetal* in them. These formulas are referred to as the fetal death rate and fetal autopsy rate. *Stillborn* and *aborted fetus* are terms commonly used to describe a fetal death. The criteria for early, intermediate, and late fetal deaths have already been specified. A fetal death indicates that no signs of life were present at the time the fetus was delivered. Newborn deaths were newborns alive at birth even though death may occur shortly after delivery. Only *intermediate* and *late fetal deaths* are included in fetal death rates. This excludes a fetus of less than 20 weeks gestation or one weighing 500 grams or less. Early fetal deaths (500 grams or less in weight or less than 20 weeks gestation) are considered insufficiently developed to sustain life outside the womb.

Formula for Fetal Death Rate:

$$\frac{\text{Total number of intermediate (int) and late fetal deaths for a period}}{\text{Total number of births (live births and int and late fetal deaths) for the period}} \times 100$$

NOTE: This is another formula that does not use discharges in the denominator. The rationale for this is that every conceptus can be expelled (born) either dead or alive, and the outcome is known at the moment of birth. By applying the *rate formula* and asking the number of times it could happen, it becomes apparent that with each birth there is a chance the infant or fetus could be born with or without signs of life. Since only intermediate and late fetal deaths are included in a fetal death rate, they must also be included in the denominator. Also, the term *births* is often used to designate newborn admissions.

EXAMPLE: Newborn data for the first quarter of the year include a total of 505 live births and 515 live discharges. Deaths included three newborn deaths, six early fetal deaths, four intermediate fetal deaths, and two late fetal deaths. To find the fetal death rate, add the number of intermediate and late fetal deaths (4 + 2 = 6) and divide by the number of live births plus the total intermediate and late fetal (505 + 6 = 511) deaths for a fetal death rate of 1.17% (6 ÷ 511 = 0.0117 × 100 = 1.17%).

 SELF-TEST 7-3

Calculate answers to two decimal places.

1. Delivery room data:

Births:	238	
Discharges:	236	
Deaths (newborn):	1	(under 48 hours)
Deaths (fetal):	3	(1 early; 1 intermediate; 1 late)

    Calculate: a. Fetal death rate.
    b. Newborn death rate.

2. Neonatal nursery data for May:

Bassinet count:	18	Fetal deaths: 6 (1 of 12 weeks gestation)
Admissions:	265	(1 of 14 weeks gestation)
Discharges:	260	(1 of 20 weeks gestation)
Deaths:	2	(1 of 24 weeks gestation)
		(1 of 28 weeks gestation)
		(1 of 30 weeks gestation)

    Calculate: a. Fetal death rate for May.
    b. Newborn death rate for May.

3. Neonatal nursery data for October:

Bassinet count:	20	Fetal deaths: 5 (1 weighed 465 grams)
Admissions:	305	(1 weighed 528 grams)
Discharges:	311	(1 weighed 936 grams)
Deaths:	2	(1 weighed 1,001 grams)
IPSDs:	565	(1 weighed 1,055 grams)

    Calculate: a. Fetal death rate for October.
    b. Newborn death rate for October.

D. CESAREAN SECTION RATES

Many hospitals determine the percentage of deliveries performed by Cesarean section (C-section) as compared to vaginal deliveries. During the past decade, a slight decrease was seen in the C-section rate, but the rate seems to be on the rise again.

1. Cesarean Section Rate

Formula for Cesarean Section Rate:

$$\frac{\text{Total number of Cesarian sections performed in a period}}{\text{Total number of deliveries for the period}} \times 100$$

Do not confuse newborn births with deliveries. A delivery can result in a live birth or a dead fetus. In addition, a delivery may result in multiple births. Each delivery is either vaginal or via a C-section. Note the use of deliveries in the denominator.

EXAMPLES:

EX 1. A total of 220 deliveries are recorded by the OB department, of which 50 were performed by C-section. The rate is determined by dividing 50 by 220 and converting to a percentage ($50 \div 220 = 0.2273 \times 100$) for a 22.73% C-section rate.

EX 2. The obstetrical unit lists 100 admissions for February. Discharges on the OB unit total 103. There were 77 deliveries, of which 22 were by C-section. Twins were born to two mothers, and one gave birth to triplets. However, only the total number of deliveries are important in determining the C-section rate. The calculation results in a 28.57% C-section rate ($22 \div 77 = 0.2857 \times 100 = 28.57\%$).

 SELF-TEST 7-4

Answers should be correct to two decimal places.

1. July OB Data:

Admissions:	451
Discharges:	456	Deaths: 3
Deliveries:	446	(includes 4 sets of twins)
Undelivered:	7
C-sections:	90

   Calculate: Cesarean section rate for July.

2. October OB Data:

Admissions:	65
Discharges:	61	Deaths: 1
Undelivered:	5

Delivered		Total	Number Delivered by C-Section
Live	Single infant	50	15
	Twins	3 sets	1 set
	Triplets	1 set	0
Dead	Stillborn	1	1
	Aborted	1	0

Calculate: a. Number of newborn births recorded in October.

             b. Total number of deliveries in October.

             c. Total number of newborn deaths in October.

             d. C-section rate for October.

3. May OB Data:

Admissions: 78	Discharges: 72	Deaths: 0	Undelivered: 4	
Delivered	**Total**		**Delivered by C-Section**	**NB Deaths**
Live	Single	40	15	1
	Twins	4 sets	1 sets	
Dead	Early fetal	3	0	
	Intermediate	1	0	
	Late fetal	1	1	

Calculate: a. Number of newborn admissions recorded in May.

             b. Number of newborn deaths recorded in May.

             c. Total deliveries recorded in May.

             d. C-section rate for May.

4. A hospital reported 150 deliveries during October 15 performed by C-section. Of the deliveries, 35 mothers were primiparae of which five delivered by C-section.

Determine: a. A formula for calculating the percentage of women who delivered for the first time.

             b. Percentage of mothers who delivered for the first time.

             c. A formula for calculating the percentage of first-time mothers who had a C-section.

             d. Percentage of all C-sections performed on first-time mothers.

             e. Percentage of first-time mothers who had a C-section delivery.

             f. C-section rate for October.

2. VBAC (Vaginal Birth after C-Section) Rate

Some facilities determine the number of women who delivered vaginally if the previous delivery was via C-section. This rate is mentioned in passing, but no computations or additional mention will be included throughout the remainder of this text.

Formula for VBAC Rate:

$$\frac{\text{Total number of vaginal deliveries in those with previous C-section}}{\text{Total number who previously delivered via C-section}} \times 100$$

EXAMPLE: During the past year, a total of 800 deliveries were reported. Of this number, 570 were vaginal deliveries and 230 were by C-section. Of the 800 deliveries, 300 delivered for the first time. Of the remaining 500, 120 had a previous C-section, of which 15 delivered vaginally during this reporting period. Therefore, 15/120, or 12.5% delivered vaginally following a C-section.

E. SUMMARY

1. A delivery refers to giving birth, either to a living child or a dead fetus.
2. Multiple births constitute one delivery.
3. A live birth shows signs of life at the time of birth.
4. A live born baby is considered an infant until one year of age.
5. The term *fetal death* is preferred over the terms *stillborn, abortion,* or *aborted fetus.*
6. Maternal/OB terms:
   a. A direct maternal death is a death related to pregnancy. Only direct maternal deaths are used in a maternal death formula.
   b. An indirect maternal death is a death of a pregnant female but caused by a previously existing condition or an acquired illness or accident, aggravated by the pregnancy.
   c. Puerperium is a period of 42 days (6 weeks) following delivery.
   d. A delivery includes the expelling of the contents of a womb; a delivery can result in single or multiple births either live or dead.
   e. Undelivered refers to a pregnancy-related admission in which the mother did not give birth during the admission.
   f. Partum refers to childbirth; antepartum is prior to childbirth; postpartum is after childbirth.
7. Neonatal terms:
   a. Neonates are newborns.
   b. A newborn is any live infant born in the hospital at the time of birth.
   c. A live born baby is considered an infant until one year of age.
   d. Three neonatal periods have been established. The periods extend from birth up to the beginning of the 28th day of life. Period I extends from birth up to 24 hours following birth; Period II extends from one day old up to seven days old; Period III extends from one week up to four weeks of age.
   e. Fetal deaths are classified by the number of weeks of gestation, counted from the last menstrual period (LMP) as: early (less than 20 weeks gestation); intermediate (20 weeks up to 28 weeks gestation); and late (28 or more weeks gestation).
   f. Fetal deaths are also classified by gram weight: early (500 grams or less); intermediate (501 grams to 1,000 grams); late (1,001 grams or more).
8. Rates:
   a. Direct maternal death rate: Direct maternal (OB) deaths divided by OB discharges.
   b. Newborn death rate: Newborn (NB) deaths divided by NB discharges.
   c. Fetal death rate: Intermediate and late fetal deaths divided by total births plus intermediate and late fetal deaths.
   d. C-section rate: Number of C-sections divided by the number of deliveries.
9. Direct maternal death rates should be low and are generally determined only on a yearly basis.

Name _____   **Date** _____

F. CHAPTER 7 TEST

All calculations should be correct to two decimal places.

1. State the gestational age for the following fetal deaths using ACOG guidelines.

    a. Early term
    b. Full term
    c. Late term

2. State the gram weight for the following fetal deaths using ACOG guidelines.

    a. Early
    b. Intermediate
    c. Late

3. Define how each of the following are different:

    a. delivered: undelivered
    b. puerperium: antepartum
    c. neonate: infant
    d. neonatal: perinatal: postnatal

4. OB Unit Data for the Year: (E—early; int—intermediate; L—late)

Admissions:	492
Discharges:	495
Deaths (direct maternal):	1
Deaths (indirect maternal):	1
Deliveries:	476 (482 live births; 8 fetal deaths—early, 5; intermediate, 2; late, 1)
Undelivered:	12

    Calculate: a. Yearly maternal death rate.
    b. Yearly fetal death rate.

5. OB Unit Data for the Year:

Admissions:	2,389	
Discharges:	2,387	
Deliveries: Live newborn:	2,288	(OB deaths—3 direct; 1 indirect)
Aborted (dead) fetus:	73	(OB deaths—1 direct) (early, 49; intermediate, 19; late, 5)
Undelivered:	27	

    Calculate: a. Yearly maternal death rate.
    b. Yearly fetal death rate.

6. Newborn Data:

	<48 Hours	>48 Hours	Early	Intermediate	Late
Births (Live):		300			
Discharges:		291			
Deaths:		3	2	1	
Fetal deaths:		26	18	6	2

    Calculate: a. Newborn death rate.
    b. Fetal death rate.

7. Newborn Data:

Births (live):   86

Discharges: 75

Deaths: 2

Fetal deaths: 10 (Weeks gestation: 15, 18, 16, 28, 31, 25, 22, 14, 27, 20)

Calculate: a. Newborn death rate.
            b. Fetal death rate.

8. Woodland Hospital (July data):

	A&C	NB	<48 Hours	>48 Hours	Early	Intermediate	Late
Bed/bassinet count	225	20					
Admissions	1,138	134					
Discharges	1,143	131					
Deaths: A&C			6	4			
NB			1	0			
Fetal					4	2	1
IPSDs	5,722	503					

Calculate: a. Newborn death rate.
            b. Fetal death rate.
            c. *(R9)* Gross death rate.
            d. *(R9)* Net death rate.
            e. *(R5)* A&C occupancy percentage.
            f. *(R5)* Newborn occupancy percentage.

9. Regional Hospital (March Data):

Unit	Bed/Bass count	Adm	Disch	Death	<48 Hrs	>48 Hrs	Early	Intermediate	Late
OB	18	188	115	1	0	1			
NB	15	110	107	2	1				
Fetal deaths							5	3	1

Calculate: a. Newborn death rate.
            b. Maternal death rate.
            c. Fetal death rate.

10. OB (October Data):

Admissions: 65   Discharges: 61

Deaths: 1 (direct)

Undelivered: 7

Delivered	Total	Vaginal	C-Section	NB Deaths
Live: Single infant	50	35	15	2
Twins	3 sets	2 sets	1 set	0
Triplets	1 set		1 set	0
Dead	2	1	1	

Calculate: a. Total number of newborn births recorded in October.
            b. Total number of deliveries recorded in October.
            c. Total number of newborn deaths recorded in October.
            d. C-section rate for October.
            e. Maternal death rate for October.

11. Serendipity Hospital (July Data for OB Unit): Bed count: 18

Admissions:	110	Delivered:	87 single infants; 2 sets of twins
Discharges:	102	Undelivered:	12
Deaths:	1 (direct)	C-sections:	27

Calculate: a. Maternal death rate.
　　　　　　b. C-section rate.

12. Rainbow Hospital (June Data for OB Unit):

	Total	Vaginal Delivery	C-Section	NB Deaths
Admissions	283			
Discharges	281			
Deaths	2 (1 direct)			
Undelivered	21			
Delivered (live): Single	221	156	65	2
Twins	3 sets	2 sets	1 set	0
Triplets	1 set	1 set		0
Fetal deaths:	17	17	0	
Early				
Intermediate	8	8	0	
Late	2	2	0	

Calculate: a. Total number of: (1) live births; (2) deliveries; (3) newborn deaths.
　　　　　　b. C-section rate for June.
　　　　　　c. Percent discharged undelivered.

13. Riverview Hospital—OB unit (June 10 Data):

Mother	NB/Fetus Sex	Delivered via Vag.	Delivered via C-Section	NB Weights #1	NB Weights #2	Deaths NB/Maternal
Adams, A	M	*		8 lb 4 oz		
Brown, B	M		*	7 lb 9 oz		
Crane, C	F	*		6 lb 8 oz		
Davis, D	F	*		6 lb 11 oz		
Evans, E	M twins	*		5 lb 10 oz	6 lb 3 oz	
Foster, F	M aborted	*		450 gm		
Grant, G	F	*		7 lb 3 oz		
Hovis, H	F abort	*		850 gm		
Ingals, I	M		*	9 lb 1 oz		
Jones, J	M	*		5 lb 1 oz		NB 10:55 A.M.
Krebs, K	F	*		8 lb 2 oz		
Long, L	M		*	8 lb 9 oz		

Calculate: a. Total number of newborn admissions.
　　　　　　b. Total number of newborn deaths.
　　　　　　c. Total number of deliveries.
　　　　　　d. C-section rate.
　　　　　　e. Fetal death rate.
　　　　　　f. Percent of live births that are male.
　　　　　　g. Average birth weight of live born males.
　　　　　　h. Average birth weight of live born females.

14. Serenity Hospital—OB unit (August 8 Data):

Mother	NB/Fetus Sex	Delivered via Vag.	C-Section	NB Weights #1	#2	Deaths NB/Maternal
Steel, B	M		*	7 lb 2 oz	6 lb 12 oz	
Runo, T	M		*	6 lb 9 oz		
Ryan, C	F	*		8 lb 1 oz		
Novak, T	F	*		6 lb 3 oz		
Bollinger, J	M twins	*		4 lb 12 oz	5 lb 4 oz	
Redfern, S	M aborted	*		375 gm		
Jennings, V	F	*		8 lb 8 oz		
Hohman, D	F abort	*		625 gm		
Portier, Z	M		*	9 lb 6 oz		
McAfee, D	M	*		4 lb 13 oz		NB 12:55 A.M.
Sultan, K	F	*		8 lb 12 oz		
Herman, L	M		*	6 lb 3 oz		

Calculate:
  a. Total number of newborn admissions.
  b. Total number of newborn deaths.
  c. Total number of deliveries.
  d. C-section rate, correct to one decimal place.
  e. Fetal death rate.
  f. Percent of live births that are male, correct to one decimal place.
  g. Average birth weight of live born males, correct to two decimal places.
  h. Average birth weight of live born females, correct to two decimal places.

Miscellaneous Clinical and Nonclinical Statistics

8

LEARNING OBJECTIVES

After studying this chapter, the learner should be able to:

Miscellaneous Clinical Statistics

 Distinguish clearly between nosocomial and community-acquired infections.

 Compute the following rates:
  a. Infection rates:
   (1) Nosocomial
   (2) Community-acquired
   (3) Postoperative
   (4) Hospital
  b. Consultation rates
  c. Complication rate
  d. Comorbidity rate

Miscellaneous Nonclinical Statistics

 Identify nonclinical statistics.

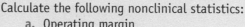 Calculate the following nonclinical statistics:
  a. Operating margin
  b. Days in accounts receivable
  c. Employee turnover
  d. Budget-to-actual variance
  e. Nurse-to-patient ratio

Health care facilities often compute clinical and nonclinical statistics in addition to those introduced in the previous chapters. Never has this been more important than now, as the rules of reimbursement are changing, with tremendous emphasis being places on the quality of patient outcomes as well as on the efficiency of how health care operations are managed. Reimbursements have been declining over the past few decades, and the ability to run efficiently while still achieving targeted quality outcomes is essential for health care providers to be successful.

These rates use the same "basic rate formula," the ratio of the number of times something *does* happen compared to the number of patients to whom it *could* happen. The reader is encouraged to attempt to originate the formula for each of the rates in this chapter prior to searching for the rate in the section under discussion. With the increased capacity for collecting health care data electronically, a wide array of rates and percentages can be more easily ascertained. Facilities can now calculate anything from the rate of readmissions to the percentage of patients seen in consultation to employee turnover. The rates discussed in this chapter are just some of those routinely calculated in many health care facilities.

A. MISCELLANEOUS CLINICAL RATES

1. Infection Rates

Health care facilities diligently try to prevent hospital-borne infections from infecting their patients. Sterilized instruments are used, contaminated materials appropriately discarded, and other measures instituted to prevent the spread of infection. However, the danger of acquiring a hospital-borne infection (also called a nosocomial infection) is always present. Infection control committees are charged with preventing and investigating nosocomial infections. Determining the incidence of infection requires medical judgment, and proper control measures need to be instituted. Suspected cases are reviewed by the infection control committee, which sets criteria and evaluates each case by the established criteria. All types of infections—such as respiratory, gastrointestinal, skin, urinary tract, surgical wound, septicemias, and infections related to insertion of catheters—may be included.

Infection rates may include hospital-wide infection rates as well as more specific rates such as infection rates for independent clinical units (pediatrics, orthopedics) or rates for various types of infection (urinary tract infections or respiratory infections). Ideally, the percentages will be low for infection rates. Rates should fall below 10% and optimally below 5%. It is recommended that rates be rechecked (especially for placement of decimal places) when results are higher than expected.

Hospitals determine infection rates to study the types of infections present within a community or health care facility. Infection rates are one determinant in evaluating the quality of care provided.

In addition, it should be noted that a patient's immune response is a factor in developing infections. Risk factors, such as a patient's age, compromised immune response due to medical treatment or disease (for example, medications, chemotherapy, or AIDS), and the severity of disease, may increase a patient's susceptibility of developing an infection. Whenever infections (of any type) are present, they generally increase the patient's length of stay, increase the cost of treatment, and decrease the quality and speed of recovery.

a. Nosocomial Infection Rate

A nosocomial infection is an infection that pertains to or originates in a hospital. Thus, a nosocomial infection is also called a hospital-acquired infection. Nosocomial infections *include* postoperative infections, as they are also hospital acquired.

The distinguishing factor between hospital-acquired (nosocomial) infections and community-acquired infections is the time frame within which the infection is manifested. Infections manifested within 72 hours of admission were most likely present in the patient at the time of admission. A nosocomial infection, on the other hand, is considered to be one that is manifested *more* than 72 hours post-admission and is more likely to have been acquired during the patient's hospitalization.

Formula for Nosocomial Infection Rate:

$$\frac{\text{Total number of infections}}{\text{Total number of discharges (including deaths)}} \times 100$$

EXAMPLE: A total of 1,000 discharges (including deaths) were reported during the past month. During that same period, a total of 10 nosocomial infections (including postoperative infections) were recorded. Therefore, the nosocomial infection rate for the month is 1% ($10 \div 1,000 = 0.01 \times 100 = 1\%$).

EXAMPLE: In March, St. Joseph Hospital had 350 discharges and deaths. Thirteen of these patients had hospital-acquired infections. The nosocomial infection rate is 3.7% (($13/350) \times 100 = 3.7\%$).

b. **Community-Acquired Infection Rate**

An infection that arises within 72 hours of admission is considered a community-acquired infection—in other words, an infection already present in the patient upon the patient's admission to the health care facility. If the health care facility finds a high community-acquired infection rate, it may develop community-wide prevention programs such as administering vaccines or health education programs aimed at preventing the spread of the infection. Gastrointestinal infections may result from ingesting contaminated food, and the local health department may be recruited to assist in locating the source of contamination.

Formula for Community-Acquired Infection Rate:

$$\frac{\text{Total number of community-acquired infections} < 72\,\text{hours after admission}}{\text{Total number of discharges (including deaths)}} \times 100$$

EXAMPLE: If a total of 20 community-acquired infections were reported out of 1,000 total discharges (including deaths), then the community-acquired infection rate for the period would be 2% ($20/1,000 = 0.02 \times 100 = 2\%$).

EXAMPLE: In May, a hospital had 1,500 discharges (including deaths), 30 patients developed a urinary tract infection, and 15 patients were classified as having a community-acquired infection. The community-acquired infection rate would be 1% ($15/1,500 \times 100 = 1\%$).

c. **Postoperative Infection Rate**

A postoperative infection is, as the name states, an infection that develops after an operation. A postoperative infection is also a nosocomial infection and is included in nosocomial infection rates. The postoperative infection rate is primarily a tool to document a problem and to help ascertain the cause and assist in future prevention. The rate serves to aid a health care facility in pinpointing types of infections occurring postoperatively and the surgical procedures most at risk, and to establish protective measures in hopes of preventing recurrences. The surgical team takes great care to prevent infections resulting from a surgical procedure. A copious amount of antibiotics is employed for wound irrigation during an operation to prevent the onset of a postoperative infection.

Surgical Terms

Surgical Procedure.

Any single, separate, systematic manipulation upon or within the body that can be complete in itself, normally performed by a physician, dentist, or other licensed practitioner, either with or without instruments, is considered a surgical procedure. Surgical procedures are done to restore disunited or deficient parts, to remove diseased or injured tissues, to extract foreign matter, to assist in obstetrical delivery, or to aid in diagnosis.

Surgical Operation.

One or more surgical procedures, performed at one time, for one patient, using a common approach or for a common purpose, is a surgical operation. An operation may include more than one procedure, but the procedures would have to be related or performed for the same common purpose. A salpingo-oophorectomy is considered one operation but includes two procedures, carried out at the same time through the same surgical approach. A patient undergoing a debridement and repair of a facial laceration and a surgical repair of a right wrist fracture is undergoing two unrelated procedures, as is a patient undergoing a colonoscopy and an endoscopic cholecystectomy.

Formula for Postoperative Infection Rate:

$$\frac{\text{Total number of postoperative infections in clean surgical cases}}{\text{Total number of surgical operations performed}} \times 100$$

NOTE: Clean surgical cases are those not infected at the time of surgery. Wounds with prior contamination and infection would be excluded in this formula. Postoperative infection rates are based on infection in which the infectious agent was most likely introduced at the time of surgery. Also, note that the denominator in a postoperative infection rate is the number of *surgical operations*, not the number of patients operated on. A patient may have more than one surgical operation, and each operation includes the possibility of acquiring an infection. The number of patients operated on was used in the postoperative death rate.

EXAMPLE: A total of 10 postoperative infections were recorded during the past month and a total of 250 surgical operations were performed. Therefore, the postoperative infection rate is 4% (10 ÷ 250 = 0.04 × 100 = 4%).

 SELF-TEST 8-1

Careful Hospital (Surgical Data for December):

    Surgical admissions: 150
    Surgical discharges: 142

Surgical Deaths	Total	<48 Hours >48 Hours	<10 Days Postop >10 Days Postop
Total	4	1	
Postoperative	2		2
Anesthesia	1		
Surgical autopsies	3		

Surgical data:

    Patients operated on: 138

    Surgical operations performed: 164

    Anesthetics administered: 144

    Infections: Nosocomial: 4

    Postoperative: 2

Calculate: a. Nosocomial infection rate.

           b. Postoperative infection rate.

           c. *(R8)* Postoperative death rate.

           d. *(R8)* Anesthesia death rate.

d. Hospital (Total) Infection Rate

The hospital infection rate includes all infections manifested during a patient's hospital stay. The hospital infection rate includes nosocomial (including postoperative infections) and community-acquired infections.

Formula for Hospital Infection Rate:

$$\frac{\text{Total number of infections}}{\text{Total number of discharges (including deaths)}} \times 100$$

EXAMPLE: A hospital recorded a total of 50 infections (20 nosocomial and 30 community acquired). The total number of discharges during the period was 2,000. Therefore, the hospital infection rate for the period was 2.5% ($50/2{,}000 = 0.025 \times 100 = 2.5\%$).

 SELF-TEST 8-2

1. Good Time Hospital (Yearly Data):

A&C:			NB:		
Admissions:	3,015		Admissions:	457	
Discharges:	3,021		Discharges:	453	
Deaths:	42		Deaths:	2	
Infections (total):	61		Infections (total):	21	
IPSDs:	20,500		IPSDs:	1,505	

Calculate: a. Hospital infection rate for the year.

           b. A&C hospital infection rate for the year.

           c. NB hospital infection rate for the year.

2. Neonatal Nursery (Yearly Data):

Admissions:	661	Discharges:	650
Infections:	36	Deaths:	5
IPSDs:	1,718		

   Calculate: a. Neonatal nursery infection rate.
   b. *(R9)* Neonatal nursery death rate.

3. Good Fellow Hospital (January–February Data):

Clinical Service	Adm	Disch	Deaths	IPSDs	Hospital Infections
Medical	364	361	14	10,555	8
Surgical	206	200	10	6,821	10
OB	62	64	2	2,485	4
BN	40	42	1	1,718	3
Orthopedic	88	85	7	3,002	6

   Calculate: a. Hospital infection rate for the period.
   b. Percentage of surgical patients who developed an infection.
   c. Clinical service with the highest infection rate.
   d. Clinical service with the lowest infection rate.

2. Consultation Rates

A consultation has been defined as a deliberation by two or more physicians with respect to the diagnosis or treatment in any case. A patient's attending physician may request a consulting physician to see his or her patient and offer an opinion, either to confirm a diagnosis or to treat a condition not in the attending physician's area of expertise. The consultant evaluates the patient and prepares a consultation report that includes the findings and recommendations for treating the patient's condition.

There are two types of consultation rates. One rate depicts the ratio of patients receiving consultations (subsequently referred to as "patients seen") to the number of patients discharged. The other consultation rate shows the ratio of the total number of consultations provided to the number of patients discharged. Patients may be seen by more than one consultant during a specific hospitalization. This second formula assesses the utilization of consultants in the health care facility. It may be used by accrediting organizations (The Joint Commission) to identify the percentage of consultations provided.

a. **Formula for Patients Seen in Consultation:**

$$\frac{\text{Total number of consultations provided}}{\text{Total number of patients discharged}} \times 100$$

b. **Formula for Consultations Provided:**

$$\frac{\text{Total number of consultations provided}}{\text{Total number of patients discharged}} \times 100$$

EXAMPLE: A pediatric unit discharged 100 patients during the past month. Of these, 33 were seen by one or more consultants during their hospital stay, and a total of 45 consultations were recorded. Using the first consultation formula (patients seen), the consultation rate is 33% (33/100 = 0.33 × 100 = 33%). Using the second formula (total consultations provided), the consultation rate is 45% (45/100 = 0.45 × 100 = 45%).

✔ SELF-TEST 8-3

1. Greenbriar Hospital (first quarter data):

	A&C	NB
Admissions	3,375	635
Discharges	3,568	621
Deaths	32	2
Patients seen in consultation	861	102
Total number of consultations provided	1,067	155
IPSDs	20,333	4,052

Calculate:
a. Percentage of patients seen in consultation during the first quarter.
b. Percentage of consultations provided during the first quarter.
c. Percentage of A&C patients seen in consultation during the period.
d. Percentage of newborns seen in consultation during the period.
e. Percentage of consultations provided to A&C patients during the period.
f. Percentage of consultations provided to NB patients during the period.

2. Sacred Heart Hospital:

Clinical Service	Adm	Disch	Deaths	Pts Seen in Consult	Consults Provided
Medical	998	991	13	312	501
Surgical	604	607	11	204	346
OB	378	372	1	85	121
NB	345	346	2	36	75
Psychiatric	207	202	1	44	69

Calculate:
a. Percentage of patients seen in consultation.
b. Percentage of consultations provided.
c. Percentage of A&C patients seen in consultation.
d. Percentage of NB patients seen in consultation.
e. Percentage of consultations provided to A&C patients.
f. Percentage of consultations provided to NB patients.
g. Clinical unit with the lowest percentage of patients seen in consult.
h. Clinical unit with the highest percentage of patients seen in consult.
i. Clinical unit with the lowest percentage of consults provided.
j. Clinical unit with the highest percentage of consults provided.

3. Pediatric unit—12 beds (May data):

		Deaths			Consultations			
Adm	Disch	<48 Hours	>48 Hours	Autopsies	Pts Seen	Provided	IPSDs	DD
98	106	1	1	1	29	45	303	310

Calculate:
- a. Percentage of pediatric patients seen in consultation in May.
- b. Percentage of consultations provided to pediatric patients in May.
- c. *(R4)* Average daily inpatient census for the pediatric unit in May.
- d. *(R5)* Percentage of occupancy for the pediatric unit in May.
- e. *(R6)* Average length of stay of pediatric patients in May.
- f. *(R9)* Gross death rate for the pediatric unit in May.
- g. *(R9)* Gross autopsy rate for the pediatric unit in May.

3. Complication Rate

A complication has been described as a condition that occurs during the patient's hospital stay that extends the length of stay by at least *one day* in 75% of cases. A complication rate is another indicator of quality of care. This rate can aid in determining development of complications and thus assist in finding measures to prevent recurrences. More simply, a complication is an additional disorder that arises after admission to the hospital and that modifies the course of the patient's illness or the need for additional medical care. Infections, hemorrhages, wound disruptions, adverse drug reactions, and transfusion reactions are all examples of complications. There is also concern for falls, burns, and medication administration errors (recorded in incident reports). Complication data and rates may be compiled monthly to assess trends and to take appropriate corrective action to reverse occurrences whenever possible.

Formula for Complication Rate:

$$\frac{\text{Total number of complications for a period}}{\text{Total discharges for the period}} \times 100$$

EXAMPLE: A total of 60 complications were recorded for the first quarter, along with 1,000 discharges. Therefore, the complication rate is 6% (60/1,000 = 0.06 × 100 = 6%).

 SELF-TEST 8-4

Mammoth Medical Center data indicated a total of 85 patients had an abdominal surgical procedure in July. Of these, five developed complications, requiring additional treatment, from the surgery. Calculate the complication rate.

4. Comorbidity Rate

Comorbidity is defined as a *preexisting* condition that will, because of its presence with a principal diagnosis, increase the length of stay at least *one day* in 75% of cases. Preexisting conditions (such as diabetes, hypertension, obesity, emphysema) may also affect the outcome of care.

Formula for Comorbidity Rate:

$$\frac{\text{Total number of comorbidities for a given period}}{\text{Total discharges for the period}} \times 100$$

EXAMPLE: A total of 120 comorbidities were reported in the first quarter of the year out of a total of 1,000 discharges. The resulting comorbidity rate was 12% (120/1,000 = 0.12 × 100 = 12%).

B. MISCELLANEOUS NONCLINICAL STATISTICS

1. Importance of Nonclinical Statistics

To manage any operation, it is important to monitor performance. Key performance metrics are established by the board of directors and senior management. Up to this point, we have discussed statistics related to patient outcomes and population health. But another important aspect of a health care facility is its overall performance—analyzed through financial, employee, and utilization of resources measurements. Over the past few decades, it has become clear that all health care facilities within the industry must operate as any business, monitoring revenues and expenses to earn a profit and remain a sustainable ongoing concern. These statistics can be looked at across an entire hospital or other facility, or at a departmental level. Through monthly, quarterly, and annual review of performance health care businesses can better assess if financial and quality goals are being met and can determine areas where there are opportunities for improvement.

2. Use of Dashboards to Track Organizational Performance

Hospitals operate within a highly regulated industry, required to meet many clinical quality outcomes to remain eligible for Medicare and Medicaid funding. There are numerous financial targets that have been established by the board of directors that facility managers work to achieve on a monthly or an annual basis. Additionally, there are other indicators that are tracked to determine how well staff is retained, trained, and involved in promotions within an organization. Given these important measures to track, many organizations have developed what has been called a *scorecard* to track these statistics monthly. There are numerous software packages that assist in collecting, analyzing, and presenting this information that allow senior executives to understand their operation's performance and where efforts may need to be directed to make improvements. Dashboards can identify those measures that are within a normal expected range, others that are just outside of this normal range and should be focused on, as well as those measures that are far beyond normal limits and require immediate attention to correct.

3. Organizational Statistics

Many nonclinical statistics that are tracked summarize the overall performance of either an inpatient or outpatient operation. Examples of these measures include operating margin, days in accounts receivable, and employee turnover.

a. Operating Margin

A key performance measure for any business operation is the amount of money that is left over after all operating expenses have been paid. *Operating margin* is defined as the ratio of *operating income* (or loss) to *total operating income*. In health care, operating income is determined by subtracting total operating expenses from net patient revenue. The higher this ratio is, the better the performance. This statistic helps an organization understand how profitable they are, based on their core business. (Other revenue from investments, sale of land, donations, etc., are handled separately in determining the "bottom line.")

Formula for Operating Margin:

(Net patient revenue-operating expenses)/total operating income

EXAMPLE: Year-end financials show that a medical center had $25,500,000 in net patient revenue and $24,300,000 in operating expenses. Operating income would be calculated by subtracting expenses from net patient revenue ($25,500,000 − $24,300,000 = $1,200,000). Operating margin would then be determined by dividing $1,200,000 by $25,500,000 which equals 4.7%.

b. **Days in Accounts Receivable**

Days in accounts receivables measures the turnaround time from billing submission to receipt of funds from a third-party payer. The health care industry is unique in that fees for services rendered are not usually collected at the point of service but at some date in the future. Generally, this period can range from 45 to 120 days, depending on the quality of the business office operation. The shorter the time period is to receive funds, the better it is for an organization to meet its short-term financial obligations, such as payroll and invoices from supply vendors. On the other hand, the older a receivable is, the harder it becomes to collect. This statistic is calculated by taking net patient receivables and dividing by net credit revenue divided by the number of days in a period.

Formula for Days in Accounts Receivable:

Net patient receivables/(net credit revenue/number of days in a year)

EXAMPLE: A hospital's business office was calculating its annual days in accounts receivable. Key data gathered for this analysis included net receivables of $300,000 and net credit revenue of $2,500,000. (The year in question is a non-leap year.) The formula would be $300,000/($2,500,000/365) = $300,000/$6,849 = 43.8 days.

c. **Employee Turnover**

Organizations routinely monitor the number of staff that leave an organization to determine how well they are doing in retaining personnel. Although some level of turnover is to be expected (such as 5% to 10%), higher levels can indicate a problem—especially when it involves the loss of key, experienced people who are critical to the success of an organization and who are very costly to replace (recruiting, training, etc.). This ratio is calculated by taking the number of employees who leave an organization and dividing by the total number of staff.

Formula for Employee Turnover:

Number of employees who left organization/
total number of employees at start of period

EXAMPLE: A hospital's human resource department's records indicate that the organization started the last year with 3,230 employees. During the 12 months that followed, 392 employees left the organization for a variety of reasons. The turnover rate would be computed by dividing 392 by 3,230 (392/3,230), resulting in a turnover rate of 12.14%.

4. Departmental Statistics

Department managers have a primary responsibility to monitor their monthly budget numbers compared to their actual performance, specifically in terms of expenses. This assessment is called a variance analysis. The difference in the budgeted and actual numbers is calculated and then turned into a percentage. Positive differences in revenues and negative differences in expenses are desirable.

On clinical units, managers will calculate their nurse-to-patient ratio to determine if they are within their organization's guidelines for that type of unit. Medical and surgical floors have higher ratios versus intensive care units that often have nurse-to-patient ratios of 1:1 or 1:2, depending on patient acuity. Managers can also look at their own employee turnover numbers and compare to other departments in their facilities, as discussed in the previous section.

Formula for Budget Variance:

Actual amount ($$) − budgeted amount ($$) = variance ($$)
Formula for Budget Variance Percentage:
Variance ($$)/budgeted amount ($$) = variance percentage (%)

EXAMPLE 1 (VARIANCE ANALYSIS): A department manager has just received her monthly financials for the prior month. Supply expenses were budgeted at $1,800, and actual supply expenses were $1,930. The variance would be calculated as follows: $1,930 − $1,800 = $130. As actual expenses are greater than what was budgeted, this would be considered a positive (unfavorable) variance. The variance percentage would be calculated as follows: $130/$1,800 = 72%.

Formula for Nurse-to-Patient Ratio:

Number of registered nurses: number of patients =
nurse:patient ratio (reduced to lowest common denominators)

EXAMPLE 2 (NURSE-TO-PATIENT RATIO): A medical nursing unit has 36 patients on the floor and has four registered nurses (RNs) on duty. The nurse-to-patient ratio would be calculated by reducing the ratio of 36/4 to 9/1. This can be translated into one nurse for every nine patients or, more commonly, nine patients per one nurse.

5. Internal and External Benchmarking

To conclude this chapter, it is important to note that for an organization to truly understand its performance, it is critical that statistics be compared to some type of benchmark. For organizational statistics, external benchmarks are appropriate. Comparing performance against similar facilities or, even better, with best-practice facilities allows management to understand how they are really operating and/or if there are areas where improvements can be made. External benchmarks can be located through professional organizations and other proprietary sources. At the department level, either internal or external benchmarks can be used for this same purpose. Top performing organizations have adopted a corporate philosophy of continuous process improvement to remain at the leading edge in their industry.

C. SUMMARY

1. Rates can be devised by dividing the number of times something happens by the number of times it could happen.
2. A surgical procedure is a single manipulation that can be complete in itself. A surgical procedure may or may not include the use of instruments—steps required to accomplish a desired result.
3. A surgical operation is one or more surgical procedures, performed on one patient at one time, via a common approach or to achieve a common purpose.
4. A complication is a disorder arising *after* admission that lengthens the patient's stay at least one day in 75% of cases.
5. A comorbidity is a *preexisting* condition that lengthens the patient's stay at least one day in 75% of cases.
6. Nosocomial infections are hospital-acquired infections—infections arising more than 72 hours after admission.
7. Community-acquired infections are infections with manifestations less than 72 hours after admission.
8. Postoperative infections are infections developing after a surgical operation; postoperative infections, in addition, are nosocomial infections.
9. A hospital infection rate includes both nosocomial and community-acquired infections.
10. A consultation is the result of the patient's attending physician requesting another physician or health care provider to provide recommendations and/or opinions regarding the care of a particular patient. A patient may be seen by more than one consulting physician during the patient's hospitalization.
11. All rates in this chapter, except for the postoperative infection rate, include total discharges in the denominator.
12. Rates in which the denominator includes total discharges:
    a. Nosocomial infection rate: Hospital-acquired infections >72 hours post-admission divided by discharges.
    b. Community-acquired infection rate: Infections arising <72 hours post-admission divided by discharges.
    c. Hospital (total) infection rate: Total number of infections divided by discharges.
    d. Complication rate: Complications divided by discharges.
    e. Comorbidity rate: Comorbidities divided by discharges.
    f. Consultation rate:
       (1) Patients seen in consultation divided by discharges.
       (2) Total consultations provided divided by discharges.
13. Postoperative infection rate: Total postoperative infections in clean surgical cases divided by the number of surgical operations.
14. Nonclinical statistics play an essential role in the management of any health care facility.

15. Dashboards are frequently used to display key performance indicators and highlight those indicators that are performing well, those that may need some attention, and others that are critically in need of improvement.
16. Some nonclinical statistics assess the overall performance of a facility, such as operating margin, days in accounts receivable, and employee turnover.
17. Other nonclinical statistics are done at the departmental level to help managers better understand their specific operation and to identify areas in need of improvement.
18. Benchmarks, both internal and external, as needed to more clearly understand an organization's or department's performance in terms of industry averages or best practice.

NOTES

Name _____   **Date** _____

D. CHAPTER 8 TEST

All computations should be correct to two decimal places.

1. Identify the value placed in the denominator for the following rates:

    a. Nosocomial infection rate.
    b. Community-acquired infection rate.
    c. Postoperative infection rate.
    d. Hospital infection rate.
    e. Consultation rate.
    f. Complication rate.

2. What timeline is used to distinguish nosocomial infections from community-acquired infections?

3. Two rates include a statement regarding *lengthening the patient's stay by at least one day*.

    a. In what percentage of cases?
    b. Name the two applicable rates.

4. Name the term that applies to:

    a. Disorder arising after admission.
    b. Disorder present *(preexisting)* upon admission that affects a patient's stay.

5. Skyline Hospital Surgical Data (January):   Surgical units bed count: 40

Admissions:	176
Discharges:	172
Deaths (total):	5 2 (<48 hours); 3 (>48 hours)
Postoperative:	2 2 (<10 days)
Anesthesia:	1
Infections (total):	6 (3 postop); (1 com-acq); (5 nosocomial)
Patients operated on:	156
Surgical operations performed:	166
Anesthetics administered:	160
Consultations (patients seen):	48

    Calculate: a. Postoperative infection rate for January.
    b. Nosocomial infection rate for January.
    c. Consultation rate for January.
    d. Surgical unit hospital infection rate for January.
    e. *(R8)* Postoperative death rate for January.
    f. *(R8)* Anesthesia death rate for January.
    g. *(R8)* Gross death rate for the surgical unit for January.
    h. *(R8)* Net death rate for the surgical unit for January.

6. Regional Medical Center (October data):

Admissions:	2,055	Infections (total):	58
Discharges:	2,050	Nosocomial (total):	25
Surgical operations:	222	Postoperative:	9
Comorbidities:	240	Community-acquired:	33
Complications:	110		
Consultations (patients seen):	363	Consultations (provided):	658

    Calculate: a. Complication rate for October.
    b. Nosocomial infection rate for October.
    c. Postoperative infection rate for October.

    d. Community-acquired infection rate for October.
    e. Hospital infection rate for October.
    f. Comorbidity rate for October.
    g. Consultation rate for October:
        (1) Patients seen.
        (2) Consultations provided.

7. Cascade Hospital (August data):

Clinical Unit	Adm	Disch	Deaths	Autopsies HP	Autopsies Cor	Consults	Hospital Infections	Surgical Operations
Medical	401	390	18	5	1	105	5	
Surgical	88	81	2	1	0	47	2 (postop)	84
Pediatrics	51	48	0	—	—	18	1	
OB	268	269	1	1	0	44	4	
Orthopedic	60	58	2	1	0	18	3	
NB	241	239	1	0	0	9	2	

Calculate:
    a. Hospital consultation rate for August.
    b. Clinical unit with the highest consultation rate for August.
    c. Hospital infection rate for August.
    d. Clinical unit with the highest infection rate for August.
    e. Postoperative infection rate for August.
    f. *(R8)* Gross death rate for August.
    g. *(R10)* Gross autopsy rate for August.
    h. *(R10)* Net autopsy rate for August.

8. Surgical data (January through March). Bed count: 36
Admissions: 360 Discharges: 348 Patients seen in consultation: 120

Month	Deaths Anes	Deaths Postop	Deaths Other	Infections Noso	Infections Postop	Infections Com-Acq	Patients Oper on	Surg Oper	Anes Adm
January	1	1	1	6	1	5	108	120	110
February	0	1	1	3	1	7	95	98	97
March	0	2	2	4	2	8	123	133	125

Calculate:
    a. Postoperative infection rate for the first quarter.
    b. Month with the highest postoperative infection rate.
    c. Nosocomial infection rate for the first quarter.
    d. Consultation rate for the first quarter.
    e. Hospital infection rate for the first quarter.
    f. *(R8)* Postoperative death rate for the first quarter.
    g. *(R8)* Anesthesia death rate for the first quarter.
    h. *(R8)* Gross death rate for the first quarter.

9. Windhaven Hospital (September surgical data):

Type of Surgery	Adm	Disch	Deaths	Patients Oper on	Consults	Postop Infections	Complications
GI	36	35	1	34	12	1	2
Gyn	45	44	0	43	3	0	1
C-section	21	22	0	20	1	0	0
Orthopedic	47	46	2	47	20	5	3
ENT	18	18	0	18	1	0	1
Urological	27	25	0	26	1	1	2
CV	48	45	3	46	22	6	4
Other	19	20	1	18	6	2	1

Additional statistics: a. Surgical procedures 271
                                  b. Surgical operations 248
                                  c. Anesthetics administered 255

Calculate: a. Consultation rate for September.
                  b. Postoperative infection rate for September.
                  c. Complication rate for September.
                  d. Type of surgery with the highest complication rate for September.
                  e. *(R8)* Type of surgery with the highest gross (September) death rate.

10. Hillcrest Hospital (July autopsies data):

Clinical Unit	Adm	Disch	Deaths	HP	Cor	Infec	Comorbidity	Consults
Medical	862	860	33	5	1	5	303	298
Surgical	333	331	16	4	2	3	98	122
OB	257	255	2	1	0	2	62	21
NB	221	218	3	2	1	4	5	11

Calculate: a. Hospital infection rate for July.
                  b. Consultation rate for July.
                  c. Comorbidity rate for July.
                  d. Surgical unit infection rate for July.
                  e. Medical unit infection rate for July.

11. Crestview Hospital (October data):

Clinical Unit	Disch	Comor-bidity	Complic	Consults Pts Seen	Consults Provided	Infections Noso	Infections Com-Acq	Infections Postop
Medical	302	99	41	89	123	21	30	
Surgical	178	57	20	66	77	19	14	11
Psych	53	14	8	8	14	3	1	
Orthopedics	111	48	12	27	38	16	7	
OB	219	36	19	31	46	18	6	
NB	202	9	33	12	22	20	0	

Surgical information: Patients operated on 215
                          Surgical operations performed 238
                          Anesthetics administered 244

Calculate: a. Complication rate for October.
                  b. Consultation rate for October:
                      (1) Patients seen.
                      (2) Consults provided.
                  c. Hospital infection rate for October.
                  d. Nosocomial infection rate for October.
                  e. Community-acquired infection rate for October.
                  f. Postoperative infection rate for October.
                  g. Comorbidity rate for October.
                  h. Medical unit complication rate for October.
                  i. Surgical unit comorbidity rate for October.
                  j. Psych unit nosocomial infection rate for October.
                  k. Orthopedic unit community-acquired infection rate for October.
                  l. OB unit consultation rate (patients seen) for October.
                  m. NB consultation rate (total provided) for October.

12. Explain the importance of nonclinical statistics, provide examples, and describe how they would be used by managers to more effectively monitor their operations.

13. Mountain Health Care reported net receivables of $6,766.300 and net credit revenue of $45,530,000 in the past year, which was a leap year.

   Calculate the days in accounts receivable to one decimal place.

14. Seaside Hospital has year-end financials that show the medical center had $25,500,000 in net patient revenue and $24,300,000 in operating expenses.

   Calculate the operating margin to one decimal place.

15. Liberty Medical Center started the year with 5,646 employees. Through the year, 723 employees left the organization.

   Calculate the employee turnover rate (to one decimal place) for this facility.

16. The manager of the HIM department has just received monthly financials for her department. Actual labor expenses for this period were $5,734, while budgeted expenses were $5,300.

   Calculate the labor expense variance and variance percentage (to one decimal place). Indicate if this is a positive or negative variance.

17. An outpatient surgery manager has just received monthly financials for his department. Actual revenues for the department were $750,340 with budgeted revenue of $685,000.

   Calculate the revenue variance and variance percentage (to one decimal place). Indicate if this is a positive or negative variance.

18. The nurse manager of a surgical intensive care unit has 14 patients in her unit and six nurses on duty.

   Calculate the nurse:patient ratio to one decimal place.

End-of-Life Statistics: *Mortality and Autopsy Rates*

9

CHAPTER OUTLINE

LEARNING OBJECTIVES

After studying this chapter, the learner should be able to:

Part I: Mortality Rates

 Define mortality.

 Distinguish clearly between:
   a. Net versus gross
   b. Newborn death/infant death/fetal death

 Identify deaths excluded in gross and net death rates.

Compute the following death rates:
   a. Gross death rate
   b. Net death rate
   c. Newborn death rate
   d. Surgical postoperative death rate
   e. Anesthesia death rate

Part II: Autopsy Rates

 Distinguish clearly between:
   a. Autopsy versus hospital autopsy versus hospital inpatient autopsy
   b. Net versus gross autopsy

Describe the types of deaths that most likely are coroner's cases.

 Describe when coroner's cases are included in hospital autopsies.

 Distinguish which autopsies are included in hospital autopsies.

 Compute the following autopsy rates:
   a. Gross autopsy rate
   b. Net autopsy rate
   c. Hospital autopsy rate
   d. Newborn autopsy rate
   e. Fetal autopsy rate

PRELIMINARY QUESTIONS

1. Define mortality.
2. Distinguish between a newborn death and a fetal death.
3. Distinguish between the terms *net* and *gross*.
4. How should death rates be considered when reporting discharge data?
5. If 10 patients are discharged on June 1 and one of the 10 expired, what is the death rate? What value was included in the numerator and what value made up the denominator?

6. Should adults/children and newborns be combined in the same death rate? Explain.
7. Explain the difference, if any, between a coroner and a medical examiner?
8. When should autopsies be performed?
9. Are consents required for all autopsies?

Part I: Mortality Rates: Although discharges include deaths, the first portion of this chapter is concerned with the percentage of deaths that occur during inpatient hospitalization. Inpatient deaths are deaths that occur during a patient's inpatient hospitalization. Outpatient deaths are those that occur when being treated by the hospital's medical staff but not during the time of a person's inpatient stay. A patient who dies during outpatient treatment or an outpatient procedure is an outpatient death. An unresponsive patient treated in the emergency department of a medical center, unable to be revived, or expires during treatment, is an out-patient death and is *not* included in inpatient death rates.

In the previous chapters, adults and children rates were not combined with newborn rates. When computing death rates, it is common to combine the two sets of data unless the A&C or newborn rate is specified. Death rates can be important in identifying causes of death and bringing attention to their causes. It may be that a community is seeing an increase in handgun deaths or an increase in cancers due to environmental conditions, which may spark community action. It may also be determined that certain ethnic populations have an increased risk of dying due to certain conditions that can be addressed. Not all deaths are preventable, but the inpatient death rate should be low.

Part II: Autopsy Rates: Autopsies are most commonly performed to determine the cause of death. Autopsies are also valuable learning tools for studying disease processes and to characterize the extent or type of changes wrought by disease and treatment. Hospital autopsies can improve clinical knowledge and can serve as a means of educating physicians. An autopsy is the examination of a dead body to determine the cause of death. An autopsy can be performed on the entire body or just a particular body organ. An autopsy is a postmortem examination.

A. TERMS

1. Mortality

Mortality refers to death or being fatal—a fatality. A mortal is subject to death or is destined to die. Mortality rates are death rates.

2. Inpatient Death

A patient who expires while an inpatient in a hospital is an inpatient death. An inpatient death indicates the patient expired after admission as an inpatient but prior to being discharged during the same hospitalization.

3. Newborn Death

A newborn death occurs only in infants who have signs of life at the time of birth. Therefore, any infant or fetus born dead is a fetal death—never a newborn death. Any sign of life, no matter how tenuous, results in a live newborn. Should the newborn expire, even minutes after birth, the newborn is classified as a newborn death and is included in inpatient death rates. It is important not to confuse a newborn death with a fetal death.

4. Outpatient Death

Outpatient deaths include patients who expire while receiving care (that is, treatment or a procedure) on an outpatient basis. Also included are patients receiving care on a continuing outpatient basis by a member of the medical staff. A hospice patient who is receiving care at home and is considered an outpatient who expires at home is an outpatient death. As mentioned, outpatient deaths are recorded but not included in inpatient statistics. ER deaths and DOAs are outpatient deaths.

5. Hospital Fetal Death

A hospital fetal death is death *prior* to the complete expulsion or extraction from its mother, in a hospital facility, of a product of human conception (fetus and placenta)—irrespective of the duration of the pregnancy—without any signs of life. Fetal deaths are *never* included in hospital mortality rates, except separate fetal death rates.

6. Net versus Gross

Whenever the term *gross* is used statistically, it represents an amount before anything is subtracted. One often hears the terms *gross pay* and *net pay*. The gross pay is the amount you would have received prior to any taxes and insurance being taken out by your employer. If an employee is hired to work 40 hours a week at the rate of $10.00 per hour, the employee is earning $400.00 a week. However, the paycheck the employee receives is somewhat lower due to the deductions (federal and state income taxes, social security tax, health insurance, retirement fund, etc.) taken out by the employer. The amount after the deductions is the employee's net pay. There are two primary inpatient death rates—a gross death rate and net death rate. When calculating net death rates, there will be deaths subtracted from the gross death rate. Gross minus something equals net.

B. DEATH RATES

Discharge data include all patients who died during their inpatient hospitalization. In general, discharge data include deaths, but should the term *live* precede the word discharges (live discharges), the reader will have to add the deaths to the live discharges to derive the total discharges. When computing all rates, keep in mind that all rates are the ratio of the number of times something happens to the number of times it could happen. If 15 patients were discharged on January 20 and 2 were deaths, then 13 were live discharges.

1. Helpful Hints

a. Death Rates Should Be Low

In previous calculations, high percentages were considered advantageous. A hospital hopes to have high census figures, inpatient service data, and high occupancy percentages. The opposite is true for death rates. A result of 90% (or even 20%) would clearly indicate a miscalculation and alert the statistician to look for errors. In many

NOTES

instances, the death rate will be less than 1%, resulting in a decimal figure (for example 0.67%). Carefully check the placement of the decimal point in computing death rates. A misplaced decimal point can make an enormous difference.

b. **Death rates Should Be Carried to Three (Rounded to Two) Decimal Places**

This will result in a death rate correct to two or at least one decimal place. For example, if the calculation were 0.00673 then the result would be 0.673%, rounded to 0.67%. A tenth of a percent of a large number is less significant than a tenth of a percent of a small number. Since death rates will typically be low, calculations should be carried out farther than the calculations introduced up to this point.

c. **Death Rates Generally Use Discharge Data**

Remember, if a patient is hospitalized, there is a chance the patient may die. Discharge data is used unless noted in the appropriate death rate.

d. **Most Death Rates Combine Newborn and Adults and Children Data**

Death rates for each patient category (A&C and NB) are also calculated, but in the majority of cases they are combined. This contrasts with census data and occupancy percentages.

2. **Gross Death Rate**

Formula for Gross Death Rate:

$$\frac{\text{Total number of IP deaths (including NB) for a period}}{\text{Total number of discharges (including deaths) for the period (NB and A\&C)}} \times 100$$

EXAMPLE: If 200 patients were discharged in March and of these, three died, the result is a death rate of 1.5% (3 divided by 200 = 0.015 × 100 = 1.5%).

3. **Net Death Rate**

This is also referred to as Institutional Death Rate.

Formula for Net Death Rate:

$$\frac{\text{Total IP deaths (including NB) minus deaths less than 48 hours (for a period)}}{\text{Total discharges (including NB) minus deaths less than 48 hours (for a period)}} \times 100$$

It was thought, historically, that a patient who expires within the first 48 hours of admission had insufficient time to be diagnosed and respond to treatment for a life-threatening disorder and that only emergency and stabilizing treatment could be provided during such a short period of time. For this reason, the net death rate or institutional death rate came into use. The feeling was that the net death rate reflected more accurately the hospital's ability to save lives. Today, the net death rate has lost its significance but is still requested by some reporting or accrediting agencies.

Hospital deaths—especially unexpected deaths—may be reviewed by a medical staff committee. Procedures and appropriate patient care may be reviewed in hopes of saving lives in the future. This points to an important role that hospital statistics can play in addition to the role in aiding administrative decisions. Statistics are important for peer review and better patient care.

Because not all hospitals use the net death rate, it is assumed the gross death rate is to be used unless otherwise indicated. Because net deaths exclude deaths less than 48 hours in the numerator, they must also be excluded in the denominator.

NOTES

EXAMPLES:

EX 1. A total of five patients expired in June, of which two died less than 48 hours following admission. A total of 450 inpatients were discharged in June. The *gross* death rate includes all deaths (five) divided by the total discharges (450) for a result of 0.011. Converted to a percentage, the gross death rate is 1.1%.

EX 2. The *net* death rate subtracts two deaths from both the numerator and the denominator $(5 - 2 \div 450 - 2)$, resulting in a ratio of 3/448 or 0.0067, multiplied by 100, the net death rate computes to 0.67%.

4. Newborn Death Rate

Formula for Newborn Death Rate:

$$\frac{\text{Total number of NB deaths (for a period)}}{\text{Total number of NB discharges (including deaths) (for a period)}} \times 100$$

NOTE: A newborn death has already been described—alive at the time of birth and born during the same admission in which the birth occurred. A neonatal death includes newborns under 28 days of age. No fetal deaths are included. Rates and definitions of terms relating to neonatal deaths, post-neonatal deaths, and infant deaths are included in Chapter 7. The formula for newborn death rate applies only to newborns born alive in the hospital who expire during that admission.

EXAMPLE: A total of two newborns died during December. There were a total of 102 live newborn discharges (104 total discharges). To determine the newborn death rate, two deaths are placed in the numerator with 104 discharges in the denominator. The newborn death rate is 1.92% $(2 \div 104) = 0.0192 \times 100 = 1.92\%$.

SELF-TEST 9-1

Compute all answers correct to one decimal place.

1. Snowflake Hospital Statistics for May:

			Deaths	
	Admissions	**Discharges**	**<48 Hours**	**>48 Hours**
A&C	686	691	4	8
Newborn	58	60	1	2

Calculate:

a. Gross death rate.
b. Net death rate.
c. Newborn mortality rate.

2. November data (deaths):

| Service | Admissions | Deaths | | Discharges |
		<48 Hours	>48 Hours	
Medical	250	2	5	261
Surgical	105	2	4	103
Pediatric	33	0	1	35
Obstetric	36	1	0	34
Psychiatric	47	1	1	45
Newborn	40	1	1	38

Calculate:

a. Gross death rate.
b. Net death rate.
c. Newborn death rate.
d. Net death rate for the medical service.
e. Clinical service with the lowest gross death rate.

3. Newborn nursery data for February:

Bassinet count:	15
Births (admissions):	88
Discharges:	84
Newborn deaths:	2 (1 less than 48 hours; 1 greater than 48 hours)
Fetal deaths:	5 (2 early; 2 intermediate; 1 late)
Inpatient service days:	398

Calculate:

a. Gross death rate for the newborn nursery in February.
b. *(R5)* Occupancy percentage for the newborn nursery in February.

4. Morris County Hospital—November Data:

| | Admission | Discharges | Deaths | |
			<48 Hours	>48 Hours
Adults/Children	386	388	2	5
Newborn	91	95	1	1

Calculate:

a. Gross death rate for November.
b. Net death rate for November.
c. Newborn mortality rate for November.
d. Gross death rate for A&C for November.
e. Net death rate for A&C for November.

5. June Statistics:

	Admissions	Discharges	Deaths Total	Deaths <48 Hours	Deaths >48 Hours
Adults/Children	650	647	12	3	9
Newborn	55	57	2	1	1
Service					
Medical		332	8	2	6
Surgical		217	3	1	2
Pediatric		98	1	0	1
Newborn		*57*	2	1	1

Calculate:

a. Gross death rate for June.
b. Net death rate for June.
c. Newborn death rate for June.
d. A&C gross death rate for June.
e. A&C net death rate for June.
f. Newborn net death rate for June.
g. Clinical service with the lowest gross death rate.
h. Clinical service with the lowest net death rate.

6. A newborn nursery reports a total of 234 births during July. During the same month, there were a total of four deaths—two newborn and two fetal deaths. One of the newborn deaths occurred less than 48 hours after admission; the other occurred more than 48 hours after admission. During July, a total of 238 newborns were discharged. The bassinet count for July was 15. Calculate the newborn death rate for July.

5. Surgical Death Rates

Two surgical death rates (postoperative and anesthesia death rates) are *not* based on discharges and therefore are an exception to the rates just discussed. These surgical death rates are not computed by all hospitals. When referencing surgical data, there is a difference between a surgical operation and a surgical procedure. A *surgical operation* is one or more surgical procedures performed at one time for one patient using a common approach or for a common purpose. A *surgical procedure* is a single manipulation that can be complete in itself. A closed reduction to align a broken bone is a procedure, as is a forceps delivery of a fetus. A patient undergoing heart bypass surgery has not only an incision made in the chest, but, in addition, a vein removed from another part of the body (such as the leg). Although two incisions are made, it is one operation. However, a patient undergoing a splenectomy and an open reduction for a broken wrist following an accident is undergoing two surgical operations. The surgical death rates are the postoperative death rate and anesthesia death rate.

a. Postoperative Death Rate

Whether the postoperative death rate is of value has been questioned. It is included here because it is still used frequently by some hospitals. However, determining death rates for specific operations can provide more valuable information. Determining the number of patients who expire as the result of a cholecystectomy or hemicolectomy can be more meaningful than stating the postoperative death rate was 3%. In addition, very few surgical patients nowadays are still hospitalized 10 days postop except patients in critical condition or patients who develop major complications.

Formula for Postoperative Death Rate:

$$\frac{\text{Total surgical deaths (within 10 days postoperative) for a period}}{\text{Total patients operated upon for the period}} \times 100$$

NOTE: This formula is an exception to the rule of dividing by the number of discharges. In this formula only, the number of patients operated on during the 10-day period is used in the calculation. This is in accordance with the stated rate formula—the number of times a death occurs to the number of times it could happen. Patients who expire later in the postoperative period (greater than 10 days) are considered most likely to have died as the result of a medical condition rather than because of complications due to surgery.

EXAMPLE: A total of three postoperative deaths (within 10 days postoperative) were reported in March. During the same period of time, 375 patients underwent an operative procedure. Using the formula for postoperative death rate, 3 deaths are placed in the numerator and 375 in the denominator (patients operated on). The computation is $3 \div 375 = 0.008 \times 100 = 0.8\%$ postoperative death rate.

 SELF-TEST 9-2

Compute all rates correct to two decimal places.

1. July surgical data:

Patients admitted:	185
Patients operated on:	187
Patients discharged:	183
Total deaths on surgical unit:	6
Total deaths postoperatively:	4
Total deaths within 10 days postop:	2
Total surgical procedures performed:	193
Total anesthetics administered:	188

Calculate: Postoperative death rate for July.

2. Feel Good Hospital—August Surgical Data:

Admissions:	193	
Discharges:	189	
Deaths:	3	(1 less than 10 days; 2 more than 10 days)
		(0 less than 48 hours; 3 more than 48 hours)
Operations performed:	210	
Patients operated on:	188	

Calculate: Postoperative death rate for August.

b. Anesthesia Death Rate

Anesthesia deaths occur infrequently, and the rate is generally only computed annually. Because it is difficult to prove a death occurred from an anesthetic agent, these deaths can only be determined by a physician. When keeping statistics on anesthesia deaths, it may be more meaningful to classify them by specific anesthetic agent rather than all anesthetics. Include deaths attributed to all anesthetic agents (local and general).

Formula for Anesthesia Death Rate:

$$\frac{\text{Total deaths caused by anesthetic agents for a period}}{\text{Total number of anesthetics administered for the period}} \times 100$$

EXAMPLE: A total of 1,400 anesthetic agents were administered during the past year. It was determined that one death resulted from an anesthetic agent. The yearly anesthesia death rate computation is $1 \div 1{,}400 = 0.0007 \times 100 = 0.07\%$. Be sure to check the placement of the decimal point in anesthesia death rates.

SELF-TEST 9-3

Compute the answers correct to two decimal places.

1. Chastity Hospital reports the following surgical data for the year:

Admissions:	1,843
Discharges:	1,849
Deaths:	30

    (7 less than 48 hours; 23 greater than 48 hours)

    (12 less than 10 days postop; 18 greater than 10 days postop)

    (1 reported due to anesthetic agent)

Operations performed:	2,010
Patients operated on:	1,852
Anesthetics administered:	1,854

    Calculate:
    a. Anesthesia death rate for the year.
    b. Postoperative death rate for the year.
    c. Gross death rate for surgical patients for the year.
    d. Net death rate for surgical patients for the year.

2. In July, Blessing Hospital reported the following surgical data:

Admissions:	258
Discharges:	262
Deaths (surgical):	9

    (3 less than 48 hours; 6 greater than 48 hours)

    (2 less than 10 days postop; 7 greater than 10 days postop)

    (0 due to anesthetic agent)

Anesthetics administered: 298
Surgical procedures performed: 301
Patients operated on: 260

Calculate:
a. Anesthesia death rate for July.
b. Postoperative death rate for July.
c. Gross death rate for surgical patients for July.
d. Net death rate for surgical patients for July.

PART II: AUTOPSY RATES

C. TERMS

1. Autopsy

An autopsy is the inspection and partial dissection of a dead body to learn the cause of death and the nature and extent of disease—a post-mortem examination.

2. Hospital Autopsy

A hospital autopsy is a postmortem examination performed—either by a hospital pathologist or by a physician on the medical staff to whom the responsibility has been delegated—on the body of a person who at some time had been a hospital patient. These patients include inpatients, outpatients, and former patients. Note that no mention is made as to where the examination is to take place.

a. Inpatients

A hospital inpatient autopsy is a postmortem examination on the body of a patient who died during inpatient hospitalization. The examination is performed by a hospital pathologist or a physician on the medical staff to whom the responsibility has been delegated. If an inpatient is a coroner's case (see definition of coroner's case) but the body is autopsied by the hospital pathologist, it is still credited as a hospital autopsy. Only if the body is removed by the coroner and the body is unavailable for autopsy is it excluded.

b. Outpatients

According to the definition of a hospital autopsy, outpatients can also be included in hospital autopsies if the autopsy is performed by a member of the hospital's medical staff. If an outpatient dies during outpatient treatment, and an autopsy is performed by a member of the hospital staff, it is included in a hospital autopsy rate.

c. Former Patients

Patients who have received treatment by the hospital's medical staff either as an inpatient or an outpatient in the past but are not currently undergoing treatment and whose bodies are autopsied by the hospital's pathologist are included in a hospital's autopsy rate. For example, a patient who underwent coronary bypass surgery, received cardiac rehabilitation as an outpatient, recovered completely, and suddenly died may be included in hospital autopsy rates if the autopsy is carried out by the hospital's medical staff. All patients who were treated by the hospital's medical staff and are autopsied by the designated medical staff member are included in a *hospital autopsy rate*.

3. Coroner

A coroner is a duly elected or appointed official whose primary function is to investigate any death in which the cause of death is uncertain or not due to natural causes. An inquest before a jury may be part of the inquiry. The investigation is directed at determining the manner, means, and cause of death.

4. Medical Examiner

A medical examiner is a physician (most commonly a pathologist) officially authorized by a governmental unit (such as a city or a county) to ascertain causes of death, especially those *not* occurring under natural circumstances. Not all jurisdictions have both a coroner and a medical examiner. In areas other than major urban areas of the country, the medical examiner's job may be performed by the hospital pathologist or another designated physician on the medical staff at the request of the coroner.

D. CORONER'S CASES

Most deaths occurring in a hospital are deaths due to illness or natural causes. However, certain patients may be admitted following a gunshot wound or attempted suicide. Should these patients expire while under the hospital's care, the deaths become known as *coroner's cases* and must be reported to the coroner's office. Most coroners are elected officials who do not have a medical degree and whose primary responsibility is to gather evidence surrounding the death. The deaths reportable to the coroner's office include deaths due to:

(1) Criminal or violent means (for example homicides).

(2) Suicides; suspected suicides.

(3) Sudden deaths, following apparent health (to rule out foul play, such as poisoning, strangulation, suffocation, or even a fall).

(4) Suspicious or unusual circumstances.

(5) Accidents, including those that occur on the job (arising from employment).

The deaths most likely to fall under the jurisdiction of the coroner's office include deaths due to blows, burns, crushing, cuts or stab wounds, drowning, electric shock, explosions, firearms, falls, poisoning (carbon monoxide, food, etc.), hanging, heat-related deaths, strangulation, suffocation, and all types of vehicle accidents (car, bus, train, bicycle, and motorcycle).

In addition, criminal or self-induced abortions are also to be reported to the coroner, including stillbirths if suspicious in nature due to illegal interference. Each state has its own laws regarding deaths reportable to the coroner, and it is important that health care practitioners are knowledgeable about the laws in the state in which they are practicing.

When computing autopsy rates, it is important to know which deaths are included. The gross autopsy rate and the net autopsy rate include *only inpatient* deaths autopsied by the authorized hospital physician. Only the *hospital autopsy rate* includes autopsies performed on inpatients, outpatients, and former patients as described earlier. A patient who expires during examination or treatment in the emergency department and whose body is autopsied is only included in the *hospital autopsy rate* as only inpatients are included in gross and net autopsy rates.

> **NOTE:** Throughout the computations in this text, all references to deaths reportable to the coroner will be called *coroner's cases* and, unless specifically indicated, will be those cases *not* autopsied by the designated physician on the hospital's medical staff, and claimed by the coroner.

E. AUTOPSY INFORMATION

1. Who Performs an Autopsy?

A hospital autopsy, as previously stated, is an autopsy performed by the hospital's designated physician, most commonly the pathologist. If the death is a coroner's case and the coroner is not a medical examiner, the coroner contracts with a physician to perform the autopsy. A physician performs the autopsy, but the circumstances of the death are investigated by the coroner's office. If the physician hired by the coroner is the hospital's pathologist and the patient was a hospital patient, the autopsy is included in hospital autopsy rates. In subsequent data and computations, the abbreviation HP will refer to an autopsy performed by the hospital pathologist, and the abbreviation cor will refer to a coroner's case.

2. Site for Performing an Autopsy

Most hospitals have a morgue to which the dead bodies are taken at the time of death, and it is here that most hospital autopsies are *performed* by the hospital pathologist. If on-site facilities are not provided, a designated place is generally specified for carrying out the autopsy.

3. Deaths Autopsied

a. Inpatients

Any inpatient who expires during hospitalization is a potential autopsy case. Autopsies not only identify and establish the cause of death but also provide information that may prove helpful to future care.

b. Outpatients

Some autopsies are performed on outpatients, but only one autopsy rate (hospital autopsy rate) includes autopsies on outpatients.

c. Former Patients

Some autopsies are performed on patients previously treated at the hospital, either as inpatients or outpatients. These patients may include hospice or home care patients. Autopsies on former patients are only included in a *hospital autopsy rate*.

d. Fetal Deaths

As mentioned throughout the entire text, fetal statistics are *never* included or combined with other groups in any statistical formula, and they are excluded from the hospital autopsy rate. Fetal autopsies, however, are reported separately and included in a fetal autopsy rate.

e. Coroner's Cases

As reported, deaths reportable to the coroner may or may not be included, depending on who performs the autopsy. If the hospital pathologist performs the autopsy at the request of the coroner, the autopsy is included with the other autopsies; otherwise, the autopsy is excluded.

4. Report Requirements

Whenever a hospital autopsy is performed, a report must be filed in the patient's medical record and the hospital laboratory. Tissue specimens from the patient must also be placed on file in the hospital, usually in the hospital laboratory.

5. Consent

A physician obtains permission from the patient's next of kin to perform an autopsy. The autopsy is performed prior to the release of the body to the funeral home. Consent is not required for a coroner's case.

6. Combining A&C and NB

As with death rates, autopsy rates combine newborns and adults/children in the appropriate autopsy rate.

 SELF-TEST 9-4

For each of the following examples, indicate if the example is applicable to a *hospital autopsy*. Circle yes or no for each example.

1. The patient dies in the hospital. The body is autopsied by the hospital pathologist in the hospital morgue.   Yes   No

2. The patient dies in the hospital. The body is taken to the local morgue and the hospital pathologist performs the autopsy.   Yes   No

3. The patient dies in the hospital. The body is released to the medical examiner who performs the autopsy.   Yes   No

4. The patient dies at home three weeks following inpatient discharge from the hospital. The body is brought to the hospital, and the hospital pathologist performs an autopsy.   Yes   No

5. Three months after inpatient hospitalization, the patient is brought to the emergency room of the hospital, where the patient is pronounced DOA. The hospital pathologist performs the autopsy.   Yes   No

6. The patient is admitted to the hospital after having received a stab wound to the abdomen. The patient expires during hospitalization; and the body is released to the medical examiner, who performs the autopsy.   Yes   No

7. The patient is admitted to the hospital and dies 4 hours after admission. No sign of violence or suicide is present, but the patient had not been under a physician's care. The coroner removes the body and designates someone other than the hospital pathologist to perform the autopsy. Yes No

8. The patient is brought to the emergency room following a car accident and dies prior to inpatient admission. The coroner authorizes the hospital pathologist to perform the autopsy. Yes No

9. A cancer patient had been receiving cobalt therapy on an outpatient basis. Between scheduled outpatient visits, the patient died at home. The body was brought to the hospital for autopsy, which was performed by the hospital pathologist. Yes No

10. The hospital pathologist is taking a two-week vacation, and a staff physician is taking on autopsy duty during the interim. During this time, a home care patient expires, and the designated physician does the autopsy. Yes No

11. A late fetal death is autopsied by the hospital pathologist. Yes No

---

NOTE: Carefully consider the data prior to computing autopsy rates. Total autopsies are placed in the numerator, and deaths (those to whom it could happen) are included in the denominator. Both numerator and the denominator will generally be small numbers, but the percentage is generally larger than death rates. Adults/children and newborns are generally combined in autopsy rates.

F. AUTOPSY RATES

1. Gross Autopsy Rate

Remember, gross means all—no subtractions or deletions.

Formula for Gross Autopsy Rate:

$$\frac{\text{Total autopsies performed on IP deaths for a period}}{\text{Total IP (A \& C and NB) deaths}} \times 100$$

EXAMPLE: During the first three months of the year, 18 inpatient deaths were recorded. Two of these were coroner's cases and fell under the coroner's jurisdiction. Of the remaining 16, an autopsy was performed on four patients. Four outpatient deaths were also reported, and two of these were autopsied. Since only inpatients are included in a gross autopsy rate, all outpatient data can be disregarded. Of the inpatients, four of the 18 deaths were autopsied. Therefore, the gross autopsy rate is 22.2% ($4 \div 18 = 0.2222 \times 100 = 22.2\%$). The two deaths released to the coroner are included in the deaths, even though their bodies were not available for autopsy.

SELF-TEST 9-5

Compute all rates correct to two decimal places. Coroner's cases refer to cases removed by the coroner for examination, and the autopsy was not performed by a member of the hospital's medical staff.

1. In November, one newborn death, eight adults/children deaths, and three intermediate/late fetal deaths were recorded. Three OP deaths were also recorded. A total of six autopsies were carried out by the hospital pathologist: one newborn, three adult/children, one late fetal death, and one outpatient death. Total discharges for the month included 331 A&C and 67 newborns. Total admissions were 335 A&C and 65 newborns.

   Calculate:
   a. Gross autopsy rate for November.
   b. Gross death rate for November.

2. Pleasant Valley Hospital (first-quarter inpatient data):

	A&C	NB	Fetal
Admissions	715	174	
Discharges	721	172	
Deaths (total)	16	2	3 early; 2 intermediate; 1 late
Autopsies	6	1	

   Calculate: Gross autopsy rate.

3. Silver City Hospital (last-quarter data):

Inpatient	A&C	NB	OP	Fetal
Admissions	1,035	221		
Discharges	1,044	228		
Deaths	35	2	6	4 early; 2 intermediate; 1 late
Autopsies (hospital)	18	1	5	1 intermediate
Coroner's cases	5	1	1	

   Calculate:
   a. Gross autopsy rate.
   b. Gross death rate.
   c. Fetal death rate.

2. Net Autopsy Rate

(Only inpatients are included in this rate and the coroner's cases are the cases released to legal authorities.)

Formula for Net Autopsy Rate:

$$\frac{\text{Total autopsies (performed on IP deaths) for a period}}{\text{Total IP deaths} - \text{unautopsied released to the coroner for a period}} \times 100$$

Again, the use of the term *net* refers to the exclusion (subtraction) of certain patients. In this formula, the cases released to legal authorities (coroner/medical examiner) are excluded, as they are not available for hospital autopsy and the cases are subtracted from the total inpatient deaths. However, should the coroner authorize the hospital pathologist to carry out the autopsy, it is included and therefore not subtracted. Only cases *unavailable* for autopsy by the hospital's designated physician are excluded. Also, no outpatients or former patients are included in a net autopsy rate.

EXAMPLE: Ten inpatient deaths are reported for March. Five of these deaths are autopsied by the hospital pathologist. Two are coroner's cases, and the coroner requests that the hospital pathologist autopsy one of them. Therefore, a total of six inpatients are autopsied by the hospital pathologist out of a total of 10 inpatient deaths, of which only nine were available for autopsy $(10 - 1 = 9)$ for a net autopsy rate of $(6/9 = 0.6666 \times 100 = 66.7\%)$.

A net rate (whether net death rate or net autopsy rate) will be higher than a gross rate. The exclusion or subtraction occurs in the denominator and may or may not affect the numerator. If the gross autopsy rate had been determined in the example, the rate would be $(6/10 = 0.60 \times 100 = 60\%)$.

 SELF-TEST 9-6

Compute rates correct to two decimal places.

1. General Hospital (second-quarter data):

	Month	Deaths	Hospital Autopsy	Coroner's Case
IP:	April	7	4	1
	May	6	3	0
	June	9	4	2
OP:	April	3	2	1
	May	4	2	1
	June	5	2	2

Calculate:
a. Net autopsy rate for the period.
b. Gross autopsy rate for the period.

2. Happiness Hospital (July through December data):

	Bed Count: 300 Bassinet Count: 35		
	A&C	NB	Fetal
IP: Admissions	1,800	957	
Discharges	1,822	963	
Deaths: 48 hours	9	2	6 early; 3 intermediate; 2 late
48 hours	23	2	
Autopsies:	10	2	2 intermediate; 1 late
Coroner's cases	4	1	1 intermediate; 1 late
OP: Deaths	8		
Autopsies	5		
Coroner's cases	2		

Calculate:

a. Net autopsy rate for the period.
b. Gross autopsy rate for the period.
c. Gross death rate for the period.
d. Newborn death rate for the period.
e. *(R9)* Fetal death rate for the period.

3. Hospital Autopsy Rate (Adjusted)

This is the only autopsy rate that includes inpatients, outpatients, and former patients autopsied by the hospital pathologist or by a designated member of the medical staff.

Formula for Hospital Autopsy Rate:

$$\frac{\text{Total number of } \textit{hospital} \text{ autopsies for a period}}{\begin{array}{c}\text{Total number of deaths of hospital patients whose bodies are}\\ \text{available for hospital autopsy for the period}\end{array}} \times 100$$

EXAMPLES:

EX 1. A hospital had 215 inpatient admissions in August and 205 discharges, of which 12 were deaths. Eight of these deaths were autopsied by the hospital pathologist. Two former patients died at home and were brought to the hospital and autopsied. To calculate the hospital autopsy rate, add all the autopsies performed in the hospital (IP, OP, and former patients) and divide by the total deaths of patients available for autopsy. The hospital autopsy rate is 71.4% (8 IP + 2 former patients = 10 autopsies) ÷ (12 IP deaths + 2 former patients available for autopsy = 14 deaths) or (10 ÷ 14 = 0.7143 × 100 = 71.4%).

EX 2. In June, eight adults, one child, and one newborn died. A total of 240 admissions and 245 discharges were recorded in June. There were also two fetal deaths (one intermediate; one late). Autopsies were performed on four adults, the child, and the newborn, as well as the late fetal death. During June, one patient died in the ER and was autopsied, and two home care patients died and were taken to the hospital, where an autopsy was carried out. The hospital autopsy rate includes all autopsies performed except the late fetal death (6 IP + 1 ER + 2 home care = 9 autopsies). Totaling the deaths available for autopsy, 10 IP + 1 ER + 2 home care = 13 deaths. Dividing 9 autopsies by 13 deaths and multiplying by 100 equals a rate of 69.23%.

EX 3. A total of 303 patients were admitted to the hospital in May, and 305 patients were discharged. Included in the discharges were five deaths. Three of the five deaths were autopsied by the hospital pathologist, one death was not autopsied, and one death was a coroner's case and was unavailable for autopsy. In addition, five outpatient deaths were reported, of which three were also autopsied by the hospital pathologist and two were coroner's cases and unavailable for autopsy. The hospital autopsy rate includes six autopsies (3 IP + 3 OP) out of seven deaths available for autopsy (4 IP + 3 OP), for a hospital autopsy rate of 85.71% (6/7 = 0.8571 × 100 = 85.71%).

NOTES

> **NOTE:** Never include fetal autopsies in a hospital autopsy rate, and subtract any bodies not available for autopsy due to the removal of the body by the coroner/medical examiner (what will be referred to as unautopsied coroner's cases). However, coroner's cases autopsied by the hospital pathologist are included.

 SELF-TEST 9-7

All computations should be correct to two decimal places.

1. A hospital with 250 beds recorded six inpatient deaths for September. During September, there were 315 discharges of adults/children. The bassinet count was 18, and 95 newborns were discharged as well, with no newborn deaths recorded. The outpatient department recorded three outpatient deaths, two of which were reported from the emergency room. Autopsies were performed on three inpatients and three outpatients, and one inpatient death was a coroner's case and unavailable for autopsy.

   Calculate:
   a. September hospital autopsy rate.
   b. Gross autopsy rate for September.
   c. Net autopsy rate for September.
   d. Gross death rate for September.

2. June statistics reveal the following:

	A&C	NB	OP
Admissions	475	75	
Discharges	472	72	
Deaths	9	1	2
Autopsies	5	1	2
Coroner's cases	1	0	0

   Calculate:
   a. June hospital autopsy rate.
   b. Gross autopsy rate for June.
   c. Net autopsy rate for June.
   d. Gross death rate for June.

3. Hillside Hospital (January through June data):
   Bed count: 175 Bassinet count: 15

	A&C					NB				
	Total	<48	>48	HP	Cor	Total	<48	>48	HP	Cor
IP: Admissions	9,598					801				
Discharges	9,641					810				
Deaths	77	21	56			16	5	11		
Autopsies				31	7				3	2
IPSD	28,872					2,610				

	A&C					NB				
	Total	<48	>48	HP	Cor	Total	<48	>48	HP	Cor
Fetal deaths:										
Early	18			0	2					
Intermediate	10			2	2					
Late	8			1	1					
OP: Deaths	9									
Autopsies				8	1					

Calculate:

a. Gross autopsy rate.
b. Net autopsy rate.
c. Hospital autopsy rate.
d. Gross death rate.
e. Net death rate.
f. Newborn death rate.
g. *(R9)* Fetal death rate.
h. *(R4)* Average A&C daily inpatient census.
i. *(R4)* Average NB daily inpatient census.
j. *(R5)* A&C occupancy percentage for the period.
k. *(R5)* Newborn occupancy percentage for the period.

4. Seven out of a total of 441 discharges in June were listed as deaths. Of these, three were autopsied by the hospital pathologist, and two additional deaths were coroner's cases. The coroner requested the hospital pathologist perform one of these autopsies, which he did. In addition, three outpatients died; two were autopsied by the hospital pathologist, and the third body was removed by the coroner.

Calculate:

a. June hospital autopsy rate.
b. Gross autopsy rate for June.
c. Net autopsy rate for June.

4. Newborn Autopsy Rate

Formula for Newborn Autopsy Rate:

$$\frac{\text{Autopsies performed on NB deaths for a period}}{\text{Total NB deaths for the period}} \times 100$$

EXAMPLE: Seventy-four births occurred during July, and a total of 72 newborns were discharged. One newborn expired shortly after birth. Five fetal deaths were also reported during July—three were intermediate fetal deaths, and two were late fetal deaths. An autopsy was performed on the newborn death and three of the fetal deaths (one intermediate and two late). Again, the fetal deaths can be ignored in the newborn autopsy formula, resulting in a newborn autopsy rate of 100% (dividing 1 newborn autopsy by the 1 newborn death and multiplying by 100 equals a rate of 100%).

NOTES

 SELF-TEST 9-8

Compute all rates correct to two decimal places.

1. Newborn data for October:

Admissions:	223	Fetal deaths:	5 (2 early; 2 intermediate; 1 late)
Discharges:	225	Fetal autopsies:	1 (late fetal)
Deaths:	2		
Autopsies:	1		

   Calculate:
   a. Newborn autopsy rate for October.
   b. *(R8)* Newborn death rate for October.

2. A neonatal unit records two newborn deaths and two term infants who were stillborn. An autopsy was performed on the two newborns and one of the stillborn. A total of 315 newborns were born, and 312 were discharged during the same month.

   Calculate: Newborn autopsy rate for the month.

3. Out of 211 discharges in a neonatal unit, one death was reported, and the death was autopsied by the hospital pathologist. A mother delivered in a taxicab on the way to the hospital, and she and the infant were admitted upon arrival at the hospital. However, the baby died shortly after admission. An autopsy was performed on this infant as well.

   Calculate: Newborn autopsy rate for the period.

---

5. **Fetal Autopsy Rate**

   Formula for Fetal Autopsy Rate:

   $$\frac{\text{Autopsies performed on (intermediate and late) fetal deaths for a period}}{\text{Total (intermediate and late) fetal deaths for the period}} \times 100$$

   > **EXAMPLE:** Ten fetal deaths were logged by the obstetric unit, of which four were early fetal deaths, four were intermediate fetal deaths, and two were late fetal deaths. Of these, the two late fetal deaths were autopsied. Since only intermediate and late fetal deaths are included, six fetal deaths were recorded for the period. Of these, only the two late fetal deaths were autopsied for a fetal autopsy rate of 33.33% (2 ÷ 6 = 0.3333 × 100 = 33.33%).

 SELF-TEST 9-9

Compute all rates correct to two decimal places.

1. Five fetal deaths were recorded in January. Also recorded were 233 live births and 240 newborn discharges. One newborn death was also recorded. Of the five fetal deaths, three were early fetal deaths and two were intermediate fetal deaths. Autopsies were done on the newborn death and one intermediate fetal death.

Calculate:

a. Fetal autopsy rate for January.
b. Newborn autopsy rate for January.
c. *(R9)* Fetal death rate for January.
d. Newborn death rate for January.

2. In December, 10 fetal deaths were reported. One of the fetal deaths was a stillborn term infant. Of the remaining, one was a late fetal death and two were intermediate fetal deaths; the others were early fetal deaths. One of the intermediate fetal deaths was of a suspicious nature and was removed by the coroner. Of the remaining fetal deaths, an autopsy was performed on the stillborn and on the late fetal death by the hospital pathologist. A total of 351 live births, 348 live newborn discharges, and one newborn death (not autopsied) were recorded in December.

Calculate:

a. Fetal autopsy rate for December.
b. Newborn autopsy rate for December.
c. *(R9)* Fetal death rate for December.
d. Newborn death rate for December.

3. Serendipity Hospital (January through March data):
    Bed count: 175 Bassinet count: 15

	A&C			NB			Fetal		
	Total	**HP**	**Cor**	**Total**	**HP**	**Cor**	**Early**	**Intermediate**	**Late**
IP:									
Admissions	5,001			413					
Discharges	4,997			409					
Deaths	29			7					
Autopsies		12	1		3	1			
Fetal							3	2	1
Deaths									
Autopsies							0	0	1HP
OP: Deaths	3								
Autopsies		2	1						

Calculate:

a. Gross autopsy rate.
b. Net autopsy rate.
c. Hospital autopsy rate.
d. Newborn autopsy rate.
e. Fetal autopsy rate.
f. Gross death rate.
g. Newborn death rate.
h. *(R9)* Fetal death rate.

G. SUMMARY

1. Inpatient deaths are deaths occurring during a patient's hospitalization as an inpatient, prior to discharge.
2. Outpatient deaths are deaths that occur:
   a. In the emergency room prior to inpatient hospitalization.
   b. In outpatients. This includes series patients who return routinely for treatment (chemotherapy, radiotherapy, rehabilitation, etc.) or outpatient surgery.
   c. In home care or hospice patients seen routinely in their homes.
3. Deaths *not* included in routine death rates include outpatient deaths, ER deaths, DOAs, and fetal deaths.
4. Adults/children and newborn deaths are combined (included) in the same death rate. Separate rates may also be determined but they are frequently combined.
5. The numerator in all death rates is the total number of deaths pertaining to that rate.
6. Helpful hints:
   a. Include only inpatient deaths—exclude OPs, DOAs, and fetal deaths.
   b. Death rates should be low.
   c. Death rates should be carried to two or three decimal places.
   d. Gross and net death rates include discharges in the denominator.
   e. Net death rates exclude deaths occurring less than 48 hours after admission.
   f. Postoperative death rates include only deaths less than 10 days postoperative. Postoperative death rates are based on the number of patients operated on.
   g. Anesthesia death rates should be extremely low and are generally computed on a yearly basis and are based on the number of anesthetics administered.
7. Rates:
   a. Gross death rate: Deaths divided by discharges.
   b. Net death rate: Total deaths minus any deaths less than 48 hours divided by total discharges minus deaths less than 48 hours.
   c. Newborn death rate: NB deaths divided by NB discharges.
   d. Postoperative death rate: Postop deaths within 10 days postop divided by the number of patients operated on.
   e. Anesthesia death rate: Anesthesia deaths divided by the number of anesthetics administered.
8. An autopsy is a postmortem examination of a body, the inspection and partial dissection of a dead body.
9. A hospital autopsy is performed by a physician designated by the hospital, most commonly the hospital pathologist, on the body of a person who has, at some time, been a hospital patient.
10. A coroner is a duly elected or appointed official whose primary function is to investigate any death in which the cause of death is uncertain or not due to other natural causes.
11. A medical examiner is a physician authorized by a governmental unit to ascertain the cause of death, especially those not due to natural causes.
12. Coroner's/medical examiner's cases include any deaths suspicious in nature or that may involve violence. Cases include drowning, poisonings, suicides, stabbings, gunshot wounds, burns, and abortions.

13. Adults/children and newborns are most commonly combined in autopsy rates.

14. A hospital autopsy rate is the only autopsy rate that includes autopsies performed on outpatients or former patients, if the autopsy was performed by the hospital's designated physician.

15. Fetal death autopsies are only included in a fetal autopsy rate.

16. Bodies removed by the coroner/medical examiner are not included in a net autopsy rate or a hospital autopsy rate. Only bodies autopsied by the hospital's designated physician are included in autopsy rates; this includes autopsies on coroner's cases, should the coroner request the hospital to perform the autopsy.

17. The numerator in all autopsy rates is the total number of autopsies performed, related to the specified rate (gross, hospital, etc.).

18. The denominator in all autopsy rates is comprised of deaths, although some deaths are excluded in certain autopsy rates.

19. Rates:

    a. Gross autopsy rate: IP autopsies divided by IP deaths.

    b. Net autopsy rate: IP autopsies divided by IP deaths, minus the unautopsied coroner's cases.

    c. Newborn autopsy rate: NB autopsies divided by NB deaths.

    d. Fetal autopsy rate: Intermediate and late fetal death autopsies divided by the number of intermediate and late fetal deaths.

    e. Hospital autopsy rate: IP, OP, and former patient autopsies divided by the total number of hospital patients (IP, OP, former patients) whose bodies are available for hospital autopsy.

NOTES

Name _____   Date _____

H. CHAPTER 9 TEST

Note: Compute all answers correct to two decimal places.

1. Which inpatient deaths are excluded in each of the following death rates:

    a. Gross death rate.
    b. Net death rate.
    c. Postoperative death rate.
    d. Anesthesia death rate.

2. Which death rates include something other than discharges in the denominator? Indicate the statistic used in place of discharges.

3. Which death rate is also called an institutional death rate?

4. Do most death rates separate newborn and adult/children deaths?

5. Emerald Valley Hospital (September):

		Deaths	
	Total	**Less than 48 Hours**	**Greater than 48 Hours**
Deaths: A&C	36	30	6
NB	5	1	4
Discharges: A&C	778		
NB	71		

Calculate:

    a. Gross death rate.
    b. Net death rate.

6. Elmwood Valley Hospital:

		Deaths		
Clinical Unit	**Discharges**	**Total**	**<48 Hours**	**>48 Hours**
Medical	310	10	4	6
Surgical	196	6	2	4
Pediatrics	38	1	0	1
Obstetrics	71	1	1	0
NB	80	2	1	1

Calculate:

    a. Gross death rate.
    b. Net death rate.

7. During July, the following surgical data were recorded:

Admissions: 1,015
Discharges: 997
Deaths: 7

Deaths:	**Total**	**<48 Hours**	**>48 Hours**	**<10 Days Postop**	**>10 Days Postop**
	7	1	6	2	5

Patients operated on: 975
Surgical procedures: 1,018

Calculate:

a. Postoperative death rate.
b. Net death rate.

8. Newborn Data:

		<48 Hours	>48 Hours	Early	Int	Late
Newborn births (live):	300					
Newborn discharges:	228					
Newborn deaths:	4	3		1		
Fetal deaths:	7			4	2	1

Calculate:

a. Newborn death rate.
b. Newborn net death rate.

9. Lee Memorial County Hospital (November data):

	Admissions	Discharges	Deaths	<48 Hours	>48 Hours
A&C	511	505	8	3	5
NB	83	80	1	0	1

Calculate:

a. Gross death rate.
b. Net death rate.
c. Newborn death rate.

10. Surgical Unit (yearly data):

		Deaths			
	Total	<10 Days Postop	>10 Days Postop	Anesthesia
Admissions:	354				
Discharges:	347				
Deaths:		5	3	1	1
Patients operated on:	334				
Operations performed:	372				
Anesthetics administered:	321				

Calculate:

a. Surgical unit gross death rate.
b. Postoperative death rate.
c. Anesthesia death rate.

11. Charity Hospital (February data):

	A&C	NB	Total	<48 Hours	>48 Hours
Bed/bassinet count:	225	20			
Admissions:	1,138	134			
Discharges:	1,143	132			
Deaths: A&C			7	5	2
NB			2	1	1
Fetal			3		
IPSD	5,722	503			

Calculate:

a. Gross death rate.
b. Net death rate.
c. Newborn death rate.

12. Milwaukee Memorial Hospital (May data):

Clinical Unit	Bed/Bass		Adm	Disch	Deaths	<48 Hours	>48 Hours	<10 Days	>10 Days	IPSDs
Medical	44		142	143	3	1	2			1,280
Surgical	20		81	78	3	1	2	2	1	518
Pediatric	8		66	61	0	0	0			118
Obstetrics	18		118	115	1	1	0			495
Neuropsych	10		44	42	1	1	0			261
Newborn		15	110	105	1	0	1			466
Totals:	100	15	561	544	9	4	5	2	1	3,208

Additional statistics:

Anesthesia deaths: 1

Anesthetics administered: 77

Patients operated on: 70

Calculate:

a. Gross death rate.
b. Net death rate.
c. Newborn death rate.
d. Net death rate for medical service.
e. Clinical service with the lowest gross death rate.
f. Clinical service with the highest gross death rate.
g. Postoperative death rate.
h. Anesthesia death rate.

13. Which autopsy rate may include outpatients as well as inpatients?

14. Who is authorized to perform a hospital autopsy?

15. What types of death fall under the jurisdiction of the coroner/medical examiner?

16. Which deaths, even though autopsied, are excluded in hospital autopsy rates?

17. Do gross, net, and hospital autopsy rates combine adult/children and newborn data?

18. Is a body autopsied by the medical examiner included in a hospital autopsy rate if the medical examiner is not on the hospital medical staff?

19. What is excluded in a net autopsy rate that is included in a gross autopsy rate?

20. Atlanta Women and Children's Hospital (April data):

	Deaths	Autopsies		
		HP	No Autopsy	Coroner
Inpatient:				
A&C	37	4	31	2
NB	2	2		
Outpatient:	2	2		

Calculate:

a. Gross autopsy rate.
b. Net autopsy rate.
c. Newborn autopsy rate.
d. Hospital autopsy rate.

21. All Souls Hospital (December data):

	A&C	NB	HP	No Autopsy	Coroner
Beds/Bassinets:	250	30			
Admissions:	1,210	205			
Discharges:	1,205	200			
Deaths:	9	2			
Autopsies: A&C			5	3	1
NB			1		1
IPSD	6,252	701			

Calculate:

a. Newborn gross autopsy rate.
b. Gross autopsy rate for A&C.
c. Gross autopsy rate.
d. Net autopsy rate.
e. *(R5)* Bed occupancy percentage for February.

22. Mystic Bay Hospital (November data): Bed count: 85; Bassinet count: 10

	A&C			NB		
	Total	HP	Cor	Total	HP	Cor
IP: Admissions	441			74		
Discharges:	450			78		
Deaths:	11			3		
Autopsies:		5	1		1	1

	OP/Former Patient				Fetal		
	Deaths	HP	Cor	Type	Deaths	HP	Cor
DOA:	3	1	2	Early	6	0	0
ER death:	2	1	1	Intermediate	3	1	1
Home care:	1	1	0	Late	2	1	1
Other:	1	0	1				

Calculate:

a. Gross autopsy rate.
b. Net autopsy rate.
c. Hospital autopsy rate.
d. Newborn autopsy rate.
e. Fetal autopsy rate.

23. Mountain Medical Center (first-quarter data):

	Admissions		Discharges		Deaths		Autopsies A&C			Autopsies NB		
	A&C	NB	A&C	NB	A&C	NB	HP	No	Cor	HP	No	Cor
Jan.	801	165	797	162	9	2	3	5	1	1	1	0
Feb.	788	151	775	146	7	1	2	4	1	1	0	0
Mar.	818	161	801	157	11	1	4	4	2	1	0	0

Calculate:

a. Gross autopsy rate for the first quarter.
b. Net autopsy rate for the first quarter.
c. Newborn autopsy rate for the first quarter.
d. January gross autopsy rate.
e. February net autopsy rate.
f. March newborn autopsy rate.

24. Adventist Hospital (May data):

Unit	Bed/Bass	Adm	Disch	Deaths	Autopsies HP	Autopsies No	Autopsies Cor	Fetal Ear	Fetal Int	Fetal Late
Medicine	45	150	148	5	2	1	2			
Surgery	20	120	124	3	1	1	1			
Pediatrics	10	62	60	1	1	0	0			
Obstetrics	12	73	71	1	0	0	0			
Newborn	10	61	58	1	1	0	0			
Fetal: Deaths								3	2	1

Autopsies HP: 1 (late) cor: 2 (intermediate)

Calculate:

a. Gross autopsy rate.
b. Net autopsy rate.
c. Newborn autopsy rate.
d. Fetal autopsy rate.

Community Health Statistics

CHAPTER OUTLINE

LEARNING OBJECTIVES

After studying this chapter, the learner should be able to:

 Identify the major vital statistics certificates collected by the National Center for Health Statistics.

 Compute obstetrical-related vital statistics for mortality rates of the following populations:
   a. Maternal
   b. Infant
   c. Neonatal
   d. Perinatal
   e. Post-neonatal
   f. Fetal

 Compute rates for prevalence and incidence of diseases.

 Compute population mortality rates:
   a. Crude death rate
   b. Age-specific death rate
   c. Cause-specific death rate
   d. Cause-race-specific death rate
   e. Proportional mortality rate
   f. Case fatality rate

 Compute measures of fertility:
   a. Crude birth rate
   b. General fertility rate

The term *vital statistics*, as previously mentioned, refers to data that record significant events and dates in human life. Births, adoptions, marriages, divorces, and deaths (including fetal deaths) are the primary sources of vital statistics data. The majority of births occur in some type of health care facility. The facility may vary from a conventional obstetrical unit to the establishment of "birthing centers" in a health care facility that has more of a homelike setting. Since over 90% of births occur in health care facilities, the health care provider is the primary source of the data recorded on a birth certificate. Births resulting in a fetal death, whether induced or due to natural causes, may also require a certificate, just as deaths require a death certificate. The United States does *not* have a uniform birth and death certificate, as registration and certification fall under the jurisdiction of each state. All states have laws regarding vital statistics certificates and the information to be entered into this database. Certificates are reported to the registrar in the state in which the birth or death occurs, where they are permanently maintained. Although the birth certificate may vary in appearance from state to state, there are key elements that are present on all certificates, and each state may add elements they deem as vital. Nationwide birth and death registration has been present since 1933.

The National Center for Health Statistics (NCHS) is the governmental agency responsible for vital statistics data. NCHS is a part of the Center for Disease Control and Prevention (CDC) based in Atlanta, Georgia. The NCHS recommends and updates standards for birth certificates, although the states are under no obligation to issue a certificate consistent with the recommended standards. The NCHS collects a sample of data (births and deaths) from each state and publishes a monthly publication titled *Vital Statistics Report*. These data are then compiled into an annual publication titled *Vital Statistics of the United States,* containing many detailed tables and demographic characteristics. Another companion report with the same title, *Vital Statistics of the United States,* has data on marriage and divorce. Although each state can determine the format and contents of a birth certificate, the NCHS recommends standards, most of which are adopted.

A. CERTIFICATES

1. Live Birth Certificates

Live birth certificates serve as proof of citizenship, age, birthplace, and parentage. Physicians and health care personnel provide the information recorded on the birth certificate. Accuracy and completeness are paramount for certificate completion. Most certificates are now available online, and information is transferred electronically to the state registrar. A live birth is a fetus, irrespective of gestational age, that, after complete expulsion or extraction, is found to have some sign of life. Such signs include a heartbeat, respirations, pulsation of the umbilical cord, or movement of voluntary muscles.

Data on a birth certificate often include birth weight, mother's age and ethnic background, pregnancy history, congenital anomalies of the child, clinical estimate of gestation, date last normal menses began, month pregnancy prenatal care began, number of prenatal visits, medical risk factors for pregnancy, other risk factors for pregnancy (smoking, alcohol use), complications of labor and/or delivery, obstetric procedures, method of delivery, and abnormal conditions of the newborn.

Although the official birth certificate is filed with the state registrar, a copy is placed in the mother's medical record. An individual needing a copy of a birth certificate should contact the state in which the birth occurred; the state applies the official state seal to the copy of the birth certificate to signify authentication.

2. Death Certificates

Death certificates are required for burial and cremation and to settle estates and insurance claims. All deaths that occur in the hospital require the attending physician to provide whatever information is requested, although the certificate is generally filed by the funeral director. Although the cause of death is frequently stated on a death certificate, the true cause of death can only be ascertained through an autopsy. Autopsies have declined in frequency in some areas of the country due to the added expense of the procedure. Some families, however, request an autopsy, in which case the expense is generally borne by them.

Some elements present on the death certificate include information regarding the decedent (name, sex, race, age, date of birth, birthplace, marital status, surviving spouse, social security number, usual occupation, residence, education, father's name and birthplace, mother's maiden name and birthplace); information regarding the place of death (county, city, town or location, name of facility—if the death occurred in a health care facility, it is indicated if the deceased was DOA, died as an OP, IP, or in the ER). If the death did not occur in a health care facility, the street address or location of death is requested; medical certification (immediate cause of death, including the interval between onset and death, other significant conditions, whether an autopsy was performed, and whether autopsy findings were available prior to completion of cause of death). For deaths from external causes, information includes date and time of injury, how the injury occurred (whether the injury occurred at work), place of injury, and location of injury. Disposition information includes method of disposition, name and location of cemetery or crematory, name of funeral director, and name and address of funeral home.

3. Fetal Death Certificates (Termination of Pregnancy)

Death certificates are issued in certain circumstances for fetal deaths. The definition of a fetal death has already been described—with no signs of life present at the time of expulsion or extraction from the mother's womb. State laws vary on requirements for reporting fetal deaths. Most states use the gestation period as the basis for determining whether a fetal death certificate is to be filed. The gestation period specified is generally 17 to 21 weeks or more. Some states require a certificate if delivery included multiple births in which a liveborn is present, and some require a certificate if the fetus is to be interred. Elements on the fetal death certificate include cause of fetal death (whether fetal or maternal), other significant conditions of the fetus or mother, and when the fetus died (before labor, during labor or delivery, or unknown).

4. Induced Termination of Pregnancy Certificates

The elements related to the completion of this certificate include pregnancy information as well as the place where the induced procedure occurred—place of induced termination (name and address of the facility), and date of termination. Pregnancy information includes previous pregnancies (previous live births, now living, and now dead) and other terminations (spontaneous and induced); date last normal menses began; physician's estimate of gestation; and type of termination procedure. Patient identification information includes such items as the patient's age, marital status, residence, race, and education.

B. OBSTETRICAL-RELATED MORTALITY RATES

Hospital-related mortality rates have already been discussed in previous chapters, including obstetrical-related mortality rates. The formulas in this chapter apply to a larger population and are the basis for local, state, and national data. The data compiled become the basis for the *Vital Statistics of the United States*. Since the population of the United States is now over 300 million, the numbers applicable in these formulas will be much larger than the data used in previous chapters to compute hospital statistics. The majority of formulas include a multiplier larger than 100; and most often a multiplier of 1,000, 10,000, or even 100,000 is used. A multiplier is used to indicate how often something occurred per 1,000 population or per 100,000. A multiplier decreases the use of minute decimal fractions and, it is said, increases data comprehension. The multiplier chosen should result in a rate expressed—for example, as "10 deaths per 10,000 population." The smaller the rate, usually the larger the multiplier.

NOTE: In certain rates to follow, rather than indicating a specific multiplier (such as 1,000 or 100,000), the letter M will be used for multiplier so that the most appropriate multiplier can be selected to facilitate comprehension of the data.

EXAMPLE: A rate with a numerator of 190,000 and a denominator of 23,000,000 results in a value of 0.00826. Using a multiplier of 1,000, the same data can be expressed as 8.3 per 1,000 population. If the multiplier had been 10,000, the resultant value becomes 82.6 per 10,000 population.

1. Maternal Mortality Rate

The maternal mortality rate is defined as the total number of deaths assigned to puerperal causes in a calendar year divided by the number of live births in that same year, with the quotient multiplied by 100,000.

Formula for Maternal Mortality Rate:

$$\frac{\text{Deaths due to pregnancy-related conditions during a given period}}{\text{Number of live births for the same given period}} \times 100,000$$

The fact that fetal deaths are not represented in this formula has a N tendency to inflate the rate, since only live births are included in the denominator. Another factor is related to multiple births, which inflate the denominator but have no effect on the numerator. These are considerations to keep in mind when this rate is used.

EXAMPLE: If the yearly deaths due to puerperal causes was 250 and the total number of live births recorded was 3,600,000 in the same year, then the maternal death rate for the year is recorded as 6.9 maternal deaths per 100,000 live births (250 ÷ 3,600,000 = 0.0000684 × 100,000 = 6.94). If 1,000 deaths were reported for 3,600,000 live births, the maternal death rate could be stated as one maternal death for every 3,600 live births, but the standard reporting method is to state the death rate to the base 10 (100, 1,000, 10,000, etc.). Therefore, the correct answer is 27.77 maternal deaths per 100,000 live births (1,000 ÷ 3,600,000 = 0.0002777 multiplied by 100,000 = 27.77).

2. Infant Mortality Rate

The infant mortality rate is defined as the number of deaths of persons age zero to one (birth to one year of age) in a calendar year, divided by the number of live births in that year, with the quotient multiplied by 1,000.

Formula for Infant Mortality Rate:

$$\frac{\text{Total deaths (under one year of age) during a given period}}{\text{Total number of live births during the same period}} \times 1{,}000$$

The major consideration when using this rate is regarding a population with a fluctuating or rapidly changing birth rate, insofar as an infant who died this year could have been born in the previous year and one born this year can die next year. However, with a large, stable population (like that of the United States) these differences tend to cancel each other out.

EXAMPLE: A state reported 4,593 infant deaths and 401,581 live births in the past year. The infant mortality rate would be 11.4 infant deaths per 1,000 live births in the state during the past year ($4{,}593 \div 401{,}581 = 0.0114372 \times 1{,}000 = 11.4$).

3. Neonatal Mortality Rate/Proportion

The neonatal mortality rate is defined as the number of deaths of neonates (infants under 28 days of age) that occurred in a calendar year divided by the number of live births that same year, with the quotient multiplied by 1,000.

Formula for Neonatal Mortality Rate:

$$\frac{\text{Total number of deaths of neonates (} < 28 \text{ days of age) for a given period}}{\text{Total number of live births for the same given period of time}} \times 1{,}000$$

EXAMPLE: A total of 347,000 live births were reported in a state during the past year. Also reported were a total of 3,600 infant deaths, 2,143 neonatal deaths, and 4,231 fetal deaths. Only the neonatal deaths are included in the neonatal mortality rate resulting in a neonatal mortality rate of 6.2 deaths per 1,000 live births for the past year ($2{,}143 \div 347{,}000 = 0.00618 \times 1{,}000 = 6.2$).

NOTE: Most of infant deaths occur within a short interval following birth.

4. Perinatal Mortality Rate/Proportion

The perinatal mortality rate is defined as the number of fetal deaths (intermediate and late) plus neonatal deaths (under 28 days of age) divided by the number of live births plus fetal deaths, with the quotient multiplied by 1,000.

Formula for Perinatal Mortality Rate:

$$\frac{\text{Total fetal (intermediate and late) and neonatal deaths during a period}}{\text{Total live births} + \text{intermediate \& late fetal deaths during the same period}} \times 1{,}000$$

All neonatal deaths (deaths occurring within the first 28 days of birth) are included, but fetal deaths include only those previously referred to as *intermediate* or *late fetal deaths*—deaths in a fetus of at least 20 weeks gestation.

EXAMPLE: During the past year, a total of 347,000 live births were recorded. Deaths within the same period included 2,911 intermediate and late fetal deaths, 2,743 neonatal deaths, and 3,667 infant deaths. Adding the fetal deaths (2,911) and the neonatal deaths (2,743) results in a total of 5,654 deaths in the numerator of the perinatal mortality rate formula. The denominator adds the total number of live births (347,000) to the intermediate and late fetal deaths (2,911) for a total of 349,911. Dividing the numerator (5,654) by the denominator (349,911) results in a perinatal mortality rate of 16.2 perinatal deaths per 1,000 fetal deaths plus live births ($0.0162 \times 1,000 = 16.2$) for the year.

5. Post-Neonatal Mortality Rate

The post-neonatal mortality rate is defined as the number of live births minus neonatal deaths, with the quotient being multiplied by 1,000.

Primary Formula for Post-Neonatal Mortality Rate:

$$\frac{\text{Total post-neonatal deaths (28 days to 1 year) for a given period}}{\text{Total live births} - \text{neonatal deaths for the same period}} \times 1,000$$

EXAMPLE: A state with a population of 20 million reported the following data for the past year: 342,000 live births, 2,600 post-neonatal deaths, and 2,500 neonatal deaths. Calculating the post-neonatal mortality rate, it is determined there were 7.7 post-neonatal deaths per 1,000 live births minus neonatal deaths for the past year (2,600 divided by ($342,000 - 2,500 = 339,500$) or $2,600 \div 339,500 = 0.00766 \times 1,000 = 7.7$).

NOTE: The post-neonatal mortality rate is occasionally determined without subtracting the neonatal deaths in the denominator. Both versions of this rate are used. However, for computations within this book, the primary formula is to be used.

Secondary Formula for Post-Neonatal Mortality Rate:

$$\frac{\text{Total post-neonatal deaths (28 days to 1 year) for a given period}}{\text{Total number of live births during the same period}} \times 1,000$$

6. Fetal Death Rate

The fetal death rate is defined as the number of intermediate and late fetal deaths divided by the number of live births during a specified period. Again, fetal deaths refer to fetuses completing 20 weeks gestation (intermediate and late fetal deaths). No reporting is generally required for early miscarriages (spontaneous abortions or early fetal deaths less than 20 weeks gestation).

NOTE: This formula does *not* add in the intermediate and late fetal deaths in the denominator as was done in the hospital fetal death rate.

Formula for Fetal Death Rate:

$$\frac{\text{Total fetal deaths (intermediate and late) during a given period}}{\text{Total live births during the same time period}} \times 1,000$$

EXAMPLE: A total of 348,000 live births were recorded in the past year in a state with a total population of 20 million. The total deaths included 2,915 intermediate and late fetal deaths, 2,100 neonatal deaths, 1,900 post-neonatal deaths, and 4,000 infant deaths (neonatal and post-neonatal). The fetal death rate for the state in the past year was 8.4 fetal deaths per 1,000 live births ($2,915 \div 348,000 = 0.00838 \times 1,000 = 8.4$).

Since the number of fetal deaths is grossly underreported nationally, the fetal death rate is grossly underestimated.

7. Induced Termination of Pregnancy Rate/Ratio

The following rates are for reference purposes only. National statistics on induced terminations of pregnancy are grossly underreported, resulting in greatly underestimated rates. The rates are included for reference purposes only. All three rates use a multiplier of 1,000.

a. *Induced Termination of Pregnancy Rate/Ratio: Ratio I*

$$\frac{\text{Induced pregnancy terminations}}{\text{Live births}} \times 1,000$$

b. *Induced Termination of Pregnancy Rate/Ratio: Ratio II*

$$\frac{\text{Induced pregnancy terminations}}{\text{Induced pregnancy terminations} + \text{live births} + \text{fetal deaths}} \times 1,000$$

c. *Induced Termination of Pregnancy Rate:*

$$\frac{\text{Induced pregnancy terminations}}{\text{Female population 15--44 years of age}} \times 1,000$$

 SELF-TEST 10-1

1. Identify the obstetrical-related mortality rate:
   a. Most likely to use a multiplier other than 1,000.
   b. Multiplier most commonly used in that rate.

2. What statistic comprises the denominator in all obstetrical-related mortality rates?

3. In which obstetrical-related mortality rate are intermediate and late fetal deaths included in the rate other than the fetal death rate?

4. In the past year, a total of 300 deaths due to pregnancy conditions were reported along with 3,500,000 live births. Calculate the maternal mortality rate for the year.

5. In the past year, a state reported a population of 20 million residents in the past year. A total of 5,000 infant deaths and 500 fetal deaths were recorded in the past year, along with 400,000 live births and 150 maternal deaths. Calculate the infant mortality rate for the year.

6. A state reported a population of 20 million residents in the past year, and the death totals included 5,000 infants under the age of 1 and 2,500 newborn deaths less than 28 days of age. The live births for the year totaled 350,000.

NOTES

Calculate:

a. Neonatal mortality rate for the year.

b. Percentage of infant deaths that were neonatal deaths.

7. The state population in the past year was 20 million residents, and a total of 350,000 live births were also recorded in the past year. The death total included 3,000 fetal deaths (intermediate and late), 2,500 neonatal deaths, 2,500 post-neonatal deaths, and 5,000 infant deaths. Calculate the perinatal mortality rate for the year.

8. The past year's state population total was 20 million with a recorded total of 324,600 live births. Death totals for the year included 3,244 fetal deaths (intermediate and late), 2,200 neonatal deaths, 2,700 post-neonatal deaths, and 4,900 infant deaths. Calculate the post-neonatal mortality rate for the year.

9. State yearly data include a population of 20 million with 350,000 live births in the past year. The yearly death statistics included 3,000 fetal deaths (intermediate and late), 1,800 neonatal deaths, 1,600 post-neonatal deaths, and 3,400 infant deaths. Calculate the fetal death rate.

C. MORBIDITY DATA AND RATES

Morbidity data, although equally as important as mortality data, are less precisely recorded and more difficult to analyze. Morbidity refers to disease (including injuries and a deviation from normal health). There are countless illnesses throughout the world; and some measures have been devised to assess the frequency of occurrences, the prevalence of the disease, and the seriousness of disease. Diseases are often referred to under broad categories such as communicable (infectious) diseases, cancers, blood disorders, or mental disorders, to name a few. Nationally and worldwide, efforts are being made to track disorders and gather data in hopes of finding ways to prevent diseases and to find cures. With vaccinations, many diseases that previously ravaged populations have been brought under control, and measures to diminish the spread of disease are as important as treatment of the disease. Morbidity data are far more difficult to gather and interpret than mortality data. Until there are standardized reporting requirements, morbidity data will undoubtedly be underreported.

1. Collecting Morbidity Data

In the United States, the Centers for Disease Control and Prevention (CDC), a component of the Department of Health and Human Services (DHHS), is the clearinghouse for morbidity data on both communicable and noncommunicable diseases. The CDC may also be called upon to aid in diagnosing disease, especially communicable disease. Each time a food-borne illness erupts in the United States, the CDC leads the effort to find the offending food source. Legionnaires' disease, Lyme disease, and the West Nile virus are other examples in which the CDC played the major role in determining the cause of the disease. The CDC works with state and local agencies and provides consultation, education, and training related to communicable diseases. The CDC has worked tirelessly to minimize the spread of AIDS. Although much data has been collected on a myriad of diseases, it is believed the data are underreported in many cases. A serious disease, such as rabies, is more likely to be reported than a less serious disease. In 2006, the nation was alerted by the CDC to an increase in mumps in young adults. Young adults who had not received their second dose of the mumps vaccine (part of the MMPR vaccination that protects against measles, mumps, pertussis, and rubella) were encouraged to see their health care provider to receive the proper protection.

Data, like that gathered in the United States, are available for most of the developed world, and attempts are made to gather data in third-world countries by various relief organizations and through the United Nations. Local health departments collect and tally reported cases of a communicable disease and forward the results to the appropriate state health department. The state information is relayed to the CDC in Atlanta, Georgia. The CDC publishes the *Morbidity and Mortality Weekly Report (MMWR)*.

Due to chronic underreporting of health data, other data systems were devised to aid in determining the general health status of the population. Surveys of all kinds have been designed to aid in compilation of data. These data are available in *Vital and Health Statistics*.

Hospital records are another source of morbidity data. However, a uniform reporting system among all hospitals has not been established. Health care insurers (such as Medicare) receive data regarding patients insured under Medicare, but a nationwide reporting system is still lacking. Registries have taken on a major role in collecting morbidity data. Cancer registries (tumor registries) have become universal throughout the United States. Other chronic diseases have followed suit, and there are now specialized registries for such diseases as AIDS, cardiovascular disease, TB, diabetes, and psychiatric disease. Data are also collected in a trauma registry as well as a registry on birth defects.

2. **Terms**

   a. **Epidemic**

   An *epidemic* is a disease that attacks many people in a region at the same time, usually spreading rapidly; it is also defined as a disease of high morbidity, which is only occasionally present in the community. Due to its rapid spread, many individuals in an area are infected. One hundred years ago, infectious disease was the leading cause of death. Vaccines and antibiotics have decreased the death rate from these diseases in developed countries, but they continue to be an ongoing problem in developing countries.

   b. **Epidemiology**

   Epidemiology originated as the study of epidemics and epidemic disease. The branch of study developed as the result of great epidemics that occurred in various parts of the world over the centuries. These epidemics included cholera, plague, typhus, and influenza, to name a few. Today, *epidemiology* is defined as the observation of the occurrences of disease in populations. Epidemiology is concerned with both small and large numbers of cases. The cause of a single, isolated case of a disease is often as difficult to ascertain as the cause of a massive outbreak. Because of this, epidemiology is often thought of as investigative medicine.

   Epidemiological data have also illustrated changing disease trends. Plotting these trends has shown a decrease in certain cancers and an increase in other cancers. In studying disease, a strong link was identified between smoking and lung cancer, although it cannot be said that all smokers develop carcinoma of the lung.

c. Endemic Disease

An *endemic disease* is a disease that is commonly found in a particular area/region. It is a disease that is present in a community but can have low morbidity and be constantly present yet clinically diagnosed in only a few. Malaria is an endemic disease in the tropics, and histoplasmosis is endemic to the Midwestern farm belt.

3. Rates

a. Prevalence

Prevalence refers to something widely or commonly occurring or existing. Regarding morbidity, it is defined as the number of existing cases (including those newly diagnosed) of a disease in each population. The existing cases of a disease (per period) are divided by the population at that time, and the quotient is multiplied by a factor (1,000, 100,000, or 1,000,000) to determine the prevalence of a disease in each population.

Formula for Prevalence:

$$\frac{\text{Known (new and existing) cases of a disease for a given period}}{\text{Population for the same period}} \times M$$

EXAMPLE: If a total of 400,000 people are alive with a diagnosis of AIDS in the year the U.S. population was recorded at 300 million, the prevalence of AIDS in the United States would be 1.33 cases per 1,000 population (400,000 divided by 300 million = 0.001333 × 1,000 = 1.33). Had the multiplier been 10,000, the answer would be stated as 13.33 per 10,000 population; with a multiplier of 100,000, the stated rate would be 133.3 per 100,000 population.

b. Incidence

Incidence refers to frequency or extent, as in the phrase "there is a high incidence of malaria in the tropics." When a population is followed for a period of time, incidence of disease can be calculated. Incidence of disease is the number of *new* cases of a disease per unit of time. The newly reported cases of a disease (per given period) are divided by the population on July 1 of that year, with the quotient multiplied by a convenient factor (as previously stated) to determine the incidence rate.

Formula for Incidence:

$$\frac{\text{Newly reported cases of a disease for a given period}}{\text{Population at the mid period}} \times M$$

EXAMPLE: If the number of new cases of tuberculosis in the United States was 21,700 when the population reached 290 million in the middle of the year, the incidence would be 0.0748 new cases of tuberculosis per 1,000 population in that year. However, to establish a rate of at least 1 (a non-decimal number), the multiplier would have to be increased. A multiplier of 10,000 still results in a decimal amount (0.748 per 10,000). However, using 100,000 as the multiplier, the rate becomes 7.48 new cases per 100,000 population.

NOTE: In the two examples above, it was impossible to divide by 300 million or 290 million with a handheld calculator. The fractions in both examples had to be reduced to get an accurate reading.

 SELF-TEST 10-2

1. A state has a midyear population of 25 million. A total of 13,500 new cases of gonorrhea were reported during that year. Calculate the incidence of gonorrhea in the state that year.

2. In the past year, a total of 450,000 females were reported to have been either newly diagnosed or had a history of breast cancer out of a population of 305 million. Calculate the prevalence of breast cancer in the total population for the year.

D. VITAL STATISTICS MORTALITY RATES

The subsequent rates are based on the basic rate formula and apply to the number of people in a population experiencing an event during a specified time period or more specifically:

Vital Statistics Mortality Rate:

$$\frac{\text{Number } \textit{experiencing} \text{ the event}}{\text{Number } \textit{at risk} \text{ of experiencing the event}} \times M$$

Vital statistics rates commonly come in three forms:

1. **Crude Rates.** Crude rates generally include the entire population. Differences that may be important factors in development of a disease (such as age, sex, race, etc.) are disregarded—hence the name crude.

2. **Specific Rates.** Specific rates include a specific factor (age, sex, race, etc.). In specific rates, some variable is included. If the factor is age, the rate is referred to as an age-specific rate; if the factor is race, the rate is race-specific.

3. **Adjusted/Standardized Rates.** These rates are used for comparison purposes between two or more groups possessing different variables (such as different ages). The computation of these rates will not be included in this text.

As with hospital mortality data, the numerator in vital statistics mortality rates is the number of deaths occurring in a specified time period in each population. Population size is often the population at midyear (July 1). Using the population figures at midyear is considered a reasonable estimate of the population, since population figures vary—generally increasing, decreasing, or remaining stable. The midyear population is the population *at risk* if the specified time period is one year. Conventionally, if this criterion is not met, the resulting calculation should be referred to as a proportion rather than a rate. However, this distinction is commonly ignored, and all determinations are considered rates. The term *annual* usually precedes a rate to indicate the rate is based on yearly data.

1. Crude Death Rate

The crude death rate is a commonly used rate; but as the name indicates, it is a crude rate, giving only an approximation of the number of deaths in a population. No factor (such as age, sex, or race) is taken into consideration in determining a crude rate.

Formula for Crude Death Rate:

$$\frac{\text{Total deaths in a population for a specified time period}}{\text{Estimated population for the same specified time period}} \times 1,000$$

EXAMPLE: A state has a population of 25 million. A total of 200,000 deaths were reported in the past year. The crude death rate is 8 deaths per 1,000 population for the past year $(200,000 \div 25,000,000 = 0.008 \times 1,000 = 8)$.

2. Specific Rates

a. Age-Specific Death Rate

In this formula, the age group is specified and therefore the population total is the census data for that specified population.

Formula for Age-Specific Death Rate:

$$\frac{\text{Total deaths in a specified age group for a specified time period}}{\text{Estimated population (of specified age group) for the same time period}} \times 1,000$$

EXAMPLE: Using the age group of 25 to 34 years and a one-year time period, assume the estimated population (ages 25–34) to be 36 million. The total deaths reported in this age group was 50,000. Therefore, the 25–34 age-specific death rate is 1.4 deaths per 1,000 population $(50,000 \div 36,000,000 = 0.00139 \times 1,000 = 1.39)$.

b. Cause-Specific Death Rate

This formula specifies the cause of death.

Cause-Specific Death Rate:

$$\frac{\text{Total deaths due to a specific cause during a specified time period}}{\text{Estimated population for the same specified time period}} \times 100,000$$

EXAMPLES:

EX 1. The estimated state population in the past year was 22 million. The cause of death to be investigated is accidents (including motor vehicle accidents) with a reported death total of 10,000. The accident death rate is 4.5 deaths per 10,000 population $(10,000 \div 22,000,000 = 0.00045$ multiplied by $1,000 = 0.45$ deaths per 1,000 or 4.5 deaths per 10,000).

EX 2. *Cancer Mortality Rate.* The cancer mortality rate is a cause-specific death rate. The total deaths are cancer deaths during a specified period of time. The denominator is the estimated population during the specified time period. If the estimated population is 20 million in the past year and a total of 50,000 cancer deaths were reported in the state in the past year, the state cancer mortality rate is 2.5 per 1,000 population ($50,000 \div 20,000,000 = 0.0025 \times 1,000 = 2.5$ cancer deaths per 1,000).

c. **Cause-Race-Specific Death Rate**

This time, both the race (such as white vs. nonwhite) and the cause of death are considered.

Formula for Cause-Race-Specific Death Rate:

$$\frac{\text{Total deaths of a specific race for a specific cause during a specified period}}{\text{Estimated population of the specific race for the specified time period}} \times M$$

EXAMPLE: The cause of death is accidents and the state chooses to evaluate the data between white males and nonwhite males. The total state population is 3,500,000 nonwhite males and 6,500,000 white males for a total of 10 million males. The accident deaths were 6,500 white males and 4,000 nonwhite males. The rate for white males is 1.0 death from accidents per 1,000 white males; the rate for nonwhite males is 1.14 deaths from accidents per 1,000 nonwhite males in the past year ($6,500 \div 6,500,000 = 0.001 \times 1,000 = 1$ death/1,000; $4,000 \div 3,500,000 = 0.00114 \times 1,000 = 1.14$ deaths/1,000).

d. **Proportional Mortality Rate**

This rate is easy to compute and therefore is often used to ascertain the relative importance of a specific cause of death. Since the entire population is used in the denominator, it is not deemed to be as reliable an indicator as the cause-specific death rate but serves as an estimator when the denominator data for the cause-specific rate are unavailable.

Formula for Proportional Mortality Rate:

$$\frac{\text{Total deaths due to a specific cause in a specified period}}{\text{Total deaths (from all causes) in the same specified time period}} \times 100$$

EXAMPLE: In the past year, 400,000 people died of malignant neoplasms. In addition, 2 million deaths were also reported in the past year from all causes. The proportional mortality rate for the year is 20% ($400,000$ divided by $2,000,000 = 0.20 \times 100 = 20\%$). Twenty percent of all deaths in the past year were due to malignant neoplasms.

e. **Case Fatality Rate**

The case fatality rate is defined as the number of deaths assigned to a given cause in a certain period, with the quotient being multiplied by 100. The case fatality rate is an indicator of the seriousness of a disease. It is often used as a means of showing the relative effectiveness of various forms of treatment.

Formula for Case Fatality Rate:

$$\frac{\text{Total deaths for a given disease in a specified time period}}{\text{Total cases of the disease reported during the specified period}} \times 100$$

EXAMPLE: During the past year, the national population was 300 million. The total number of deaths from hepatitis A (infectious hepatitis) was 510 out of a total of 32,000 cases of hepatitis A reported nationwide. The case fatality rate for the past year is 1.6% (510 ÷ 32,000 = 0.0159 × 100 = 1.6%). A total of 1.6% of reported cases of hepatitis A died from the disease in the past year.

 SELF-TEST 10-3

A state has a population of 6 million. Data for the past year included the following:

Age Group	Males	Females	Total Deaths Males	Total Deaths Females	Deaths Due to Cancer Males	Deaths Due to Cancer Females
80+	90,000	150,000	5,780	6,420	1,930	2,170
60–79	340,000	500,000	5,630	5,160	1,860	1,720
40–59	620,000	700,000	5,340	5,070	1,800	1,690
20–39	700,000	800,000	4,550	4,190	1,300	1,260
0–19	1,000,000	1,100,000	4,100	3,760	960	870

Calculate:
a. Crude death rate for the state.
b. Age-specific death rate for 40- to 59-year-olds.
c. Cause-specific (cancer) death rate for males.
d. Cause-specific (cancer) death rate for females.
e. Proportional mortality cancer rate for the total population.
f. Age-specific death rate for males, 60–79.
g. Age-specific death rate for females, 20–39.
h. Age-specific death rate for population, 60–79.

E. MEASURES OF FERTILITY

Measures of fertility are helpful in designing programs related to maternal and child health services. They may be helpful to school boards to plan for future needs, such as school facilities and teachers.

1. Crude Birth Rate

Crude rates can be used to make approximations, particularly in stable populations.

Formula for Crude Birth Rate:

$$\frac{\text{Total number of live births for a given community in a specified time period}}{\text{Estimated population (July 1) for the community during the same period}} \times 1,000$$

EXAMPLE: A community reported a population at midyear (July 1) of 250,000 along with a total of 3,400 live births. The crude birth rate is 13.6 live births per 1,000 population for the community that year $(3,400 \div 250,000 = 0.0136 \times 1,000 = 13.6$ live births$)$.

NOTE: Although the crude birth rate is commonly used as an estimator, it should be noted that the denominator includes both males and females rather than only those capable of childbearing. A more significant rate is the general fertility rate. However, the data figures needed for their computations are not as readily obtained.

2. General Fertility Rate

The general fertility rate is based on the number of females capable of childbearing in a specified year.

Formula for General Fertility Rate:

$$\frac{\text{Total number of live births in a calendar year}}{\text{Total number of females, ages 15–44 at midyear}} \times 1,000$$

EXAMPLE: A community, population of 200,000 in the past year, reported 33,000 females of childbearing age (15–44) at midyear. A total of 2,100 live births were also recorded. The general fertility rate of the community is 63.6 live births per 1,000 women ages 15–44 per year $(2,100 \div 33,000 = 0.0636 \times 1,000 = 63.6)$.

3. Additional Measures of Fertility

Listed are two other fertility measures, neither of which will be included in this text. However, the rates follow the same principles as other age-specific or age-adjusted rates.

a. *Age-Specific Fertility Rate*

b. *Age-Adjusted Fertility Rate*

 SELF-TEST 10-4

1. A state had a midyear population of 1 million in the past year; data included the following:

	Males	Females	Females (15–44)	Live Births
Population	490,000	510,000	200,000	12,200
Deaths	810	770		

Calculate:

a. Crude birth rate for the state for the year.

b. General fertility rate for the state for the year.

2. County data in the past year included a total midyear population of 500,000.

	Males	Females	Females (15–44)	Live Births
Population	243,000	257,000	105,000	6,800

Calculate:

a. Crude birth rate for the county for the year.
b. General fertility rate for the county for the year.

3. A city had a population of 150,000 at midyear (data for the past year):

	Males	Females	Females (15–44)	Live Births
Population	74,000	76,000	38,000	2,400
Deaths	155	125		

Calculate:

a. Crude birth rate for the city for the past year.
b. General fertility rate for the city for the past year.

F. SUMMARY

1. Vital statistics data are a record of significant events and dates in human life, including births, adoptions, marriages, divorces, and deaths.
2. The National Center for Health Statistics (NCHS), a branch of the Centers for Disease Control and Prevention (CDC), is the governmental agency responsible for collection and reporting of vital statistics data.
3. Certificates of live birth, death, and—in certain instances—fetal death and induced termination of pregnancy are issued by states for legal purposes.
4. Vital statistics rates generally include a multiplier of 1,000, 10,000, or 100,000 to aid comprehension of data.
5. Fetal deaths include only intermediate and late fetal deaths.
6. Obstetrical-related mortality rates for a specified period include:
   a. Maternal: A ratio of pregnancy-related deaths to live births.
   b. Infant: A ratio of infant deaths to live births.
   c. Neonatal: A ratio of neonatal deaths to live births.
   d. Perinatal: A ratio of fetal and neonatal deaths to live births and fetal deaths.
   e. Post-neonatal:
      (1) Primary—ratio of post-neonatal deaths to live births–neonatal deaths.
      (2) Secondary—ratio of post-neonatal deaths to live births.
   f. Fetal: A ratio of fetal deaths to live births.
7. Morbidity data refer to disease (including injuries and any deviation from normal health).
8. The CDC is the clearinghouse for morbidity data.
9. An epidemic is a disease that attacks many people in a region at the same time, usually spreading rapidly.
10. An endemic disease is a disease commonly found in an area, usually due to environmental factors.
11. Epidemiology is the study of the occurrence of disease in populations.

12. Prevalence of disease is the known (new and existing) cases of a disease (per period) divided by the population at that time, with the quotient multiplied by a convenient factor.

13. Incidence of disease is the newly reported cases of a disease (per period) divided by the population at midpoint of the period, with the quotient multiplied by a convenient factor.

14. The crude death rate is the ratio of deaths to the estimated population.

15. Specific mortality rates include a specific factor (age, sex, race, cause of death) in the calculation. The cancer mortality rate is a cause-specific mortality rate and is the ratio of cancer deaths to the estimated population.

16. A proportional mortality rate is the ratio of cause-specific deaths to deaths from all causes.

17. The case fatality rate is the ratio of deaths due to a certain cause to the total diagnosed cases of the disease.

18. All vital statistics rates are computed for a specified time period, most commonly yearly.

19. The crude birth rate and general fertility rate tend to estimate the increase in population due to the birth rate.

NOTES

Name _____   Date _____

G. CHAPTER 10 TEST

1. List and briefly describe the four major vital statistics certificates collected by the National Center for Health Statistics.

2. A community has 60,000 inhabitants, 35,000 of which are female. Of the female population, 525 have been diagnosed with osteoporosis. What is the prevalence rate?

3. In the same community, the number of new cases of osteoporosis reported in the past year was 76. What is the incidence rate in this community, correct to the nearest whole number?

4. State population statistics for the year include the following:

Population of state	2,555,000
Female population (15–44)	35,000
Maternal deaths	50
Live births	380,000
Infant deaths (<1 year)	3,293
Neonatal deaths (<28 weeks)	2,007
Fetal deaths (>20 weeks)	2,345
Post-neonatal deaths	1,286

Calculate:

a. Maternal mortality rate.
b. Infant mortality rate.
c. Neonatal mortality rate.
d. Percentage of all infant deaths that are neonatal deaths.
e. Perinatal mortality rate.
f. Post-neonatal mortality rate.
g. Fetal death rate:
h. Without fetal deaths in the denominator.
i. Including fetal deaths in the denominator.

5. State Health Department data for the past year: Population: 3,620,000

Disease	New Cases	Deaths
Diphtheria	22	1
Hepatitis A	7,882	4
Hepatitis B	3,444	3
Mumps	33	2
Rubella	78	0
Rubeola	56	0

Calculate:

a. State incidence of diphtheria per 1,000 population.
b. State incidence of hepatitis B per 10,000 population.
c. State case fatality ratio of hepatitis A.
d. State cause-specific death rate for mumps per 100,000 population.
e. State cause-specific death rate for hepatitis B per 100,000 population.

6. State cancer registry data for colorectal cancer:

	Total	Males	Females
Population	1,570,000	780,000	790,000
Newly diagnosed cases	793	415	378
Residents with "history of"	12,548	6,983	5,665

Calculate:

a. State prevalence of colorectal cancer in males (per 10,000).
b. State incidence of colorectal cancer in females (per 10,000).

7. State Health Department (data for the past year): State population: 5,610,000

Disease	Newly Diagnosed Cases	Deaths
Pertussis	168	1
Salmonellosis	9,820	4
Shigellosis	550	1
Syphilis (all stages)	1,410	6
Chlamydia	9,995	1
Gonorrhea	7,000	1
AIDS	2,006	8

Calculate:

a. State incidence of Chlamydia (per 1,000 population).
b. Case fatality rate of syphilis.
c. Cause-specific death rate of AIDS (per 10,000 population).
d. Proportional mortality rate for Salmonellosis.

8. A total of 500,000 males were reported to have been newly diagnosed or have a history of prostate cancer during the past year. Of these, 38% were white males and 62% were black males. The U.S. population was reported as 300 million, of which 145 million were males and 155 million were females. Among the male population, 110 million were white, and 35 million were black.

Calculate:

a. Prostate cancer prevalence (per 100,000 population).
b. Prostate cancer prevalence (per 100,000 white males).
c. Prostate cancer prevalence (per 100,000 black males).

9. A community has a population of 76,000. A total of 3,650 deaths were reported during the past year. Which of the following adequately describes the crude death rate?

a. 48 per 1,000
b. 4.8 per 1,000
c. 0.04 per 1,000
d. 48 per 10,000
e. 4%

10. The multiplier used in vital statistics rates can also be designated as a power of 10 (10 to the nth power). The power is the number of zeros following the number one. The multiplier 100,000 is 10 to the fifth power; 10,000 is 10 to the fourth power, and so forth. Identify the nth power for: a. 100; b. 1.

11. State Population: 1 million (yearly data):

Ages	White			Black		
	Males	Females	Total	Males	Females	Total
75+	9,000	15,000	24,000	2,000	4,000	6,000
65–74	23,000	30,000	53,000	7,500	9,500	17,000
45–64	91,000	94,000	185,000	29,000	36,000	65,000
0–44	243,000	247,000	490,000	75,000	85,000	160,000
Deaths:	Prostate	White males	471	Black males	250	
	Breast	White females	526	Black females	202	

Ages:	75+		65–74		45–64		0–44	
Deaths:	White	Black	White	Black	White	Black	White	Black
Prostate	120	71	215	73	105	68	31	18
Breast	95	46	187	81	168	53	76	22

Calculate:

a. Cause-race-specific prostate cancer death rate for blacks.
b. Cause-race-specific prostate cancer death rate for whites.
c. Cause-race-specific breast cancer death rate for blacks.
d. Cause-race-specific breast cancer death rate for whites.
e. Cause-age-race-specific prostate cancer death rate for blacks, 45–64.
f. Cause-age-race-specific prostate cancer death rate for whites, 65–74.
g. Cause-age-race-specific breast cancer death rate for blacks, 45–64.
h. Cause-age-race-specific breast cancer death rate for whites, 65–74.
i. Cause-age-race-specific prostate cancer death rate for blacks, 0–44.
j. Cause-age-race-specific breast cancer death rate for whites, 75+.

12. Shelby county reported a population of 1,500,000 in 2017 and live births of 25,000. The county also reported 400,000 females of childbearing age (15–44).

Compute:

a. Crude birth rate, correct to one decimal place.
b. General fertility rate, correct to one decimal place.

Statistics: *Learning the Basics*

LEARNING OBJECTIVES

After studying this chapter, the learner should be able to:

✓ Distinguish between the measures of central tendency and identify the distributions in which they are most representative.

✓ Distinguish a bilaterally symmetrical (normal) bell-shaped curve from an asymmetrical skewed curve and describe positive and negative skewness.

✓ Describe the effect of skewness on measures of central tendency.

✓ Define and identify the measures of dispersion—range, variance, and standard deviation.

✓ Compute the following:
   a. Range, median, and mode
   b. Mean from an ungrouped and grouped distribution
   c. Variance and standard deviation from an ungrouped and grouped distribution

✓ Identify the empirical rule—the relationship of standard deviation to the area under a normal curve.

Throughout most of the previous chapters, we have computed some type of average, which is also called the *mean*. Each time the average census, average occupancy percentage, average death rate, or average length of stay was calculated, a measure of *central tendency* was calculated. Measures of central tendency refer to scores most commonly called *measures* or *values* that are typical or representative of a set of data. These measures tend to lie near the center of a distribution when the data are arranged according to magnitude and are, therefore, commonly referred to as *measures of central tendency*.

Frequency distributions, tables, charts, and graphs have been discussed previously, and they are important tools in displaying data. However, it is also important to describe the main characteristics of a data set. These characteristics include identifying the center and spread of a distribution. A table or graph represents the data for an entire group but often one wants to know the average for the group. For example, it is interesting to note the income of everyone in a city, but it is often more beneficial to know what the average or "typical" family earns in the community. The spread of the distribution of incomes helps identify the relative position of a family's income within the city.

The most commonly reported measures of central tendency include the mean, median, and mode. If the frequency distribution is a bilaterally symmetrical, unimodal distribution, then all three measures of central tendency will be equal. Each of these measures has advantages and disadvantages, depending on the data and their intended purpose.

Lastly, it is important to note that most of the calculations that will be discussed in this chapter can be done easily with computer software packages such as Microsoft Excel. Although this may be the method used in the real world to perform data analysis, it is also important to understand how these calculations are made and how they are best used to collect and report information necessary for decision making.

A. MEASURES OF CENTRAL TENDENCY

1. Mean

a. Arithmetic Mean

The *mean* (more correctly known as the *arithmetic mean*) is an arithmetical average. It is computed in the same manner as all the averages computed in previous chapters. It is derived by adding all the scores in a distribution and dividing by the total number of scores in the distribution. There are additional means (harmonic and geometric), but only the arithmetic mean is used in this text. Therefore, when the term *mean* is used, it refers to the arithmetic mean. The arithmetic mean is the most commonly used measure of central tendency.

Formula for Arithmetic Mean:

$$\frac{\Sigma \text{ scores}}{N} \quad (N = \text{total number of scores})$$

EXAMPLE: Seven patients were discharged from the hospital today, and the number of days each was hospitalized was reported as 5, 3, 7, 12, 2, 4, and 2 days. The average length of stay for these seven patients was five days $[(5 + 3 + 7 + 12 + 2 + 4 + 2) = 35 \div 7 \,(\text{seven patients}) = 5 \,\text{days}]$.

 SELF-TEST 11-1

Twenty-five patients were seen in the emergency room yesterday. The number of clinical laboratory and X-ray procedures performed on each patient were recorded as: 5, 3, 7, 4, 6, 7, 2, 1, 4, 6, 3, 3, 2, 2, 5, 7, 4, 5, 3, 6, 2, 1, 4, 3, 5. Calculate: Mean (arithmetic) number of lab and X-ray procedures per patient.

b. Weighted Mean

If certain scores are more significant than others, they can be assigned a weight (W), depending on their importance.

Weighted Mean Formula:

$$\frac{W(\Sigma S1) + W(\Sigma S2) + \ldots + W(\Sigma S_x)}{W1 + W2 + \ldots + W} = \frac{\Sigma W(S_x)}{\Sigma W_x}$$

EXAMPLE: A final exam (FE) in a course is weighted three times as much as a quiz (Q), and a regular exam (Ex) is weighted twice as much as a quiz. If three regular exams, five quizzes, and a final exam are administered throughout a course, then the formula for the weighted mean would be:

Arithmetic Mean Formula:

$$\frac{3\ FE + 2\ Ex1 + 2\ Ex2 + 2\ Ex3 + Q1 + Q2 + Q3 + Q4 + Q5}{3 + 2 + 2 + 2 + 1 + 1 + 1 + 1 + 1}$$

or

$$\frac{3(FE) + 2(Ex1 + 2\ Ex2 + 2\ Ex3) + (Q1 + Q2 + Q3 + Q4 + Q5)}{3(1) + 2(3) + 1(5)}$$

 SELF-TEST 11-2

In the previous example, using the following test scores: FE = 85; Ex1 = 95; Ex2 = 90; Ex3 = 82; Q1 = 80; Q2 = 88; Q3 = 94; Q4 = 96; Q5 = 73. Calculate: Average grade for the weighted mean, correct to two decimal places.

c. **Mean Computed from Grouped Data**

Chapter 3 dealt with grouped and ungrouped data sets. Ungrouped data include individual information on each member of a population or sample, whereas grouped data aggregate the individual scores within a class interval. When scores are grouped into a frequency distribution, all values that fall within a class interval are considered to coincide with the midpoint of the interval. In an interval whose limits are 60–62, all scores within that interval are considered to be 61 (midpoint) for computation purposes.

EXAMPLE: Heights (in centimeters) for 100 males participating in a heart study are recorded. The frequency distribution includes:

Heights (in centimeters) for 100 males participating in a heart study:

Heights (cm)	Midpoint	Frequency	Frequency × Midpoint
175–179	177	2	354
170–174	172	12	2,064
165–169	167	25	4,175
160–164	162	32	5,184
155–159	157	20	3,140
150–154	152	9	1,368
		Total: 100	16,285

To compute the mean from a grouped frequency distribution:

(1) Multiply the frequency in each interval by its respective midpoint.
(2) Total the (frequency × midpoint) column.
(3) Divide the (frequency × midpoint) column by N.

Therefore, the average height is 162.85 cm (16,285 ÷ 100 = 162.85 cm) for the 100 patients in the heart study.

NOTES

SELF-TEST 11-3

Age at the time of death is recorded for 90 patients:

Age	Midpoint (mp)	Frequency (f)	mp × f	Age	mp	f	mp × f
90–99	94.5	3		40–49	44.5	8	
80–89	84.5	15		30–39	34.5	5	
70–79	74.5	19		20–29	24.5	4	
60–69	64.5	15		10–19	14.5	3	
50–59	54.5	13		0–9	4.5	5	

Calculate: Mean age at the time of death to the nearest whole number.

NOTE: Some difference may be seen between the mean computed from a grouped distribution compared to an ungrouped distribution. The size of the discrepancy depends on the width of the class interval as well as the number of observations within each interval. With a smaller class interval size and a large sample size, the discrepancy is negligible.

A major drawback of the mean is that it is very sensitive to *outliers*. Outliers are extreme values—a few very small or a few very large values. In health care, outliers are seen when looking at patient length of stay (LOS); most patients may have a LOS of three to five days, but there may be one or two outliers with lengths of stay at 40 or 50 days. The effect of outliers is noted in an upcoming section on skewed curves, where it is addressed in more detail. It is mentioned here to point out that the mean is not always the best measure of central tendency because of the effect of outliers on its value. If a data set contains outliers, a *trimmed mean* is recommended. When calculating the value of a trimmed mean, drop the small percentage of values from both ends of the distribution (smallest score and largest score) and then calculate the mean from the remaining scores.

One property of the mean is that if we know the means and sample sizes of two (or more) data sets, a *combined mean* can be calculated.

Formula for Combined Mean:

$$\frac{n(\text{mean 1}) + n(\text{mean 2})}{n + n} \quad n = \text{sample size}$$

EXAMPLE: Instructor A administers a test to her class of 30 students, and the mean score is 85. Instructor B administers the same test to her class of 40 students, and the mean score is 81. The combined mean for the two classes is [82.7 (30 × 85) + (40 × 81) = 2,550 + 3,240 = 5,790 ÷ 70 (40 + 30) = 82.7], or a score of 83 for the combined mean of the two classes.

SELF-TEST 11-4

A class of 48 HIM majors went to buy a statistics textbook. One group of 22 students bought their text at Bookstore A for an average price of $120 per book. The other group of 26 purchased their text at Bookstore B for an average price of $136 per book.

Calculate the combined mean for the 48 textbooks.

2. Median

The median is the middle score of a distribution when the scores are arranged in order of magnitude (high to low or low to high). The median is the *midpoint* of a distribution, or the point above which 50% of the scores lie and below which the other 50% lie. The median divides the distribution into halves. It is considered relatively easy to calculate and takes the entire distribution into account. The median is not influenced by outliers and is preferred over the mean for data sets with outliers.

Formula for Median:
a. If N is *odd*—the median is the middle score.
b. If N is *even*—the median is the average of the two middle scores.

EXAMPLES:

EX 1. Ten patients are seen for glaucoma screening. The intraocular pressures are: 14, 18, 20, 16, 24, 28, 10, 15, 21, 12. Arranging the scores from high to low: 28, 24, 21, 20, 18, 16, 15, 14, 12, 10. Since 10 is an even number, the median is the average of the fifth (18) and sixth (16) scores for an average intraocular pressure of $17 (18 + 16 = 34 \div 2 = 17)$.

EX 2. The number of colonoscopies performed each day for a week include: 4, 8, 10, 9, 12, 9, 11. Scores by magnitude are: 12, 11, 10, 9, 9, 8, 4. The *median* number of colonoscopies for the week is 9 (the fourth score of 7). The *mean* for the same seven scores is $9 (63 \div 7 = 9)$.

 SELF-TEST 11-5

Fourteen new cases of cancer were reported during the previous week. Age at the time of diagnosis was: 18, 35, 50, 64, 88, 49, 75, 28, 61, 59, 47, 77, 66, 48.

Calculate:
a. Median age, at diagnosis, correct to one decimal place.
b. Mean age, at diagnosis, correct to one decimal place.

3. Mode

The mode of a set of numbers is the score that occurs with the greatest frequency—that is, the most common value in a data set. It is quite possible to have no mode in a distribution. Even if a mode does exist, it may not be unique. A distribution with a single mode is *unimodal*; a distribution with two modes is *bimodal*; a data set with more than two modes is *multimodal*. The mode score is located at the high point of a curve and in a truly normal distribution, the mode score value is in the center of that curve. The mean, median, and mode will all be equal in a normal, unimodal, symmetrical, bell-shaped curve. The mode's weak points include that it may not be descriptive of the distribution, it may not be unique, and the entire distribution is not represented. An advantage of the mode is that it can be calculated for both quantitative and qualitative data. The mean and median are only appropriately used with quantitative data.

EXAMPLE: Twenty cases of measles (rubella) were reported during the past month by the state health department. The reported ages of the patients were: 12, 14, 18, 17, 20, 21, 9, 19, 22, 20, 19, 16, 21, 23, 21, 18, 10, 20, 21, 19. Since the mode is the age that occurs most often, the mode is 21 (four cases being reported in this age group).

 SELF-TEST 11-6

Prior to the start of a low-impact aerobics class for females, the participants' resting heart rates were recorded. Fifteen females made up the class, and their ages ranged from 20 to 25. The resting heart rates were: 73, *77*, 80, 83, 73, 82, 75, 73, *77*, 84, 76, 81, 75, 79, 70.

Calculate:

a. Mode (heart rate).
b. Median (heart rate).
c. Mean (heart rate), correct to the nearest whole number.

NOTE: No measure of central tendency is universally preferred; each is better under certain situations. The most used measure is the mean followed by the median. The mean uses each value of the data set. The median is a better representation when outliers are present. The mode is simple to locate but is impractical for most situations. The measure of central tendency that best represents various kinds of data is:

a. Skewed distribution—median
b. Nominal scores—mode
c. Ordinal scores—median
d. Interval scores—mean

B. CURVES OF A FREQUENCY DISTRIBUTION

1. Bilaterally Symmetrical Curves

A bilaterally symmetrical curve is one that, when folded down the center vertically, is identical on both sides of the fold. In a bilaterally symmetrical curve, all three measures of central tendency (mean, median, and mode) will be identical. These three measures will lie at the center of the distribution and thus are called *measures of central tendency*.

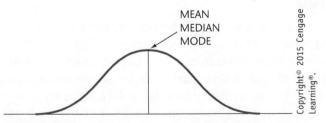

**Relationship of Measures of Central Tendency
to a Normal Bell-Shaped Curve**

a. Normal Bell-Shaped Curve

A bell-shaped curve is generally considered the mathematical ideal. It is a curve with a certain proportion and in which a certain percentage of scores lie at certain intervals along the curve. A bell-shaped curve is also referred to as a *normal curve*. The bell-shaped curve represents a "normal" distribution. In a normal distribution, the data lie within certain parameters.

b.   Other Symmetrical Curves

These curves resemble the bell-shaped curve and are symmetrical, but they vary in their ratios of height to width. Some are referred to as "peaked" curves, and others as "flat" curves.

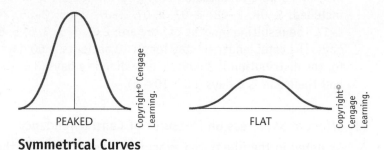

PEAKED   FLAT

Symmetrical Curves

2.   Additional Curves

a.   Skewed Curves

Not all curves are symmetrical in shape. Curves that have scores concentrated at either the high or low end of the curve are called skewed curves. The direction of skewness refers to the location of the tail, rather than the end where the height of the curve (where scores tend to be concentrated) occurs. A curve skewed to the right is one with the tail to the right end; a curve skewed to the left has a tail extending to the left.

Skewness also affects the location of the measures of central tendency. Instead of all three measures being representative and identical, the location of these three measures shifts. A curve skewed to the right has its mean shifted to the right, and a curve skewed to the left has its mean shifted to the left. Curves skewed to the right are termed *positive skewness* and curves skewed to the left are termed *negative skewness*.

In addition to the displacement of the mean, the median and mode take on another relationship as well. Since the mode is the most recurring score in a distribution, it will shift to the high point of the curve or away from the tail. Therefore, the mode shifts to the right with negative skewness and shifts to the left with positive skewness. The median will lie between the mean and the mode.

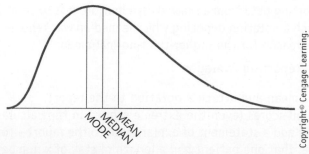
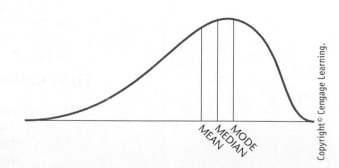

Skewed Curves

EXAMPLE: The most common example of skewness in hospital statistics occurs when reporting and plotting lengths of stay, especially when one or more patients have an exceptionally long stay compared to others in the same group. If the average length of stay is less than a week and a patient accrues a length of stay of several weeks, the extended stay results in a positive skewness (skewed to the right), thus raising the mean for all patients. To illustrate, the following discharges were reported on February 10, 2012. The admission dates included: 2–08, 2–08, 2–07, 2–07, 2–07, 2–05, 2–05, 2–04, 2–03, 1–17. The resulting lengths of stay are: 2, 2, 3, 3, 3, 5, 5, 6, 7, and 24 days. The total length of stay for all 10 patients is 60 days. The mode for the distribution is 3 days, the median is 4 days ($3 + 5 = 8 \div 2 = 4$), and the mean is 6 days ($60 \div 10 = 6$).

(1) Effect of Skewness on Measures of Central Tendency

As noted in the illustrated example, skewness affects the measures of central tendency and is of importance to the mean as it is the measure most commonly computed. However, it must be pointed out, average lengths of stay are usually computed for more than 10 patients. The small number was included here for illustrative purposes only. The illustration was used to show the influence of a nonrepresentative score on the mean of a distribution and to show the relationship between the three measures of central tendency, especially in skewed distributions. The reader should also be made aware that statistics must be taken with a "grain of salt" and that careful judgments must be made when reading or interpreting data.

(2) Reporting Measures of Central Tendency from a Skewed Distribution

The term *average* is synonymous with the arithmetic mean, and the proper measure of central tendency should be used when indicating a value such as the mean age or the median age. Income statistics are often reported in the United States every year, and there is great variation between the reported average (mean) income and the average (median) income of U.S. residents. The high-income earners skew the distribution positively, and the median is generally considered the better measure of average income. If data are symmetrically distributed, either the mean or the median will be representative of the data. For a series with a large amount of data, the mean is easier to compute, whereas for a small series, the median is more easily determined. Median determination is generally very time consuming unless a computer is used to more easily sort data by magnitude. For skewed data, the median is the more representative measure of central tendency. When reporting data from a skewed distribution, it is generally advisable to attach a notation denoting why the median was reported or to explain the reason for the higher-than-normal mean.

(3) Suggestions for Reporting Averages

a. Calculate the mean and attach a notation to the report.
   1. Include all scores (even the extreme scores) in the calculation, and add a statement of explanation to the report—for instance, that one patient had a length of stay of x number of days.

2. Exclude the extreme scores (outliers) but include a statement regarding the exclusion—for instance, that one patient had a stay of x number of days and was excluded in the computation of the mean. A trimmed mean can also be reported, with a proper notation included.

3. Calculate both ways (including and excluding the extreme score), and attach a note explaining the difference in the two means.

    EXAMPLE: Using the previous example for illustrative purposes, the notation might state that the average (mean) length of stay for all patients was 6 days, but one patient had a length of stay of 24 days; by excluding that patient, the mean length of stay for all patients was 4 days.

4. Calculate the median and attach a notation to the report. Explain in the notation that one patient had an extended stay of x number of days, and, therefore, the median was chosen as most representative of the average length of stay.

b. *Other curves.* Shown are other types of curves that may be encountered in graphical representations of data. They are included here for reference purposes only.

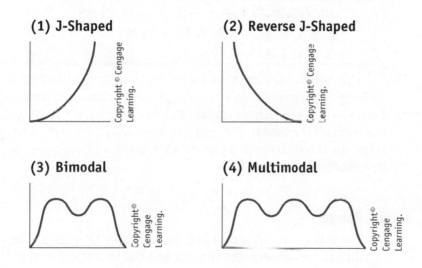

(1) J-Shaped

(2) Reverse J-Shaped

(3) Bimodal

(4) Multimodal

C. MEASURES OF DISPERSION (VARIABILITY)

The measures of central tendency (mean, median, and mode) do not reveal the whole picture of the distribution of a data set. Two data sets with the same mean may have completely different characteristics—the spread displayed in one data set may be much larger or smaller than for the second data set. The terms *dispersion, spread,* and *variation* have the same meaning.

EXAMPLE: Two different HIM departments each have eight employees. The ages of employees at department A are: 18, 27, 30, 34, 51, 58, 60, 62. The ages of employees at department B are: 34, 35, 39, 41, 42, 48, 50, 51. The total of all the ages for department A is 340, as is the total for department B. Therefore, the mean age is the same for both departments, 42.5 years.

If the only thing known about the two departments were the average age, without knowing the individual ages, one may deduce that the employees at these two departments have a similar age distribution.

Even the median ages are not greatly dissimilar, with a median age of 43 for department A and a median age of 41.5 for department B. However, the spread or variability in age is much greater in department A than in department B. Thus, it is usually insufficient to report only the mean, median, and mode of a data set. A measure of variation provides valuable additional information. The measures of central tendency and dispersion taken together provide a better picture of a data set than the measures of central tendency alone. Although the measures of central tendency are helpful indicators of a data set, it is often useful to know if the data from one distribution are similar (homogeneous) or dissimilar with considerable variation (heterogeneous). This section discusses the three measures of dispersion: range, variance, and standard deviation.

EXAMPLE: An instructor has three classes of 10 students each. The identical 10-point quiz is given to each class. The quiz scores for each of the classes are as follows, with the scores listed from high to low.

Class	Scores	Range	Mean	Median
A	10, 9, 8, 8, 6, 5, 5, 4, 4, 1	$10 - 1 = 9$	6	5.5
B	9, 9, 8, 7, 6, 6, 5, 4, 3, 3	$9 - 3 = 6$	6	6.0
C	8, 8, 8, 6, 5, 5, 5, 5, 5, 5	$8 - 5 = 3$	6	5.0

The results indicate that the means are identical for all three classes. However, the range is much broader in Class A than in the other two classes. Class C has a very narrow range, but all three have a mean score of 6, and the medians are similar. The measure of variation, however, varies. Variability refers to the difference between each score and every other score in the distribution.

1. **Range**

   The range was discussed and computed in Chapter 3. The range is the difference between the highest and the lowest value in a data set. It is the easiest measure of variation to compute, but only the high and low scores are used in the computation. As the sample size increases, the range also tends to increase. However, a major disadvantage of the range is the fact that it does not include all scores (only the largest and the smallest) in the distribution in its calculation. The range, like the mean, has the disadvantage of being influenced by outliers. Consequently, the range is not a good measure of dispersion to use for a data set that contains outliers and is not regarded as a satisfactory measure of dispersion.

   Formula for Range:

   range = largest value − smallest value

2. **Variance and Standard Deviation in Ungrouped Data**

   Variance and standard deviation consider all values in a data set, not just the two extremes. Variance is determined by comparing each score value with the mean of the distribution. Once the mean has been determined, every score in the distribution is subtracted from the mean and the number squared. The most commonly used measure of dispersion is standard deviation, and standard deviation is obtained from the variance (square root of the variance). The value of the standard deviation tells how closely the values of a data set are clustered around the mean. In general, the smaller the standard deviation for a data set, the smaller the variation around the mean—a more compact distribution or less dispersion. The greater the deviations for the values from the mean, the greater the variance.

Officially, different symbols are used to designate *population data* from *sample data*. *Population* data use σ^2 (lowercase sigma squared) to denote variance; therefore, σ represents the standard deviation of the distribution as the standard deviation is the square root of the variance; lowercase x indicates the score value; μ represents the mean; and uppercase N represents the number of scores in the distribution. *Sample* data use lowercase s^2 (s squared) to denote variance; therefore, s represents the standard deviation; lowercase x, again, indicates the score value; $\bar{x}$ (called x-bar) represents the mean; and lowercase n represents the number of scores in the distribution. However, whatever symbols are used, the calculations are identical except that 1 is subtracted from n (n − 1) when computing variance from sample populations.

Basic Formulas for Variance:

a. Population $\sigma^2 = \dfrac{\Sigma(x - \mu)^2}{N}$

b. Sample $s^2 = \dfrac{\Sigma(x - \bar{x})^2}{n - 1}$

The quantity $(x - \mu)$ or $(x - \bar{x})$ in the basic formulas for variance is called the *deviation* of the x-value from the mean. The sum of the deviations of the x-values from the mean is always zero; that is, $\Sigma(x - \mu) = 0$ and $\Sigma(x - \bar{x}) = 0$.

EXAMPLE: The midterm scores of a sample of four students are 82, 95, 67, and 92. The mean for this sample is 84 ($82 + 95 + 67 + 92 = 336 \div 4 = 84$). Subtracting each score from the mean (deviation of the four scores) is: $82 - 84 = -2$; $95 - 84 = +11$; $67 - 84 = -17$; and $92 - 84 = +8$. Note that the sum of the subtractions $(-2) + (+11) + (-17) + (+8) = 0$.

Computationally, it may be easier and more efficient to use *shortcut formulas* to calculate the variance and standard deviation; the formulas are:

Shortcut Formulas for Variance:

a. Population $\sigma^2 = \dfrac{\Sigma x^2 - \dfrac{(\Sigma x)^2}{N}}{N}$

b. Sample $\Sigma^2 = \dfrac{\Sigma x^2 - \dfrac{(\Sigma x)^2}{N}}{n - 1}$

NOTE: Except for the symbols used, the only difference between calculating population variance and standard deviation is that the denominator for population data is N, and for sample data is n − 1.

EXAMPLES:

EX 1. Basic method of variance and standard deviation calculation using the quiz score data from a previous example—three classes of 10 students each, all with a mean of 6.

Class	Scores	Mean
A	10, 9, 8, 8, 6, 5, 5, 4, 4, 1	6
B	9, 9, 8, 7, 6, 6, 5, 4, 3, 3	6
C	8, 8, 8, 6, 5, 5, 5, 5, 5, 5	6

(Dif is the difference between the mean and the class score—each score subtracted from the mean.)

Class A			Class B			Class C		
$(x-\mu)$	Dif	$(x^2-\mu)$	$(x-\mu)$	Dif	$(x^2-\mu)$	$(x-\mu)$	Dif	$(x^2-\mu)$
10 − 6	4	16	9 − 6	3	9	8 − 6	2	4
9 − 6	3	9	9 − 6	3	9	8 − 6	2	4
8 − 6	2	4	8 − 6	2	4	8 − 6	2	4
8 − 6	2	4	7 − 6	1	1	6 − 6	0	0
6 − 6	0	0	6 − 6	0	0	5 − 6	−1	1
5 − 6	−1	1	6 − 6	0	0	5 − 6	−1	1
5 − 6	−1	1	5 − 6	−1	1	5 − 6	−1	1
4 − 6	−2	4	4 − 6	−2	4	5 − 6	−1	1
4 − 6	−2	4	3 − 6	−3	9	5 − 6	−1	1
1 − 6	−5	<u>25</u>	3 − 6	−3	<u>9</u>	5 − 6	−1	<u>1</u>

Had the results been based on a larger sample, it could be said that the students in Class C are more homogeneous in ability than the students in the other two classes; or that the students in Class A are more heterogeneous than those in either Class B or Class C.

Note: The total deviations above could have been divided by 10 (N) instead of 9 (n − 1). A small grouping of data was used for illustrative purposes only. Most populations will include more than 10 scores in each of the three classes.

Steps in computing variance and standard deviation from ungrouped data:

a. Calculate the mean.

b. Calculate the difference between each score and the mean $(x-\mu)$.

c. Square all the differences $(x-\mu)^2$.

d. Sum all the differences squared $\Sigma(x-\mu)^2$.

e. Divide by N or n − 1 (depending if the data is a population or sample); this calculation results in the variance.

f. To calculate the standard deviation, obtain the square root of the variance.

Reminder: When multiplying one negative number by another negative number, the result is a positive number (−2 times −4 equals $+8$); or the negative sign can be ignored, thus using what is referred to as the *absolute value*.

EX 2. Shortcut formulas for variance and standard deviation calculation (in ungrouped data) using the same data in the example above—three classes, 10 quiz scores for each class.

Note: To use the formula, it is important to remember there is a difference between $\Sigma(x^2)$ and (Σx^2). In the first instance, each *score* is squared (multiplied by itself), and then a total is determined. In the second case, all the scores in the data set are totaled, and then the *total* is squared.

To calculate $(\Sigma x)^2/N$: The total of all 10 scores in each of the three classes was 60; therefore, $(\Sigma 60)^2 = 3{,}600$. The $(\Sigma x)^2$ $(3{,}600)$ divided by $N(10) = 360$ for all three classes.

To calculate Σx^2: Each score (in each class) must be squared and the result totaled:

Class A	Class B	Class C
x^2	x^2	x^2
100	81	64
81	81	64
64	64	64
64	49	36
36	36	25
25	36	25
25	25	25
16	16	25
16	9	25
1	9	25
Total: 428	Total: 406	Total: 378

Then, applying the shortcut formula, the numerator for each class is:

$428 - 360 = 68; \quad 406 - 360 = 46; \quad 378 - 360 - 18$

Note: The numerator totals (68, 46, and 18) are identical to the results computed using the basic formula.

Again, each value is divided by 9 ($n - 1$), and the square root is obtained. Had the population formula been used, the divisor in both applications would be 10 ($N = 10$), and the square root would be obtained. In either case, the results derived via the standard (basic method) and the shortcut formula, if computed accurately, will be identical.

Additional Information:

(a) The values of the variance and standard deviation are never negative. In all calculations, the numerator in the shortcut formula should never produce a negative value. If a data set has no variation, then the variance and standard deviation are both zero. If four people in a group are all the same age, there is no variation in age.

(b) The measurement units of variance are always the square of the measurement units of the original data. If data are in thousands of dollars, then the variance and standard deviation are in thousands of dollars.

(c) If the data involve *all* students or employees, the population formula is used; if only a certain number are included, the sample formula is used.

(d) A numerical measure (such as mean, median, mode, range, variance, or standard deviation) calculated for a population data set is called a *population parameter*, or simply a *parameter*. A population mean is called a population parameter.

(e) A summary measure calculated for a sample data set is called a *sample statistic*, or simply a *statistic*. A mean calculated from a sample is a sample statistic.

3. Coefficient of Variation

One disadvantage of the standard deviation as a measure of dispersion is that it is a measure of absolute variability and not of relative variability. Sometimes it becomes necessary to compare the variability of two different data sets that have different units of measurement. Suppose a study is carried out regarding the salaries of all employees in the HIM department. Another study calculates the years of experience for the same HIM employees. A coefficient of variation or relative variation can be determined. The coefficient of variation is defined as the ratio of the standard deviation to the mean, expressed as a percentage.

Formula for Coefficient of Variation:

$$CV = \frac{\text{standard deviation}}{\text{mean}} \times 100 \text{ (or) } \frac{\sigma}{\mu} \times 100 \quad \frac{s}{\bar{x}} \times 100$$

EXAMPLE: The coefficient of variation depicts the size of the standard deviation relative to its mean. The primary use of the coefficient of variation is to compare the relative variation of unrelated quantities. A researcher may desire to know whether the variation of blood glucose readings is greater or less than the variation of serum cholesterol levels. If it was determined that the mean blood glucose reading was 152, the standard deviation for blood glucose was 55, the mean serum cholesterol was 216, and the standard deviation was found to be 39, the coefficient of variation (CV) can be calculated. The coefficient of blood glucose is 36% (55 ÷ 152 equals 0.3618 × 100 = 36%). The coefficient of serum cholesterol is 18% (39 ÷ 216 = 0.1806 × 100 = 18%). The computations indicate that the variation in blood glucose is relatively greater than that for serum cholesterol.

 SELF-TEST 11-7

1. The yearly salaries of all 20 employees of a HIM department has a mean of $30,500 and a standard deviation of $5,000. The 20 employees have a mean of 12 years of experience with a standard deviation of 2 years. Is the relative variation in salaries larger or smaller than that in years of experience for these employees?

2. Two classes of 15 students each were given identical tests. The ranked scores are:

    Class A: 25, 24, 21, 20, 20, 18, 18, 17, 16, 15, 14, 14, 14, 11, 8

    Class B: 20, 19, 19, 19, 18, 17, 17, 15, 15, 15, 15, 14, 14, 12, 11

    Using ungrouped population statistics, calculate:

    a. Mean score for each class.
    b. Median score for each class.
    c. Mode score for each class.
    d. Range for each class.
    e. Variance for each class.
    f. Standard deviation for each class.

4. Variance and Standard Deviation for Grouped Data

The mean has already been calculated from both ungrouped and grouped data. The same can be accomplished in calculating variance and standard deviation. Again, the midpoint of the class interval represents all scores within the interval, and the midpoint is again multiplied by the frequency of the interval.

Basic Formula for Variance for Grouped Data:

a. Population　　　　　b. Sample

$$\sigma^2 = \frac{\Sigma f (m-x)^2}{N} \qquad s^2 = \frac{\Sigma f (m-x)^2}{n-1}$$

Standard Deviation: square root of the variance

EXAMPLE: (computation of variance and standard deviation using the *basic formula*) *A* total of 50 females were diagnosed with breast cancer in the past year. The age, at time of diagnosis, for each patient was recorded. The ages in descending order are as follows:

　　84 82 81 *77* 75 74 74 72 72 71 71 70 70 67 66 66 65 64

　　64 63 63 62 62 61 58 *57* 57 56 56 *55 55 55* 54 53 52 51

　　50 49 48 48 46 44 43 39 38 36 36 34 28 26

A frequency distribution grouping of the ages with an interval size of 5:

Interval	Midpt	f	Midpt × f	$x - \mu$	$(x-\mu)$ $(x-\mu)^2$ (f)
80–84	82	3	246	$82 - 58 = 24$	$576(3) = 1{,}728$
75–79	77	2	154	$77 - 58 = 19$	$361(2) = 722$
70–74	71	8	576	$72 - 58 = 14$	$196(8) = 1{,}568$
65–69	67	4	268	$67 - 58 = 9$	$81(4) = 324$
60–64	62	7	434	$62 - 58 = 4$	$16(7) = 112$
55–59	57	8	456	$57 - 58 = 1$	$1(8) = 8$
50–54	52	5	260	$52 - 58 = 6$	$36(5) = 180$
45–49	47	4	188	$47 - 58 = 11$	$121(4) = 484$
40–44	42	2	84	$42 - 58 = 16$	$256(2) = 512$
35–39	37	4	148	$37 - 58 = 21$	$441(4) - 1{,}764$
30–34	32	1	32	$32 - 58 = 26$	$676(1) = 676$
25–29	27	2	54	$27 - 58 = 31$	$961(2) = 1{,}922$
Totals:					10,000

Mean: $\Sigma\,(\text{midpt} \times f) \div N = 2{,}900 \div 50 = 58$ years of age.

Variance $\Sigma(x - \mu)^2(f) \div N = 10{,}000 \div 50 = 200 = T^2$

Standard deviation: $\sigma = \sqrt{200} = 14.14$ years

Shortcut Formula for Variance for Grouped Data

      a. Population   b. Sample

$$\sigma^2 = \frac{\Sigma m^2 f - \dfrac{(\Sigma m\, b)^2}{N}}{N} \qquad s^2 = \frac{\Sigma m^2 f - \dfrac{(\Sigma m\, b)^2}{n}}{n-1}$$

EXAMPLE: (Computation of variance and standard deviation using the *shortcut* formula; same data as in the previous example.)

NOTE: *m* indicates the midpoint of the interval. Instead of dealing with individual scores, all scores within an interval are assumed to coincide with the midpoint of the interval, as previously mentioned.

Interval	(m)	f	mf	m²	m²f
80–84	82	3	246	6,724	20,172
75–79	77	2	154	5,929	11,858
70–74	72	8	576	5,184	41,472
65–69	67	4	268	4,489	17,956
60–64	62	7	434	3,844	26,908
55–59	57	8	456	3,249	25,992
50–54	52	5	260	2,704	13,520
45–49	47	4	188	2,209	8,836
40–44	42	3	84	1,764	3,528
35–39	37	4	148	1,369	5,476
30–34	32	1	32	1,024	1,024
25–29	27	2	54	729	1,458
Totals: 50					178,200

Formula: $\dfrac{178{,}200 - (2{,}900)^2 / 50}{50}$

$$\frac{(178{,}200 - 8{,}410{,}00)/50}{50}$$

$$\frac{178{,}200 - 168{,}200}{50}$$

$$\frac{10{,}000}{50}$$

$\Sigma^2 = 200 \quad \sigma = \sqrt{200}$

$\sigma = 14.14$ years

Results: Identical to the basic grouped computation—Mean = 58 years of age; Variance = 200; and Standard deviation = 14.14 years.

NOTE: Values of the variance and standard deviation for grouped data are approximations. The exact values of the variance and standard deviation can only be obtained from ungrouped data.

 SELF-TEST 11-8

A group of 80 students took a statistics exam, and the following scores were recorded:

68 84 75 82 68 90 62 88 76 93 73 79 88 73 58 93 71 59 58 51

61 65 75 87 74 62 95 78 63 72 66 96 79 65 74 *77* 95 85 78 86

71 78 78 62 80 67 69 83 76 62 71 75 82 89 67 58 73 74 73 65

81 76 72 75 92 97 57 63 68 83 81 82 53 85 94 52 78 88 *77* 71

Calculate:

a. Range.
b. Mean exam score.
c. Median exam score.
d. Mode exam score.
e. Variance and standard deviation from a grouped distribution with the lowest score interval limits of 50–54.

5. Uses of Standard Deviation

By using the mean and standard deviation, the proportion or percentage of the total scores (observations) that fall within a given interval about the mean can be determined.

a. Empirical Rule

In a normal, bell-shaped curve, a certain proportion of scores fall within a designated standard deviation from the mean. In the diagram, area A encompasses all scores that lie within one standard deviation from the mean. The baseline numbers indicate the standard deviation, and the numbers in the sections labeled, A, B, and C indicate the percent of scores that fall within each standard deviation. As indicated, 68.26% of scores fall in each area marked A, which is one standard deviation of the mean (−1 SD to +1 SD). Also, in a normal curve, approximately 95% of scores fall within two standard deviations (−2 SD to +2 SD), and 99% lie within three standard deviation (−3 SD to +3 SD). The relationship percentages related to the normal, bell-shaped curve is called the *empirical rule* and only applies to a normal curve.

Normal Bell-Shaped Curve

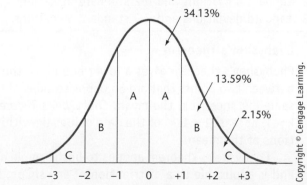

A frequency distribution of measured variables—such as blood pressure, respiratory rate, pulse rate, and height—when plotted, generally take the shape of a normal distribution.

Normal distribution features include the following:

(1) Shape. The distribution has the appearance of a symmetrical, bell-shaped curve as in the diagram. However, not every bell-shaped curve is a normal distribution—refer to the other symmetrical curves shown in a previous section.

(2) Area under the curve. As seen in the diagram, the area under established markers (standard deviation intervals) is always the same.

(3) The distribution is defined by the mean and standard deviation.

EXAMPLES:

EX 1. According to the National Center for Health Statistics, the average height of a white male in the United States is 5 feet 9.5 inches (69.5 inches) with a standard deviation (SD) of 2.8 inches. Therefore, a white male 6 feet 5 inches (77 inches) in height is in the 99th percentile.

EX 2. An age distribution data set has a sample of 5,000 people. The mean of the distribution is 40 years, and the standard deviation is 12. Therefore, we know approximately 68% of people are between the ages of 28 and 52 (40 − 12 and 40 + 12); also, 95% are between the ages of 16 and 64 (28 − 12 and 52 + 12).

 SELF-TEST 11-9

1. If the prices of all college textbooks follow a bell-shaped distribution and the mean price is $105 with a standard deviation of $20, using the empirical rule, find the percentage of all college textbooks with a price between:
   a. $85 and $125.
   b. $65 and $145.

2. A total of 1,000 patients in a fitness study were tested for serum cholesterol. The results indicated a mean of 216.96 milligrams per cent and standard deviation of 38.82 milligrams per cent. Indicate the values for the following:
   a. −1 standard deviation and +1 standard deviation.
   b. −2 standard deviations and +2 standard deviations.
   c. −3 standard deviations and +3 standard deviations.

b. Chebyshev's Theorem

Chebyshev's theorem gives a lower bound for the area under a curve between two points that are on opposite sides of the mean and at the same distance from the mean. *Chebyshev's Theorem:* For any number $k > 1$, at least $1 - 1/k^2$ of the data values lie within k standard deviations of the mean.

Chebyshev's theorem applies to both sample and population data and is applicable to a distribution of any shape, but only for $k > 1$.

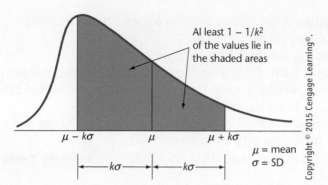

Al least $1 - 1/k^2$ of the values lie in the shaded areas

$\mu - k\sigma$ μ $\mu + k\sigma$

$\leftarrow k\sigma \rightarrow | \leftarrow k\sigma \rightarrow$

μ = mean
σ = SD

EXAMPLE:

1. If $k = 2$, then the formula reads:
   $1 - 1/k^2 = 1 - 1/2^2 = 1 - 1/4 = 1 - 0.25 = 0.75$ or 75%

2. If $k = 3$, then the formula reads:
   $1 - 1/k^2 = 1 - 1/3^2 = 1 - 1/9 = 1 - 0.11 = 0.89$ or approximately 89% indicating at least 89% of the values lie within three standard deviations of the mean.

3. The average systolic blood pressure for 4,000 women, screened for hypertension, was found to be 187 mm Hg with a standard deviation of 22. Using Chebyshev's theorem, $\mu = 187$ and $\sigma = 22$. If asked to find the percentage of women with a systolic blood pressure between 143 and 231 mm Hg, the first step is to determine k. The value of k is obtained by dividing the distance between the mean and each point by the SD. Therefore, $187 - 143 = 44$; likewise, $231 - 187 = 44$ (each point lies 44 units from the mean). Dividing 44 by 22 (SD) $= 2 = k$. Using the formula above:

   $$1 - 1/k^2 - 1 - 1/2^2 = 1 - 1/4 = 1 - 0.25 = 0.75 \text{ or } 75\%$$

   According to Chebyshev's theorem, at least 75% of women in the study have a systolic blood pressure between 143 and 231 mm Hg.

 SELF-TEST 11-10

The mean monthly mortgage payment for homeowners in the local community was $2,365, and the standard deviation was $340. Using Chebyshev's theorem, calculate the percentage of homeowners in this town who pay between $1,685 and $3,045.

D. SUMMARY

1. The mean (arithmetic), median, and mode are referred to as measures of central tendency—they tend to lie near the center of a data set. Although the term *average* is often associated with them, only the arithmetic mean is a true average.
2. The (arithmetic) mean is the arithmetic average of the distribution.
3. A weighted mean is used if certain components are more significant than others.
4. A mean can be computed from ungrouped or grouped data; grouped data employ the midpoint of an interval as the representative value for each score in the interval.

5. The median is the middle score in a data set when scores are arranged in order of magnitude.
6. The mode is the most frequently occurring score.
7. A trimmed mean drops a small percentage of scores (outliers) from both ends of a distribution and then calculates the mean from the remaining scores. (Outliers are extreme values.)
8. A combined mean computes the mean when the means and sample sizes of two or more data sets are known.
9. Certain types of data are best represented by different measures of central tendency:
    a. Skewed distribution—median
    b. Nominal scores—mode
    c. Ordinal scores—median
    d. Interval scores—mean
10. A frequency distribution can be plotted as a curve. Curves may be symmetrical or skewed. The bell-shaped curve, also called a normal curve, is the ideal.
11. Skewed curves are referred to as skewed to the right (positive skewness) or skewed to the left (negative skewness).
12. Skewed distributions affect measures of central tendency, moving the mean in the direction of the skewness and moving the median between the mean and the mode.
13. Measures of dispersion (variation) include the range, variance, and standard deviation.
14. The range is the difference between the largest value and the smallest value, and has limited use in describing a distribution.
15. Variance and standard deviation consider all values in a data set; Variance is the sum of the squared differences of each score in a distribution from the mean divided by N for population statistics and divided by $n - 1$ for sample statistics.
16. Standard deviation is the square root of the variance of all scores in the distribution.
17. The coefficient of variation is the ratio of the standard deviation to the mean, expressed as a percentage.
18. Variance and standard deviation can be calculated from either ungrouped or grouped data; with grouped data, the scores within an interval are represented by the midpoint of the interval.
19. The empirical rule applies to a normal, bell-shaped curve (distribution) and indicates the percentage of scores that lie within each standard deviation from the mean; within ± 1 SD $= 68\%$; ± 2 SDs $= 95\%$; and ± 3 SDs $= 99.7\%$.
20. Chebyshev's theorem applies to both sample and population data and gives a lower bound for the area under a curve between two points on opposite sides of the mean and at the same distance from the mean, for any number if $k > 1$.

Name _____ Date _____

E. CHAPTER 11 TEST

1. Select the best or most representative measure of central tendency for the following:

    a. Bell-shaped distribution of interval data.
    b. A positively skewed distribution of interval data.
    c. A distribution of coded, nominal data.
    d. Middle measure of central tendency in a skewed distribution.
    e. Measure whose value is the highest in a negatively skewed distribution.

2. A patient's reaction time to certain stimuli was tested by a psychologist. The times were: 0.53, 0.46, 0.50, 0.49, 0.52, 0.53, 0.44, and 0.55 seconds. Calculate the mean reaction time.

3. Three instructors of medical terminology reported mean grades of 75, 83, and 80. The classes consisted of 32, 25, and 17 students, respectively. Calculate the mean grade for the combined classes.

4. An index is to be computed using the following weighted scores: resting diastolic blood pressure, 3; resting heart rate, 2; serum cholesterol, 1. Weekly readings were taken, and the averages were recorded as: diastolic pressure, 82; heart rate, 62; cholesterol, 164. Calculate the weighted mean.

5. Forty children, under the age of 5 years, were diagnosed with acute lymphoblastic leukemia (ALL) during the past year. The age of each child was recorded (in months) at the time of diagnosis. Listed are the ages from youngest to oldest: 13, 15, 16, 18, 18, 20, 21, 23, 24, 24, 25, 25, 27, 28, 30, 32, 32, 32, 34, 36, 37, 38, 40, 40, 41, 42, 44, 45, 45, 47, 48, 48, 49, 50, 52, 53, 55, 57, 58, 58.

    Calculate:

    a. Range.
    b. Mode.
    c. Median.
    d. Mean from an ungrouped distribution.
    e. Mean from a grouped distribution, correct to the nearest whole number, with the lowest interval, 11–15.
    f. Variance from a grouped distribution, with the lowest interval, 11–15, using the grouped mean correct to the nearest whole number.
    g. Standard deviation from a grouped distribution, with the lowest interval, 11–15.

6. Thirty patients were tested for systolic blood pressure in a heart study at the local hospital. The readings, in mm of mercury, were as follows:

    102 112 116 118 166 138 146 143 157 128 152 136 134 120 118

    134 126 118 154 186 134 108 178 110 176 134 130 122 138 116

    Calculate:

    a. Range.
    b. Mode.
    c. Median.
    d. Mean from an ungrouped distribution.
    e. Mean from a grouped distribution with the lowest interval, 100–109.
    f. Variance from the grouped distribution, using the decimal value of the grouped mean, with the lowest interval, 100–109.
    g. Standard deviation from the grouped distribution.

7. The same 30 patients (from question 6) had their weight recorded in kilograms. Weights in ascending order:

   47 51 55 56 56 59 59 59 60 61 62 62 64 65 66 66 66 66

   66 66 70 70 71 73 73 75 75 80 83 91

   Calculate:

   a. Mode.
   b. Median.
   c. Mean from the ungrouped distribution.
   d. Mean from a grouped distribution with the lowest interval, 45–49, correct to the nearest whole number.
   e. Variance from the grouped distribution, using the grouped mean correct to the nearest whole number, with the lowest interval, 40–49.
   f. Standard deviation from the grouped distribution.

8. Calculate the coefficient of variation for questions 6 and 7. Which frequency distribution has the greater relative variation—systolic blood pressure or weight?

9. The recorded lengths of stay for patients with a coded diagnosis for either poisoning or burns is listed in descending order:

   25 22 18 17 16 14 14 13 13 12 11 11 10 10 10 9 9 9 9 8

   8 8 8 7 7 7 7 7 6 6 6 6 6 6 5 5 5 5 4 4 4

   4 3 3 3 3 3 2 2 2 2 2 2 1 1 1 1 1 1 1 1

   Calculate:

   a. Mode.
   b. Median.
   c. Mean from the ungrouped distribution.
   d. Variance from the ungrouped distribution.
   e. Standard deviation from the ungrouped distribution.
   f. Is the distribution skewed to the right or to the left?

10. During the past year 40 females were diagnosed with breast cancer. The age of each patient, at the time of diagnosis, was recorded. The ages in descending order are as follows:

    81 79 78 76 75 74 73 72 69 68 67 66 64 64 63 62 61 59 58 58

    58 57 56 55 54 53 52 49 48 47 46 44 43 41 39 39 38 34 32 28

    Calculate:

    a. Mode.
    b. Median.
    c. Mean from an ungrouped distribution.
    d. Mean from a grouped distribution, correct to the nearest whole number, with the lowest interval, 25–29.
    e. Variance from the ungrouped distribution using the ungrouped mean to the nearest whole number, with the lowest interval, 25–29.
    f. Standard deviation from the grouped distribution, with the lowest interval, 25–29, correct to the nearest whole number.
    g. Value for −1 SD and +1 SD and −2 SD and +2 SD, using the whole number value for the mean and SD.
    h. Actual percentage of cases that fall within one standard deviation of the mean; the percentage that normally fall within one standard deviation of the mean according to the empirical rule.

12

Organizing Data for Analysis

CHAPTER OUTLINE

LEARNING OBJECTIVES

After studying this chapter, the learner should be able to:

✓ Construct a frequency distribution for qualitative data.

✓ Determine the relative frequency for quantitative data.

✓ Determine the cumulative frequency for quantitative data.

✓ Construct a frequency distribution for quantitative data.

✓ Determine score limits and intervals for frequency distributions.

✓ Explain the difference between rankings made in percentiles, deciles, and quartiles.

✓ Compute values within percentiles.

✓ Calculate percentile ranks for scores.

PRELIMINARY QUESTIONS

1. A group of 80 students took a statistics exam, and the following scores were recorded:

68 84 75 82 68 90 62 88 76 93 73 79 88 73 60 93 71 59 85 75
61 65 75 87 74 62 95 78 63 72 66 96 79 65 74 77 95 85 78 86
71 78 78 62 80 67 69 60 76 62 71 75 82 89 67 73 73 74 79 65
81 76 72 75 61 97 57 63 68 83 76 75 53 85 94 75 78 88 77 60

   a. Determine: (1) Highest score _____; (2) Lowest score _____; (3) Range _____
   b. Rank the scores from high to low, listing each score only once and placing a tally mark beside each score.
   c. Determine: (1) Most frequently occurring score _____; (2) Middle score _____; (3) Percentage of scores 90 or higher _____; (4) Percent less than 65 _____; (5) Percent from 80 to 89 _____; (6) 70–79 _____; (7) 60–69 _____; (8) below 60 _____

2. Would you expect a score of 85 to fall above or below the 85th percentile? _____ Would you expect a score of 70 to fall above or below the 60th percentile? _____

3. What is the average of all scores? _____

4. Using the grouped array of scores below, complete the tally and frequency columns.

Scores	Tally	Frequency	Scores	Tally	Frequency
95–99			70–74		
90–94			65–69		
85–89			60–64		
80–84			55–59		
75–79			50–54		

When data are collected, the information obtained from each member of the population or sample is recorded in the sequence as obtained. These data have no order, are unranked and un-grouped, and are referred to as *raw data*. However, analyzing the data in a meaningful manner facilitates drawing interpretations from the data. This chapter will focus on a variety of methods used in organizing and displaying data.

A. TABLES

Data are most frequently displayed in tabular form. Charts and graphs are another frequently used method to display data; however, a data table most often is the basis for a graphic representation. Tables are used to present large amounts of text-based quantitative data via a matrix of columns and rows with associated headings and labels to identify the data. Tables allow a user or an audience to easily compare quantitative values with similar qualitative values. A well-designed table allows the reader to quickly identify similarities, differences, and trends that the table represents.

Tables can range from simple to complex. A simple format is more effective if the table is to be used for a presentation at a meeting or a conference. A complex table, presented on such an occasion, may result in the audience's concentration focusing on attempting to understand the table rather than on the point the presenter is trying to make. If, however, a presenter needs to present a large amount of data in a minimal amount of space, a more complex and well-designed table may be more effective. This text will focus on developing simple tables, though the design process is the same whether the table is simple or complex. A table should be self-explanatory. If a table were removed from its accompanying text, it should still convey all the information necessary for the reader to clearly understand the table.

1. Basic Table Format

TABLE 12.1 Basic Table Format

Stub (Series)	Column/Category	Column/Category	Column/Category
Heading _____	Heading _____	Heading _____	Heading _____
Stub	Cell (Data)	Cell (Data)	Cell (Data)
Stub	Cell (Data)	Cell (Data)	Cell (Data)
Stub _____	Cell (Data) _____	Cell (Data) _____	Cell (Data) _____
Total:			

2. Table Elements

a. Table Number

Not all tables require a table number. A table number (such as Table 1 or Table 11.1) is used to aid the reader in accessing the data.

b. Table Title

A table title is an important component of a table. A well-written title should clearly answer the following questions:

(1) What do the data represent? Do the data represent annual hospital discharges, annual death rates by disease category, or newly diagnosed cancers for the year?

(2) What is the source of the data? Were the data collected at Mountain View Medical Center or the State Health Department, or were they compiled from regional tumor registries?

(3) When were the data collected? What time period is represented? The time period is most commonly reported by data, such as 2012 or July through December 2012.

    In addition, codes, abbreviations, acronyms, or symbols should be avoided in the table title as these might be misinterpreted by the reader, particularly if the audience is unfamiliar with the codes, abbreviations, acronyms, or symbols.

    Generally, it is best to avoid their use even with a professional audience. If their use is unavoidable, it is important to provide an explanatory footnote.

c. Table Headings

(1) Stub (series) heading. A stub (series) heading is the heading of the first column and indicates how the data were interpreted. This could be months of the year, ages, sex of participants, or score limits of a frequency distribution.

(2) Column/category headings. These are the subheadings related to the stub heading. Each heading should clearly state what is being displayed.

Again, it is best to avoid codes, abbreviations, acronyms, or symbols when labeling the data to prevent misinterpretation.

d. Table Cells (Data)

The appropriate data elements are entered in the table under the appropriate heading.

e. Additional Information

(1) Footnote. If codes, abbreviations, acronyms, or symbols are unavoidable, an explanatory footnote should be included.

(2) Units of Measure. Units of measure (pounds or grams, ages in months or years) should be documented to prevent misinterpretation of the data presented.

(3) Totals. Totaling data in rows and columns often provides a simple method of cross-checking the accuracy in a table. If percentages are used, it is recommended they be presented as whole numbers and the total (100%) indicated.

NOTES

3. Designing a Table

Listed below are some guidelines in designing a table:

a. Determine table contents. Before creating a table, a presenter needs to decide what data should be presented and how it should be presented.

b. Create the table title.

c. Label the headings—stub (series) and column/category.

d. Enter and align the data in the appropriate cells. Proper data alignment makes a table easier and more appealing to read. There are different standards for text and numbers:

(1) Text. Text can be right-justified, left-justified, or centered, depending on how the table is formatted.

(2) Numbers. Numbers should be aligned in relation to the decimal place. Whole numbers most often are right justified, but decimal numbers must be aligned by the decimal point and have the same number of decimal places.

EXAMPLES:

TABLE 12.2 Monthly Percentage of Occupancy General Hospital 2011–2012

Month	2011	2012
January	85	78
February	87	82
March	82	85
April	79	86
May	75	80
June	70	77
July	75	72
August	78	70
September	80	75
October	82	72
November	85	80

TABLE 12.3 Percent of Cigarette Smokers 18 Years of Age or Older in the United States by Decade

	1970	1980	1990	2000
All persons	42.4	37.1	30.1	24.7
All males	51.9	43.1	32.6	27.0
All females	34.0	32.5	28.2	22.8

TABLE 12.4 Percent of Current Cigarette Smokers 18 Years of Age or Older in the United States, 2000

Males				Females		
Ages	All	White	Black	All	White	Black
18–24	27.8	28.4	14.6	21.8	24.9	8.8
25–34	29.5	29.9	25.1	26.4	27.3	26.7
35–44	31.5	31.2	36.3	27.1	27.0	31.9
45–64	27.1	26.3	33.9	24.0	24.0	27.5
65	14.9	14.1	28.5	11.5	11.7	13.3

Copyright© 2015 Cengage Learning®.

TABLE 12.5 Annual Hospital Discharges by Third-Party Payer and Hospital Service Anytown Hospital, Anytown, USA, 20XX

Hospital Service	Government		Private		
	Medicaid	Medicare	MCO	Other	Totals
Medicine	1,098	890	1,113	345	3,446
Obstetrics	1,145	234	488	765	2,632
Orthopedics	1,234	675	932	789	3,630
Pediatrics	1,212	10	799	234	2,255
Surgery	543	765	911	345	2,564
Totals	5,232	2,574	4,243	2,478	14,527

Copyright© 2015 Cengage Learning®.

B. FREQUENCY DISTRIBUTIONS FOR QUALITATIVE DATA

A frequency distribution for *qualitative* data lists all categories and the number of elements (scores) that belong in each category. The term *frequency* refers to the number of times the score appears in the array. When done manually, tally marks are recorded for each score in the array, and the total tally marks becomes the frequency for each class or category. The fifth score when tallying is noted by a slash mark through the first four scores to more easily sum the total of all scores.

EXAMPLE: The 30 employees in a health information management department were asked how stressful their jobs were. The employees' response choices were: *very* stressful, *somewhat* stressful, and *not* stressful. The results are as follows:

somewhat	not	somewhat	very	very	not
very	somewhat	somewhat	very	somewhat	somewhat
somewhat	very	very	somewhat	not	somewhat
very	somewhat	not	very	not	somewhat
somewhat	very	somewhat	somewhat	very	not

Frequency Distribution
Job Stress in the HIM Department

Stress on Job	Tally	Frequency (f)
Very	//// ////	10
Somewhat	//// //// ////	14
Not	//// /	6

To determine *relative frequency*, divide the frequency by the sum of all frequencies (total scores in the distribution). In the example, the relative frequency for the "very stressful" category is 10 divided by 30, and so forth. To calculate *frequency percentage*, each relative frequency is multiplied by 100. (The "very stressful" relative frequency (0.333) multiplied by 100 equals 33.3%.)

Ungrouped Frequency Distribution. An ungrouped distribution consists of raw data or a listing of scores from high to low or low to high.

Grouped Frequency Distribution. When a large number of scores are obtained, it becomes necessary to group and tally scores to facilitate analysis of the data. In scanning the data, it is often noted that several scores are identical, and these scores can be grouped under a single heading—that is, all students who scored 92 on an exam are placed under the same heading. In addition, with large distributions, it often becomes necessary to group several *different* scores—for example, combining scores of 80, 81, and 82 into the same interval. Combining scores within a distribution results in a grouped frequency distribution. However, most statistics texts state that a grouped distribution must include a grouping of two or more *different* scores.

Grouping data has been facilitated with the aid of high-speed computers, and data are easily sorted by many software packages available for personal computers (PCs), including Microsoft Excel.

Although the grouping process generally destroys much of the original detail of the data, it is often the most effective way to handle a large array of data and still obtain a clear overall picture of the obtained data and the vital relationship made evident by those data.

When the number of different scores exceeds a certain number, say 25, it is generally conceded that consolidation of scores becomes desirable. There are two main reasons for classifying data into a grouped frequency distribution:

5. Bring order to chaos. Listing scores according to size reduces the disorganization present in the original array of data.
6. Condense data to a more readily grouped form—more concise and useful.

Scores are generally listed from the highest score to the lowest score in the distribution, but occasionally the reverse is correct, especially if a low score is better than a high score.

Relative Frequency and Percentage Frequency
HIM Department Job Stress

Stress on Job	Relative Frequency	Frequency Percentage
Very	10/30 = 0.333	0.333 (100) = 33.3%
Somewhat	14/30 = 0.467	0.467 (100) = 46.7%
Not	6/30 = 0.200	0.200 (100) = 20.0%

Note: *The sum of all relative frequencies should always add up to 1.00.*
The sum of all frequency percentages should always add up to 100.

 SELF-TEST 12-1

1. A group of 25 people signed up for a weight-loss class. All participants were
    asked why they wanted to lose weight. The choices were H (health reasons),
    C (cosmetic reasons), or O (other). The results were as follows:

    H H C H O C C H C OO H C H H C H H O H H O C H C

    Construct a frequency distribution to include a frequency column, relative
    frequency column, and frequency percentage column.

2. Twenty pediatric patients were asked if they live with both parents (B), their
    mother only (M), their father only (F), or someone else (S). The responses
    were as follows:

    M B B M F S B M F M B F B M M B B F B M

    Construct a frequency distribution table to include a frequency column, a rela-
    tive frequency column, and frequency percentage column for all categories.

C. FREQUENCY DISTRIBUTIONS FOR QUANTITATIVE DATA

A frequency distribution for *quantitative* data is similar to that for qualitative data.

1. Terms

There are several terms associated with a grouped frequency distribution.

a. Range

The range is the interval spanned by the data. It is computed by
finding the difference between the largest score in the distribution
and the smallest. If the highest score is 108 and the lowest score is
18, the *range* is 90 (108 − 18 = 90).

b. Class

A class is a category into which a score can be placed. It is a single
score in a small distribution and a grouping of scores in a grouped
distribution; it is an interval that includes all the values that fall
within two numbers, the lower and upper limits. For instance, one
class could include all heights from 60 to 64 inches, the next class
would include heights from 65 to 69 inches, and so on. Each one of
these is called a *class interval*.

EXAMPLE: On a final exam, the student scores ranged from a high of 100 down to a low of 56; therefore, the *range* is 44. If it were decided to subdivide the range by 15, three different scores would be included in each interval (the range, 44, divided by 15 yields 3 scores per interval). The lowest interval could include the scores of 56–57–58, in which case the uppermost interval would include all scores of 98–99–100.

Usually the number of classes for a frequency distribution varies from 5 to 20, depending mainly on the data in the data set. The greater the size of the data, generally, the more classes established.

c. **Class Width**

It is preferable to have the same width for all classes, though there are instances when classes of different sizes are used. For all the exercises in this text, equal class sizes will be assumed.

To approximate class width, divide the range by the number of classes desired. (Refer to the previous example in which the number of classes chosen was 15.) This calculation will approximate the class width for the distribution.

The more detailed the interpretation one needs, the smaller the class interval width should be; and as the interval size increases, the more that detail is lost. If high descriptive precision is needed or desired, if fluctuations in frequency over small parts of the range are to be studied, and if the number of scores tabulated is large enough to permit such detailed study, then the interval should be small. If just a very rough picture of the distribution of scores is needed, a very broad interval may be quite satisfactory.

d. **Class Limits**

Each class will have a *lower limit* and an *upper limit*. Any convenient number, equal to or less than the smallest value in the data set, can be used to set the lower limit for the first class. The class width determines the *upper* limit. The class limits are set in sequence until all scores are included.

EXAMPLE: A health care facility decides to track the number of daily requests received, for a period of one month, from former patients requesting a copy of their health record. The totals are recorded as:

8   25 11 15 29 22 10 5   17 21 22 13 26 16 18 12 9
26 20 16 23 14 19 23 20 16 27 16 21 14

The minimum value is 5, and the maximum value is 29. A decision is made to group the data into five classes of equal width. The range, 24 (29 − 5 = 24), is divided by 5, resulting in a class width of 4.8 scores, which rounds to 5 scores.

Should 5 be chosen as the lower limit of the first class, the class limits are: 5–9, 10–14, 15–19, 20–24, 25–29.

A frequency table reads:

Monthly Requests for Records: Requests, Tally, Frequency

Requests	Tally	Frequency
25–29	////	5
20–24	//// ///	8
15–19	//// ///	8
10–14	/////	6
5–9	///	3

e. Class Boundaries

The class boundaries of a frequency distribution are recorded in decimal values. The class boundary is the midpoint of the upper limit of one class and the lower limit of the next class. Class boundaries are therefore 0.5 below the lower-class limit to less than 0.5 (most commonly written 0.4) above the upper-class limit of each interval. When measuring heights, a person recorded as 5 feet 6 inches tall lies between 5 feet 5.5 inches and below 5 feet 6.5 inches in height. A class interval limit of 60 to 64 inches theoretically includes all measurements from 59.50 inches up to, but not including, 64.50 inches (often recorded as 64.49 inches). These decimal numbers represent the class boundaries. Again, the smaller number is the *lower-class boundary,* and the larger number the *upper-class boundary.* Class boundaries are also referred to as real or actual class limits or true class limits.

f. Class Midpoint

The class midpoint is obtained by dividing the sum of the two limits (or the two boundaries of a class) by 2.

In the frequency table, the class limits of the lowest interval (5–9) has class boundaries of 4.5 to less than 9.5. The class midpoint is 7 ($5 + 9 = 14$ divided by $2 = 7$).

g. Relative Frequency and Percentage

The relative frequencies and percentages for quantitative data are calculated similarly as for qualitative data. To calculate the relative frequency for a class, divide the frequency (f) for that class by the sum of all frequencies (total scores in the distribution). The percentage is determined by multiplying the relative frequency by 100.

EXAMPLE: Using the data in the previous example the table would read:

Monthly Requests for Records: Requests, Class Boundaries, Relative Frequency, Percentage

Requests	Class Boundaries	Relative Frequency	Percentage
25–29	24.5 to less than 29.5 (29.4)	5/30 = 0.167	16.7
20–24	19.5 to less than 24.5 (24.4)	8/30 = 0.267	26.7

Requests	Class Boundaries	Relative Frequency	Percentage
15–19	14.5 to less than 19.5 (19.4)	8/30 = 0.267	26.7
10–14	9.5 to less than 14.5 (14.4)	6/30 = 0.200	20
5–9	4.5 to less than 9.5 (9.4)	3/30 = 0.100	10

Using this table, it can be noted that the number of requests totaled 10 or more in that month 90% of the time.

h. Cumulative Frequency

The cumulative frequency is the sum of the frequencies, starting at the lowest interval and including the frequencies within that interval. This column is prepared by adding in successive class frequencies from the bottom to the top. The entry opposite the lowest interval is the frequency in that interval; the entry opposite the second interval is the sum of the frequencies in the first and second intervals; the entry opposite the third interval is the sum of the frequencies in the first, second, and third intervals; and so on. The entry opposite the top interval equals the total number (N) in the distribution. Cumulating frequencies is most commonly done from bottom to top, but it is also possible to cumulate from the top downward.

EXAMPLE: Listed are the final test scores for 100 students at Studious State University (Table 2.6). The recorded scores are as follows:

```
58 68 73 61 66 96 79 65 86 69 94 84 79 80 65 78 78 62
80 67 74 97 75 88 75 82 77 89 67 73 73 83 82 82 73 87
75 61 97 74 57 81 81 69 68 60 74 94 75 78 88 72 75 88
85 90 93 62 77 95 85 78 63 94 92 71 62 71 95 69 60 76
62 76 84 92 88 59 60 78 74 79 65 76 75 92 84 76 85 63
68 72 83 71 53 85 96 95 93 75
```

Highest score = 97; lowest score = 53; range = 44 (97 − 53 = 44)

Ranked Listing:

```
97 97 96 96 95 95 95 94 94 94 93 93 92 92 92 90 89
89 88 88 88 88 87 86 85 85 85 85 84 84 84 83 83 82
82 82 81 81 80 80 79 79 78 78 78 78 78 77 77 76 76
76 76 75 75 75 75 75 75 75 74 74 74 74 73 73 73 73
72 72 71 71 71 69 69 69 68 68 68 67 67 66 65 65 65
63 63 62 62 62 62 61 61 60 60 60 59 58 57 53
```

Grouping the data into a table with a class size of 3 is shown below:

TABLE 12.6 Frequency Table of Final Scores: Elementary Statistics Studious State University Spring, 20xx

Score Limits	Tally	Frequency (f)	Cumulative Frequency (cf)
96–98	////	4	100
93–95	//////	8	96
90–92	////	4	88
87–89	/////	6	84
84–86	//////	8	78
81–83	//////	7	70
78–80	/////	10	63
75–77	////////	13	53
72–74	/////	10	40
69–71	/////	6	30
66–68	/////	6	24
63–65	////	5	18
60–62	/////////	9	13
57–59	///	3	4
54–56		0	1
51–53	/	1	1

 SELF-TEST 12-2

The following are the scores of 30 students on a statistics test:

75 52 80 96 65 79 71 87 93 95 69 72 81 61 7686 79 68 50
92 83 84 77 64 71 87 72 92 57 98

a. Determine the range.
b. Set up the distribution using 10 classes with 50 as the lower limit of the first interval, including a column for each of the following:

(1) Class limits
(2) Class boundaries
(3) Tallies
(4) Frequency
(5) Cumulative frequency
(6) Relative frequency

2. Frequency Distribution Table

A table of the data in a frequency distribution generally includes a score column and a frequency column. A cumulative frequency column may also be added.

When data are grouped with a class interval size of 2 or greater, remember a score can only be listed in one interval. It is inappropriate to have class limits of 5–10, 10–15, 15–20, and so forth, since some data—such as the numbers 10 and 15—can be placed in either two classes. Therefore, the limits should have read 5–9, 10–14, 15–19, and so forth.

Listed are some reminders to facilitate frequency distribution design:

(a) The number of classes should generally be from 5 to 15.
(b) Include all scores in the distribution—the entire range.
(c) Each data entry should fall into only one category.
(d) An equal class size is preferred.

Limits of 1–5, 6–10, 11–15, indicate a class interval size of 5.
Limits of 1–5, 6–8, 9–15 indicate unequal interval sizes.

3. General Rules for Creating a Frequency Distribution

(a) Determine range.

Occasionally it may be helpful to sort the scores from high to low or from low to high.

(b) Establish the number of class intervals.

For most types of data, it is commonly recommended that the number of class intervals be at least 5 but no more than 20. Many statistical texts state that around 15 is the preferred average. However, the number is only a rule of thumb, and the number must be based on the data and the interpretations to be drawn from these data.

Although grouped data can account for a grouping error, the error is generally regarded to be so small or negligible that it can be ignored unless an interval size results in a very small number of classes—say, below 10. Therefore, 15 class intervals seem to be a good compromise for an overall choice. Some data require more class intervals, and other data can be condensed without being affected by grouping error.

(c) Set class limits.

There is no universal rule governing the setting of class limits. Some common methods are included, but it should be remembered that these are suggestions and that the limits should be representative of the grouped data. Some statisticians recommend setting limits by beginning with the lowest interval, and others recommend starting at the top interval.

(1) Suggested methods include the following:
    (a) *Lower limit is a multiple of interval size.* A rather common method of setting the lower limit is to make the lower limit a multiple of the interval size. If the lowest score in a distribution is 19 and the interval size is determined

to be three, the lower score limit of the lowest interval would be 18 and the upper score limit 20.

(b) *Multiple of highest score appears as the middle score of the interval.* In this method, a multiple of the highest score is found, and this multiple should be the middle score of the interval. If the highest score is 178 and the interval size is three, the multiple computes to 177. In setting the score limits, the limits would read 176–178.

(2) Departures from convention: The practice of beginning a class interval as a multiple of class size or making the middle score of the uppermost interval a multiple of the highest score is a rule of thumb. There are instances when setting other limits is more beneficial and grouping is facilitated by choosing other limits. It is much easier to group large numbers of scores in multiples of 5 or 10. Score limits of 35–39 or 30–39 are much easier to work with than limits of 32–36 or 28–37. Therefore, limits are often set by considering all the factors that facilitate construction of the distribution and yet are representative of scores in the distribution. A little thought is required when setting class limits. However, in abandoning the rule, it is also possible that a bias can occur if the scores are not equally representative of the midpoint of the interval because the midpoint is used in making computations from grouped data. However, these errors will *not* be addressed in this text, and the reader is referred to a more comprehensive statistics text for further analysis.

EXAMPLE:
TABLE 12.7 Frequency Table Congestive Heart Failure Age at Initial Diagnosis of Helpful Hospital, 20xx

Age Range	f	cf	%f	%cf
85	3	80	3.75	100.00
80–84	7	77	8.75	96.25
75–79	8	70	10.00	87.50
70–74	11	62	13.75	77.50
65–69	15	51	18.75	63.75
60–64	13	36	16.25	45.00
55–59	7	23	8.75	28.75
50–54	5	16	6.25	20.00
45–49	4	11	5.00	13.75
40–44	2	7	2.50	8.75
35–39	2	5	2.50	6.25
30–34	1	3	1.25	3.75
25–29	2	2	2.50	2.50

4. Rules for Subsequent Computations

For the sake of maintaining consistency among the computations that follow, the following rules will apply:

(a) Desired number of class intervals: 15 (or between 12 and 20)

(b) Preferred class sizes: 1, 2, 3, 5, 7, 10, 15 (or any higher multiple of 5)

(c) Setting lower limits. Determine the class size. If the class size is an

 (1) *Odd* number: Find a multiple of this number nearest to the lowest score in the distribution. This multiple should be the lowest score in the interval. Other limits will be determined automatically from this.

 (2) *Even* number: Find a multiple of this number, and set the lower limit as a multiple of this number.

> **EXAMPLE:** If the scores in a distribution ranged from a high of 109 to a low of 18, the range would be 90. To find the number of intervals, the range is divided by 15 to approximate the number of scores to be grouped within each class for a distribution of approximately 15 intervals. Dividing 90 by 15 results in a class size of 6 (90/15 = 6). However, 6 is not a preferred class size, so 5 or 7 would more likely be used. Using 7 as the class size, the lower limit of the lowest class would be 14, a multiple of 7. The limits of this class interval would be 7–13. The resultant limits of the remaining classes are: 14–20, 21–27, 28–34, 35–41, 42–48, 49–55, 56–62, 63–69, 70–76, 77–83, 84–90, 91–97, 98–104, 105–111.
>
> If the upper class had been established first by using a multiple of the highest score as the middle score in the interval, then the top interval would read 102–108 because 105 is a multiple of 7 and becomes the middle score of the interval, with the remainder of the score limits following in succession as stated earlier.

 SELF-TEST 12-3

1. For the scores that follow, and using the preferred class interval sizes, determine:
    a. The most appropriate class interval size for each range of scores.
    b. The approximate number of class intervals for these scores without setting score limits.
    c. Score Limits a. Interval Size b. Number of Class Intervals

   (1) 1 through 45
   (2) 72 through 136
   (3) 43 through 237
   (4) 0.12 through 0.38

2. Determine approximately the number of resulting classes if:
   a. A class interval of 5 is used for a range from 1 through 55.
   b. A class interval of 5 is used for a range from 172 through 366.
   c. A class interval of 3 is used for a range from 88 through 124.
   d. A class interval of 10 is used for a range from 12 through 160.

3. Determine the range for the following high and low scores:
   a. 345 and 118 _____
   b. 137 and 15 _____
   c. 0.88 and 0.25 _____

4. Indicate the class boundaries for the following class limits:
   a. 56 through 58 _____ to _____
   b. 25% through 75% _____ to _____
   c. 0.28 through 0.30 _____ to _____

5. For the following distribution, indicate the class boundaries, frequency, and cumulative frequency for each interval.

   Scores: 56 51 47 58 55 52 53 52 49 55 54 53 47 51
   57 49 50 50 48 56 58 47 57 51 54 57 49 56

   Score Limits Class Boundaries Tally Frequency Cumulative Frequency
   a. 56–58
   b. 53–55
   c. 50–52
   d. 47–49

6. Set the class score limits for the uppermost and lowest intervals for a distribution in which 88 is the lowest score and 166 the highest.

D. RANKS/QUARTILES/DECILES/CENTILES/PERCENTILES

It is not at all uncommon for an individual to be ranked in relation to other members of a group. Everyone has, at one time or another, been told they ranked, for example, 10th out of 30 participants who took an exam, came in 10th out of a field of 30 contestants in a race, and so forth. Most people are also familiar with a percentile ranking, such as placing in the top 10% of a class or a group (or in the lower 10%).

1. Terms

   a. **Rank**

   Rank indicates the relative status in a group. The rank of a score indicates its position in a series when all scores have been arranged in order of magnitude. A rank of 30, for example, indicates that the score is 30th in the distribution when all scores were ranked in order of magnitude.

   The meaningfulness of any designated rank depends upon the number of scores in the series or distribution. To rank 30th in a group of 50 is not the same as ranking 30th in a group of 100 or 30th in a group of 30. For this reason, ranks are more appropriately expressed in more relative terms as percentiles.

   b. **Percentiles (Centiles)/Deciles/Quartiles**

   Percentiles divide the distribution into 100 equal segments. The data should be ranked in increasing order to compute percentiles.

Deciles divide the data into 10 equal parts. The first decile includes one-tenth or 10% of the data in the distribution; the second decile another tenth (20%), and so on. There are 10 deciles in a distribution.

Quartiles divide the data into four equal parts (25%, 50%, etc.). The middle score in a distribution is referred to as the median and the score at the second quartile mark (equivalent to the fifth decile) is also the median of the distribution.

c. **Percentile Rank**

The percentile rank is the percentile for a specific score. For example, someone who scores a 67 on a test may rank at the 90th percentile. However, a score of 15 on another test may also be ranked at the 90th percentile.

d. **Percentile Score**

The percentile score represents the score that one must attain to reach a specific percentile. For example, to rank at the 90th percentile, an individual may need a score of 67.

2. **Importance of Percentiles**

A raw score, reported as 43, may not be meaningful to a participant. If, in addition, the participant is told the score placed him or her at the 85th percentile and that out of the entire group of participants only 15% got a higher score, the participant has a better understanding as to how his or her performance measured up to the rest of the group.

EXAMPLE: A group of arthritic patients is undergoing daily range-of-motion exercises in the physical therapy department. One test involves standing upright and bending forward to touch the toes. Scores are recorded to the nearest half-inch and are based on how close the fingers come to touching the floor. If 60% get to within two inches of the floor, any person attaining this level of achievement has a better indication of how he or she did as compared to others in the group.

3. **Weakness of Percentiles**

Percentile scores are *not* equally divided up and down a percentile scale. If 10 score points separate the 70th and 80th percentiles, this does *not* mean that the 10 score points separate each decile level, because scores often tend to be clustered near the middle, with less spread within this range. Special statistical treatment is required to figure specific scores from a percentile score. In percentiles:
   (1) The number of score points that separate each percentile level is equal.
   (2) The score ranges between percentiles may be unequal.

4. **Cumulative Frequency Related to Percentiles**

Cumulative frequencies related to percentiles are computed in the same fashion as any frequency distribution—adding each frequency to the previous frequency and accumulating frequencies from one end of the frequency distribution to the other. Each row should be a total of all frequencies up to that row.

5. **Calculating Percentiles and the Percentile Rank of a Value**

    a. **Calculating Percentiles**

        (1) *Ungrouped distribution*. Multiply the percentile (P) desired by n (sample size) and divide by 100. This result indicates the approximate location of the percentile score.

        > **EXAMPLE:** Scores reported are:
        >   7 8 9 10 11 12 13 13 14 17 17 45
        >   To find the value of the 42nd percentile, multiply 42 (P) times 12 (n) and divide by 100, which equals 5.04 or the fifth ranked score in the distribution, which is a score of 11 in the array.

   SELF-TEST 12-4

Sixteen people sign up for a weight-loss class, and the amount of weight lost at the end of the two-month period (in pounds) is as follows:

5 10 8 7 25 12 5 14 11 10 21 9 8 11 18 10

   a. What is the value of n?
   b. Compute the (approximate) value of the 82nd percentile.

        (2) *Grouped distribution*. Since a grouped distribution originated from ungrouped (raw) data, it is generally possible to use the ranked ungrouped data to calculate a percentile. However, the percentile can be estimated directly from grouped data as well. Referring to the grouped data of the test scores from Studious State University (Table 2.6), it was noted that n = 100. To calculate a given percentile from *grouped data*:

            (a) Designate the percentile (P) desired (10th, 25th, 85th, etc.).
            (b) Multiply the desired percentile (P) by n.
            (c) Subtract this number from the cumulative frequency below that interval.
            (d) Divide the difference by the frequency within the interval within which the score lies.
            (e) Multiply the quotient by the interval size.
            (f) Add this result to the lower-class boundary of the interval, and correct the result to the nearest whole number.

EXAMPLES:

   EX 1. To determine the value of the first decile (10th percentile) using the data from the Studious State grouped frequency distribution, the computation would be:

            (a) Percentile (10% of 100).
            (b) 0.10 (100) 10.
            (c) The 10th score lies in the class interval 60–62; the cumulative frequency (cf) below that interval is 4; therefore 10 − 4 = 6.
            (d) Dividing the result (6) by the frequency (f) within the interval (9) yields a result of 6/9 or 2/3.
            (e) The result, 2/3, multiplied by the interval size (3) = 2.
            (f) The lower-class boundary of the interval (59.5) added to 2 = 61.5 or 62. Therefore, the 10th percentile score is 62.

EX 2. Again, using the same frequency distribution, to determine the first quartile score, the computations are:

(a) Percentile (25% of 100).
(b) $0.25(100) = 25$.
(c) The 25th score lies within the class interval 69–71; the cf below that interval is 24, therefore, $25 - 24 = 1$.
(d) The frequency of the desired interval is 6; the result is 1/6.
(e) The result 1/6 multiplied by the interval size $(3) = 0.5$.
(f) $68.5 + 0.5 = 69$.

Therefore, a student who scored 69 on the final exam scored at the 25th percentile or first quartile, meaning 25% of test takers got a lower score and 75% received a higher score.

Shortcut: Once the basic computation is understood, the process can be streamlined as follows, using the 6th decile for illustrative purposes.

6th decile = lower limit + difference/f × interval size

$D6 = 77.5 + (7/10 \times 3) = 77.5 + 21/10 = 77.5 + 2.1 = 79.6 = 80$.

A student with an exam score of 80 scored at the 60th percentile.

 SELF-TEST 12-5

For instructions, see Self-Test 12-4, Grouped Distribution. Using the frequency distribution from question 1 of the preliminary test (scores on a statistics exam taken by 80 students), determine:

a. 8th decile score
b. 3rd quartile score
c. 9th decile score
d. 55th percentile score

---

b. Calculating the Percentile Rank (r) of a Score

Formula for Percentile Rank:
Divide the number of values less than r by the total number of values (n) in the data set and multiply by 100.

EXAMPLE: USING THE VALUES FROM A PREVIOUS EXAMPLE:

7 8 9 10 11 12 13 13 14 17 17 45
To find the percentile rank for a score of 14: $8/12 = 2/3 \times 100$
$= 66.67 = $ 67th percentile.

 SELF-TEST 12-6

Using the frequency distribution from question 1 of the preliminary test (statistics exam scores of 80 students), determine the percentile rank for the following scores:

a. 84
b. 66
c. 77
d. 61

E. SUMMARY

1. Tables can present large amounts of text-based quantitative data.
2. Frequency distributions organize data so they become more meaningful.
3. Qualitative data can be tallied and the frequency, relative frequency, and frequency percentage can be determined.
4. Tables can present data in a more usable form. They should be self-explanatory and clearly labeled.
5. Tables should include a title, headings, data in data cells, and any additional information needed such as a footnote, units of measure, totals, and possibly a table number.
6. Quantitative data can be displayed in an ungrouped or a grouped frequency distribution.
7. To prepare a frequency distribution, determine the range and establish the class interval (which includes class width, class limits, class boundaries, and class midpoint).
8. Preferred class sizes are 1, 2, 3, 5, 7, 15, and multiples of 5. The preferred number of classes is generally 5 to 15 or 20.
9. A frequency distribution table must include all scores in a distribution and each score should fall into only one class interval.
10. Rank indicates relative status in a group.
11. Percentiles (centiles, deciles, quartiles) divide a distribution into equal segments (100, 10, 4).
12. Percentiles have strengths and weaknesses that need to be considered before they are used.
13. Percentiles (P) can be determined from a grouped or an ungrouped frequency distribution. To calculate a percentile (P):

    Ungrouped distribution: multiply the desired percentile (P) by n and divide by 100 ($P \times n \div 100$). This computation designates the rank order in the distribution; then find the score from its rank.

    Grouped distribution: P = lower limit + difference divided by $f \times$ interval size.

14. Percentile rank (r) = divide the number of values less than r by n × 100; (# of values < r) ÷ n multiplied by 100.
15. Tables can be generated on many basic software programs (such as Microsoft Word).

Name _____ Date _____

F. CHAPTER 12 TEST

1. Surgical technology students were surveyed in their last academic term as to how well prepared they believed they were to enter the workforce upon graduation. Students could choose from the following levels of preparation: very (V), moderately (M), slightly (S), not at all (N). A total of 20 student responses were collected as follows:

    V M N S S V V V M V S M M V V M M V N S

    Construct a qualitative frequency distribution and include a frequency column, relative frequency column, and frequency percentage column.

2. A questionnaire was given to all patients discharged from a rehabilitation facility. The respondents were asked to rate the care or service they received. The choices included excellent (E), good (G), fair (F), and poor (P). A total of 75 responses were tabulated as follows:

    E G G E F E G G E F E E G G P E G F   E GGG   E E P

    E G G G E G F E G G F E E P E G GGP E G G   E F E

    E E G G F E F G E E G GGGGG   P E E F G   E E F G

    Construct a qualitative frequency distribution and include a frequency column, relative frequency column, and frequency percentage column.

3. Determine the approximate number of classes resulting if:

    a. A class interval size of 5 is used for a range of 20 to 85.
    b. A class interval size of 3 is used for a range of 8 to 50.
    c. A class interval size of 7 is used for a range of 43 to 113.
    d. A class interval size of 2 is used for a range of 131 to 160.

4. Indicate the class boundaries for a class limit of:

    a. 1 to 5
    b. 70.5 to 80.5
    c. 6.75 to 7.25

5. The number of laboratory tests carried out on 48 patients during their hospital stay (discharged last week) included the following:

    17 2   15 22 31   11 18 5   7   17 3   16 1   12   9   4   6   44 7   18 4   10 14
    12 8   13 3   38 8   11 25 29 9   21   36 2   5   6   17 8   3   9   13 9   6   5   9   14

    a. Construct a frequency distribution with the lower score limits of 0–2. Include both a frequency column and a cumulative frequency column.
    b. What was the average number of tests performed on the 48 patients?

6. A total of 320 patients were treated at a clinic in the past year for sexually transmitted diseases (STDs). Excluding 32 cases that resulted from congenital transmission or sexual abuse, construct the limits for a frequency distribution of the remaining cases (288) if the oldest patient was 88 and the youngest 12 years of age.

7. Blood glucose levels were recorded for all males over the age of 40, admitted with a diagnosis of coronary artery disease (a total of 755 diagnosed cases). The lowest blood glucose level recorded was 58 and the highest, 442. Using a class interval size of 25, set the score limits for each interval.

8. The ages of all patients diagnosed with cancer during the past year (255 new cases) were recorded. The youngest patient was 3 years old and the oldest was 92.

    a. Construct score limits for each class interval, using an interval size of 7 years and a lower limit of 2 for the lowest interval.
    b. Determine the number of class intervals.

9. A blood sample was drawn from 50 smokers between the ages of 45 and 65 and the serum cholesterol level recorded. The values are as follows:

291	285	273	270	268	260	260	256	254	252	251	248	247	243	241
240	240	239	238	238	238	235	234	233	233	231	230	229	227	227
226	223	222	221	221	219	217	214	212	209	207	205	199	198	188
185	179	177	165	158										

a. Calculate the range.
b. Calculate the number of class intervals if 10 scores are grouped in each interval.
c. Construct a frequency distribution starting with the lowest interval of 150–159.
d. Record the frequency and cumulative frequency for each interval.

10. The diastolic blood pressures (in mm Hg) of 84 patients with hypertension were as follows:

88	98	78	84	77	81	90	82	75	72	92	85	92	77	84	77	82	100
92	88	74	80	95	90	87	80	83	77	86	80	88	90	79	82	93	100
80	85	96	85	90	84	82	95	88	97	80	88	94	92	88	96	90	103
88	86	84	90	98	88	86	95	97	88	75	82	90	98	84	97	84	102
88	78	80	82	86	90	85	95	88	86	90	101						

a. Calculate the range.
b. Construct a frequency distribution with a class interval size of 3 starting with an interval of 71–73. Indicate score limits, score boundaries, frequency, and cumulative frequency.
c. Calculate the value of:
   (1) First quartile score.
   (2) Third quartile score.
   (3) 90th percentile score.
   (4) Percentile rank of a score of 81.
   (5) Percentile rank of a score of 87.

11. The number of days a patient was hospitalized with a diagnosis of traumatic injury was recorded as follows:

20	19	18	18	17	17	17	15	15	14	14	14	13	13	12	11	11	10 10 10
10	9	9	8	8	8	8	8	7	7	7	6	6	6	6	6	6	6 5 5 5 5 5 5 5 5 5 4
4	4	4	4	4	3	3	3	3	3	3	2	2	2	2	2	2	2 2 2 2 2 1 1 1 1 1 1

a. What is the value of N?
b. Construct a frequency distribution starting with the lowest class interval of 1–2, including a frequency column and a cumulative frequency column.
c. Calculate:
   (1) Percentage of scores with stays greater than one week.
   (2) Percentage of scores with stays greater than two weeks.
d. Calculate:
   (1) Percentile rank for a stay of nine days.
   (2) Percentile rank for a stay of three days.

12. The age of a patient at the time of diagnosis of colon cancer was tracked for 50 males and 50 females. The ages are as follows:

M:	91	87	87	85	83	81	80	79	78	77	75	75	74	73	72	72	71	71
	70	69	69	68	66	66	65	63	63	63	62	62	62	61	61	61	60	60
	59	59	57	56	55	55	53	53	51	48	45	39	38	29				
F:	94	93	92	90	89	88	87	86	86	85	85	83	81	79	79	78	77	77
	76	76	76	76	75	74	74	73	72	72	71	70	68	68	67	66	66	65
	65	65	64	64	64	63	60	59	58	55	54	53	51	48				

a. Calculate the range for:
   (1) Males
   (2) Females
   (3) Males and females combined.
b. Calculate the average age for males.
c. Complete the table below:

Age at Diagnosis of Colon Cancer in a Group of 50 Males and 50 Females

		Males		Females		Combined	
Score Limits	Midpt.	f	cf	f	cf	f	cf
90–99							
80–89							
70–79							
60–69							
50–59							
40–49							
30–39							
20–29							

d. Calculate the value for:
   (1) 85th percentile for the combined ages.
   (2) Percentile for an age of 60 for females.
   (3) Percentile for an age of 75 for males.

13. Explain the difference between rankings made in percentiles, deciles, and quartiles, using examples to demonstrate the differences.

Displaying Data for Analysis

CHAPTER OUTLINE

LEARNING OBJECTIVES

After studying this chapter, the learner should be able to:

 Determine the type of chart/graph appropriate for presenting various types of data.

 Construct the following using computer software:
   a. Bar chart/column chart
   b. Stack bar/column chart
   c. Percent stack bar/column chart
   d. Pie chart
   e. Line chart

 Construct the following types of graphs:
   a. Histogram
   b. Frequency polygon

PRELIMINARY QUESTIONS

1. Name the two axes of a chart/graph and the type of information represented on each axis.
2. What is the difference between a bar chart and a column chart?
3. Approximately what height-to-width ratio is most appropriate for chart construction?
4. What type of chart is most appropriate for presenting qualitative data?
5. What type of chart is most appropriate for presenting quantitative continuous data?
6. What popular software includes graphing capabilities?

Everyone has heard the expression, "a picture is worth a thousand words." Once data collection has been completed and analyzed to determine what is meaningful, it is generally helpful to convey the data in some form of graphic display. Data are collected to provide information to the user; but, more often, this information is to be shared with others—staff, an administrator, an outside agency, a presentation to a group, a presentation in a journal, and so forth. The likelihood that statistical data will attract a reader's attention is greatly enhanced if data are displayed in graphic or tabular form. The type of presentation is often dependent on the target audience that the presenter hopes to reach. The type of data presentation, whether a table or graph, is also often dependent on the reader's background, knowledge, and degree of sophistication in reading and interpreting data. Data are displayed or presented in two major forms: (1) tables and (2) charts/graphs.

Tables, as presented in the previous chapter, are used to present large amounts of text-based quantitative data via a matrix of columns and rows with associated headings and labels to identify the data. Charts and graphs are a more visual form of data presentation; they are pictorial representations of the analyzed data. The proper chart or graph enables an audience to more quickly assimilate and understand the material being presented.

The presentation of data, using tables and graphs, has been greatly facilitated through the availability of software packages currently available on most personal computers (PCs). Data information can be fed directly into a PC, and a very professional-looking graph, chart, or table can be generated automatically. The important decision is the selection of the proper presentation tool. When using data analysis software on a PC, good table design is the first step in producing informative graphical presentations. Most programs require that data be entered into a table before a chart or a graph can be generated.

Included below is a cursory review of data terms identified in Chapters 1 and 12:

1. *Qualitative* data are data that cannot assume a numerical value but can be classified into two or more nonnumeric categories.

2. *Quantitative* data are data that can be measured numerically.

3. *Discrete* data are a type of quantitative data whose values are countable and finite with no intermediate values (no fractions or decimal numbers).

4. *Continuous* data are also quantitative data, but the values can assume any numerical value over a certain interval or intervals.

5. *Nominal* data are qualitative data—nonnumeric data—observations are organized into categories without any recognition of order.

6. *Ordinal* data are qualitative data—data ordered in some meaningful way, as in levels of severity (e.g., from minor to fatal)—or data from surveys in which the choices range from strongly agree to strongly disagree.

7. *Ranked* data are a type of ordinal data where the observations are ranked according to magnitude, such as in the 10 leading causes of death in the United States.

A. CHARTS AND GRAPHS

Many types of charts and graphs are employed in presenting statistical data. The choice of graph or chart is dependent on the nature of the data and the purpose for which the graph or chart is intended. The terms *graph* and *chart* are most often used interchangeably, though there are subtle differences in the two types of graphic presentation techniques.

Chart: A chart illustrates data using only one quantitative coordinate. Charts are most appropriate for quantitatively comparing discrete categories or groups of data. The most common charts are column, bar, line, and pie charts.

Graph: A graph is a method of relating one qualitative variable to another quantitative variable, usually time. The most common graphs are histograms and frequency polygons. Charts and graphs are pictorial presentations of the relationship between variables.

Charts and graphs catch the eye of the reader, help the reader grasp information more quickly, and tend to be easier to comprehend than tables since they are a more visual means of presentation than a table. However, charts and graphs often lack the detail that can be presented in a table.

The basic design characteristics and principles for both charts and graphs are very similar. The different charts and graphs are mostly variations of each other. This chapter addresses the most common categories of charts—which include bar, column, line, and pie charts—and the most common graphs—which include histograms and frequency polygons.

1. General Rules/Guidelines

A chart or a graph should:

a. Be appropriate. The chart or graph should be appropriate for the type of data to be presented or conveyed.

b. Be self-explanatory and well labeled. Graphs, like tables, should be self-explanatory and should include a descriptive title, labeled axes, and a clear indication of the units displayed.

c. Be easily comprehended. Avoid overly complex charts or graphs. They should be clean in appearance and not attempt to overwhelm the reader with so much information that comprehension is difficult.

d. Include a legend or key if necessary.

e. Use scale proportion. The scale refers to the proportion or distribution of the two axes—height and width in relationship to one another. As a rule, the *height* of the vertical axis should have a ratio of approximately 3:5—or more commonly, 3:4—of the *length* of the horizontal axis. Thus, a chart or a graph should be greater in length than in height.

f. Acknowledge and credit each outside source.

2. Fundamentals of a Chart/Graph

Axes. Most charts and graphs use rectangular coordinates that have two lines, called axes, that intersect at a right angle (Figure 13-1).

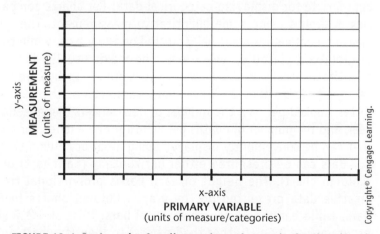

FIGURE 13-1 Rectangular Coordinates (x- and y-axes) of a Chart/Graph

X-axis—horizontal axis. The lowest values are generally located on the left and the highest values are located to the right. The x-axis usually represents the primary variable (independent variable).

Y-axis—vertical axis. Along this axis are the values used to measure the primary variable (frequency, number of cases, cost, or other quantitative measure). The lowest values are listed at the bottom and the highest at the top.

Scale. The vertical scale should begin at zero to avoid misleading the reader (Figure 13-2). If the data lend themselves to a different lower value (other than zero), a broken line or other means of interruption should be drawn at the bottom of the vertical axis. This broken line should be employed as well at the bottom of each frequency rectangle to indicate clearly that the *zero-frequency* rule was circumvented.

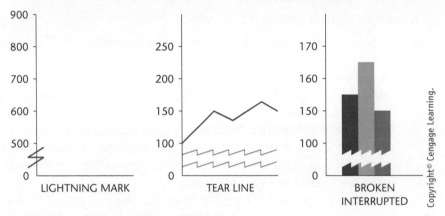

FIGURE 13-2 Interrupted Vertical Scale

Labeling. Each axis is labeled with both the name of the variable and the units in which the variable was measured.

B. CHARTS

1. Bar Chart/Column Chart

Bar charts are one of the most common data presentation tools. A bar chart is particularly useful for displaying data such as gender, ethnicity, occupation, types of discharges, and treatment categories. Bar charts are appropriate for displaying categorical data. Bar charts compare categories or groups using some quantitative measurement. The quantitative measurement values are usually plotted on the y-axis, while the category or group are placed on the x-axis. The x-axis usually does not have a quantitative scale. If quantitative values are used, they are presented in categories (e.g., ages 25–34, 35–44). Data such as the number of cigarettes smoked per day, the number of new cancers diagnosed in the past year, and the number of deaths per month for an entire year are examples that can be conveniently displayed using a bar or column chart.

Bars can be presented either horizontally (bar chart) or vertically (column chart). The height of each bar is proportional to the quantitative data presented on the y-axis. Column charts have vertical bars, while bar charts have horizontal bars. Most statistical software programs use icons (rather than names) to identify chart options. The decision as to which type of chart (bar or column) to use is left to the discretion of the person creating the chart.

a. Single Bar/Column Charts

The simplest bar chart displays data from a one variable table. Each category is represented by a bar on the x-axis. Categories may be arranged in alphabetical order or in increasing or decreasing bar height. The height or length of the bar on the y-axis is associated with its quantitative unit of measure. Space is left between bars to alert the reader to the fact that no continuity is indicated. The y-axis should begin at zero, or an interruption of the scale should be used as previously indicated.

EXAMPLES:

Ex 1. Column Chart. A simple column chart is displayed in Table 13-1. The graphic presentation of data makes it easy to compare and identify the hospital service with the highest and lowest discharges (Figure 13-3).

TABLE 13-1 Hospital Discharges by Service, Anytown Hospital, Anytown, USA, 20XX

Service	Discharges
Medicine	3,446
Obstetric	2,632
Orthopedic	3,630
Pediatric	2,255
Surgery	2,564
Totals	**14,527**

Copyright © Cengage Learning.

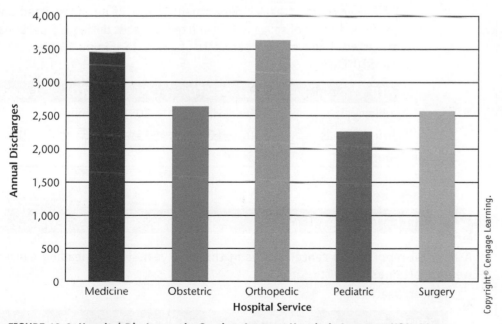

FIGURE 13-3 Hospital Discharges by Service, Anytown Hospital, Anytown, USA, 20xx

b. Bar Chart

The bar chart in Figure 13-4 was created from the same data as previously shown; however, instead of vertical bars (column chart), the bars extend horizontally to produce a bar chart.

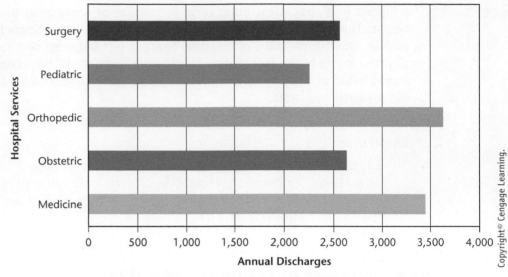

FIGURE 13-4 Hospital Discharges by Service, Anytown Hospital, Anytown, USA, 20xx

Vertical column charts are frequently used to illustrate that data are increasing or decreasing, represented by the height of the column. However, if labels are too long to fit on a horizontal axis, a horizontal bar chart makes the labels easier to read. It is important to note that when a horizontal bar chart is used, the categorical data are still on the x-axis, the x-axis is simply rotated to the vertical position, and the y-axis is moved to the horizontal position. The axes are moved, *not* the data.

Ex 2. Bar chart. A health department report of newly reported and confirmed cases of sexually transmitted diseases during the past year are listed, followed by a bar chart of the data (Figure 13-5):
STD/Cases

STD	Cases	STD	Cases	STD	Cases
Chlamydia	120	HPV	30	Syphilis	3
Trichomonas	90	HSV-2	15	AIDS	1
Gonorrhea	45				

 SELF-TEST 13-1

A hospital reported 60 cancer deaths in the past year. The six leading cancers were reported as follows:
Cancer/Deaths

Cancer	Deaths	Cancer	Deaths
Breast	15	Colorectal	10
Lung	14	Leukemias	5
Prostate	12	Lymphomas	4

Construct a bar or column chart to represent the data.

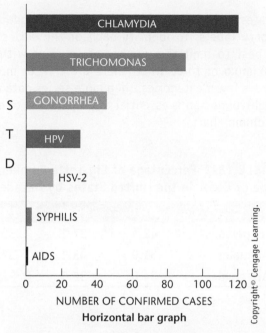

NUMBER OF CONFIRMED CASES
Horizontal bar graph

FIGURE 13-5 Sexually Transmitted Diseases, Health Department, 20XX

c. Comparison Bar/Column Charts

Occasionally, two or more sets of data are plotted on the same chart, using the same axes. This method is most commonly employed when comparisons are to be shown, especially between two related items. For example, one might choose to compare one hospital with another hospital or one country with another country and, therefore, plot both sets of data on the same chart. Comparisons are more easily visualized when displayed in this fashion (Figure 13-6).

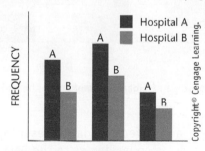

FIGURE 13-6 Side-by-Side Comparison Column Chart

(1) Multiple Side-by-Side Charts

The design concept is similar to simple bar charts.

EXAMPLES:

Ex 1. Referring to the data in Table 13-2 (percentage of cigarette smokers in the United States by decade), the data can be displayed on a single multiple column chart (Figure 13-7). The x-axis lists the decades and the y-axis the percentages. Comparisons are quickly visible. The columns, representing smokers by category, are clustered by decade to illustrate their comparative use rates over time. A legend is required, in addition to the x-axis category labels, to identify each of the series representatives. It is best to limit the number of columns within a category to a maximum of *three* when there are five or more categories. If there are fewer categories, then more series data can be presented. Thoughtful design is essential to preparation of effective multiple bar/column charts.

TABLE 13-2 Percentage of Cigarette Smokers: 18 Years of Age or Older in the United States by Decade

	1970	1980	1990	2000
All persons	42.4	37.1	30.1	24.7
All males	51.9	43.1	32.6	27.0
All females	34.0	32.5	28.2	22.8

Copyright © Cengage Learning®.

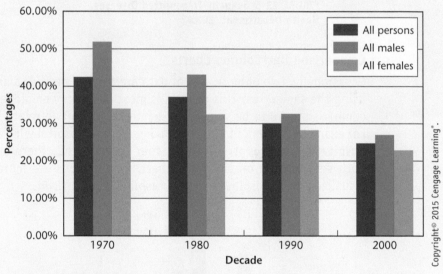

Copyright© 2015 Cengage Learning®.

FIGURE 13-7 Percentage of Cigarette Smokers in the United States (18 or Older) by Decade

Accurate and effective data presentation requires critical thinking and decision making as to the best format for presenting data. The software cannot determine which axis is the better axis on which to place data. The software does not let the operator know whether the chart created is too cluttered or confusing. A computer is a tool that can create many different charts, but the person creating the chart must select the appropriate chart that best illustrates the information to be presented by the statistical data.

Ex 2. A hospital wishes to compare (by quarter) the percentage of occupancy over the past two years (Figure 13-8).

Quarter	2010	2011	Quarter	2010	2011
1	82%	89%	3	79%	70%
2	74%	81%	4	70%	78%

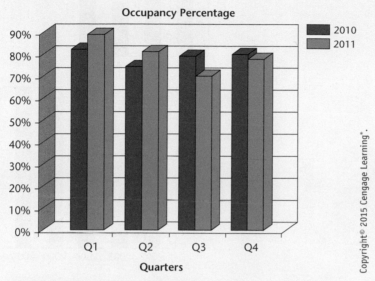

FIGURE 13-8 Comparison of Occupancy Percentage (by Quarter)

 SELF-TEST 13-2

The local health department reports the following number of confirmed cases of measles and mumps over the past decade. Construct a comparison chart for the data.

Year/Measles/Mumps

Year	Measles	Mumps	Year	Measles	Mumps
2002	13	9	2007	3	3
2003	3	5	2008	6	8
2004	1	5	2009	3	13
2005	1	3	2010	3	5
2006	3	3	2011	11	4

(2) Stack Bar/Column Chart

A stack bar/column chart compares categories composed of series data. The visual emphasis is on the comparison of the total quantitative values of each data category along the x-axis. The stack bar format allows the viewer to see the series variables that contribute to the total value of the category.

EXAMPLES:
Percent Stack Column Chart
EX 1. a. Basic stack column chart.

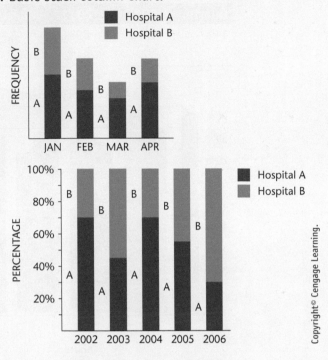

b. Basic percent stack column

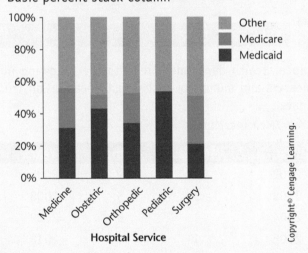

EX 2. Table 13-3 is an example of a stack bar chart with emphasis on comparing total discharges by hospital service and payer. The basic design characteristics and principles of stack bar/column charts are the same as the multiple bar chart. The only difference lies in the chart presentation format that emphasizes comparison of the categorical axis on the x-axis.

TABLE 13-3 Hospital Discharges by Hospital Service and Payer, Anytown Hospital, Anytown, USA, 20xx

Service	Discharges (by Payer)			
	Medicaid	Medicare	Other Payers	Totals
Medicine	1,098	890	1,558	3,546
Obstetrics	1,145	234	1,253	2,632
Orthopedics	1,234	675	1,721	3,630
Pediatrics	1,210	10	1,035	2,255
Surgery	543	765	1,256	2,564

(3) Percent Stack Bar/Column

The percent stack bar chart is useful for comparing the relative contribution of the series data in each of the categorical variables. The chart is used to standardize the series data when the total category values are unequal. The percent stack bar is a variation of a stack bar chart in which percentage comparisons of the component series variables are used. Because each of the bars is standardized, based on 100%, all the categorical bars are the same height. The component series data are presented as a percentage of the total rather than as actual quantitative values. The percent stack bar chart is used when the main categorical variables have significantly different values and when it is necessary to compare the contribution of the series variables.

EXAMPLE: The percent stack column chart is based on data in the previous example, but note that all columns are the same height.

Hospital Discharges by Hospital Service and Payer, Anytown Hospital, Anytown, USA, 20xx

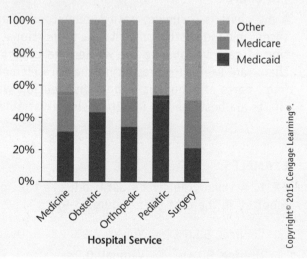

d. Guidelines for Constructing a Bar Chart

(1) Arrange the data into categories that reflect a natural order. (Alphabetical; increasing or decreasing in value.)

(2) Use either column or bar charts, whichever best illustrates the data.

(3) Limit the number of category and series variables presented when multiple bar charts are used. This allows for easier comparative analysis.

(4) Use colors, or geometric designs in black-and-white charts, to clearly differentiate the series bars from each other.

(5) Use space between bars to alert the reader that no continuity is indicated and to reduce the possibility of implying continuity.

 SELF-TEST 13-3

A report from six midwestern states included the number of reported cancers (per 100,000 population) in three sites as follows:

State	Lung	Colorectal	Lymphoma (non-Hodgkin's)
Iowa	139	120	40
Missouri	164	113	38
Nebraska	132	118	40
Oklahoma	172	108	37
North Dakota	114	109	37
South Dakota	126	114	39

Construct a stack bar/column chart for the data.

2. Pie Chart

A pie chart is a simple, easily understood chart. The size of the "pie slices" in a pie chart represents the proportional or percentage contribution of each variable to the whole data category being presented. Pie charts are useful for presenting the data elements for a single variable (e.g., parts of a budget, ethnic distribution within a population). Pie charts are best used to illustrate single-variable tables.

EXAMPLES:

EX 1. A tumor registrar's data indicate the following female cancers reported in the past year (Figure 13-9):

Cervical, 50.0%   Vulvar, 2.2%   Ovarian, 16.5%

Uterine, 30.4%   Vaginal, 0.9%

A pie chart of the data illustrates percentage relationships.

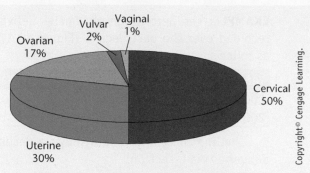

FIGURE 13-9 Percentage of Female Cancers, ABC Hospital, 20xx

EX 2. Figure 13-10 illustrates the percentage distribution of discharges by hospital service via a pie chart.

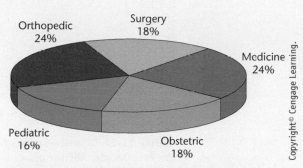

FIGURE 13-10 Percent Distribution of Discharges by Hospital Service, Anytown Hospital, Anytown, USA, 20xx

 SELF-TEST 13-4

A hospital recorded the marital status (at the time of admission) of patients over the age of 14 during the past year. The percentages are as follows:

Single (never married)	18.8%	Married	55.2%
Widowed	10.5%	Divorced	15.5%

Construct a pie chart to illustrate the data.

3. Line Chart

A line chart illustrates patterns or trends of quantitative data over some variable, usually time. When analyzing health care data, this type of chart is commonly used to show time-related series data and to compare several series to each other. A line chart is the method of choice for plotting data over time.

a. Basic, Single Line Chart

A single line chart is particularly effective in showing an increase or decrease over time.

EXAMPLE: The percentage of females delivering via C-section was recorded over the past decade (Figure 13-11). The percentages are as follows:

Year	%	Year	%	Year	%	Year	%	Year	%
2002	44	2003	42	2004	38	2005	38	2006	35
2007	35	2008	33	2009	35	2010	30	2011	27

The line chart of the data shows a decline in the percentage of deliveries via C-section.

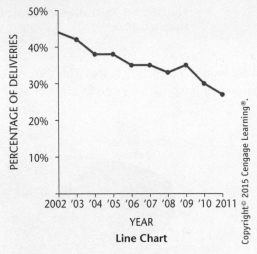

FIGURE 13-11 Cesarean Section Rates for the Past Decade, ABC Hospital

b. Multiple Comparison Line Chart

A multiple line chart superimposes several sets of data on the same chart. Each line should be distinguished by using different colors or a variation in the type of line drawn (Figure 13-12). Again, a legend should be included to indicate what is represented by each line.

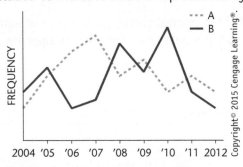

FIGURE 13-12 Comparison Line Chart

EXAMPLE: A comparison is to be made of the monthly deaths of males and females over the past year (Figure 13-13). The deaths were reported as follows:

Month	M	F	Month	M	F	Month	M	F
January	19	17	May	18	15	September	20	24
February	13	15	June	21	12	October	18	22
March	20	12	July	22	15	November	19	20
April	15	18	August	25	22	December	24	18

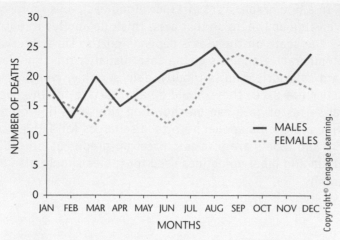

FIGURE 13-13 Comparison Line Chart of Monthly Gender Deaths, ABC Hospital, 20xx

EXAMPLE: Table 13-4 summarizes annual discharges by hospital service over a period of five years at Anytown Hospital. The data from the table are then plotted in a line graph format (Figure 13-14).

TABLE 13-4 Annual Discharges by Hospital Service, 2007–2011, Anytown Hospital, Anytown, USA

	Year				
Service	**2007**	**2008**	**2009**	**2010**	**2011**
Medicine	3,098	2,890	3,126	2,987	3,446
Obstetric	2,145	2,234	2,143	2,345	2,632
Orthopedic	2,234	2,675	2,167	2,765	3,630
Pediatric	2,212	2,210	2,232	2,567	2,255
Surgery	2,543	2,765	2,324	2,587	2,564
Totals	**12,232**	**12,774**	**11,992**	**13,251**	**14,257**

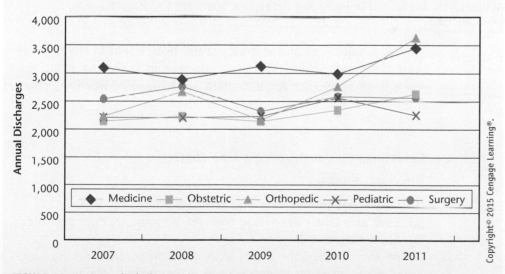

FIGURE 13-14 Annual Discharges by Hospital Service, 2007–2011, Anytown Hospital, Anytown, USA 2012

NOTE: In a line graph, a set distance along each axis represents the same quantitative value anywhere on that axis. This rule applies to both the x-axis and the y-axis. The scale on the x-axis depends on the time intervals to be presented for a comparative analysis of the data. Usually, the time data are presented in standard categorical units (hourly, daily, weekly, monthly, or annually). Whatever units are used, they should be appropriate for the data being presented. Several series of data can be shown on the same line graph. In Figure 13-14, each line represents annual hospital discharges for a given service. Appropriate headers and labels are just as critical on graphs as on tables and charts. The same title and label guidelines used for tables should also be applied to charts and graphs.

EXAMPLE: The data in the chart in Figure 13-15 are identical to the previous example, but the data reflects greater variation in the data. Try to determine the reason for the apparent greater variation in the data before continuing with this section.

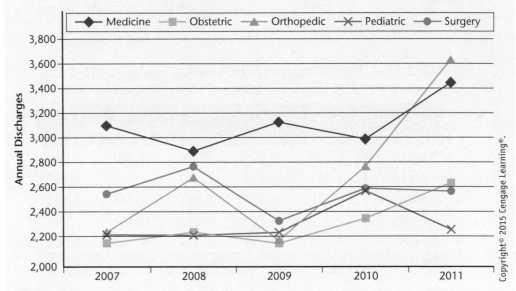

FIGURE 13-15 **Annual Discharges by Hospital Service, 2007–2011 Anytown Hospital, Anytown, USA**

The problem lies on the y-axis scale. Notice that in the original chart the y-axis scale starts at 0, whereas in the above chart the y-axis begins at 2,000. Accurate data are misleading when the chart or graph is inaccurately constructed.

c. **Guidelines for Constructing a Line Chart**

The y-axis should:

(1) Have titles that explain who or what, where, and when.
(2) Have axis labels describing the variables and units of measure.
(3) Always start at 0.
(4) Be shorter than the x-axis with good proportion. An x:y ratio of 5:3 is often recommended and is the default setting for most spreadsheet programs.

(5) Have a range of values in standard units (10s, 100s, etc.), with the last unit slightly larger than the largest data unit presented on the chart. In Figure 13-15, the largest y-value is 3,630 in 2011, and the scale value was rounded up to 4,000.

(6) Have data intervals that adequately illustrate the important details of the data.

(7) Have lines that are distinguished differently (different colors or variation in lines) with a legend to indicate what each line represents.

 SELF-TEST 13-5

Construct a comparison line chart of the comparative measles and mumps data in Self-Test 13-2.

4. Pictograph/Pictogram

Pictographs make use of pictures in their display of data. A common representative picture is a stick figure that represents a certain number of people. Pictograms often show great originality and ingenuity on the part of the presenter and, because they are eye-catching, can often draw the reader's attention to the displayed data.

EXAMPLE: Hospital records indicate that a total of 136 patients were admitted for inpatient treatment of an infectious disease during the past year. The infections and their recorded frequency are listed and depicted in a pictogram (Figure 13-16).

Bacterial Infection	f	Bacterial Infection	f	Viral Infection	f
Intestinal	49	Strep throat	7	Exanthems	7
TB (respiratory)	9	Septicemia	14	Hepatitis	15
TB (non-respiratory)	4	Other bacterial	7	Other viral	24

Depiction of Data in Pictograph Form:

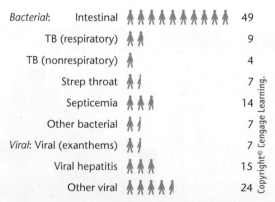

FIGURE 13-16 Inpatient Treatment of Infectious Disease, ABC Hospital, 20xx (Each figure represents five people.)

C. GRAPHS

Quantitative continuous data are displayed via a graph. The two most commonly employed graphs are the histogram and the frequency polygon. If comparisons are to be made on the same graph, the frequency polygon is the preferred graph. Frequency distributions were discussed in Chapter 3. If cholesterol values were taken from a group of vegetarians and a group of nonvegetarians and the results were compared, the frequency polygon would be the graph of choice.

The axes for graphs are similar to chart axes. The x-axis is the horizontal axis, and the y-axis is the vertical axis. The horizontal axis (x) usually shows the values of the independent (or x) variable. The vertical axis (y) is used to show the dependent (or y) variable, which is usually a frequency measure. Each axis is labeled accordingly with the name of the variable and the units in which it is measured.

1. Histogram

A histogram is a pictorial or graphic representation of a frequency distribution table in which each frequency is shown by the height of the column for each class interval. A true histogram presents quantitative continuous data. The horizontal axis is composed of the class boundaries/limits or midpoints of the class interval. The vertical axis depicts the relative frequency of the cases within the class interval. A histogram is similar in appearance to a bar graph except all bars are contiguous, reflecting continuous quantitative data.

A histogram is created by grouping data into two or more data ranges with limits. A plot is generated by creating rectangles with the data ranges along the x-axis and the relative frequencies determining the height.

Smaller class interval sizes provide a more detailed graph. Larger class intervals smooth out the data and generally promote an accurate representation, despite slight imperfections in the data sample. A wide data range may be desirable where the data vary only slightly, but a smaller data range may be used when the distribution makes more drastic changes.

The area under each rectangle also corresponds to the percentage of total scores. To get a proper representation of data, it is imperative that the size of class intervals within a distribution be identical. A histogram will be distorted if unequal class interval sizes are used.

EXAMPLE: Basic Histogram (Figure 13-17)

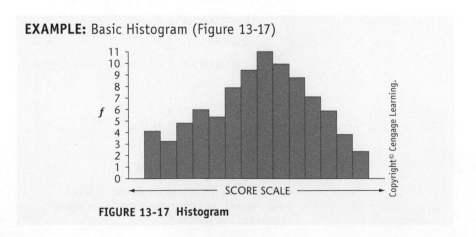

FIGURE 13-17 Histogram

NOTE: Unlike a bar chart, the data represented by the height and width of the bar are data-dependent. An accurate histogram cannot be drawn with a standard charting program, because bar width is not taken into consideration. Given the height and area requirements of the bars in a histogram, the data must be statistically analyzed and graphed accordingly. Most statistical programs (SPSS, Minitab, Math Stat, etc.) offer a statistical tool to accurately construct a histogram. These programs are used primarily for advanced statistical analysis, which is beyond the scope of this text. Health data analysts will find that bar charts are appropriate for most health data presentation applications.

Summary for Constructing a Histogram:
(1) The vertical scale should begin at zero.
(2) Use correct proportion—the height of the vertical axis should be approximately 3:5 or 3:4 the length of the horizontal axis.
(3) Generally, avoid unequal class intervals. Histograms are most commonly used for class intervals of equal size, as the area under each rectangle is proportional to the class frequency. If class intervals are unequal in size, the heights or widths must be adjusted. How this is done is not discussed in this text.
(4) Generally, the horizontal axis represents class boundaries, with the midpoint of the interval in the center; the vertical axis represents the relative frequency.

EXAMPLES:

EX 1. Thirty-six morbidly obese people signed up for a weight-loss class that included a strict diet for a month. The participants' initial weight and weight at the end of the month were recorded in pounds. The number of pounds lost was plotted in a frequency distribution (Figure 13-18). The recorded weight loss (in descending order) is:

28, 27, 27, 26, 25, 24, 24, 23, 22, 22, 22, 22, 21, 20, 20, 18,

18, 17, 17, 17, 16, 15, 15, 15, 14, 14, 13, 13, 13, 13, 12, 12,

11, 11, 10, 8

Weight Lost (in pounds) on a Strict Diet Program for One Month for a Group of Morbidly Obese Patients (n = 36)

Frequency Distribution

Class Boundaries	Midpoint	Frequency
27.5–29.4	28.5	1
25.5–27.4	26.5	3
23.5–25.4	24.5	3
21.5–23.4	22.5	5
19.5–21.4	20.5	3
17.5–19.4	18.5	2
15.5–17.4	16.5	4
13.5–15.4	14.5	5

Class Boundaries	Midpoint	Frequency
11.5–13.4	12.5	6
9.5–11.4	10.5	3
7.5–9.4	8.5	1

Histogram

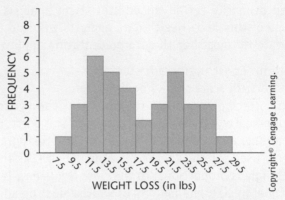

FIGURE 13-18 One-Month Weight Loss (on liquid diet) by a Group of Morbidly Obese Patients, ABC Hospital, 20xx

EX 2. Traumatic Hyphema ABC Clinic (March 2012) (Figure 13-19)

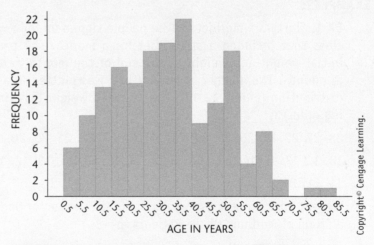

FIGURE 13-19 Traumatic Hyphema Diagnoses, ABC Clinic, March 20xx

EX 3. Variations in histogram construction (Figure 13-20).

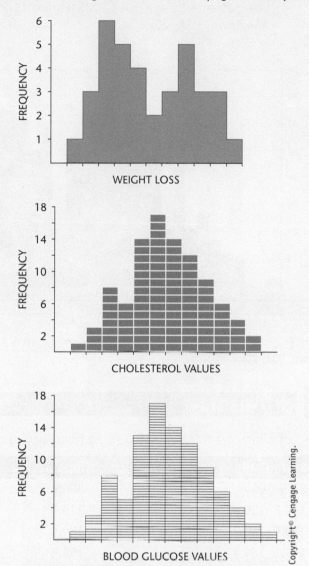

FIGURE 13-20 Variations in Histogram Construction

EX 4. Illustration of a computer-generated histogram of breast cancer patients by age (n = 1,208) (Figure 13-21) at Anytown Hospital, Anytown, USA, 20xx.

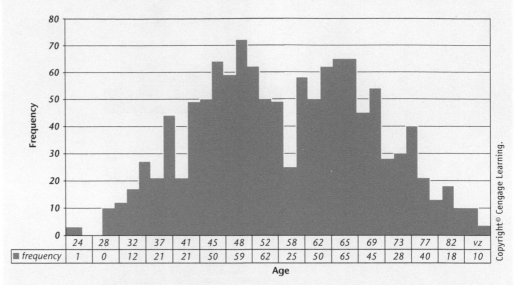

	24	28	32	37	41	45	48	52	58	62	65	69	73	77	82	vz
■ frequency	1	0	12	21	21	50	59	62	25	50	65	45	28	40	18	10

Age

FIGURE 13-21 Histogram of Breast Cancer Patients by Age (n = 36), Anytown Hospital, Anytown, USA, 20xx

 SELF-TEST 13-6

Construct a histogram from the following frequency distribution:

Systolic Blood Pressure	Midpoint	Frequency
89.5–109.4	99.5	16
109.5–129.4	119.5	37
129.5–149.4	139.5	29
149.5–169.4	159.5	12
169.5–189.4	179.5	4
189.5–209.4	199.5	2

2. Frequency Polygon

A frequency polygon is another statistical graph. It uses the same data as a histogram but resembles a line chart, in that it connects the midpoints of each data interval with a line. Like line charts, the lines of frequency polygons are effective for comparing multiple sets of frequency data. Multiple frequency polygons can be superimposed, much like a line chart, comparing two or more frequency distributions. Since a frequency polygon is a form of histogram, most statistical software programs offer a feature to accurately construct a frequency polygon. Again, the application of these programs is beyond the scope of this text.

The axes (x and y) are the same as those used in the histogram. At the top of each relative frequency (midpoint), a dot is placed, and a line connects adjacent dots. To bring the figure to the baseline, dots are placed at the zero-frequency level at the two ends of the distribution, extending the line to the horizontal axis.

EXAMPLES:

EX 1. Frequency polygon of the weight-loss data reported in the histogram section (Figure 13-22).

Weight Loss (in pounds) on a **Strict Diet Program** (for a month) for a Group of Morbidly Obese Patients **(n = 36)**

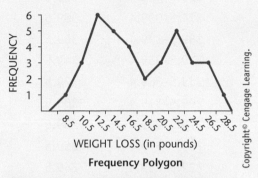

Frequency Polygon

FIGURE 13-22 One-Month Weight Loss (on liquid diet) by a Group of Morbidly Obese Patients, ABC Hospital, 20xx

EX 2. Example of a computer-generated frequency polygon (Figure 13-23).

Breast Cancer Patients by Age (n = 1,208)

Anytown Hospital, Anytown, USA, 20xx

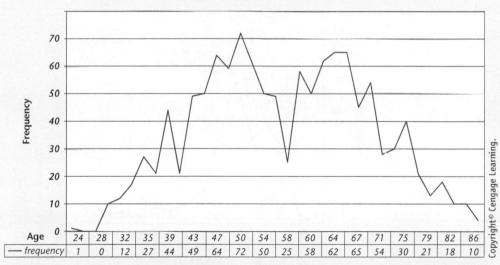

Age	24	28	32	35	39	43	47	50	54	58	60	64	67	71	75	79	82	86
— frequency	1	0	12	27	44	49	64	72	50	25	58	62	65	54	30	21	18	10

FIGURE 13-23 Frequency Polygon of Breast Cancer Patients by Age (n = 1,208), Anytown Hospital, Anytown, USA, 20xx

EX 3. Comparison frequency polygon. Serum cholesterol levels were taken of 150 males and 150 females between the ages of 20 and 100 (Figure 13-24). The values ranged from a high of 415 to a low of 135.

Comparison of Serum Cholesterol in Males and Females Ages 20–100, ABC Hospital, 20xx

Frequency Distribution

Cholesterol Values	Midpoint	Male Frequency	Female Frequency
399.5–419.4	409.5	1	0
379.5–399.4	389.5	0	1
359.5–379.4	369.5	2	0
339.5–359.4	349.5	3	2
319.5–339.4	329.5	2	2
299.5–319.4	309.5	4	2
279.5–299.4	289.5	3	2
259.5–279.4	269.5	5	5
239.5–259.4	249.5	8	5
219.5–239.4	229.5	22	18
199.5–219.4	209.5	35	45
179.5–199.4	189.5	21	27
159.5–179.4	169.5	24	30
139.5–159.4	149.5	18	10
119.5–139.4	129.5	2	1

Comparison Frequency Polygon

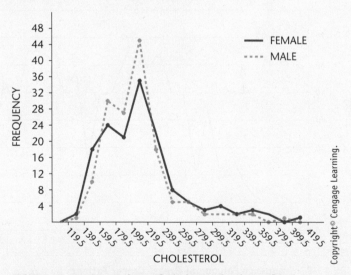

FIGURE 13-24 Comparison of Cholesterol Values of Males and Females (ages 20–100), ABC Hospital, 20xx

 SELF-TEST 13-7

Construct a frequency polygon for the data (systolic blood pressure) in Self-Test 13-6.

D. SUMMARY

1. Data should be reviewed for completeness and accuracy prior to analysis.
2. A chart illustrates data using only one quantitative coordinate.
3. Charts are most appropriate for quantitatively comparing discrete categories or groups of data.
4. The most common charts are bar/column, line, and pie charts.
5. Bar/column charts can be single, multiple (comparison), or stacked.
6. A bar chart has a bar extending horizontally.
7. A column chart has a bar extending vertically.
8. A line chart illustrates patterns or trends of quantitative data over some variable, usually time.
9. Line charts can be singular or multiple (comparison) charts.
10. Charts and graphs have a horizontal axis (x-axis) and a vertical axis (y-axis).
11. Charts and graphs are pictorial presentations of the relationship between variables.
12. Charts and graphs convey information more quickly than tables; however, charts and graphs often lack the detail that can be presented in a table.
13. Charts and graphs should be simple, clear, and uncomplicated so that the message is clear to the viewer.
14. Appropriate and descriptive titles and labels should accompany all charts and graphs.
15. A graph illustrates continuous quantitative data.
16. The most common graphs are the histogram and frequency polygon.
17. Most charts can be created using a spreadsheet software program (such as Excel).
18. To accurately create a graph (histogram and frequency polygon), special statistical software (such as SPSS, Minitab, or Math Stat) is required.
19. The maximum number of data elements illustrated in a chart or a graph should be five. Data elements with multiple subcategories should have less than five.
20. Colors and patterns are useful to emphasize a point, not to make a chart or a graph look "pretty."
21. The type of data determines the type of chart/graph to be constructed.
    a. Bar/column charts are best used to compare categorical data.
    b. Line charts are best for illustrating and comparing trends.
    c. Pie charts are used to illustrate percentage distributions.

Name _____   **Date** _____

F. CHAPTER 13 TEST

1. Identify the graphic technique used to display quantitative continuous data.

   a. Bar chart
   b. Stack bar chart
   c. Line chart
   d. Histogram
   e. All of the above

2. Identify the graphic technique that presents data as percentages.

   a. Bar chart
   b. Line chart
   c. Stack bar chart
   d. Frequency polygon
   e. Pie chart

3. Identify the graphic technique used to compare quantitative continuous data.

   a. Stack bar chart
   b. Percent stack bar chart
   c. Line chart
   d. Frequency polygon
   e. All of the above

4. The number of deaths due to colon cancer during the past decade is to be presented graphically. Identify the chart/ graph to best display the data.

   a. Bar chart
   b. Histogram
   c. Frequency polygon
   d. Pie chart

5. When plotting a histogram, what is primarily plotted?

   a. Along the x-axis
   b. Along the y-axis

6. Indicate the axis for plotting the following values for each chart/graph.

Chart/Graph	Value	Axis
a. Histogram	Class interval score limits	x y
b. Line chart	Months of the year	x y
c. Frequency polygon	Relative frequencies	x y
d. Comparison bar chart	Percent of occupancy	x y
e. Column chart	Cholesterol values	x y
f. Percent stack column chart	Percentages	x y

7. A comparison is to be made of the yearly Cesarean section rates of Hospital A and Hospital B over the past five years. The data are as follows:

Year	Hospital A	Hospital B
2008	44%	35%
2009	42%	33%
2010	38%	35%
2011	38%	30%
2012	35%	27%

   Create a chart that clearly compares the rates of the two hospitals.

8. A hospital administrator wishes to compare the percentage of occupancy (by month) for the current year (2012) with that of the prior year (2011). The data are as follows:

Month	2011	2012	Month	2011	2012	Month	2011	2012
Jan	85%	78%	May	75%	80%	Sept	80%	75%
Feb	87%	82%	June	70%	77%	Oct	82%	72%
Mar	82%	85%	July	75%	72%	Nov	85%	80%
Apr	78%	86%	Aug	78%	70%	Dec	73%	80%

Create a comparison chart of the results.

9. During the past year, a hospital reported the following newborn admissions:

Month	NB	Month	NB	Month	NB	Month	NB
Jan	110	Apr	95	July	131	Oct	130
Feb	80	May	128	Aug	142	Nov	126
Mar	84	June	133	Sept	138	Dec	91

Construct a column chart for the data.

10. The admission totals (for a week in June) were reported for medical and surgical services as follows:

Service	Sun	Mon	Tues	Wed	Thur	Fri	Sat
Medical	81	61	70	66	62	55	42
Surgical	20	12	16	14	14	8	5

Construct a side-by-side comparison chart for the data.

11. Quarterly newborn admission totals were recorded by gender as follows:

	Q1	Q2	Q3	Q4
Male	181	218	238	202
Female	204	201	210	213
Total	**385**	**419**	**448**	**415**

Construct a stack column comparison chart of the data.

12. Total monthly admission data for the past year were recorded as follows:

Month	Adm	Month	Adm	Month	Adm	Month	Adm
Jan	661	Apr	560	July	563	Oct	533
Feb	572	May	546	Aug	546	Nov	558
Mar	583	June	487	Sept	484	Dec	547

Construct a line chart of the data.

13. During the past year, the number of newly diagnosed cancers was recorded. The percentage of each cancer among males and females is as follows:

Cancer	Male (%)	Female (%)	Total Percentage
Lung	60	40	100
Colorectal	55	45	100
Urinary tract	70	30	100
Oral	75	25	100
Pancreatic	50	50	100
GI*	65	35	100

Construct a percent stack bar/column chart for the data.

*Esophageal, stomach, and small intestines

14. The pathologic diagnoses of 200 females undergoing surgery for a breast lesion are as follows:

Diagnosis	N	Percentage
Fibrocystic disease	68	34
Fibroadenoma	36	18
Intraductal papilloma	12	6
Lipoma	4	2
Other benign lesions	26	13
Carcinoma of the breast	54	27

a. Construct a pie graph of the above data.
b. Construct a bar graph of the above data.

Fundamentals of Research

14

CHAPTER OUTLINE

LEARNING OBJECTIVES

After studying this chapter, the learner should be able to:

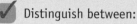 Distinguish between:
a. Basic and applied research
b. Quantitative and qualitative approach to research
c. Inductive and deductive reasoning
d. A retrospective and prospective study
e. A cross-sectional and longitudinal study
f. Random and nonrandom samples
g. Sampling and non-sampling errors

Describe key factors in common research designs:
a. Historical
b. Descriptive
c. Correlational
d. Observational
e. Evaluation
f. Experimental

Explain each of the random sampling techniques:
a. Simple random sampling
b. Systematic random sampling
c. Stratified random sampling
d. Cluster sampling

Identify several non-sampling errors.

Identify general principles of sample size selection.

Describe methods to increase the response rate in surveys.

Distinguish between:
a. Validity and reliability
b. Correlation, significance, and confidence
c. Null hypothesis and alternative hypothesis

Identify the purpose of the IRB.

List the steps followed when conducting a research study.

Distinguish between a null hypothesis and an alternative hypothesis.

D ata in and of itself can often be meaningless; data should be collected with some purpose in mind. Data collected and analyzed can prove to be useful information. Discoveries are often the result of painstaking research, whether it is to find a cure for AIDS or to reduce the spread of infection. Research is instrumental in all fields of knowledge and is extremely important to health care. Knowledge acquired through research can increase effectiveness and efficiency in the health care field. Research to reduce coding error rates improves the efficiency in both the health information department (HIM) and in overall reimbursement. Research can range from an extensive review of the literature on a specified topic to the collection of data from a 10-year study of the effectiveness of exercise on osteoporosis. Research is a scholarly approach to scientific investigation, and inquiry and is often a means to discover solutions to problems. Research is carried out in all fields of study and in a variety of ways.

A. BASIC RESEARCH-RELATED TERMS

1. Types of Research

Research is classified as basic research or applied research.

a. Basic Research

Basic research focuses on developing a theory and tends to answer the question, "why": Why are more people developing diabetes mellitus presently than in the past? Or why is the delinquency rate for chart completion increasing in the HIM department rather than decreasing? Why is one ethnic group prone to a disease like sickle cell anemia when another ethnic group is not? Basic research tends to seek answers to aid in understanding a process.

b. Applied Research

Applied research focuses on implementation. Once the answer to the question "why" has been discovered, a solution is sought as to how or what should be done to correct or solve the problem: What can be done to increase the chart completion rate? What types of preventive measures are needed to decrease the number of patients with diabetes?

2. Research Process Approaches

a. Quantitative Approach

Quantitative data, as described previously, implies that the data can be quantified with numerical data. Numerical data are collected and analyzed with statistical results. Studies can include comparisons of populations, experiments carried out on test subjects, or investigations such as counting the number of errors made on a transcribed report.

b. Qualitative Approach

The qualitative approach uses descriptions rather than numerical data. Qualitative research often includes interviews where the test subject is asked their perception through words, gestures, or images. Assessing play activities of infants is an example of a qualitative approach.

c. Mixed Approach

The mixed approach is emerging as an alternative to strictly quantitative or qualitative methods and is a combination of the two approaches.

3. **Types of Reasoning**
   a. **Inductive Reasoning**

   Inductive reasoning involves drawing conclusions based on a limited number of observations. Inductive reasoning is often referred to as the "bottom up" approach. A researcher may observe certain patterns or relationships occurring, which generates an idea to be pursued further. Provisional conclusions or theories are often drawn based on the data.

   b. **Deductive Reasoning**

   Deductive reasoning involves conclusions based on generalizations and is often referred to as "top down" reasoning. In deductive reasoning, the researcher generally starts with a hypothesis (an assumption or idea to be tested) and develops a means to test the hypothesis to either validate or invalidate the theory (hypothesis). Both inductive and deductive reasoning are important research tools. It is often the case that a researcher starts with an exploratory idea (based on inductive reasoning), which then generates into a research project to prove or disprove the initial theory (using deductive reasoning).

4. **Time Frame**

   Another aspect of any research study is the time frame of the study—whether it is a 10-year study or is completed in a matter of days or weeks.

   a. **Retrospective Study**

   Retrospective studies review information already collected; they look back in time. Examining patient health records to study disease protocol and patterns of disease for a specified group is an example of a retrospective study.

   b. **Prospective Study**

   Prospective refers to likely to happen or expected to happen. Prospective studies most often refer to studies in which a researcher wants to see if a group of subjects will develop a condition in the future. Subjects with certain risk factors are followed over a period of time to see if a disease or condition occurs.

   c. **Cross-Sectional Study**

   A cross-sectional study involves the shortest time frame, and data are collected on a one-time basis. Recording the number of medications a patient is taking at any specified time is a cross-sectional study. These studies may or may not be representative of the total population, and their primary advantage is the efficiency with which data can be collected.

   d. **Longitudinal Study**

   Longitudinal studies also occur over long periods of time, but the same group of subjects is followed over extended periods at multiple times throughout the study period.

B. COMMON RESEARCH DESIGNS

1. Historical Research

Historical research investigates the past. Historical research includes the study of past events and records, including both primary and secondary sources of information. Primary sources, again, include original sources of data or information; secondary sources include information derived from primary sources, most commonly abstracted from the original. Historical examples include research into the causes that led to the flu epidemic a century ago or the study of the factors that played a role in the spread of AIDS.

2. Descriptive Research

Descriptive research describes the present status. Descriptive research often employs a survey, or observation of a process, in the design. The most common research tools employed in descriptive research are a survey, an interview, or an observation. Descriptive research is exploratory rather than explanatory—describing the current status. Descriptive research examples include opinion polls that aid in policy decision making. Another study may determine how often patients make physician appointments via the Internet or how well satisfied patients are with the care they received.

3. Correlational Research

Correlational research involves studying the relationship between factors or variables to determine whether a strong or weak relationship or no relationship exists between the factors studied. *Correlation* refers to the relationship between two variables. Correlational research may be carried out to determine if a relationship exists between the administration of childhood vaccines and autism or if there is a correlation between eating a diet high in fat and the development of cancer.

4. Observational Research

Observational research observes a process or a behavior. The process or behavior is observed in hopes of detecting problems to be corrected. Patterns of behavior are detected and described relating to current situations. It involves observing subjects in their natural setting and recording the key characteristics without trying to manipulate the behavior. Infants are often observed as they perform a skill; the researcher tries to capture the activity in a natural setting. Some studies are carried out with the researcher on-site during the observation or with the researcher out of sight of the subject (observing on a TV screen or behind a one-way mirror). Observational research may include observing how a patient adapts to a prosthetic device following an amputation or how many times an employee is interrupted to answer the phone while completing a task.

5. Evaluation Research

In evaluation research, a process or an object is examined systematically to evaluate its effectiveness. Policies or procedures in a department can be evaluated as to their merit or their efficiency. Prior standards must be established on which the evaluation is to be conducted to eliminate as much subjectivity as possible. The criteria and standards established for the evaluation should be reproducible by other researchers. Evaluation research includes a case study evaluation of the cost-effectiveness of purchasing a new system for a department or a physician's office or to determine if a new EHR system will increase health care access to underserved populations. Evaluation research generally is carried out to improve outcomes.

6. Experimental Research

Experimental research is research conducted to observe and analyze a specific type of treatment. Experimental research is often referred to as *causal research* as it attempts to answer the question as to what causes certain things to happen—to find a cause. Once the cause for a disease has been established, then the researcher attempts to discover a cure or treatment for the disease. Experimental research discovers causes and establishes causal relationships (cause and effect). It has been well established that smoking (cause) leads to lung cancer (effect). Experimental research includes designing an experiment to make decisions. An experimental research study may be carried out to determine if there is an association between eating unhealthy food and a person's cholesterol level or a pharmaceutical company wants to check if a new medicine it developed will cure or reduce symptoms of a disease. Another researcher may design an experiment to determine if certain weight-training activities reduce the incidence of osteoporosis.

C. SURVEYS AND EXPERIMENTS

The two most common methods of obtaining data are conducting a survey and conducting an experiment. The main difference between the two types of data collection is the control the experimenter has over the result.

1. Surveys

In a survey, data are collected from the members of a population or sample in such a way that there is no control over the factors that may affect the results of the survey. If, for example, a survey was taken of residents in a community to determine the amount of money each family spent on medications in the previous month, the researcher only decides how to conduct the survey. Will a questionnaire be sent to each household, will personal interviews be conducted, or will telephone calls be placed to obtain the information? Nonetheless, many people do not like to be called at home, and those without a phone will be left out of the survey. However, surveys conducted by mail have a low response rate, as many who received the survey do not return the questionnaire. An Internet survey is another possibility but, again, certain households will be excluded. Also, the researcher has no idea if the responses are accurate. Much thought goes into developing an effective survey, and often a pilot test survey is carried out on a small group of individuals for feedback and to fine-tune the survey before it is administered.

2. Experiments

In an experiment, the researcher exercises control over some factor(s) regarding data collection. In testing a new drug to determine its effectiveness in curing a disease, an experiment is designed to test the drug on two groups—a *treatment* group and a *control* group. The treatment group receives the actual drug, and the control group receives a *placebo* (a substitute which resembles the actual drug). If neither the physicians nor the patients know to which group a patient belongs, the experiment is called a *double-blind experiment*. Then, after comparing the results, a decision is made regarding the effectiveness or ineffectiveness of the new drug.

EXAMPLES: A new drug is given to a group of patients with rheumatoid arthritis. This drug is to help reduce the joint inflammation and pain associated with this disease. After six months of usage, the researcher will evaluate the results from both the control group and the treatment group on the effectiveness or ineffectiveness of the drug. Research that is carried out on every member of a population is referred to as a *census*, and every member of the group is referred to as the *target population*. In practice, research is usually conducted on a *sample* of the target population. Three main reasons for conducting a sample survey instead of a census include the following:

a. Time. It takes less time to contact a hundred—rather than a thousand or more—participants.

b. Cost. Most researchers have a limited budget, and it becomes cost prohibitive to survey an entire target population.

c. Impossibility of contacting everyone in a target population—some cannot be located, and others may refuse to cooperate.

D. SAMPLING

Depending on how a sample is drawn, it may be a *random sample* or a *nonrandom sample*.

1. Random Sample

A *random* sample is drawn in such a way that each member of the population has some chance of being selected in the sample. A random sample is drawn in the same manner as choosing a raffle winner—all the names are placed in a bowl or a box, and a winner is drawn at random from the container. If a researcher has a list of 100 people and wants to survey 10, all 10 have an equal chance of having their names drawn for the pool of 100. If, however, the names are arranged alphabetically and the first 10 names are picked, it will be a nonrandom sample because those at the end of the alphabetical list have no chance of being selected in the sample. A random sample is usually a representative sample.

2. Random Sampling Techniques

a. Simple Random Sampling

Under this sampling technique, each sample of the same size, selected from the same population, has the same probability of being selected. As mentioned, this type of sampling often selects the participants by a lottery or drawing. Another method is to use a table of random numbers. However, this method has become outdated and it is now easier to use a statistical package such as Minitab to select a random sample.

b. Systematic Random Sampling

Simple random sampling becomes very tedious if the target population is large. Suppose a community has 50,000 households and only 100 households are to be included in the sample. The names of all 50,000 are arranged according to some characteristic (such as alphabetically). Since the sample size should be 100, the ratio of the population to the sample size is taken (50,000 divided by 100 = 500) indicating that one household out of every 500 is to be selected. If we start with number 200, the remaining members of the survey will be numbers 700, 1,200, 1,700, and so on.

c. **Stratified Random Sampling**

In stratified random sampling, the population is initially subdivided by some strata or factor. If different levels of income are to be included in the study, the population is subdivided by income such as low-, medium-, and high-income households. Then a certain number of households are selected randomly from each of these strata. The strata may include any characteristic such as income, sex, education, race, employment, or family size.

d. **Cluster Sampling**

In cluster sampling, the entire population is first divided into geographic groups called *clusters*. Each cluster is representative of the population. Then a random sample of clusters is selected, followed by a random sample of elements (subjects) from each of the selected clusters. This type of sampling is primarily carried out over a wide geographical area such as an entire state or the whole country.

3. Nonrandom Sample

In a nonrandom sample, some members of the population may not have any chance of being selected for the sample. There are several types of nonrandom samples.

a. **Convenience Sample**

In a convenience sample, the most accessible members of the populations are selected. This is done to obtain results quickly.

b. **Judgment Sample**

The members for the sample are selected from the population based on the judgment and prior knowledge of an expert. If readers of a magazine are polled on a certain topic, the survey may not be representative of the entire population. Also, selecting only respondents that watch a specific television station or television show may not be representative of the population.

c. **Quota Sample**

Selecting the same percentage of males and females as in the population is a *quota sample*. It may also be done by choosing the same percentage of blacks, whites, Asians, and Hispanics present in the entire population; or the same percentage of Republicans and Democrats.

4. Sampling and Non-Sampling Errors

The results obtained from a sample survey may contain two types of errors—sampling and non-sampling errors.

a. **Sampling or Chance Error**

Usually, all samples selected from the same population will produce different results since they are taken from different elements of the population. In addition, the results from one sample survey will not exactly match the result obtained from a census. The difference between the samples result and a census result is called the *sampling error,* assuming the sample is a random sample. The sampling error occurs due to chance and cannot be avoided. Calculating sampling error will not be discussed in this text.

b. **Non-Sampling Errors**

Non-sampling errors occur because of human mistakes and not by chance. Non-sampling errors can be minimized by careful preparation prior to conducting a survey. Some of the non-sampling errors are discussed.

1) **Selection Error**

Selection error occurs when the sample is chosen from a nonrepresentative group of the population. If names are chosen from a phone book, everyone not listed in the phone book is excluded as a possible subject.

2) **Nonresponse Error**

A nonresponse error occurs because many people fail to respond to a survey. This type of error is common with a mailed survey but occurs in other types as well. An interviewer calling on residents at home may find the subject not at home at the time of the visit. Telephone surveys may also find the subject not at home at the time of the call. To avoid nonresponses, every effort should be made to contact all people included in a survey.

3) **Response Error**

A response error occurs when people included in a survey do not provide honest answers. Many respondents will not disclose their true income or respond honestly as to their feelings on a specific topic, such as race relations, and this may depend on the race of the interviewer. Others choose not to reveal how much they weigh or what they spent for an item or services.

4) **Voluntary Response Error**

Voluntary response error occurs when a survey is published in a magazine or a newspaper and people are asked to respond to the questionnaire. Usually only people with a strong opinion about a topic will respond. In addition, if respondents must pay for a call-in order to be included in a survey, many will not want to bear this cost.

5. **Sample Size**

Most survey research is performed on a sample of the population under study. As mentioned, when choosing a sample, it is extremely important to have an accurate representation of the true population to ensure the results will be similar to the results in the population. When selecting formerly hospitalized patients, it would not be representative to choose only people under 30 or those with other certain characteristics. Certain types of software applications (such as SPSS) can be used to generate an appropriate sample size. Usually there is a trade-off between the desirability of a large sample and the feasibility of a small one. The ideal sample size is one that is large enough to represent the target population—to adequately generalize about the group being targeted in the study—and yet be small enough to be economical. A researcher must consider subject availability and the expense of carrying out the research—the time and resources necessary to adequately collect and analyze the data. In general, the larger the sample is, the smaller the magnitude of sampling error. In addition, a survey study generally will include a larger sample size than an observational or, possibly, an experimental study. Since the response rate with a questionnaire-type of survey can be quite low (20% to 30%), a large initial sample is recommended. Generally, the larger the group from which a sample can be selected, the larger the sample size can be. The availability of subjects and the costs in carrying out the survey also play a role in sample size. As a rule, it is often stated that the sample size should be the largest sample possible.

6. Response Rate

The response rate is extremely important in survey research. The response rate will vary but can be quite low. It is often necessary to follow up with the survey subjects who failed to respond. Some studies require the researcher to state the number of times survey subjects will be contacted to respond to the survey questionnaire. Follow-up reminders should include the title of the research study, when the study was initially sent, the importance of the study, and a reminder that the responses will be maintained in strictest confidence. Many studies also offer to send a copy of the results to the respondents in the survey. Some responses to surveys are returned incomplete, and a researcher must decide whether the survey can be included or disregarded in a study.

E. ADDITIONAL TERMS

1. Validity

Validity means that what was intended to be measured was measured. Validity is an indicator of accuracy. Validity answers the question, does the research measure what it was intended to measure? Validity assesses relevance and completeness as well as accuracy and correctness. The data collection instrument and the method of data collection play a significant role in determining the validity of the related data. Testing often precedes the use of an instrument for research purposes to assure it is valid. An applicant for a medical transcription job is often screened by transcribing reports dictated by a physician. This is considered a valid test to determine the ability of the applicant to be hired as a transcriptionist. However, if the opening is for a radiology transcriptionist, transcribing a radiology report would be more valid than transcribing an autopsy report. There are several types of validity.

a. Face Validity

Face validity means that if an expert were to evaluate a study, it would pass the validity test. The term *face validity* refers to the fact that the study can be taken at "face value." In some instances, face validity is a weak measure of true validity.

b. Content Validity

The content of a study undergoes rigorous scrutiny that all relevant aspects of a topic are included. Does the study adhere to the topic, or does it contain irrelevant measures to the result? Again, experts often decide on an instrument's content validity and may score each item as to whether the item is essential, useful but not essential, or not necessary.

c. Construct Validity

Construct refers to *concepts*. In construct validity, the study or instrument is judged as to the degree it adheres to the concepts being measured. Construct validity is assessed by evaluating the degree of correlation between the instrument and the variables it purportedly measures.

d. Criterion Validity

Criteria refer to accepted and established standards. Criterion validity evaluates how well the study adheres to these criteria.

2. Reliability

Reliability means consistency, reproducibility, and repeatability. In a weight loss program, subjects are weighed initially and at the completion of the program. If five different people were to weigh the same individual on the same scale, they should all record the same weight. When charts are coded in the HIM department, five people coding the same chart should all assign the same codes to the chart. The same principle holds true when conducting research. If five different recorders are doing the testing, they should all be trained ahead of time so that results are consistent. It is possible to have reliability without validity, but a study cannot be valid if it is not reliable.

3. Correlation/Correlation Coefficient

Whenever two variables (such as blood pressure and serum cholesterol) are determined for everyone in a study group, the purpose may be to see if one of these variables influences the other—is there a relationship between them? Does a diet high in saturated fat increase the susceptibility of developing cardiovascular disease? Is there a relationship between a mother's weight and the birth weight of her baby? Do oral contraceptives increase the incidence of thromboembolism? Does the amount of sun exposure in childhood play a role in developing malignant melanoma in adulthood? Is there a relationship between IQ and grade point average, or between fluoride in drinking water and cavities in children's teeth? These questions are examples of studies undertaken to determine if a relationship (correlation) exists and how great that correlation is. Questions of this kind are approached by computing the correlation coefficient. Computation of the correlation coefficient is not included in this text but can be found in a statistical textbook. Correlation coefficients range from -1 (negative correlation or an inverse relationship) to $+1$ (strong positive correlation).

A correlation coefficient indicates the strength between two variables. The higher the positive decimal is ($+0.7$ vs. $+0.1$), the greater the relationship. A correlation coefficient of 0 indicates no relationship between variables. A positive correlation has been established between cigarette smoking and increased risk of heart disease and respiratory disorders (such as COPD). Occasionally, a relationship is revealed between two entities in which the development of one condition correlates highly with another, and this is referred to as a *causal relationship*. However, most relationships between two variables are *indirect* rather than causal. One investigator noted that a positive relationship existed between a child's foot size and handwriting ability. This relationship can best be explained by the fact that as a child grows, not only does the size of the foot increase, but the ability to write also improves—an indirect relationship. However, a causal relationship has been established between cavities in children's teeth and the presence of fluoride in drinking water.

4. Inferential Statistics

Previously, it was stated that there are two types of statistics, descriptive and inferential statistics. The computations carried out throughout this text were descriptive statistics in that they described and analyzed a given group or set of data but did not draw any conclusions or inferences about a larger group. In descriptive statistics, data are gathered, organized, computed, and can be graphically displayed. In inferential statistics, there is an attempt to make inferences from data—that is, drawing inference from a sample to the general population. For inferential statistics, the correlation coefficient must be determined and found to be statistically significant at a certain level of confidence. These topics are addressed in other statistics classes. However, public policy is often based on decisions reached through inferential statistics.

EXAMPLE: Inferential statistics have found a statistically significant relationship between smoking and lung cancer to include:

a. The lung cancer death rate for cigarette smokers was 70% higher than for non smokers.

b. The lung cancer death rate increased with increased smoking.

c. The ratio of lung cancer death rates of heavy smokers vs. light smokers was greater than 100%.

d. The lung cancer mortality rate of cigarette smokers vs. nonsmokers was substantially higher for those who started to smoke before age 20 than for those who started smoking after age 25. The mortality ratio increased with more years of smoking.

e. The mortality ratio for smokers who inhaled was higher than for those who did not.

f. Persons who stopped smoking had a mortality rate 1.4 times that of persons who never smoked, while for current smokers, it was 1.7.

g. In all causes of death, smokers had a 70% greater mortality than nonsmokers. Respiratory system mortality was even higher—lung cancer was 10 times higher; emphysema 6.1 times higher.

5. Institutional Review Board

Medical facilities that carry out biomedical and behavioral research studies involving human subjects are mandated by statute to have an *Institutional Review Board*/independent ethics committee (IRB/ IEC) (also known as an *ethical review board*). This group has been formally designated to approve, monitor, and review biomedical and behavioral research studies involving humans, with the aim to protect the rights and welfare of the subjects. The U.S. mandate requires IRBs for all research that receives funding from Health and Human Services (HHS). IRBs themselves are regulated by the Office for Human Research Protections (OHRP) within HHS; IRBs are empowered to approve, require modification in, or disapprove research conducted on human subjects. IRBs were developed to prevent earlier research abuses, such as the Tuskegee Syphilis Study (1932–1972) by the U.S Public Health Service on poor, illiterate black men in the South. The chief objectives are to assess the scientific merit of the proposed research and its methods, to promote fully informed and voluntary participation of the subjects, and to maximize the safety of these subjects.

F. THE RESEARCH PROCESS

The major steps in carrying out a research study are described in this section.

1. Start with an Idea (Topic to Be Researched)

A research study generally begins with an idea (or topic) of concern to the researcher. Most research is carried out in a researcher's area of expertise or interest. A HIM manager is more likely to choose a subject related to improving the work environment—to improve a process that may be too time consuming or studying how enhanced computer technology may be beneficial to the department. Once an idea or a topic is chosen, it then must be refined. A teacher develops a lesson by devising a lesson plan. A student assigned a term paper needs to study the topic and develop a carefully thought-out approach through study and refinement to produce a coherent product.

2. Review the Literature

A review of the literature allows the researcher to systematically review previous studies and become more familiar with the topic of interest. Not only is it helpful to know whether the topic has already been studied, but often a researcher provides additional suggestions at the completion of the research for further study on the topic. All studies should also be reviewed with a critical eye—for example, for bias that may have crept into the study and affected the results. Comprehensive examination of prior research lays the foundation for additional research by identifying new ideas and approaches that may not have occurred to the researcher. The purpose of the literature review is to identify current knowledge on the topic. The bibliography that accompanies a research article can be very helpful in laying a foundation for a topic to be studied.

3. Refine the Original Idea

Once the researcher has done a thorough review of the literature, the original idea or topic needs to be refined. A research study needs to take a great many factors into account, such as the following:

a. Expertise

Researchers need to determine if they have the expertise to conduct the research. If advanced statistical application is necessary, the researcher should feel confident in the application of the more sophisticated statistical analysis necessary for the study or choose a study more within their comfort zone.

b. Skill

Does the topic fit the skill level of the researcher? If advanced training is needed to adequately carry out and analyze the topic, the researcher needs to acquire a proficient skill level for this purpose. If coding skills are to be analyzed, the researcher needs to be proficient in this area.

c. **Personal Attributes**

A study involving interviewing subjects requires a person who can establish a good rapport with people. The researcher needs to have good communication skills and the ability to make a subject feel at ease in order to get a subject to respond honestly to the interviewer. Some researchers may be better at collecting data based on an experiment.

d. **Time**

Time constraints are a major factor in deciding on a research project. Is the research going to be a pilot project or a 10-year study? Can the project be completed in days or weeks, or will it extend over a period of months or years? Time constraints apply to both the researcher and the subjects.

e. **Money**

Researchers must decide up front if the funds are available to carry out the desired research project. Subjects may need to be recruited and the researcher needs to decide if the subjects are going to be reimbursed for their participation? Does the project require the researcher to take time off work for the project, and, if so, for how long? Is special equipment required that may need to be purchased? Prior planning should alleviate the possibility that funds are depleted before completing the project.

f. **Research Subjects**

Are the subjects needed for the research readily available? How will subjects be recruited, and how many will be needed? Will they be available when needed? Have additional subjects been recruited, should they be needed? Is the pool of subjects large enough to have an adequate sample size?

g. **Define All Aspects Related to the Research**

What is the minimum number of subjects needed for an adequate representation of the research? Is a small department made up of less than 10 or 20 employees adequate? What is the coding standard needed for the project? Is a representative sample selected, or were subjects chosen because they were conveniently acquired?

4. Design the Project

Once the general idea has taken shape, the project needs to be planned out in detail and the methodology developed. The preliminary work has been done, and it is time for an outline and step-by-step detail of the project. The research subject (topic) often dictates how the project is to be carried out. Will the study be observational research, survey research, or experimental research? How many people are included; what is the time frame; will assistants be needed, and, if so, how will they be recruited and trained? If it is a survey study, what percentage of completed responses is needed, and what is the plan for follow-up on nonresponses? Has bias been eliminated as completely as possible? Has a step-by-step approach been laid out? What type of data collection and interpretation is needed? What are the aims or objectives of the project? What is the hypothesis?

a. Hypothesis

When designing a project, a researcher often establishes a hypothesis—a statement that predicts the relationship among variables. A hypothesis is a proposed statement of the intent of the research—to prove the statement correct or incorrect (positive or negative). The hypothesis is stated in measurable terms and serves as a guide to analysis of the problem. The hypothesis allows the researcher to prove a point, that is, that a relationship exists between variables or that no relationship exists. Lack of a relationship does not indicate poor research; it only indicates that no association between variables was found. For an unbiased research study, it is important to state the hypothesis prior to gathering data. The hypothesis serves to refine the research question. There are two forms of the hypothesis:

(1) *Null hypothesis*. The null (meaning none) hypothesis states there is no difference between the two variables being compared. A null hypothesis is a claim (or statement) about a population parameter that is assumed to be true until it is declared false. A non-statistical example applies to a defendant being tried for a crime in a court of law. A defendant is said to be innocent until proven guilty. Based on the evidence, the judge or jury is to decide either (1) the person is not guilty, or (2) the person is guilty of the crime. At the outset of the trial, the person is presumed not guilty and the prosecutor's job is to prove the person guilty. In statistics, the "person is not guilty" is called the *null hypothesis*. When a new medicine is being tested in a clinical trial, the new medicine may turn out to be no better than the current medicine to which it was compared.

(2) *Alternative hypothesis*. In an alternative hypothesis, the researcher tries to predict the association between the independent and the dependent variables. An alternative hypothesis is a claim about a population parameter that will be true if the null hypothesis is false. Returning to the court example, we can say that the verdict, "the person is guilty," is called the *alternative hypothesis*. In the new medicine example, the alternative hypothesis might state that the new medicine is 10% more effective than the current (control) medicine. This may or may not prove to be the case, but the outcome is predicted prior to data gathering. If voice recognition software is introduced to a group of physicians and one group receives specified training in its use and another group of physicians does not, the researcher may specify a predicted improved outcome (say 10%) for the group receiving the training than the control group (those without the training).

b. Significance and Confidence

(1) *Significance*. The term *significance* also accompanies research studies. The significance level is the criterion used for rejecting the null hypothesis. Statistical techniques exist to establish the

significance level, though they are only appropriate with random samples. Criteria to determine significance must be established prior to data collection. The significance level is also known as the alpha level, and the levels are generally indicated by 0.001, 0.01, or 0.05. A level of 0.001 is lower than a level of 0.01.

(2) *Confidence.* The confidence level states how much confidence there is that the confidence interval contains the true population parameter. Although any confidence level can be chosen to construct a confidence interval, the more common values are 90%, 95%, and 99%.

5. Collect the Data

Once the planning and preliminary work is complete, the research is ready for data collection. An instrument is selected according to how the data will be collected. Some examples of measurement instruments include checklists, various tests, rating scales, questionnaires, and interview guidelines. The data collection process should stress consistency and rigorous implementation. The quality of a research project is primarily based on how rigorous the data was collected and analyzed. A comprehensive, step-by-step plan should be in place to assure accuracy.

6. Analyze the Data and Draw Conclusions

After completing the data collection, the researcher needs to attempt to make some sense of the data collected. Researchers examine and make conclusions based on what the data results indicate. Analysis requires a great deal of thought and time. Any conclusions reached, based on the data, should be related to the hypothesis in a quantitative study. It is important to report any limitations discovered during the analysis as well as any positive findings. Suggestions for further studies, as well as what might have been done differently, are also appropriate.

7. Write/Present the Report

Following all the analysis, the researcher generally commits to writing or presenting a report. Tables, charts, and graphs are valuable aids to include in the report. Research reports can be submitted for publication, and the publication's guidelines should be followed. Some research projects are also presented at a conference or to interested groups. Every report should be well thought out and grammatically correct. Previous research papers and articles serve as an excellent basis for this phase of the project.

This chapter has only served as a basis for starting on an exploratory path to further research. A research class is invaluable in developing research skills. Most research also requires a more advanced knowledge of statistics and additional statistics classes are recommended. Reading research studies in professional publications and journals provides insight as to how previous studies were conducted and provide ideas for future research. Assisting a qualified researcher on a project is also invaluable and provides experience to the novice researcher. Anyone interested in doing research should avail themselves of a mentor, if possible, and learn to perfect written, verbal, and analytic skills in the search for answers to untested questions, as there are always new problems to be solved.

G. SUMMARY

1. The two types of research are referred to as *basic research* and *applied research*. Basic research answers the question "why"; applied research tries to discover a solution to a problem.
2. The most common approaches to research are the quantitative (using numerical data), the qualitative (descriptions), and the mixed approach (both quantitative and qualitative approaches).
3. Inductive reasoning draws conclusions based on a limited number of observations; deductive reasoning draws conclusions based on generalizations, rules, or principles.
4. A retrospective study looks back in time; a prospective study looks ahead—what is likely to happen in the future.
5. A cross-sectional study collects data on a one-time basis; a longitudinal study follows research subjects over extended periods of time and at multiple times throughout the study period.
6. Historical research investigates the past—past events and records.
7. Descriptive research describes the present status with words rather than numerical data.
8. Correlational research studies the relationship between factors or variables to see if a relationship exists.
9. Observational research observes a process or a behavior as it occurs.
10. Evaluation research examines the effectiveness of a process or an object—how well is it working?
11. Experimental research is analytical; it is often referred to as causal research in that it tries to establish a cause-and-effect relationship.
12. A survey is a common method of collecting descriptive data; opinion polls, telephone surveys, and questionnaires are common survey tools.
13. An experiment is a tool designed to collect data—a process that, when performed, results in one observation (and only one of many observations). These observations are called *outcomes* of the experiments. The collection of all outcomes for an experiment is called a *sample space*.
14. Experimental research often includes a treatment group and a control group with the former receiving a treatment and the latter a placebo.
15. A double-blind experiment is one in which neither the physicians nor the patients know to which group the patient belongs.
16. A random sample is an unbiased selection of subjects from the target population.
17. A nonrandom sample is biased in the selection of subjects through convenience (easily accessible), judgment (selected group), or quota (a certain number from several groups—e.g., blacks, whites, Asians, Hispanics).
18. Sampling errors are the difference between the population and sample due to pure chance.
19. Non-sampling errors occur because of human mistakes and not by chance. The errors include a selection error (a nonrepresentative sample), a nonresponse error (certain subjects contacted fail to respond, skewing the results), a response error (subjects are not truthful in their response), and a voluntary response error (only those with strong opinions respond).
20. Sample size refers to the number of subjects in a sample. In general, the larger the sample is, the smaller the magnitude of sampling error.

21. In survey research, the response rate to a survey is generally quite low, and follow-up reminders are recommended. Responses should be held in strictest confidence.
22. Validity means the right thing was measured: accuracy.
23. Reliability means consistency, the same results are reproducible or repeatable, and consistency of measurement.
24. A research study may be reliable but not valid, but a study cannot be valid if it is not reliable.
25. Face validity means that by looking at the instrument, it appears valid; it is a weak measure of validity.
26. Content validity means rigorous review that all relevant aspects of a topic are included.
27. Construct validity means that all constructs (concepts) are measured.
28. Criterion validity assesses an instrument against another established instrument.
29. Correlation refers to the strength of a relationship between variables.
30. Inferential statistics makes inferences about the population based on the results of a sample.
31. The Institutional Review Board (IRB) oversees research studies concerning human subjects, protecting the rights and welfare of the human subjects in the research study.
32. The research process includes starting with an idea, reviewing past studies related to the idea, refining the idea through introspection and evaluation of time and resources, designing the project, collecting the data, analyzing the data and drawing conclusions, and writing and/or presenting the report.
33. A null hypothesis states there is no relationship between the independent and the dependent variables; an alternative hypothesis states there is a difference—the predicted difference—between the two variables.
34. Significance level is the criterion used for rejecting the null hypothesis, usually expressed as 0.001, 0.01, or 0.05.
35. Confidence level states how much confidence there is that the confidence interval contains the true population parameter, usually expressed as 90%, 95%, and 99%.

Name _____ Date _____

H. CHAPTER 14 TEST

1. What are the two types of research?

   a. Basic and applied
   b. Descriptive and causal
   c. Qualitative and quantitative
   d. Theoretical and non-theoretical

2. Indicate the type of research that uses descriptive rather than numerical data.

   a. Theoretical
   b. Quantitative
   c. Qualitative
   d. Experimental

3. Indicate the type of reasoning that draws conclusions based on a limited number of observations.

   a. Deductive
   b. Inductive
   c. Observational
   d. Descriptive

4. Indicate the type of study that collects data on a one-time basis.

   a. Retrospective
   b. Prospective
   c. Cross-sectional
   d. Longitudinal

5. Indicate the type of study that follows subjects over extended periods at multiple times.

   a. Retrospective
   b. Prospective
   c. Cross-sectional
   d. Longitudinal

6. Indicate the term signifying "top down" reasoning.

   a. Deductive
   b. Inductive
   c. Observational
   d. Descriptive

7. Indicate the term for an assumption or idea to be tested through validation or invalidation.

   a. Criterion
   b. Hypothesis
   c. Sampling
   d. Correlation

8. Indicate the type of study design that investigates the past.

   a. Historical
   b. Experimental
   c. Evaluation
   d. Observational

9. Indicate the type of study design most likely to use the qualitative approach.

   a. Descriptive
   b. Correlational
   c. Evaluation
   d. Experimental

10. Indicate the term referring to the relationship between two variables.

    a. Reliability
    b. Validity
    c. Significance
    d. Confidence
    e. Correlation

11. Indicate the term often referred to as causal research.

    a. Historical
    b. Descriptive
    c. Observational
    d. Evaluation
    e. Experimental

12. Indicate the type of sample in which everyone in the target population has an equal chance of being included.

    a. Random
    b. Nonrandom

13. Indicate the type of random sampling in which everyone is listed and every 500th name is selected.

    a. Simple
    b. Systematic
    c. Stratified
    d. Cluster

14. The type of error that occurs when people do not respond to a survey is called

    a. Response error
    b. Sampling error
    c. Nonresponse error
    d. Selection error

15. Indicate the term for a study that measures what it was intended to measure.

    a. Validity
    b. Reliability
    c. Integrity
    d. Significance
    e. Confidence

16. Indicate the term related to repeatability and consistency.

    a. Validity
    b. Reliability
    c. Integrity
    d. Significance
    e. Confidence

17. Indicate the board established to protect the rights of human subjects in biomedical and behavioral research studies.

    a. FDA
    b. OHRP
    c. HHS
    d. IRB
    e. BMRB

18. Which of the following is an appropriate indicator of significance level?

    a. 0.05
    b. 5.00
    c. 5%
    d. 50%
    e. None of these

19. Which of the following is a commonly used confidence level?

    a. 0.05
    b. 5.00
    c. 5%
    d. 50%
    e. None of these

20. Indicate the random sampling technique carried out over a wide geographical area such as an entire state.

    a. Systematic
    b. Stratified
    c. Cluster
    d. Judgment

21. Indicate an appropriate range for a correlation coefficient.

    a. 0.001 to 0.05
    b. 0.5 to 5.0
    c. 10% to 20%
    d. -1 to $+1$
    e. 90% to 99%

22. All of the following are methods used in selecting sample size except

    a. Making an accurate representation of the population being surveyed
    b. Use of a statistical software package
    c. Use of as large a sample as possible, given low response rates
    d. Assuring sample subject availability
    e. Use of a small sample size to allow for easier result calculation

23. What is the most common method typically used to increase survey response rates?

24. Place the following steps in the research process in the correct order:

    a. _____Review the literature.
    b. _____Design the project.
    c. _____Analyze the date/draw conclusions.
    d. _____Write/present the report.
    e. _____Collect the data.
    f. _____Start with an idea.
    g. _____Refine the original idea.

25. Indicate the type of hypothesis in which the researcher attempts to predict a specified association between variables.

    a. Null
    b. Alternative
    c. Significant
    d. Analytical
    e. Alternative

APPENDIX I
ANSWERS TO TEXT PRELIMINARY QUESTIONS

CHAPTER 1

1. a. *Data* refers to a set of facts, whereas information is data that has been collected, analyzed, and processed to make conclusions and become useful.
   b. Population refers to an entire group, whereas a sample is a subset (a smaller portion) of a given population.
   c. Primary data are found in a patient record, but secondary data are primary data that have then been grouped with other data, such as in an index or registry.
   d. A constant is something that is assumed to not change across the distribution and has only one value, whereas a variable can change; variables such as age, sex, or diagnosis are examples of variables that can be compared within a distribution.
   e. A representative sample is chosen because it fairly represents the population under study, while a random sample merely selects by some process the number of records to be studied.
   f. Morbidity is related to disease statistics, but mortality refers to death statistics.

2. Demography is the study of human population statistics. Demographic variables include such factors as age, sex, income, and health status that are looked at within studies of human populations.

3. Vital statistics are records of significant events such as birth, death, and marriage.

4. Users of health care data include administration, governing boards, other treatment facilities, outside agencies, insurers, and researchers.

5. Health care data can be used for assessing utilization of service and quality of care, justifying the need for new equipment, and for making patient diagnoses and treatment decisions.

6. NCHS: National Center for Health Statistics; DHHS: Department of Health and Human Services; CDC: Centers for Disease Control and Prevention

7. a. IP = inpatient;
   b. OP = outpatient;
   c. DOA = dead on arrival;
   d. NB = newborn;
   e. Σ = summation of numbers that follow the sign

CHAPTER 2

1. a. $12/60 = 1/5$
   b. $27/162 = 3/18 = 1/6$
   c. $40/520 = 1/13$
   d. $7/42 = 1/6$

2. a. $70/13 = 5.38$
   b. $9246/27 = 342.44$
   c. $3/11 = 0.27$

3. a. $36/92 = 39.13\%$
   b. $54/358 = 15.08\%$
   c. $612/1348 = 45.40\%$
   d. $72/54 = 133.3\%$

4. a. $6/200 = 0.03$
   b. $7/510 = 0.01$
   c. $4/450 = 0.01$
   d. $32/75 = 0.43$

5. a. 407.5
   b. 3.53
   c. 477.09

6. a. 96
   b. $125.876 = 125.88$
   c. $349 = 300$

7. a. $2/40 = 5\%$
   b. $3/67 = 4.48\%$
   c. $762/1045 = 72.92\%$

8. a. $0.000998 = 0.10\%$
   b. $7.61546 = 761.55\%$
   c. $60.72 = 6072\%$

9. a. $8(60) + 2/3(9) - 64/6 = 480 + 6 - 10.67 = 475.33$
   b. $32.946(2) + 6.75 - 3/5(70) = 65.89 + 6.75 - 42 = 30.64$
   c. $60\%(420) - 2/3(75) - 45\%(380) = 252 - 50 - 171 = 31$

10. a. $1/2 + 3/5 + 7/10 = 5/10 + 6/10 + 7/10 = 18/10 = 1.8$
    b. $3/5 \times 15/60 = .6 \times .25 = 0.15$
    c. $3/10 \div 6/24 = 1.2$

CHAPTER 3

1. The level of care varies between a hospital and a nursing facility, with hospitals delivering acute care and nursing facilities providing extended inpatient care.

2. Encounter: direct, professional contact between a provider and a patient

   Occasion of service: a specific, identifiable service of care delivered to a patient as a result of an encounter (for example, a lab test or X-ray).

   Visit: a single encounter between a patient and a provider and all services provided therein.

   MCO: a managed care organization.

3. Medicare is a national health insurance for those 65 or older, whereas Medicaid is a national program, administered at the state level, provided to those who qualify—often those on welfare.

4. Hospice care: care for the terminally ill.

   Respite care: short-term relief for caregivers by providing care for the person in need of care.

5. Primary care centers provide care services much the same as is provided in doctors' offices by family practice, internal medicine, or pediatric physicians.

6. The most common cut-off for the designation of a child is the 14th birthday.

7. Concurrent collection of data takes place during the care of a patient, whereas retrospective data collection takes place after care has been provided and is done through a review of the patient's chart.

8. An abstract is a condensed summary of data—a common example of an abstract is a cancer registry.

9. An index is a tool used to locate information that serves as a guide in the process.

10. A register is a chronological list of data within a health care facility, whereas an index refers to the way in which data are organized, such as by patient number, physician, or disease type.

11. AIDS, birth defects, organ transplants, trauma, etc.

12. Incident reports are completed, per facility protocol, on potentially risky events—such as medication errors, patient falls, or aseptic techniques. These reports allow organizations to identify trends and opportunities for improvement in delivering high-quality care.

CHAPTER 4

1. Census is a count of a specific population—as a whole or as a subgroup.

2. Census data can be collected on a daily, weekly, monthly, yearly, or other periodic basis. Hospitals typically establish a set time of day at which point the patient population is counted.

3. An inpatient is a person who has been admitted to a hospital and for whom continuous nursing service is provided, whereas an outpatient receives a more short-term service at a facility other than a hospital or nursing care facility.

4. Patients can be transferred from one care unit to another or from one facility to another, the latter of which is called a "discharge transfer."

5. DOA is defined as dead on arrival.

6. The average number of beds occupied is 67.86 (or 68). Given that the facility has a capacity of 100 beds, 100 becomes the denominator, and the average occupancy would be 67.86% (67.86/100).

7. 365 days in a non-leap year; April, June, September, November

8. Yes; if the year is evenly divisible by the number four, then it was (is) a leap year.

CHAPTER 5

1. 60% (60/100)

2. The health care facility hopes to have a high occupancy percentage in order to better utilize resources and operate "in the black."

3. Inpatient beds for adults and children (A&C) are counted separately from newborn (NB) beds, which are often referred to as bassinets. Services and staffing levels vary greatly among these two populations of patients. Healthy newborns typically require less care and require less direct nursing service.

4. A&C and NBs should be counted separately as they fall into two different bed counts. Separating this data also makes calculation of length of stay more accurate for the adults/children population, as newborn length of stay tends to be much shorter and can skew the overall analysis of patient length of stay.

5. Health care facilities open and close units based on demand for service; staffing units is one of the highest costs within a facility, and staffing a unit that has only a few patients is not cost-effective. It is better to move patients to another unit to gain higher levels of efficiency. During times of increasing demand, on the other hand, facilities can look to expand their beds/bassinets to meet this demand in accordance with state certificate of need requirements.

CHAPTER 6

1. All calendar days are counted in a patient's length of stay, from the point of admission to discharge.

2. Yes, the 4 hours translate into a one-day stay.

3. Yes, if daily census is taken at midnight, the 1 hour prior to this would count as a day.

4. Length of stays has been decreasing in large part due to reimbursement that is calculated on diagnostic code and not the length of stay in a facility.

5. Facilities with longer lengths of stay (two months or more) include nursing homes and rehabilitation hospitals.

6. Average LOS = 4 days; 28 total days divided by 7 (denominator) = 4 days ALOS

7. They are typically not combined when calculating length of stay, as these populations are unique, and, therefore, statistics are kept separate.

CHAPTER 7, 8

(none)

CHAPTER 9

1. Mortality refers to death or being fatal.

2. A newborn death occurs after delivery where signs of life have been detected, whereas a fetal death occurs prior to delivery.

3. Net: the amount after deductions have been made

   Gross: an amount before anything is subtracted

4. Death rates should be included in discharge data as long as the discharge data are not looking at only "live discharges"; in this case, death totals would be added to live discharges in order to calculate rates.

5. 10%; 1 expired/10 total discharges

6. Again, newborn death rate data should be segregated from that of adult and children for better statistical analysis.

CHAPTER 10, 11

(none)

CHAPTER 12

1. a.   Highest score = 97; Lowest score = 53;
        Range = 53–97

1. b.

53		68	(3)	79	(3)	89	
57		69		80		90	
59		71	(3)	81		93	(2)
60	(3)	72	(2)	82	(2)	94	
61	(2)	73	(4)	83		95	(2)
62	(4)	74	(3)	84		96	
63	(2)	75	(7)	85	(3)	97	
65	(3)	76	(4)	86			
66		77	(2)	87			
67	(2)	78	(5)	88	(3)		

1. c.   1) 75; 2) 75; 3) 10% (8/80); 4) 17.5% (14/80); 5) 18.75% (15/80); 6) 41.25% (33/80); 7) 26.25% (21/80); 8) 3.75% (3/80)

2. Below;
   $85 \times 80/100 = 68$ (85 is above 68);
   $60 \times 80/100 = 48$ (70 is above 48)

3. 75

4.

Scores	Frequency	Scores	Frequency
95–99	4	70–74	12
90–94	4	65–69	10
85–89	9	60–64	11
80–84	6	55–59	2
75–79	21	50–54	1

CHAPTER 13

1. The x-axis is the horizontal axis and typically contains the primary variables. Values are shown from lowest on the left to highest on the right. The y-axis is the vertical axis and has lowest values at the bottom and highest values at the top.

2. Bar charts are used for displaying quantitative data related to categories or groups. Bar charts are presented horizontally. When a bar chart is presented vertically it is called a column chart.

3. The general rule is to use a 3:5—or, more commonly, 3:4—height to length. The graph should therefore be greater in length than in height.

4. Qualitative data are best displayed through the use of charts such as bar or column charts.

5. Quantitative continuous data are best displayed on a graph, either histogram or frequency polygon.

6. The most popular graphing software comes in the Microsoft Office Suite; it is called Excel.

7. A coroner is an elected or appointed official, and a medical examiner is a physician officially authorized by a governmental agency to rule on cause of death.

8. Any inpatient that dies in the hospital is a candidate for an autopsy. Some autopsies are performed on outpatients, former patients, and some fetal deaths. Deaths that need to be reported to the coroner's office include deaths involving criminal/violent means, suicides, sudden deaths, deaths with suspicious circumstances, and accidental deaths, including those occurring in the workplace.

9. Physicians need to retain a consent for an autopsy, but if the autopsy is considered a coroner's case, no consent is required.

CHAPTER 14

(none)

FORMULAS

Listed below are the basic formulas used for hospital statistics. They have been included in the various chapters of the text and are repeated here for easy reference.

A. CENSUS

Inpatient Census: Patients remaining at the previous census-taking time *plus* addition of new admissions and subtraction of the day's discharges (including the deaths).

Inpatient Service Days: Census plus A&Ds (those admitted and discharged the same day).

Average DIPC:

$$\frac{\text{Total IPSD for a period}}{\text{Total number of days in the period}}$$

A&C Average DIPC:

$$\frac{\text{Total IPSD (excluding NB) for a period}}{\text{Total number of days in the period}}$$

NB Average DIPC:

$$\frac{\text{Total NB IPSD for a period}}{\text{Total number of days in the period}}$$

Clinical Unit Average DIPC:

$$\frac{\text{Total IPSD for the clinical unit for a period}}{\text{Total number of days in the period}}$$

B. PERCENTAGE OF OCCUPANCY

Daily IP Bed Occupancy Percentage:

$$\frac{\text{Daily IPSD}}{\text{IP bed count for that day}} \times 100$$

Daily NB Bassinet Occupancy Percentage:

$$\frac{\text{Daily NB IPSD}}{\text{NB bassinet count for that day}} \times 100$$

IP Bed Occupancy Percentage for a Period:

$$\frac{\text{Total IPSD for a period}}{\text{Total IP bed count} \times \text{number of days in the period}} \times 100$$

NB Bassinet Occupancy Percentage for a Period:

$$\frac{\text{Total NB IPSD for a period}}{\text{Total NB bassinet count} \times \text{number of days in the period}} \times 100$$

Clinical Unit Occupancy Percentage for a Period:

$$\frac{\text{Total IPSD in a clinical unit for a period}}{\text{IP bed count total for that unit} \times \text{number of days in the period}} \times 100$$

Occupancy Percentage for a Period with a Change in Bed Count:

$$\frac{\text{Total IPSD for the period}}{(\text{Bed count} \times \text{days}) + (\text{Bed count} \times \text{days})} \times 100$$

(Days refer to number of days in the period.)

C. LENGTH OF STAY

Average Length of Stay:

$$\frac{\text{Total discharge days (including deaths but excluding NB)}}{\text{Total discharges (including deaths but excluding NB)}}$$

Average NB Length of Stay:

$$\frac{\text{Total NB discharge days (including deaths)}}{\text{Total NB discharges (including deaths)}}$$

D. HOSPITAL MORTALITY RATES

1. General

Gross Death Rate:

$$\frac{\text{Total number of IP deaths (including NB) for a period}}{\text{Total number of discharges for the period (including deaths of NB} + \text{A\&C)}} \times 100$$

Net Death Rate:

$$\frac{\text{Total IP deaths (including NB)} - \text{deaths} < 48 \text{ hours for a period}}{\text{Total discharges (including NB)} - \text{deaths} < 48 \text{ hours for a period}} \times 100$$

NB Death Rate:

$$\frac{\text{Total NB deaths for a period}}{\text{Total NB discharges (including deaths) for the period}} \times 100$$

2. Surgical Death Rates

Postoperative Death Rate:

$$\frac{\text{Total postoperative surgical deaths} < 10 \text{ days postop for a period}}{\text{Total patients operated upon for the period}} \times 100$$

Anesthesia Death Rate:

$$\frac{\text{Total deaths caused by anesthetic agents for a period}}{\text{Total number of anesthesias administered for the period}} \times 100$$

E. OB-RELATED RATES

Maternal Death Rate:

$$\frac{\text{Total direct maternal deaths for a period}}{\text{Total maternal discharges (including deaths) for the period}} \times 100$$

Fetal Death Rate:

$$\frac{\text{Total intermediate and late fetal deaths for a period}}{\substack{\text{Total live births} + \text{intermediate and late} \\ \text{fetal deaths for the period}}} \times 100$$

C-Section Rate:

$$\frac{\text{Total C-sections performed for a period}}{\text{Total number of deliveries for the same period}} \times 100$$

F. AUTOPSY RATES

Gross Autopsy Rate:

$$\frac{\text{Total autopsies on IP deaths for a period}}{\text{Total IP deaths}} \times 100$$

Net Autopsy Rate:

$$\frac{\text{Total autopsies on IP deaths for a period}}{\text{Total IP deaths} - \text{unautopsies coroner's cases}} \times 100$$

Hospital Autopsy Rate:

$$\frac{\substack{\text{Total number of hospital autopsies} \\ \text{(IP, OP, and former patients) for a period}}}{\substack{\text{Number of deaths of hospital patients whose bodies} \\ \text{are available for hospital autopsy for that period}}} \times 100$$

NB Autopsy Rate:

$$\frac{\text{Autopsies on NB deaths for a period}}{\text{Total NB deaths for the period}} \times 100$$

Fetal Autopsy Rate:

$$\frac{\text{Autopsies on intermediate and late fetal deaths for a period}}{\text{Total intermediate and late fetal deaths for the period}} \times 100$$

G. MISCELLANEOUS RATES

Infection Rates

Hospital:

$$\frac{\substack{\text{Total number of infections} \\ \text{(nosocomial and community-acquired)}}}{\text{Total number of discharges (including deaths)}} \times 100$$

Nosocomial:

$$\frac{\text{Total number of hospital-acquired infections} (>72 \text{ hours after admission})}{\text{Total number of discharges (including deaths)}} \times 100$$

Community-Acquired:

$$\frac{\text{Total number of community-acquired infections} (<72 \text{ hours of admission})}{\text{Total number of discharges (including deaths)}} \times 100$$

Postoperative:

$$\frac{\text{Total number of postoperative infections in clean surgical cases}}{\text{Total number of surgical operations performed}} \times 100$$

Consultation Rates

a. Patients Seen

$$\frac{\text{Total number of patients receiving consultation}}{\text{Total number of patients discharged}} \times 100$$

b. Consults Provided

$$\frac{\text{Total number of consultations provided}}{\text{Total number of patients discharged}} \times 100$$

Complication Rate

$$\frac{\text{Total number of complications for a period}}{\text{Total number of discharges for the period}} \times 100$$

Comorbidity Rate

$$\frac{\text{Total number of comorbidities for a period}}{\text{Total number of discharges for the period}} \times 100$$

Bed/Bassinet Turnover Rates

Direct:

$$\frac{\text{Total number of discharges (including deaths) for a period}}{\text{Average bed count during the period}} \times 100$$

Indirect:

$$\frac{\text{Occupancy rate (in decimal format)} \times \text{number of days in a period}}{\text{Average length of stay for the period}} \times 100$$

H. VITAL STATISTICS RATES (MULTIPLIERS MAY BE 1,000, 10,000, OR 100,000)

OB-Related Mortality Rates

Maternal:

$$\frac{\text{Deaths (due to pregnancy-related conditions) for a period}}{\text{Number of live births for the same period}} \times 100,000$$

Infant:

$$\frac{\text{Infant deaths} (< 1 \text{ year of age}) \text{ for a period}}{\text{Total number of live births for the same period}} \times 1,000$$

Neonatal:

$$\frac{\text{Number of neonatal deaths} (< 28 \text{ days of age}) \text{ for a period}}{\text{Total number of live births for the same period}} \times 1,000$$

Perinatal:

$$\frac{\text{Number of perinatal (intermediate and late fetal and neonatal) deaths for a period}}{\text{Total number of live births} + \text{intermediate and late fetal deaths for the same period}} \times 1,000$$

Post-neonatal:

a. Primary

$$\frac{\text{Number of post neonatal deaths} (28 \text{ days to 1 year}) \text{ for a period}}{\text{Total number of live births} - \text{neonatal deaths for the same period}} \times 1,000$$

b. Secondary

$$\frac{\text{Number of post neonatal deaths} (28 \text{ days to 1 year}) \text{ for a period}}{\text{Total number of live births for the same period}} \times 1,000$$

Fetal:

$$\frac{\text{Number of intermediate and late fetal deaths for a period}}{\text{Total number of live births for the same period}} \times 1,000$$

Induced Termination of Pregnancy Ratio/Rate

Ratio I:

$$\frac{\text{Number of induced pregnancy terminations for a period}}{\text{Total number of live births for the same period}} \times 1,000$$

Ratio II:

$$\frac{\text{Number of induced pregnancy terminations for a period}}{\text{Number of induced pregnancy terminations} + \text{live births} + \text{intermediate and late fetal deaths}} \times 1,000$$

Induced Termination of Pregnancy Rate:

$$\frac{\text{Number of induced pregnancy terminations for a period}}{\text{Female population (age 15-44) for the same period}} \times 1,000$$

NOTE: The multiplier for the following rates most commonly is 1,000, 10,000, or 100,000.

Morbidity Rates

Prevalence:

$$\frac{\text{Number of known (existing) cases of a disease for a period}}{\text{Population for the same period}} \times \text{multiplier}$$

Incidence:

$$\frac{\text{Newly reported cases of a disease for a period}}{\text{Population at midperiod}} \times \text{multiplier}$$

Additional Death Rates

Crude Death Rate:

$$\frac{\text{Number of deaths in a population for a period}}{\text{Estimated population for the same period}} \times \text{multiplier}$$

Age-Specific Death Rate:

$$\frac{\text{Number of deaths in a specified age group for a period}}{\text{Estimated population of the age group for the same period}} \times \text{multiplier}$$

Cause-Specific Death Rate:

$$\frac{\text{Number of deaths due to a specific cause for a period}}{\text{Estimated population for the same period}} \times \text{multiplier}$$

Cause-Race-Specific Death Rate:

$$\frac{\text{Number of deaths of a specific race for a specific cause for a period}}{\text{Estimated population of the specific race for the same period}} \times \text{multiplier}$$

Proportional Mortality Rate:

$$\frac{\text{Number of deaths due to a specific cause for a period}}{\text{Total deaths (from all causes) for the same period}} \times 100$$

Case Fatality Rate:

$$\frac{\text{Number of deaths for a given disease/cause for a period}}{\text{Number of cases of the disease reported for the same period}} \times 100$$

Fertility Rates

Crude Birth Rate:

$$\frac{\begin{array}{c}\text{Number of live births} \\ \text{(for a given community) for a period}\end{array}}{\begin{array}{c}\text{Estimated population (midperiod)} \\ \text{of the community for the same period}\end{array}} \times 1,000$$

General Fertility Rate:

$$\frac{\text{Number of live birth in a calendar year}}{\text{Total number of females (age } 15-44 \text{) at midyear}} \times 1,000$$

Cancer Mortality Rate:

$$\frac{\text{Deaths due to cancer for a period}}{\text{Estimated population for the same period}} \times \text{multiplier}$$

I. BASIC RATE FORMULA

$$\frac{\text{Number of times something happens}}{\text{Number of times it could happen}} \times 100$$

J. GENERAL STATISTICS

Mean

$$\frac{\Sigma \text{ scores}}{N}$$

Variance

$$s^2 = \frac{\Sigma(x - \overline{x})^2}{n-1}$$

Standard Deviation

$$s = \sqrt{\frac{\Sigma(x - \overline{x})^2}{n-1}}$$

Formula for Operating Margin

(Net patient revenue − operating expenses)/total operating income

Days in Accounts Receivable

Net patient receivables/(net credit revenue/number of days in year)

Employee Turnover

Number of employees that left organization/total number of employees at start of period

Budget Variance

Actual amount ($$) − budgeted amount ($$) = variance ($$)

Budget Variance Percentage

Variance ($$)/budgeted amount ($$) = variance percentage (%)

Nurse-Patient Ratio

Number of registered nurses: number of patients = nurse: patient ratio (reduced to lowest common denominators)

ANSWERS TO TEXTBOOK SELF-TESTS

CHAPTER 1 Health Statistics: *Why Are They Important?*

Self-Test 1-1

1. a. qualitative
   b. quantitative
   c. quantitative
2. a. discrete
   b. continuous
   c. continuous
   d. discrete

Self-Test 1-2

1. a. nominal
   b. nominal
   c. neither (interval)
   d. ordinal

Self-Test 1-3

1. a. population
   b. sample
   c. population
   d. sample
   e. sample

CHAPTER 2 Mathematics: *Reviewing the Basics*

Self-Test 2-1

1. a. 43/85
   b. $25/85 = 5/17$
   c. 12/85
   d. 5/85
2. a. 1) 3
      2) 10
      3) 6
      4) 35
   b. 1) 17
      2) 10
      3) 8
      4) 80
   c. 1) 13. Rationale: $325/25 = 13$
      2) 7. Rationale: $49/7 = 7$
      3) 200. Rationale: $1,800/9 = 200$
      4) 9. Rationale: $72/8 = 9$

Self-Test 2-2

a. 8/25. Rationale: 32 and 100 are divisible by $4 = 8/25$
b. 1/6. Rationale: 6 and 36 are divisible by 1/6
c. 1/20. Rationale: 4 will go into 4 once and 4 into 80 20 times, which equals 1/20
d. 1/8. Rationale: Both the numerator and the denominator are divisible by 7, which equals 1/8.
e. 1/5. Rationale: Both the numerator and the denominator are divisible by 15, which equals 1/5.

Self-Test 2-3

a. 0.10. Rationale: $6/60 = 1/10 = 0.10$
b. 0.004. Rationale: $4/1,000 = 0.004$
c. 0.045. Rationale: $9/200 = 0.045$
d. 0.13. Rationale: $10/77 = 0.129 = 0.13$

Self-Test 2-4

a. 24%. Rationale: $12/50 \times 100 = 24\%$
b. 40%. Rationale: $4/10 \times 100 = 40\%$
c. 0.3%. Rationale: $3/1,000 \times 100 = 0.3\%$
d. 0.52%. Rationale: $45/8,640 \times 100 = 0.52\%$

Self-Test 2-5

Death rate is 2.5%. Rationale: $(4/160) \times 100 = 2.5\%$

Self-Test 2-6

Orthopedic: 20/100 or 20%. Rationale: $20/100 \times 100 = 0.20 = 20\%$
Gynecological: 12/100 or 12%. Rationale: $12/100 \times 100 = 0.20 = 12\%$
Ophthalmological: 18/100 or 18%. Rationale: $18/100 \times 100 = 0.18 = 18\%$
Urological: 22/100 or 22%. Rationale: $22/100 \times 100 = 0.22 = 22\%$
General surgery: 28/100 or 28%. Rationale: $28/100 \times 100 = 0.28 = 28\%$

Self-Test 2-7

1. 8.14. Rationale: $(6 + 10 + 8 + 9 + 5 + 12 + 7)/7 = 8.14$
2. 3.75. Rationale: $(3 + 4 + 1 + 2 + 6 + 2 + 5 + 8 + 1 + 4 + 6 + 3)/12 = 3.75$
3. 18.55. Rationale: $575/31 = 18.55$
4. 5.8. Rationale: $1,050/181 = 5.8$
5. 2.29. Rationale: $(2 + 2 + 4 + 1 + 3 + 1 + 3)/7 = 2.29$

Self-Test 2-8

1. a. 65
   b. 66
   c. 66
   d. 71
   e. 7,051
   f. 1
   g. 38
   h. 596
   i. 148
   j. 10
   k. 16
   l. 56
2. a. 12.4
   b. 27.6
   c. 31.7
   d. 0.0
   e. 457.0
   f. 699.0
   g. 84.0
   h. 1.1
   i. 6.6
   j. 76.0
3. a. 65.70
   b. 68.64
   c. 0.01
   d. 953.80
   e. 126.00
   f. 65.67
   g. 18.00
   h. 80.00
   i. 100.06
   j. 1.15
4. a. 3,300
   b. 5.8
   c. 0.005
   d. 46.74
   e. 4,000,000
   f. 2,180
   g. 43.88

Self-Test 2-9

a. 62.5%. Rationale: $5/8 \times 100 = 62.5\%$
b. 78.3%. Rationale: $65/83 \times 100 = 78.3\%$
c. 14.3%. Rationale: $1/7 \times 100 = 14.3\%$
d. 87.5%. Rationale: $7/8 \times 100 = 87.5\%$
e. 35%. Rationale: $70/200 \times 100 = 35\%$

Self-Test 2-10

a. 33%. Rationale: $1/3 \times 100 = 33\%$
b. 64%. Rationale: $7/11 \times 100 = 64\%$
c. 83%. Rationale: $5/6 \times 100 = 83\%$
d. 65%. Rationale: $11/17 \times 100 = 65\%$
e. 25%. Rationale: $15/60 \times 100 = 25\%$

Self-Test 2-11

1. a. 125%. Rationale: $1.25 \times 100 = 125\%$
   b. 63.5%. Rationale: $0.635 \times 100 = 63.5\%$
   c. 30%. Rationale: $0.3 \times 100 = 30\%$
   d. 3%. Rationale: $0.03 \times 100 = 3\%$
   e. 0.6%. Rationale: $0.006 \times 100 = 0.6\%$
   f. 82.35%. Rationale: $0.8235 \times 100 = 82.35\%$
   g. 1.62%. Rationale: $0.0162 \times 100 = 1.62\%$
   h. 55%. Rationale: $0.55 \times 100 = 55\%$
2. a. 325%. Rationale: $3.25 \times 100 = 325\%$
   b. 46%. Rationale: $0.4567 \times 100 = 46\%$
   c. 1%. Rationale: $0.005 \times 100 = 1\%$
   d. 56%. Rationale: $0.5555 \times 100 = 56\%$
   e. 2%. Rationale: $0.0166 \times 100 = 2\%$
   f. 4%. Rationale: $0.0449 \times 100 = 4\%$

Self-Test 2-12

a. 0.05. Rationale: $5/100 = 0.05$
b. 0.114. Rationale: $11.4/100 = 0.114$
c. 0.005. Rationale: $0.5/100 = 0.005$
d. 1.25. Rationale: $125/100 = 1.25$

Self-Test 2-13

a. 3/4. Rationale: Divide each number by $25 = 3/4$
b. 17/20. Rationale: Divide each number by $5 = 17/20$
c. 3/10. Rationale: Divide each number by $10 = 3/10$
d. 11/10. Rationale: Divide each number by $10 = 11/10$
e. 1/5. Rationale: Divide each number by $20 = 1/5$
f. $84/100 = 21/25$. Rationale: Divide each number by $4 = 21/25$
g. 1/2. Rationale: Divide each number by $50 = 1/2$
h. $98/100 = 49/50$. Rationale: Divide each number by $2 = 49/50$

Self-Test 2-14

1. a. 1/4
   b. 31.25/50
   c. $6/10 = 3/5$
   d. 0.005
   e. 0.03
   f. 0.12
2. $1,060 \times 0.25 = 265$
3. $2/3 \times 100 = 67$
4. $28 \times 0.18 = 5$ are home with the flu, which means 23 are working.
5. $(350 + 225) \times 0.08 = 46$ have been diagnosed.

Self-Test 2-15

1. a. liter (1.0567 quarts)
   b. 10 km (6.2 miles)
   c. 200 lbs ($90\,kg = 198.41\,lbs$)
   d. 100 meters (100 meters $= 109.4$ yards)
2. a. 138.89 lbs
   b. 68.04 kg
   c. 18.64 miles

Self-Test 2-16

1. a. $37,440. Rationale: 52 weeks in a year $\times 40$ hours per week $= 2,080$, and $2,080$ hours $\times \$18 = \$37,440$.
   b. $15,600. Rationale: 52 weeks in a year $\times 15$ hours per week $= 780$, and 780 hours $\times \$20 = \$15,600$.

Self-Test 2-17

Two full-time coders. Rationale: 220×20 minutes $= 4,400$ minutes$/60 = 73.33$ hours of work $=$ two full-time coders, working a 40-hour week, are needed to code 220 charts.

Self-Test 2-18

2 shelving units. Rationale: $5 \times 35 = 175$ inches in one unit. $350/75 = 2$ additional units.

Self-Test 2-19

a. $2,320. Rationale: $1,600 + (3(120 \times 2)) = 1,600 + 720 = \$2,320$
b. $9,280. Rationale: $\$2,320 \times 4 = \$9,280$

Self-Test 2-20

a. 37 charts could be in non-compliance. Rationale: $0.95 \times 750 = 712.50$ needed in compliance; therefore, 37 (750 – 712.50) could fail compliance and still meet 95% standard.

Self-Test 2-21

a. Under budget. Rationale: $5,520 is less than $6,000
b. $480. Rationale: $(6,000 - 5,520) = \$480$
c. 8%. Rationale: $6,000 - 5,520 = 480$ and $(480/6,000) \times 100 = 8\%$

CHAPTER 3 Health Data across the Continuum
Self-Test 3-1

a. GI	i. Onco	q. Uro
b. Pulm	j. Hem	r. Onc
c. Neuro	k. Neuro	s. Ortho
d. GI	l. Hem/CV	t. Gyn
e. Hem	m. Ortho	u. CV
f. Neuro	n. Gyn	v. ENT
g. ENT	o. Derm	w. Ophth
h. CV	p. Gyn	x. Endo

Self-Test 3-2

a. Plastic & Recon	g. General	n. Op
b. General	h. Neurosurgery	o. General
c. General	i. Neuro	p. Uro
d. OT	j. Ortho	q. General
e. Gyn	k. Ge	r. C
f. Op	l. Ge	s. General
	m. Ot	t. CV/Thoracic

CHAPTER 4 Hospital Census
Self-Test 4-1

1. a. 469. Rationale: $456 + 58 - 45 = 469$
   b. 475. Rationale: $469 + 6 = 475$
   c. 475. Rationale: $469 + 6 = 475$
2. a. 24. Rationale: $22 + 4 - 2 = 24$
3. a. 99. Rationale: $100 - 1 = 99$
   b. 102. Rationale: $100 + 3 - 1 = 102$
   c. 102. Rationale: $100 + 3 - 1 = 102$
4. a. 151. Rationale: $150 + 3 - 2 = 151$
   b. 152. Rationale: $151 + 1$ A&D $= 152$
   c. 152. Rationale: $151 + 1$ A&D $= 152$
5. a. 1,250. Rationale: Add all IPSD columns together = 1,250
   b. 47. Rationale: There were 47 services days recorded for April 20
   c. 379. Rationale: $38 + 42 + 43 + 36 + 35 + 41 + 47 + 48 + 49 = 379$
   d. 42. Rationale: $1,250/30 = 41.6 = 42$

Self-Test 4-2

1. January–April: 379.29. Rationale: $45,515/120 = 379.29$
   May–August: 444.10. Rationale: $54,624/123 = 444.10$
   September–December: 515.49. Rationale: $62,890/122 = 515.49$
2. a. 233.55. Rationale: $7,240/31 = 233.55$
   b. 17.42. Rationale: $540/31 = 17.42$
3. a. A&C $= 135$. Rationale: $140 + 310 - 315 = 135$. NB $= 7$. Rationale: $11 + 90 - 94 = 7$
   b. A&C $= 141.2$. Rationale: $4,236/30 = 141.2$
   c. NB $= 13.7$. Rationale: $410/30 = 13.6 = 13.7$
4. a. Ped $= 11.5$. Rationale: $344/30 = 11.5$; Ortho $= 14.4$. Rationale: $433/30 = 14.4$; Psych $= 9.5$. Rationale: $284/30 = 9.5$.
   b. Ped $= 8$. Rationale: $10 + 85 - 87 = 8$; Ortho $= 11$. Rationale: $12 + 122 - 123 = 11$; Psych $= 7$. Rationale: $6 + 54 - 53 = 7$.
   c. 1,061. Rationale: $344 + 433 + 284 = 1,061$

CHAPTER 5 Hospital Occupancy
Self-Test 5-1

1. 70%. Rationale: $210/300 \times 100 = 70\%$
2. 84.71%. Rationale: $72/85 \times 100 = 84.71\%$
3. 103.33%. Rationale: $155/150 \times 100 = 103.33\%$
4. 96.2%. Rationale: $125/130 \times 100 = 96.2\%$
5. 86.7%. Rationale: $13/15 = 86.7\%$
6. a. 7. Rationale: $9 + 3 - 4 - 1 = 7$
   b. 58.3%. Rationale: $7/12 \times 100 = 58.3\%$

Self-Test 5-2

1. a. December 1 through December 10. Rationale: $165/180 \times 100 = 92.67\%$, which is the highest occupancy percentage.
   b. 90.86%. Rationale: $507/558 \times 100 = 90.86\%$
2. August through October. Rationale: $13,220/13,800 \times 100 = 95.80\%$, which is the highest occupancy percentage.
3. a. 96%. Rationale: $48/50 \times 100 = 96\%$
   b. February 4 and February 19. Rationale: Both days had 100% occupancy, 50 occupied over 50 available.
   c. 87.86%. Rationale: $1,230/1,400 \times 100 = 87.86\%$
   d. February 1–7 is 87.14%. Rationale: $305/(350) \times 100 = 87.14\%$; February 8–14 is 88.57%. Rationale: $310/(350) \times 100 = 88.57\%$; February 15–21 is 90.29%. Rationale: $316/(350) \times 100 = 90.29\%$; February 22–28 is 85.43%. Rationale: $299/(350) \times 100 = 85.43\%$
4. a. 92.38%. Rationale: $388/420 \times 100 = 92.38\%$
   b. 11. Rationale: $12 + 88 - 88 - 1 = 11$
5. a. Medical: 95%. Rationale: $2,850/3,000 \times 100 = 95\%$
   Surgical: 96.86%. Rationale: $988/1,020 \times 100 = 96.86\%$
   Pediatric: 93.78%. Rationale: $422/450 = 93.78\%$
   Orthopedic: 92.96%. Rationale: $502/540 \times 100 = 92.96\%$
   Obstetric: 90.67%. Rationale: $544/600 \times 100 = 90.67\%$
   Newborn: 97.04% $=$ Best. Rationale: $524/540 = 97.04\%$, which is the highest occupancy rate.
   b. 94.58%. Rationale: $5,306/5,610 \times 100 = 94.58\%$

Self-Test 5-3

1. a. January–March, 95.42%. Rationale: $13,325/13,965 \times 100 = 95.42\%$
   April–June, 96.07%. Rationale: $14,425/15,015 \times 100 = 96.07\%$
   July–September, 96.65%. Rationale: $16,005/16,560 \times 100 = 96.65\%$
   October–December, 96.22%. Rationale: $17,704/18,400 \times 100 = 96.22\%$
   b. January–March, 93.67%. Rationale: $843/900 \times 100 = 93.67\%$
   April–June, 90.99%. Rationale: $1,242/1,365 \times 100 = 90.99\%$
   July–September, 90.54%. Rationale: $1,666/1,840 \times 100 = 90.54\%$
   October–December, 94.78%. Rationale: $1,744/1,840 \times 100 = 94.78\%$
   c. 96.12%. Rationale: $61,459/63,940 \times 100 = 96.12\%$
   d. 92.43%. Rationale: $5,495/5,945 \times 100 = 92.43\%$
   e. July–September, 94.78%. Rationale: October–December rate is 94.78%.
2. 81.57%. Rationale: $5,710/7,000 \times 100 = 81.57\%$
3. 95.32%. Rationale: $76,006/79,740 \times 100 = 95.32\%$
4. 95.89%. Rationale: $676/705 \times 100 = 95.89\%$
5. a. 98.39%. Rationale: $4,880/4,960 \times 100 = 98.39\%$
   b. 94.07%. Rationale: $1,110/1,180 \times 100 = 94.07\%$
   c. 93.72%. Rationale: $31,657/33,780 \times 100 = 93.72\%$
   d. 91.57%. Rationale: $3,791/4,140 \times 100 = 91.57\%$
   e. 95.22%. Rationale: $62,827/65,980 \times 100 = 95.22\%$
   f. 93.63%. Rationale: $7,692/8,215 \times 100 = 93.63\%$
   g. October–December. Rationale: This quarter had a 96.97% occupancy rate, which was the highest
   h. April–June, Rationale: $21,902,300 \times 100 = 95.22\%$, which was the highest.
6. a. 96.26%. Rationale: $1,800/1,870 \times 100 = 96.26\%$
   b. 85.92%. Rationale: $3,050/3,550 \times 100 = 85.92\%$

Self-Test 5-4

1. a. 76.28%. Rationale: $69,608/(250 \times 365) \times 100 = 76.28\%$
   b. (1) 36.72 turnovers. Rationale: $9,180/250 \times 100 = 36.72$ turnovers (2) 36.31 turnovers. Rationale: $69,608/91,250 \times 100 = 76.28\%$, and $0.76 \times 365 = 277.4$, and $277.4/7.64$ days $= 36.31$ turnovers
   c. 88.51%. Rationale: $4,846/(15 \times 365) \times 100 = 88.51\%$
   d. (1) 83 turnovers. Rationale: $1,245/15 \times 100 = 83$ turnovers (2) 81.73 turnovers. Rationale: $4,846/5,475 \times 100 = 88.51\%$, and $0.88 \times 365 = 321.2$, and $321.2/3.93$ days $= 81.73$ turnovers

CHAPTER 6 Hospital Length of Stay

Self-Test 6-1

LOS: Rationale for 1–8, add each day except the last day of the stay for each group. The answer cannot be 0. Each stay is at least 1 day.

1. 1 day
2. 3 days
3. 9 days
4. 9 days
5. 10 days
6. 46 days
7. 20 days
8. 78 days

Self-Test 6-2

1. a. 4 days. Rationale: $1,252/313 = 4$
   b. 81.29%. Rationale: $1,260/(50 \times 31) \times 100 = 81.29\%$
2. a. 3.93 days. Rationale: $2,685/683 = 3.93$
   b. 88.43%. Rationale: $2,653/(100 \times 30) \times 100 = 88.43\%$
3. a. 3.4 days. Rationale: $34/10 = 3.4$ days
   b. 3.6 days. Rationale: $18/5 = 3.6$ days
   c. 4 days. Rationale: $12/3 = 4$ days
   d. 2 days. Rationale: $4/2 = 2$ days
4. a. 5.05 days. Rationale: $2,884/571 = 5.05$ days
   b. 4.91 days. Rationale: $1,516/309 = 4.91$ days
   c. 7.65 days. Rationale: $972/127 = 7.65$ days
   d. 2.93 days. Rationale: $202/69 = 2.93$ days
   e. 2.94 days. Rationale: $194/66 = 2.94$ days
   f. 81.23%. Rationale: $2,843/(125 \times 28) = 81.23\%$
5. a. 5 days. Rationale: $36,508/7,289 = 5$ days
   b. Third quarter has the lowest ALOS Rationale: $9,502/1,902 = 4.995$ days
   c. Second quarter has the highest ALOS. Rationale: $8,955/1,785 = 5.02$ days
6. a. $12,591/1,968 = 6.4$ days
   b. The type of surgery with the highest LOS for the year is Neuro with an ALOS of 9.44 days. Rationale: $1,133/120 = 9.44$ days
   c. The type of surgery with the lowest LOS for the year is EENT with an ALOS of 2.17 days. Rationale: $490/226 = 2.17$ days
   d. EENT is 2.17 days, Neuro is 9.44 days, Thoracic is 8.09 days, Abdominal is 7.02 days, GU is 5.97 days, and Other is 4.23 days.

Self-Test 6-3

1. a. 2.09 days. Rationale: $420/201 = 2.09$ days
   b. 87.74%. Rationale: $408/465 = 87.74\%$
2. a. 2.62 days. Rationale: $55/21 = 2.62$ days
   b. 2.69 days. Rationale: $35/13 = 2.69$ days
   c. 2.5 days. Rationale: $20/8 = 2.5$ days
   d. 58%. Rationale: $58/100 \times 100 = 58\%$
3. a. 2.6 days. Rationale: $13/5 = 2.6$ days
   b. 2.5 days. Rationale: $5/2 = 2.5$ days
   c. 2.67 days. Rationale: $8/3 = 2.67$ days
   d. 7 lb 5 oz. Rationale: $45/6 = 7$ lb 5 oz
   e. 8 lb 7 oz. Rationale: $17.4/2 = 8$ lb 7 oz
   f. 6 lb 9 oz. Rationale: $26.75/4 = 6$ lb 9 oz

CHAPTER 7 Hospital: Obstetric and Neonatal Statistics

Self-Test 7-1

1. 0.33%. Rationale: $4/1,255 \times 100 = 0.33\%$
2. 0.15%. Rationale: $2/1,302 \times 100 = 0.15\%$
3. 0.19%. Rationale: $2/1,033 \times 100 = 0.19\%$

Self-Test 7-2

1. 0.83%. Rationale: $2/240 \times 100 = 0.83\%$
2. 0.86%. Rationale: $3/348 \times 100 = 0.86\%$

3. a. 3.91%. Rationale: $5/128 \times 100 = 3.91\%$
   b. 5.95%. Rationale: $5/84 \times 100 = 5.95\%$
   c. 0%. Rationale: $0/44 \times 100 = 0\%$

Self-Test 7-3

1. a. 0.83%. Rationale: $2/240 \times 100 = 0.83\%$
   b. 0.42%. Rationale: $1/236 \times 100 = 0.42\%$
2. a. 1.49%. Rationale: $4/269 \times 100 = 1.49\%$
   b. 0.77%. Rationale: $2/260 \times 100 = 0.77\%$
3. a. 1.29%. Rationale: $4/309 \times 100 = 1.29\%$
   b. 0.64%. Rationale: $2/311 \times 100 = 0.64\%$

Self-Test 7-4

1. 20.18%. Rationale: $90/446 \times 100 = 20.18\%$
2. a. 59. Rationale: 50 single plus 3 sets of twins and 1 set of triplets = 59 births
   b. 56. Rationale: 50 deliveries resulting in single infants plus 3 resulting in twins, plus 1 resulting in triplets plus 1 resulting in a stillborn and 1 resulting in an abortion. One single delivery can result in multiple births. $50 + 3 + 1 + 1 + 1 = 56$
   c. 1. Rationale: There was 1 death recorded in this problem.
   d. 30.36%. Rationale: $17/56 \times 100 = 30.36\%$
3. a. 68. Rationale: 60 single and 4 sets of twins = 68
   b. 1. Rationale: There was 1 death recorded in May.
   c. 69 Rationale: $60 + 4 + 3 + 1 + 1 = 69$
   d. 24.64%. Rationale: $17/69 \times 100 = 24.64\%$
4. a. Primiparous/total deliveries
   b. 23.3%. Rationale: $35/150 \times 100 = 23.3\%$
   c. C-section primiparous/all primiparous deliveries
   d. C-section primiparous/all C-sections
   e. 14.29%. Rationale: $3/35 \times 100 = 14.29\%$
   f. 10%. Rationale: $15/150 \times 100 = 10\%$

CHAPTER 8 Miscellaneous Clinical and Nonclinical Statistics

Self-Test 8-1

1. a. 9.86%. Rationale: $14/142 \times 100 = 9.86\%$
   b. 1.22%. Rationale: $2/164 \times 100 = 1.22\%$
   c. 1.45%. Rationale: $2/138 \times 100 = 1.45\%$
   d. 0.69%. Rationale: $1/144 \times 100 = 0.69\%$

Self-Test 8-2

1. a. 2.36%. Rationale: $82/3,474 \times 100 = 2.36\%$
   b. 2.02%. Rationale: $61/3,015 \times 100 = 2.02\%$
   c. 4.64%. Rationale: $21/453 \times 100 = 4.64\%$
2. a. 5.54%. Rationale: $36/650 \times 100 = 5.54\%$
   b. 0.77%. Rationale: $5/650 \times 100 = 0.77\%$
3. a. 4.12%. Rationale: $31/752 = 100 = 4.12\%$
   b. 5%. Rationale: $10/200 \times 100 = 5\%$
   c. Newborn. Rationale: $3/42 \times 100 = 7.14\%$
   d. Medical. Rationale: $8/361 \times 100 = 2.21\%$

Self-Test 8-3

1. a. 22.99%. Rationale: $963/4,189 \times 100 = 22.99\%$
   b. 29.17%. Rationale: $1,222/4,189 \times 100 = 29.17\%$
   c. 24.13%. Rationale: $861/3,568 \times 100 = 24.13\%$
   d. 16.43%. Rationale: $102/621 \times 100 = 16.43\%$
   e. 29.9%. Rationale: $1,067/3,568 \times 100 = 29.9\%$
   f. 24.96%. Rationale: $155/621 \times 100 = 24.96\%$
2. a. 27.05%. Rationale: $681/2,518 \times 100 = 27.05\%$
   b. 44.16%. Rationale: $1,112/2,518 \times 100 = 44.16\%$
   c. 29.70%. Rationale: $645/2,172 \times 100 = 29.70\%$
   d. 10.40%. Rationale: $36/346 = 10.40\%$
   e. 47.74%. Rationale: $1,037/2,172 \times 100 = 47.74\%$
   f. 21.68%. Rationale: $75/346 \times 100 = 21.68\%$
   g. NB. Rationale: $36/346 \times 100 = 10.40\%$
   h. Surgical. Rationale: $204/607 \times 100 = 33.61\%$
   i. NB. Rationale: $75/346 \times 100 = 21.68\%$
   j. Surgical. Rationale: $346/607 \times 100 = 57\%$
3. a. 27.36%. Rationale: $29/106 \times 100 = 27.36\%$
   b. 42.45%. Rationale: $45/106 \times 100 = 42.45\%$
   c. 9.77 patients. Rationale: $303/31 = 9.77$ patients
   d. 81.45%. Rationale: $303/372 \times 100 = 81.45\%$
   e. 2.92 days. Rationale: $310/106 = 2.92$ days
   f. 1.89%. Rationale: $2/106 \times 100 = 1.89\%$
   g. 50%. Rationale: $1/2 \times 100 = 50\%$

Self-Test 8-4

5. 88%. Rationale: $5/85 \times 100 = 5.88\%$

CHAPTER 9 End-of-Life Statistics: *Mortality and Autopsy Rates*

Self-Test 9-1

1. a. 2%. Rationale: $15/751 \times 100 = 1.999\%$
   b. 1.3%. Rationale: $10/746 \times 100 = 1.3\%$
   c. 5%. Rationale: $3/60 \times 100 = 5\%$
2. a. 3.68%. Rationale: $19/516 \times 100 = 3.68\%$
   b. 2.36%. Rationale: $12/509 \times 100 = 2.357\%$
   c. 5.26%. Rationale: $2/38 \times 100 = 5.26\%$
   d. 1.93%. Rationale: $5/259 \times 100 = 1.93\%$
   e. Medical. Rationale: $7/261 \times 100 - 2.68\%$
3. a. 2.38%. Rationale: $2/84 = 2.38\%$
   b. 94.76%. Rationale: $398/420 \times 100 = 94.76\%$
4. a. 1.86%. Rationale: $9/483 \times 100 = 1.86\%$
   b. 1.25%. Rationale: $6/480 \times 100 = 1.25\%$
   c. 2.1%. Rationale: $2/95 \times 100 = 2.1\%$
   d. 1.8%. Rationale: $7/388 \times 100 = 1.8\%$
   e. 1.30% Rationale: $5/386 \times 100 = 1.295\%$
5. a. 1.98% or 2%. Rationale: $14/704 \times 100 = 1.98\%$
   b. 1.43%. Rationale: $10/700 \times 100 = 1.43\%$
   c. 3.51%. Rationale: $2/57 \times 100 = 3.51\%$
   d. 1.85%. Rationale: $12/647 \times 100 = 1.85\%$
   e. 1.40%. Rationale: $9/644 \times 100 = 1.397\%$
   f. 1.79%. Rationale: $1/56 \times 100 = 1.79\%$
   g. Pediatric. Rationale: $1/98 \times 100 = 1.02\%$
   h. Surgical. Rationale: $2/216 \times 100 = 0.93\%$
6. 0.84%. Rationale: $2/238 \times 100 = 0.84\%$

Self-Test 9-2

1. 1.07%. Rationale: $2/187 \times 100 = 1.07\%$
2. 0.53%. Rationale: $1/188 \times 100 = 0.53\%$

Self-Test 9-3

1. a. 0.05%. Rationale: $1/1,854 \times 100 = 0.05\%$
   b. 0.65%. Rationale: $12/1,852 \times 100 = 0.65\%$
   c. 1.62%. Rationale: $30/1,849 \times 100 = 1.62\%$
   d. 1.25%. Rationale: $23/1,842 \times 100 = 1.25\%$
2. a. 0%. Rationale: $0/298 \times 100 = 0\%$
   b. 0.77%. Rationale: $2/260 \times 100 = 0.77\%$
   c. 3.44%. Rationale: $9/262 \times 100 = 3.44\%$
   d. 2.32%. Rationale: $6/259 \times 100 = 2.32\%$

Self-Test 9-4

1. Yes	5. Yes	9. Yes
2. Yes	6. No	10. Yes
3. No	7. No	11. Yes
4. Yes	8. Yes	

Self-Test 9-5

1. a. 44.44%. Rationale: $4/9 \times 100 = 44.44\%$
   b. 2.26%. Rationale: $9/398 \times 100 = 2.26\%$
2. a. 38.89%. Rationale: $7/18 \times 100 = 38.89\%$
3. a. 51.35%. Rationale: $19/37 \times 100 = 51.35\%$
   b. 2.91%. Rationale: $37/1,272 \times 100 = 2.91\%$
   c. 1.34%. Rationale: $3/(221+3) \times 100 = 1.34\%$

Self-Test 9-6

1. a. 57.89%. Rationale: $11/22 - 3 \times 100 = 57.89\%$
   b. 50%. Rationale: $114/22 \times 100 = 50\%$
2. a. 38.71%. Rationale: $12/(36-5) \times 100 = 38.71\%$
   b. 33.3%. Rationale: $12/36 \times 100 = 33.3\%$
   c. 1.29%. Rationale: $36/2,785 \times 100 = 1.29\%$
   d. 0.42%. Rationale: $4/963 \times 100 = 0.42\%$
   e. 0.52% .Rationale: $5/(957+5) \times 100 = 0.52\%$

Self-Test 9-7

1. a. 75%. Rationale: $6/(9-1) \times 100 = 75\%$
   b. 50%. Rationale: $3/6 \times 100 = 50\%$
   c. 60%. Rationale: $3/5 \times 100 = 60\%$
   d. 1.46%. Rationale: $6/410 \times 100 = 1.46\%$
2. a. 66.67%. Rationale: $8/12 \times 100 = 66.67\%$
   b. 60%. Rationale: $6/10 \times 100 = 60\%$
   c. 66.67%. Rationale: $6/9 \times 100 = 66.67\%$
   d. 1.84%. Rationale: $10/544 \times 100 = 1.84\%$
3. a. 36.36%. Rationale: $34/93 \times 100 = 36.36\%$
   b. 40.48%. Rationale: $34/(93-9) \times 100 = 40.48\%$
   c. 5.65%. Rationale: $42/(102-10) \times 100 = 5.65\%$
   d. 0.89%. Rationale: $93/10,451 \times 100 = 0.89\%$
   e. 0.64%. Rationale: $67/10,425 \times 100 = 0.64\%$
   f. 1.98%. Rationale: $16/810 \times 100 = 1.98\%$
   g. 2.2%. Rationale: $18/819 \times 100 = 2.2\%$
   h. 159.51. Rationale: $28,872/181 = 159.51$

i. 14.42. Rationale: $2,610/181 = 14.42$
j. 91.15%. Rationale: $28,872/(175 \times 181) \times 100 = 91.15\%$
k. 96.13%. Rationale: $2,610/(15 \times 181) \times 100 = 96.13\%$
4. a. 75%. Rationale: $6/(10-2) \times 100 = 75\%$
   b. 57.14%. Rationale: $4/7 \times 100 = 57.14\%$
   c. 66.67%. Rationale: $4/(7-1) \times 100 = 66.67\%$

Self-Test 9-8

1. a. 50%. Rationale: $1/2 \times 100 = 50\%$
   b. 0.89%. Rationale: $2/225 \times 100 = 0.89\%$
2. 100%. Rationale: $2/2 \times 100 = 100\%$
3. 100%. Rationale: $2/2 \times 100 = 100\%$

Self-Test 9-9

1. a. 50%. Rationale: $1/2 \times 100 = 50\%$
   b. 100%. Rationale: $1/1 \times 100 = 100\%$
   c. 0.85%. Rationale: $2/235 \times 100 = 0.85\%$
   d. 0.41%. Rationale: $1/240 \times 100 = 0.41\%$
2. a. 50%. Rationale: $2/4 \times 100 = 50\%$
   b. 0%. Rationale: $0/1 \times 100 = 0\%$
   c. 1.13%. Rationale: $4/354 \times 100 = 1.13\%$
   d. 0.29%. Rationale: $1/349 \times 100 = 0.29\%$
3. a. 41.67%. Rationale: $15/36 \times 100 = 41.67\%$
   b. 44.12%. Rationale: $15/(36-2) \times 100 = 44.12\%$
   c. 47.22%. Rationale: $17/(39-3) \times 100 = 47.22\%$
   d. 42.86%. Rationale: $3/7 \times 100 = 42.86\%$
   e. 0, as there are no coroner cases
   f. 0.67%. Rationale: $36/5,406 \times 100 = 0.67\%$
   g. 1.17%. Rationale: $7/409 \times 100 = 1.17\%$
   h. 0.72%. Rationale: $3/416 \times 100 = 0.72\%$

CHAPTER 10 Community Health Statistics

Self-Test 10-1

1. a. Maternal mortality rate. Rationale: See maternal mortality rate.
   b. 100,000. Rationale: See maternal mortality rate.
2. Number of live births. Rationale: See formula.
3. Perinatal mortality rate. Rationale: See formula.
4. 8.57%. Rationale: $300/3,500,000 \times 100,000 = 8.57\%$
5. 12.5%. Rationale: $5,000/400,000 \times 1,000 = 12.5\%$
6. a. 7.14%. Rationale: $(2,500/350,000) \times 1,000 = 7.14\%$
   b. 50%. Rationale: $2,500/5,000 = 50\%$
7. 15.58%. Rationale: $5,500/353,000 \times 1,000 = 15.58\%$
8. 8.37%. Rationale: $2,700/(324,600-2,200) \times 1,000 = 8.37\%$
9. 8.57%. Rationale: $3,000/350,000 \times 1,000 = 8.57\%$

Self-Test 10-2

1. 54 per 100,000. Rationale: $13,500/25,000,000 \times 100,000 = 54$
2. 147.54 per 100,000. Rationale: $450,000/305,000,000 \times 100,000 = 147.54$

Self-Test 10-3

1. a. 8.33 per 1,000. Rationale: $50,000/6,000,000 \times 1,000$ $= 8.33$ per 1,000
   b. 7.89 per 1,000. Rationale: $10,410/1,320,000 \times 1,000$ $= 7.89$ per 1,000
   c. 2.85 per 1,000. Rationale: $7,850/2,750,000 \times 1,000$ $= 2.85$ per 1,000
   d. 2.37 per 1,000. Rationale: $7,710/3,250,000 \times 1,000$ $= 2.37$ per 1,000
   e. 2.6 per 10,000. Rationale: $15,560/6,000,000 \times 1,000$ $= 2.6$ per 1,000
   f. 16.56 per 1,000. Rationale: $5,630/340,000 \times 1,000$ $= 16.56$ per 1,000
   g. 5.24 per 1,000. Rationale: $4,190/800,000 \times 1,000$ $= 5.24$ per 1,000
   h. 12.8 per 1,000. Rationale: $10,790/840,000 \times 1,000$ $= 12.8$ per 1,000

Self-Test 10-4

1. a. 12.2 per 1,000. Rationale: $12,200/1,000,000 \times 1,000$ $= 12.2$ per 1,000
   b. 61 per 1,000. Rationale: $12,200/200,000 \times 1,000 = 61$ per 1,000
2. a. 13.6 per 1,000. Rationale: $6,800/500,000 \times 1,000$ $= 13.6$ per 1,000
   b. 64.76 per 1,000. Rationale: $6,800/105,000 \times 1,000$ $= 64.76$ per 1,000
3. a. 16 per 1,000. Rationale: $2,400/150,000 \times 1,000 = 16$ per 1,000
   b. 63.16 per 1,000. Rationale: $2,400/38,000 \times 1,000$ $= 63.16$ per 1,000

CHAPTER 11 Statistics: *Learning the Basics*
Self-Test 11-1

4. Rationale: $100/25 = 4$

Self-Test 11-2

Weighted mean, 87.14. Rationale: $3(85) + 2(95) + 2(90) + 2(82) + 80 + 88 + 94 + 96 + 73/14$

Self-Test 11-3

59.28. Rationale: $5,355/90 = 59.28$

Self-Test 11-4

$128.67. Rationale: $[(22 \times \$120) + (26 \times \$136)]/48 = \$6,176/48 = \$128.67$

Self-Test 11-5

a. 54.5. Rationale: $50 + 59/2 = 54.5$
h. 54.64. Rationale: $765/14 = 54.64$

Self-Test 11-6

a. 73. Rationale: 73 occurs three times, which is the highest frequency of the set.

b. 77. Rationale: See definition of median.
c. 77.2. Rationale: $1,158/15 = 77.2$

Self-Test 11-7

1. Smaller
2. a. Class A mean is 17. Rationale: $255/15 = 17$, Class B mean is 16. Rationale: $240/15 = 16$
   b. The median for A is 17 and the median for B is 15.
   c. The mode for A is 14 and the mode for B is 15. Rationale: See definition of mode.
   d. The range for A is 17. Rationale: $25 - 8 = 17$. The range for B is 9. Rationale: $20 - 11 = 9$
   e. Variance for A is 21.29 and variance for B is 7.29.
   f. The standard deviation for A is 4.61 and for B is 2.7.

Self-Test 11-8

1. a. 46. Rationale: $97 - 51 = 46$
   b. 75.13. Rationale: $610/80 = 75.13$
   c. 75. Rationale: $75 + 75/2 = 75$
   d. 78. Rationale: See definition of mode.
   e.

Interval	Midpoint	Frequency	Midpoint x f	x–μ	(x–μ)^2f
50–54	52	3	156	−23	1,587
55–59	57	5	285	−18	1,620
60–64	62	7	434	−13	1,183
65–69	67	10	670	−8	640
70–74	72	13	936	−3	117
75–79	77	16	1,232	2	64
80–84	82	9	738	7	441
85–89	87	8	696	12	1,152
90–94	92	5	460	17	1,445
95–99	97	4	388	22	1,936
Totals:			5,995		10,185

Variance = 25.78. Rationale: $2,062.7/80 = 25.78$. SD = 5.08. Rationale: Square root of variance (25.78) equals 5.077, rounded to 5.08.

Self-Test 11-9

1. a. 68%. Rationale: See percentages associated with bell curve.
   b. 95%. Rationale: See percentages associated with bell curve.
2. a. 178.14 and 255.78. Rationale: $216.96 - 38.82 = 178.14$ and $216.96 + 38.82 = 255.78$
   b. 139.32 and 294.6. Rationale: $216.96 - 77.64 = 139.32$ and $216.96 + 77.64 = 294.6$
   c. 100.5 and 333.42. Rationale: $216.96 - 116.46 = 100.5$ and $216.96 + 116.46 = 333.42$

Self-Test 11-10

75% of homeowners pay between $1,685 and $3,045.

CHAPTER 12 Organizing Data for Analysis
Self-Test 12-1

1.

Reason	Frequency	Relative Frequency	Frequency Percentage
Health	12	$12/25 = 0.48$	$0.48(100) = 48\%$
Cosmetic	8	$8/25 = 0.32$	$032(100) = 32\%$
Other	5	$5/25 = 0.2$	$0.2(100) = 20\%$

2.

Lives with	Frequency	Relative Fr.	Frequency %
Mother	7	$7/20 = 0.35$	35%
Both parents	8	$8/20 = 0.4$	40%
Father	4	$4/20 = 0.2$	20%
Someone else	1	$1/20 = 0.05$	5%

Self-Test 12-2

a. Range is 48. Rationale: $98 - 50 = 48$

b.

Score Limits	Frequency	Relative Frequency	Frequency Percentage (%)
50–54	2	0.07	6.67
55–59	1	0.03	3.33
60–64	2	0.07	6.67
65–69	3	0.10	10
70–74	4	0.13	13.33
75–79	5	0.17	16.67
80–84	4	0.13	13.33
85–89	3	0.10	10
90–94	3	0.10	10
95–99	3	0.10	10

Self-Test 12-3

1.

Score Limits	Interval Size	Number of Class Intervals
1–45	5	9
72–136	8	8
43–237	10	20
0.12–0.38	0.26	2

2. a. 5. Rationale: $55/11$
   b. 39. Rationale: $(366 - 172)/5 = 38.8$
   c. 12. Rationale: $(124 - 88)/3 = 12$
   d. 15. Rationale: $(160 - 12)/10 = 14.8$

3. a. 227. Rationale: $345 - 118 = 227$
   b. 122. Rationale: $137 - 15 = 122$
   c. 0.63. Rationale: $0.88 - 0.25 = 0.63$
4. a. 59 to 61
   b. 76% through 126%
   c. 0.31 to 0.33

5.

Score Limits	Class Boundaries	Frequency	Cumulative Frequency
56–58	55.5 to less than 58.5	8	100
53–55	52.5 to less than 55.5	6	92
50–52	49.5 to less than 52.5	7	86
47–49	46.5 to less than 49.5	7	79

6. 88–97, 98–107, 108–117, 118–127, 128–137, 137–146, 147–156, 157–166

Self-Test 12-4

a. $n = 16$

b. 8. Rationale: $82(P) \times 16(n)/100 = 13.12$ or the 14th ranked score, which is a score of 8 in this array

Self-Test 12-5

a. 86. Rationale: $(1/9) \times 5 = 0.55$; $85 + 0.55 = 85.55 = 86$.

b. 83. Rationale: $(4/6) \times 5 = 3.3$; $80 + 3.3 = 83.3 = 83$.

c. 91. Rationale: $(11/9) \times 5 = 6$; $85 + 6 = 91$.

d. 77. Rationale: $(10/21) \times 5 = 2.38$; $75 + 2.38 = 77.38 = 77$.

Self-Test 12-6

a. 78.75%

b. 18.75%

c. 57.75%

d. 6.25%

CHAPTER 13 Displaying Data for Analysis

1. a. Top Six Leading Cancer Deaths in 20XX—Bar Chart
   b. Top Six Leading Cancer Deaths in 20XX—Column Chart
2. Confirmed Cases of Measles and Mumps (2002–2011)—Comparison Column Chart
3. a. Reported Cancers (per 100,000 population)—Stock Bar Chart
   b. Reported Cancers (per 100,000 population)—Stock Column Chart
4. Marital Status of Patients > 14 Years Old in 20XX—Pie Chart
5. Confirmed Cases of Measles and Mumps (2002–2011)—Comparison Line Chart
6. Systolic Blood Pressure Histogram
7. Systolic Blood Pressure Frequency Polygon

CHAPTER 1 Health Statistics: *Why Are They Important?*

1. a. Population. Rationale: See definition of population.
   b. Sample. Rationale: See definition of sample.
   c. Sample. Rationale: See definition of sample.

3. a. Quantitative and discrete. Rationale: See definition of quantitative and discrete.
   b. Qualitative. Rationale: See definition of qualitative.
   c. Qualitative. Rationale: See definition of qualitative.
   d. Quantitative and continuous. Rationale: See definition of quantitative and continuous.
   e. Qualitative. Rationale: See definition of qualitative.
   f. Quantitative and discrete. Rationale: See definition of quantitative and discrete.
   g. Qualitative. Rationale: See definition of qualitative.
   h. Qualitative. Rationale: See definition of qualitative.
   i. Qualitative. Rationale: See definition of qualitative.
   j. Quantitative and discrete. Rationale: See definition of quantitative and discrete.
   k. Quantitative and discrete. Rationale: See definition of quantitative and discrete.
   l. Qualitative. Rationale: See definition of qualitative.

5. a. Variable. Rationale: See definition of variable.
   b. Death. Rationale: See definition on mortality statistics.
   c. Vital or vital statistics. Rationale: See definition of vital statistics.
   d. Inferential. Rationale: See definition of inferential statistics.
   e. Random. Rationale: See definition of random sample.

7. a. All the facts and data regarding a patient's care are entered at the point of care. Information entered relative to this care is a primary data source. Secondary Data. A secondary source is abstracted information—that is, information taken from the health record and generally recorded into another document, such as a list, a register, or an index. Cancer abstracts and indexes (such as the master patient index) are prime examples of secondary data sources. Rationale: See definition of primary and secondary data sources.
   b. A representative sample is a sample that represents the characteristics of the population as closely as possible. Rationale: See definition of representative sample and random sample.

9. a. The Center for Medicare and Medicaid Services (CMS) administers the Medicare program and the federal aspect of the Medicaid program. Rationale: See definition of CMS.
   b. The Department of Health and Human Services (DHHS). Rationale: See definition of DHHS.
   c. The Department of Health and Human Services (DHHS) is a cabinet-level position and shares information with the president of the United States. The department has many components, one of which is the Food and Drug Administration (FDA)—concerned with the safety of foods, drugs, and medical equipment. Another component of DHHS is the Center for Medicare and Medicaid Services (CMS). Rationale: See definition of DHHS and CMS.

11. a. Newborn. Rationale: See abbreviations.
    b. Intensive care unit. Rationale: See abbreviations.
    c. Length of stay. Rationale: See abbreviations.
    d. Admitted and discharged the same day. Rationale: See abbreviations.
    e. Centers for Disease Control and Prevention. Rationale: See definition of statistics.
    f. Adults and children. Rationale: See abbreviations.
    g. Sum or summation. Rationale: See abbreviations.
    h. Inpatient. Rationale: See abbreviations.
    i. Greater than. Rationale: See abbreviations.
    j. National Center for Health Statistics. Rationale: See major health care collection agencies.

13. a. The scores from highest to lowest worst are as follows (Hint: Use Excel and sort data.):

100	84	72	63
99	82	72	60
98	82	72	57
97	81	72	55
95	81	71	55
93	78	70	54
92	77	70	50
91	77	68	49
90	75	67	48
90	75	66	44
88	74	66	44
86	74	66	38
84	73		

b. Hint: Use Excel and sort data.

Score	Number of Individuals Receiving Each Individual Score
100	1
99	1
98	1
97	1
95	1
93	1
92	1
91	1
90	2
88	1
86	1
84	2
82	2
81	2
78	1
77	2
75	2
74	2
73	1
72	4
71	1
70	2
68	1
67	1
66	3
63	1
60	1
57	1
55	2
54	1
50	1
49	1
48	1
44	2
38	1

b. Hint: Use Excel.

Score	Number of Individuals Receiving Each Individual Score	Number of Scores in Interval
100	1	
99	1	3
98	1	
97	1	2
95	1	
93	1	
92	1	
91	1	5
90	2	
88	1	2
86	1	
84	2	4
82	2	
81	2	3
78	1	
77	2	
75	2	6
74	2	
73	1	
72	4	8
71	1	
70	2	
68	1	
67	1	5
66	3	
63	1	2
60	1	
57	1	
55	2	4
54	1	
50	1	1
49	1	2
48	1	
44	2	2
38	1	1

There are no scores in the interval 58–61.

CHAPTER 2 Mathematics: *Reviewing the Basics*

1. a. $35/40 = 7/8$. Rationale: 35 and 40 are divisible by 5.
   b. $8/64 = 1/8$. Rationale: 8 and 64 are divisible by 8.
   c. $25/125 = 1/5$. Rationale: 25 and 125 are divisible by 25.
   d. $18/27 = 2/3$. Rationale: 18 and 27 are divisible by 9.
3. a. $6/100 = 6\%$. Rationale: $6/100 \times 100 = 6\%$
   b. $5/10 = 50\%$. Rationale: $5/10 \times 100 = 50\%$
   c. $8/1,000 = 0.8\%$. Rationale: $8/1,000 \times 100 = 0.8\%$
   d. $73/400 = 18.25\%$. Rationale: $73/400 \times 100 = 18.25\%$
5. a. 40.64. Rationale: 40.636 rounds to 40.64.
   b. 40.67. Rationale: 40.666 rounds to 40.67.
   c. 40.70. Rationale: 40.699 rounds to 40.70.
   d. 11.00. Rationale: 10.999 rounds to 11.00.
   e. 18.56. Rationale: 18.555 rounds to 18.56.
   f. 0.10. Rationale: 0.095 rounds to 0.10.
7. a. 4,500. Rationale: 4,455 rounded to the nearest hundred is 4,500.
   b. 4.7. Rationale: 4.657 rounded to the nearest tenth is 4.7.
   c. 0.006. Rationale: 0.0055 rounded to the nearest thousandth is 1.006.
   d. 5,000,000. Rationale: 44,500,000 rounded to the million is 5,000,000.
   e. 63.90. Rationale: 63.895 rounded to the nearest hundredth is 63.90.
   f. 80. Rationale: 77.499 rounded to the nearest ten is 80.
   g. 87,000. Rationale: 87,485 rounded to the nearest thousand is 87,000.
9. a. 3/5. Rationale: 60/100 is divisible by $20 = 3/5$
   b. 4/5. Rationale: $80\% = 8/10 = 4/5$
   c. 7/13. Rationale: 36/65 is divisible by $5 = 7/13$
   d. 1/3. Rationale: 33/99 is divisible by $33 = 1/3$
   e. 1/10. Rationale: 10% is equal to 1/10.
   f. 1/20. Rationale: $5/100 = 1/20$
11. a. 0.02 and 2%. Rationale: $2/100 = 0.02 \times 100 = 2\%$
    b. 0.24 and 24%. Rationale: $6/25 = 0.24 \times 100 = 24\%$
    c. 0.19 and 19%. Rationale: $16/84 = 0.19 \times 100 = 19\%$
    d. 0.29 and 29%. Rationale: $260/900 = 0.29 \times 100 = 29\%$
13. a. 4,066 Rationale: 7/10 or 70% of patients were admitted and discharged within three days. Therefore, the remaining 30% exceeded a three-day stay. So 30% of 13,554 admissions equal 4,066.2 or 4,066 admissions.
    b. 17.6. Rationale: $0.05 \times 3,520 = 176$ patients affected.
    c. 44,372. Rationale: $0.35 \times 126,778 = 44,372.3$, or 44,372 patients seen by a consultant.
15. 72.58 kg. Rationale: $160 \times 0.4536 = 72.576$ rounded to 72.58 kg
17. a. 1,400. Rationale: $4 \times 5 = 20$ total shelves, and $20 \times 35 = 700$ total filing inches. $700/0.5 = 1,400$ records stored.
    b. 2,100. Rationale: $6 \times 5 = 30$ total shelves, and $30 \times 35 = 1,050$ total filing inches. $1,050/0.5 = 2,100$
    c. 933. Rationale: $700/0.75 = 933$
19. a. Vendor A. Rationale: $\$2,500 \times 0.05 = 125$, and $2,500 - 125 = \$2,375$

Vendor B. Rationale: $\$2,800 \times 0.10 = 280$, and $\$2,800 - 280 = \$2,520$
Vendor C. Rationale: $\$2,400 \times 0.03 = 72$, and $2,400 - 72 = \$2,328$
Vendor D. Rationale: $\$2,700 \times 0.08 = 216$, and $2,700 - 216 = \$2,484$
   b. Vendor C. $2,328
21.

2,800	2,800/23,800	11.76%
15,350	15,350/23,800	64.50%
3,660	3,660/23,800	15.38%
1,990	1,990/23,800	8.36%
23,800		100.00%

23. Experienced = $31,200, and trained with no experience is $24,960.

Coders	Hourly Rate	Daily Rate	Weekly Rate	Annual Rate
Experienced	$15.00 × 8 hours	$120.00	$600.00	$31,200.00
Experienced	$15.00 × 8 hours	$120.00	$600.00	$31,200.00
Trained and no experience	$12.00 × 8 hours	$96.00	$480.00	$24,960.00
Trained and no experience	$12.00 × 8 hours	$96.00	$480.00	$24,960.00

25. 96.29%. Rationale: $650/675 = 0.962 \times 100 = 96.29\%$
27. $2,174.60

Hourly Rate	Daily Salary	Weekly Salary	Monthly Salary
$13.10 × 8	$104.80 × 5	$524.00 × 4	$2,096.00

Rationale: Overtime is 4 hours at $19.65 (13.10 + 6.55) = $78.60. Monthly salary + overtime = $2,096 + 78.60 = \$2,174.60$
29. $17,441. Rationale: $16,300 \times 0.07 = 1,141$, and $16,300 + 1,141 = 17,441$
31. a. Full-time weekly salary is $480.00, and part-time weekly salary is $280.00. Rationale: See table.
    b. $120.00 per week for full-time employees. Rationale: See table.
    c. $12,480. Rationale: $(120 \times 2) \times 52 = \$12,480$

Employee	Hourly Wage	Hours Worked per Week	Weekly Salary	Costs to Employer
A	$12.00	40	$480.00	$120.00
B	$11.00	40	$440.00	$120.00
C	$14.00	20 (no fringe benefits)	$280.00	$0.00
			Total	**$240.00**

33. a. 98.4%. Rationale: $(1{,}250-20)/1{,}250 = 0.984 = 98.4\%$
    b. 12 charts. Rationale: $1{,}250 \times 0.99 = 1{,}237.5$, rounded to 1,238 charts, need to be correctly coded; $1{,}250 - 1{,}238 = 12$ charts that could be incorrectly coded.

CHAPTER 3 Health Data across the Continuum

1. a. The primary difference between an LTC facility and a hospital is the level of care. Long-term care patients are not considered to be in an acute phase of illness but require extended inpatient care. A skilled nursing facility provides the highest level of LTC. Rationale: See definition of hospital.
   b. An intermediate care facility (ICF) provides long-term care but provides a more limited degree of support and nursing services than are provided in the SNF. Rationale: See definition of SNF and ICF.
   c. An intermediate care facility (ICF) provides a limited degree of support and nursing services to persons with a variety of physical or emotional conditions who may still need institutional care. A residential care facility (RCF) provides custodial care to those unable to live independently. The residents may suffer from physical, mental, or emotional conditions. Rationale: See definition of ICF and RCF.
   d. Trauma centers (Level I and Level II) that are equipped to handle the most threatening emergencies. Rationale: See definition of emergency room.
3. Care provided by a primary care center is similar to care provided in physicians' offices. Many hospitals have set up and staffed such facilities either on their premises or as a satellite (off-site) operation. Basic health care is provided by a primary care physician (family practice, internist, or pediatrician). Rationale: See definition of primary care.
5. a. AMA = against medical advice, signifying a patient has left the hospital without a physician's discharge order
   b. MCO = managed care organization; an integrated health care reimbursement and delivery system
7. An adolescent is included in adult statistics. Rationale: See definition of adolescent.
9. Indexes maintained in a hospital include MPI, number, disease, procedure/operation, and physician. Rationale: See sources of statistical data.
11. An encounter is a direct, personal contact between a patient and health care provider to order or provide health care services. An occasion of service is a specified service, often the result of an encounter. A visit is a single encounter that includes all the services supplied during the encounter. Rationale: See definitions of encounter, occasion of service, and visit.
13. a. CV. Rationale: See Table 3-1.
    b. A&I. Rationale: See Table 3-1.
    c. Endo. Rationale: See Table 3-1.
    d. CV. Rationale: See Table 3-1.
    e. GI. Rationale: See Table 3-1.
    f. Pulm. Rationale: See Table 3-1.
    g. NB. Rationale: See Table 3-1.
    h. GU. Rationale: See Table 3-1.
    i. Neuro. Rationale: See Table 3-1.
    j. ENT. Rationale: See Table 3-1.
    k. GI. Rationale: See Table 3-1.
    l. Psych. Rationale: See Table 3-1.
    m. Ortho. Rationale: See Table 3-1.
    n. Onco and/or Gyn and/or CV. Rationale: See Table 3-1.
    o. Onco. Rationale: See Table 3-1.
    p. NB. Rationale: See Table 3-1.
    q. Neuro. Rationale: See Table 3-1.
    r. Hem. Rationale: See Table 3-1.
    s. GU. Rationale: See Table 3-1.
    t. Ophth. Rationale: See Table 3-1.
    u. CV. Rationale: See Table 3-1.
    v. Derm. Rationale: See Table 3-1.
    w. Neuro. Rationale: See Table 3-1.
    x. Neuro. Rationale: See Table 3-1.
    y. Gyn. Rationale: See Table 3-1.

CHAPTER 4 Hospital Census

1. The daily inpatient census refers to all patients present at CTT plus any inpatients admitted and discharged (A&D) before the next census-taking time. Inpatient census refers to the number of inpatients present at any one time. Rationale: See definition of daily inpatient census and inpatient census.
3. Adults/children and newborn data should not be combined; these two averages are calculated separately. Rationale: See average census.
5. a. No, the clinical unit transfer totals (in and out) do not need to be equal. Rationale: See transfers.
   b. Yes, the total transfers within the facility must be equal. Rationale: See transfers.
7. A newborn is considered A&D when he or she is born and died on the same day, was born and discharged on the same day, or was born and transferred to another facility on the same day. Rationale: See A&D.

9.

Clinical Unit	Bed Count	Bed Census	Admissions	Discharges	Deaths	IPSD
Urology	18	15	62	60	1	501
ENT	16	12	51	48	0	418
Orthopedics	24	20	89	87	1	607
					Total =	1,526

   a. Urology = 17. Rationale: $15 + 62 - 60$. ENT = 15. Rationale: $12 + 51 - 48$. Ortho = 22. Rationale: $20 + 89 - 87$
   b. 1,526. Rationale: $501 + 418 + 607 = 1{,}526$
   c. Urology = 16.7. Rationale: $501/30$. ENT = 13.9. Rationale: $418/30$. Ortho = 20.2. Rationale: $607/30$

11.

Census	Admissions	Discharges	A&D	DOA
January 31: 456				
February 1:	58	45	6	3

   a. Census for February 1 is 469. Rationale: $456 + 58 - 45 = 469$
   b. IPSD total for February 1 is 475. Rationale: $469 + 6 = 475$
   c. DIPC for February 1 is 475. Rationale: $469 + 6 = 475$

13. St. Peter's Hospital adults/children data for the year:

   Admissions: 998
   Discharges: 989
   IPSD: 36,440

   Average A&C daily inpatient census for the year is 99.8 or 100. Rationale: $36,440/365 = 99.8$

15. Day 1: Census 125

Day 2	Admissions	Live discharges	Deaths	A&D
	8	6	2	2

   a. Ending census on day 2 is 125. Rationale: $125 + 8 - 6 - 2 = 125$
   b. DIPC for day 2 is 127. Rationale: $125 + 2 = 127$
   c. IPSD total for day 2 is 127. Rationale: $125 + 2 = 127$

17. May 31: Census 150

Patient	Admission	Discharges
A Adams	8:00 A.M.	4:50 P.M.
B Brown	9:00 A.M.	
C Carson	10:18 A.M.	
D Davis		11:55 A.M.
E Edwards	2:40 P.M.	7:00 P.M. (TRF—another hospital)
F Funk		7:30 P.M.
G Grant	7:50 P.M.	11:39 P.M. (expired)
H Hughes	8:19 P.M.	
I Ingals		9:15 P.M.
J Jones	11:45 P.M.	
K Kohl	4:22 P.M.	
L Lamb		8:33 P.M.

   Admissions = 5
   Discharges = 4
   A&D = 3
   a. IP census on June 1 is 151. Rationale: $150 + 5 - 4 = 151$
   b. DIPC on June 1 is 154. Rationale: $151 + 3 = 154$
   c. IPSD on June 1 is 154. Rationale: $151 + 3 = 154$

CHAPTER 5 Hospital Occupancy

1. a. Percentage of occupancy for Oct is 84.96%. Rationale: $1,712/(65 \times 31) \times 100$

   b. Percentage of occupancy for Oct 25 is 96.92%. Rationale: $63/(65 \times 1) \times 100$
   c. Percentage of occupancy for Oct 1 through Oct 10 is 75.23%. Rationale: $489/(65 \times 10) \times 100$
   d. Percentage of occupancy for Oct 11 through Oct 20 is 86.62%. Rationale: $563/(65 \times 10) \times 100$
   e. Percentage of occupancy for Oct 21 through Oct 31 is 101.53%. Rationale: $660/(65 \times 11) \times 100 = 92.31$
   f. Percentage of occupancy for Oct with a change in bed count 78.71%. Rationale: $1,712/[(65 \times 10) + (70 \times 10) + (75 \times 11)] \times 100$

3. a. 14 Rationale: $13 + 4 - 3$. Inpatient service days is 15. Rationale: $14 + 1$
   b. Bassinet occupancy for January 2 is 93.75%. Rationale: $15/16$

5. a. Bed occupancy percentage for March is 80.56%. Rationale: $1,998/(80 \times 31)\,100$
   b. Bassinet occupancy percentage for March is 86.45%. Rationale: $268/(10 \times 31)\,100$
   c. Orthopedic unit occupancy percentage for March is 74.73%. Rationale: $278/(12 \times 31)100$

7. a. January 1 through February 15 is 92.15%. Rationale: $3,815/(46 \times 90)100 = 92.15\%$
      February 16 through March 31 is 92.7%. Rationale: $4,079/(100 \times 44)100 = 92.7\%$
      April 1 through April 30 is 90.48%. Rationale: $2,986/(110 \times 30)100 = 90.48\%$
      May 1 through June 30 is 77.55%. Rationale: $4,021/(85 \times 61)100 = 147.83\%$
   b. Percentage of bassinet occupancy for each period.
      January 1 through February 15 is 83.88%. Rationale: $463/(46 \times 12) = 83.88\%$
      February 16 through March 31 is 89.2%. Rationale: $314/(8 \times 44)100 = 89.2\%$
      April 1 through April 30 is 90.67%. Rationale: $272/(10 \times 30)100 = 90.67\%$
      May 1 through June 30 is 82.9%. Rationale: $708/(14 \times 61)100 = 82.9\%$
   c. Percentage of bed occupancy for January through June is 102.34%. Rationale: $(3,815 + 4,079 + 2,986 + 4,021)/(46 \times 90) + (100 \times 44) + (110 \times 30) + (85 \times 32)$
   d. Percentage of bassinet occupancy for January through June is 83.67%. Rationale: $(463 + 314 + 272 + 708)/(46 \times 12) + (100 \times 8) + (10 \times 30) + (14 \times 32) = 83.67\%$
   e. Period with the highest IP bed occupancy percentage is February 16 through March 31. Rationale: February 16 through March 31 is 92.7%. Rationale: $4,079/(100 \times 44)100 = 92.7\%$

9. a. 1,250. Rationale: Add all IPSD.
   b. 379. Rationale: $(38 + 42 + 43 + 36 + 35 + 41 + 47 + 48 + 49)$
   c. 38.9. Rationale: $389/10$
   d. 41.67 or 42. Rationale: $1,250/30 = 41.67$
   e. 83.33%. Rationale: $1,250/(50 \times 30) \times 100$
   f. 79.11%. Rationale: $1,250/(50 \times 14) + (55 \times 16) \times 100$

11. Rationale: See table

Pine Ridge Hospital—100 beds; 15 bassinets

Census Report for February

	A&C									NB					
Day	Census	Adm	TRF-In	Dis Live	Exp	TRF-Out	Census	A&D	IPSD	Beg Census	Births	Dis Live	Exp	Census	IPSD
20	77	12	3	7	0	3	82	0	82	11	3	7	0	7	7
21	82	14	2	9	1	2	86	1	87	7	6	3	0	10	10
22	86	8	2	12	0	2	82	0	82	10	5	2	0	13	13
26	82	16	6	8	0	6	90	0	90	13	3	2	0	14	14
24	90	7	3	4	0	3	93	4	97	14	1	4	0	11	11
25	93	6	4	13	1	4	85	2	87	11	2	5	0	8	8
26	85	11	2	7	0	2	89	0	89	8	2	3	0	7	7
27	89	9	3	11	0	3	87	0	87	7	4	2	1	8	8
28	87	12	5	5	1	5	93	3	96	8	5	1	0	12	12
Totals		95	30	76	3	30	93 ending census		797		31	29	1		90

A&C occupancy 67%. Rationale: $797/(100 \times 9) = 797/900 = 67\%$
NB occupancy 66.67%. Rationale: $90/(15 \times 9) = 90/135 = 66.67\%$

CHAPTER 6 Hospital Length of Stay

1. Yes, if he or she is an inpatient for at least 365 days. Rationale: See definition of discharge day.
3. The physician writes an order allowing the patient to leave the hospital and to return at a specified time, during which time the patient is absent at the census-taking time. Rationale: See definition of leave of absence.
9.

5. They are computed separately. Rationale: See average length of stay.
7. a. 5.35 days. Rationale: 4,785/895
   b. 3.84 days. Rationale: 330/86
   c. 89.26%. Rationale: $(4,820/5,400) \times 100$
   d. 75.33%. Rationale: $(339/450) \times 100$

Hopeful Hospital—Discharge List for June 3

Disc (live)	Service	Adm Date	LOS
M	Surgical	5/31	3
F	Medical	5/19	15
F	Surgical	5/23	11
M	Psychiatric	5/3	31
F	OB	5/28	10
M	Ortho	5/24	12
M	Urology	5/28	6
F	ENT	6/2	1
F	Gyn	6/3	1
M	Medical	5/29	5
M	Urology	5/30	4
F	Gyn	5/27	7
F	Ortho	5/28	6

Hopeful Hospital—Discharge List for June 3			
Disc (live)	Service	Adm Date	LOS
M	Surgical	5/26	8
Death			
M	Medical	5/29	5
TOTAL			**91**

ALOS for A&C	7.93 days
ALOS for males	9 days
ALOS for females	6.71 days
ALOS for surgical	7.33 days
ALOS for medical	8.33 days
ALOS for ortho	8 days

CHAPTER 7 Hospital: Obstetric and Neonatal Statistics

1. a. Less than 20 weeks gestation. Rationale: See definition.
   b. 20 weeks to no less than 28 weeks. Rationale: See definition.
   c. 28 or more weeks. Rationale: See definition.
3. a. A woman admitted to the hospital that does not deliver a baby is considered undelivered, versus an admission that results in the delivery of an infant.
   b. The puerperium is the 42-day period following delivery, whereas antepartum is the period before giving birth.
   c. A neonate is a baby up to 28 days of age, whereas an infant refers to a newborn up to one year of age.
   d. Perinatal refers to the period surrounding birth, neonatal refers the first 28 days of life for an infant, and postnatal refers to the period from the end of the neonatal period up to one year of age.
5. a. 0.16%. Rationale: $4/2{,}387 \times 100$
   b. 1.04%. Rationale: $(19 + 5)/(2{,}288 + 24) \times 100$
7. a. 2.67%. Rationale: $2/75 \times 100$
   b. 3.37%. Rationale: $3/(86 + 3) \times 100$
9. a. 1.87%. Rationale: $2/107 \times 100$
   b. 0.87%. Rationale: $1/115 \times 100$
   c. 3.51%. Rationale: $4/114 \times 100$
11. a. 0.98%. Rationale: $1/102 \times 100 = 0.98\%$
    b. 30.34%. Rationale: $27/89 \times 100 = 30.34\%$
13. a. 11. Rationale: Exclude those aborted
    b. 1. Rationale: baby Jones
    c. 12. Rationale: Include those aborted
    d. 25%. Rationale: $3/12 \times 100$
    e. 8.3%. Rationale: $1/12 \times 100$
    f. 63.64%. Rationale: $7/11 \times 100$
    g. 7.25 lbs. Rationale: $50.8/7$
    h. 7.1 lbs. Rationale: $28.41/4$

Mother	NB/Fetus Sex	Vaginal	C-Section	NB #1 Weight	NB#2 Weight	NB/Maternal Deaths
Adams	male	×		8 lbs. 4 oz.		
Brown	male		×	7 lbs. 9 oz.		
Crane	female	×		6 lbs. 8 oz.		
Davis	female	×		6 lbs. 11 oz.		
Evans	male twins	×		5 lbs. 1 oz.	6.3	
Foster	male aborted	×		450 grams		
Grant	female	×		7 lbs. 3 oz.		
Hovis	female aborted	×		850 grams		
Ingals	male		×	9 lbs. 1 oz.		
Jones	male	×		5 lbs. 1 oz.		10:55 A.M.
Krebs	female	×		8 lbs. 2 oz.		
Long	male		×	8 lbs. 9 oz.		

CHAPTER 8 Miscellaneous: Clinical and Nonclinical Statistics

1. Identify the value placed in the denominator for the following rates:
   a. Total number of discharges (including deaths). Rationale: See formula.
   b. Total number of discharges (including deaths). Rationale: See formula.
   c. Total number of surgical operations performed. Rationale: See formula.
   d. Total number of discharges (including deaths). Rationale: See formula.
   e. Total number of patients discharged. Rationale: See formula.
   f. Total discharges for the period. Rationale: See formula.
3. a. 75% of cases. Rationale: See definition for complication and comorbidity.
   b. Complication and comorbidity. Rationale: A complication is a disorder arising after admission that lengthens the patient's stay at least one day in 75% of cases. A comorbidity is a preexisting condition that lengthens the patient's stay at least one day in 75% of cases.

5. Skyline Hospital, surgical data (January): Surgical units bed count: 40

Admissions:	176
Discharges:	172
Deaths (total):	52 (<48 hrs); 3 (>48 hrs)
Postoperative:	22 (<10 days)
Anesthesia:	1
Infections (total)	6 (3 postop); (1 comacq); (5 nosocomial)
Patients operated on:	156
Surgical operations performed:	166
Anesthetics administered:	160
Consultations (patients seen):	48

   a. 1.81%. Rationale: $3/166 \times 100 = 1.81\%$
   b. 2.91%. Rationale: $5/172 \times 100 = 2.91\%$
   c. 27.91%. Rationale: $48/172 \times 100 = 27.91\%$
   d. 3.49%. Rationale: $6/172 \times 100 = 3.49\%$
   e. 1.28%. Rationale: $2/156 \times 100 = 1.28\%$
   f. 0.63%. Rationale: $1/160 \times 100 = 0.63\%$
   g. 2.91%. Rationale: $5/172 \times 100 = 2.91\%$
   h. 1.76%. Rationale: $(5-2)/(172-2) \times 100 = 1.76\%$

7. Cascade Hospital (August data):

				Autopsies			Hospital	Surgical
Clinical Unit	Adm	Disch	Deaths	HP	Cor	Consults	Infections	Operations
Medical	401	390	18	5	1	105	5	
Surgical	88	81	2	1	0	47	2 (postop)	84
Pediatrics	51	48	0	—	—	18	1	
OB	268	269	1	1	0	44	4	
Orthopedic	60	58	2	1	0	18	3	
NB	241	239	1	0	0	9	2	

   a. 22.21%. Rationale: $241/1,085 \times 100 = 22.21\%$
   b. Surgical. Rationale: $41/81 \times 100 = 58.02\%$
   c. 1.57%. Rationale: $17/1,085 \times 100 = 1.57\%$
   d. Orthopedic. Rationale: $3/58 \times 100 = 5.17\%$
   e. 2.38% .Rationale: $2/84 \times 100 = 2.38\%$
   f. 2.21%. Rationale: $24/1,085 \times 100 = 2.21\%$
   g. 33.33%. Rationale: $8/24 \times 100 = 33.33\%$
   h. 34.78%. Rationale: $8/24 - 1 \times 100 = 34.78\%$

   c. 14.55%. Rationale: $155/1,065 \times 100 = 14.55\%$
   d. 9.12%. Rationale: $97/1,065 \times 100 = 9.12\%$
   e. 5.45%. Rationale: $58/1,065 \times 100 = 5.45\%$
   f. 4.62%. Rationale: $11/238 \times 100 = 4.62\%$
   g. 24.7%. Rationale: $263/1,065 \times 100 = 24.7\%$
   h. 13.58%. Rationale: $41/302 \times 100 = 13.58\%$
   i. 32.02%. Rationale: $57/178 \times 100 = 32.02\%$
   j. 5.66%. Rationale: $3/53 \times 100 = 5.66\%$
   k. 6.31%. Rationale: $7/111 \times 100 = 6.31\%$
   l. 14.16%. Rationale: $31/219 \times 100 = 14.16\%$
   m. 10.89%. Rationale: $22/202 \times 100 = 10.89\%$

9. Windhaven Hospital (September surgical data):
   a. 25.88%. Rationale: $66/255 \times 100 = 25.88\%$
   b. 6.05%. Rationale: $15/248 \times 100 = 6.05\%$
   c. 5.49%. Rationale: $14/255 \times 100 = 5.49\%$
   d. CV. Rationale: $4/45 \times 100 = 8.89\%$
   e. CV. Rationale: $3/45 \times 100 = 6.67\%$
11. a. 12.49%. Rationale: $133/1,065 \times 100 = 12.49\%$
    b. Consultation rate for October:
       1) 21.88%. Rationale: $233/1,065 \times 100 = 21.88\%$
       2) 30.05%. Rationale: $320/1,065 \times 100 = 30.05\%$

13. 54.4 days. Rationale: $\$6,766,300/(\$45,530,000/366) = 6,766,300/124,399 = 54.39 = 54.4$ days
15. 12.8%. Rationale: $723/5,646 = 0.1280 = 12.8\%$
17. Revenue variance = $\$65,340$; variance % = 9.5%; positive variance. Rationale: $\$750,340 - \$685,000 = \$65,340$; $\$65,340/\$685,000 = 0.0953 = 9.5\%$; positive variance as actual revenue is greater than budget

CHAPTER 9 End-of-Life Statistics: *Mortality and Autopsy Rates*

1. a. None. Rationale: See definition.
   b. Deaths under 48 hours. Rationale: See definition.
   c. Deaths within 10 days of the postoperative period. Rationale: See definition.
   d. None. Rationale: See definition.
3. Net death rate. Rationale: See definition.
5. a. 4.83%. Rationale: $(30+6+1+4)/(778+71) \times 100$
   b. 1.22%. Rationale: $(30+6+1+4-31)/(778+71-31) \times 100$
7. a. 0.21%. Rationale: $2/975 \times 100$
   b. 0.60%. Rationale: $(7-1)/(997-1) \times 100$
9. a. 1.54%. Rationale: $(3+5+1)/(505+80) \times 100$
   b. 1.03%. Rationale: $(3+5+1-3)/(505+80-3) \times 100$
   c. 1.25%. Rationale: $1/80-100$
11. a. 0.71%. Rationale: $9/1,275 \times 100$
    b. 0.24%. Rationale: $3/1269$
    c. 16.67%. Rationale: $2/132 \times 100$
13. Hospital autopsy rates. Rationale: See definition of hospital autopsy rate.
15. The deaths reportable to the coroner's office include deaths due to: (1) criminal or violent means (homicides, for example); (2) suicides; suspected suicides; (3) sudden deaths, following apparent health (so as to rule out foul play—such as poisoning, strangulation, suffocation, or even a fall); (4) suspicious or unusual circumstances; (5) accidents, including those which occur on the job (arising from employment). The deaths most likely to fall under the jurisdiction of the coroner's office include deaths due to blows, burns, crushing, cuts or stab wounds, drowning, electric shock, explosions, firearms, falls, poisoning (carbon monoxide, food, etc.), hanging, heat-related deaths, strangulation, suffocation, and all types of vehicle accidents (car, bus, train, bicycle, and motorcycle). Rationale: See definition of coroner's cases.
17. Yes, they are combined. Rationale: See definitions for gross, net, and hospital autopsy rates.
19. Unautopsied coroner's cases. Rationale: See definition of net autopsy rate.
21. a. 50%. Rationale: $1/2 \times 100 = 50\%$
    b. 55.56%. Rationale: $5/9 \times 100 = 55.56\%$
    c. 54.55%. Rationale: $6/11 \times 100 = 54.55\%$
    d. 66.67%. Rationale: $6/9 \times 100 = 66.67\%$
    e. 89.31% for A&C and 83.43% for NB. Rationale: A&C $(6,252)/(250 \times 28) \times 100$; NB $(701)/(30 \times 28) \times 100$
23. a. 38.71%. Rationale: $12/31 \times 100 = 38.71\%$
    b. 44.4%. Rationale: $12/(31-4) \times 100 = 44.4\%$
    c. 75%. Rationale: $3/4 \times 100 = 75\%$
    d. 36.36%. Rationale: $4/(9+2) \times 100 = 36.36\%$
    e. 42.86%. Rationale: $3/(7+1-1) \times 100 = 42.86\%$
    f. 100%. Rationale: $1/1 \times 100 = 100\%$
25. a. 56%. Rationale: $14/25 \times 100 = 56\%$
    b. 60.87%. Rationale: $14/(25-2) \times 100 = 60.87\%$
    c. 66.67%. Rationale: $18/(31-4) \times 100 = 66.67\%$
    d. 100%. Rationale: $1/1 \times 100 = 100\%$
    e. 40%. Rationale: $2/5 \times 100 = 40\%$
    f. 1.91%. Rationale: $25/1,308 \times 100 = 1.91\%$
    g. 0.36%. Rationale: $1/275 \times 100 = 0.36\%$

CHAPTER 10 Community Health Statistics

1. (1) Live birth certificates—proof of citizenship, age, birthplace, and parentage; (2) death certificates—required for burial/cremation services and to settle estates and insurance claims; (3) fetal death certificates—usually required for fetal deaths from 17–21 weeks or more, provide information on cause of death, other significant conditions, and when the fetus died; and (4) induced termination of pregnancy certificates—includes information on place of induction, date of termination, other various pregnancy information, and type of termination procedure.
3. 2 per 1,000. Rationale: $76/35,000 = 0.002 \times 1,000 = 2$ per 1,000
5. a. 0.006 per 1,000. Rationale: $22/3,620,000 \times 1,000 = 0.006$ per 1,000
   b. 9.51 per 10,000. Rationale: $34,444/3,620,000 \times 1,000 = 9.51$ per 10,000
   c. 5.07 per 1,000. Rationale: $4/7,882 \times 100 - 5.07$ per 1,000
   d. 6,060.6 per 100,000. Rationale: $2/33 \times 100,000 = 6,060.6$ per 100,000
   e. 87.1 per 100,000. Rationale: $3/3,444 \times 100,000$
7. a. 1.78 per 1,000. Rationale: $9,995/5,610,000 \times 1,000$
   b. 4.26 per 1,000. Rationale: $6/1,410 \times 1,000$
   c. 39.89 per 10,000. Rationale: $8/2,006 \times 10,000$
   d. 18.8% or 188 per 1,000. Rationale: $4/22 \times 100$
9. 48 per 1,000. Rationale: $3,650/76,000 \times 1,000$

11.

	White				Black		
State Population: 1 Million (yearly data)							
Ages	Males	Females	Total		Males	Females	Total
75+	9,000	15,000	24,000		2,000	4,000	6,000
65–74	23,000	30,000	53,000		7,500	9,500	17,000
45–64	91,000	94,000	185,000		29,000	36,000	65,000
0–44	243,000	247,000	490,000		75,000	85,000	160,000

State Population: 1 Million (yearly data)

Deaths	Prostate:							
	White males 471							
	Black males 250							
	Breast							
	White females 526							
	Black females 202							

Ages:	75+		65–74		45–64		0–44	
Deaths:	White	Black	White	Black	White	Black	White	Black
Prostate	120	71	215	73	105	68	31	18
Breast	95	46	187	81	168	53	76	22

a. 2.2 deaths per 1,000. Rationale: $250/(2,000 + 7,500 + 29,000 + 75,000) \times 1,000$

b. 1.29 deaths per 1,000. Rationale: $471/(9,000 + 23,500 + 91,000 + 243,000) \times 1,000$

c. 1.5 deaths per 1,000. Rationale: $202/(4,000 + 9,500 + 36,000 + 85,000) \times 1,000$

d. 1.36 deaths per 1,000. Rationale: $526/(15,000 + 30,000 + 94,000 + 247,000) \times 1,000$

e. 2.34 deaths per 1,000. Rationale: $68/29,000 \times 1,000$

f. 9.35 deaths per 1,000. Rationale: $215/23,000 \times 1,000$

g. 1.47 deaths per 1,000. Rationale: $53/36,000 \times 1,000$

h. 6.23 deaths per 1,000. Rationale: $187/30,000 \times 1,000$

i. 0.24 deaths per 1,000. Rationale: $18/75,000 \times 1,000$

j. 6.3 deaths per 1,000. Rationale: $95/15,000 \times 1,000$

CHAPTER 11 Statistics: *Learning the Basics*

1. a. Mean. Rationale: See measures of central tendency.
   b. Median. Rationale: See measures of central tendency.
   c. Mode. Rationale: See measures of central tendency.
   d. Median. Rationale: See measures of central tendency
   e. Median. Rationale: See measures of central tendency.
3. 78.85. Rationale: $(75 \times 32) + (83 \times 25) + (80 \times 17) = 5,835/74 = 78.85$
5. a. Range is 45. Rationale: $58 - 13 = 45$
   b. Mode is 32. Rationale: See definition of mode.
   c. Median is 36.5. Rationale: $(37 - 36)/2 = 36.5$
   d. Mean from an ungrouped distribution is 36. Rationale: Add all numbers and divide by 40.

e. 36. Rationale: $1,430/40 = 35.75$ (correct to the nearest whole number)

f. 172.5. Rationale: $6,900/0 = 172.5$

g. 13.13. Rationale: $= 13.13$

Class Intervals	Frequency (f)	Midpoint (Mp)	Mp × f
11–15	2	13	26
16–20	4	18	72
21–25	6	23	138
26–30	3	28	84
31–35	4	33	132
36–40	5	38	190
41–45	5	43	215
46–50	5	48	240
51–55	3	53	159
56–60	3	58	174
Total	**40**		**1,430**

7. a. Mode is 66. Rationale: See definition of mode.
   b. Median is 66. Rationale: See definition of median.
   c. Mean from the ungrouped distribution is 65.77. Rationale: See definition of mean.
   d. Mean from a grouped distribution is 66.33. Rationale: $1,990/30 = 66.33$
   e. Variance is 91.33. Rationale: $2,740/30 = 91.33$ (see table)
   f. SD is 9.64. Rationale: $2,785.83/30 = 92.86$ and $\sqrt{91.33} = 9.56$ (see table)

Class Intervals	Frequency (f)	Midpoint (Mp)	Mp × f		$x - \mu =$		$x - \mu^2$ (f)	
45–49	1	47.5	47.5	47.5	65.77	−18.27	333.79(1)	333.79
50–54	1	53.5	53.5	53.5	65.77	−12.27	150.55(1)	150.55
55–59	6	57.5	45	57.5	65.77	−8.27	63.4(6)	410.36
60–64	5	63.5	317.5	63.5	65.77	−2.27	5.15(5)	25.76
65–69	7	75.5	528.5	75.5	65.77	9.73	94.67(7)	662.71
70–74	5	73.5	367.5	73.5	65.77	7.73	59.75(5)	298.76
75–79	2	77.5	155	77.5	65.77	11.73	137.59(2)	275.19
80–84	2	83.5	167	83.5	65.77	17.73	314.35(2)	628.71
85–89	0	87.5	0	87.5	65.77	21.73	0	0.00
90–94	1	93.5	93.5	93.5	65.77	27.73	768.95(1)	768.95
Total	**30**		**2,075**					**2,785.83**

9. a. Mode is 1. Rationale: See definition of mode.
   b. Median is 6. Rationale: See definition of median.
   c. Mean from the ungrouped distribution is 7. Rationale: See definition of mean.
   d. Variance from the ungrouped distribution is 26.33. Rationale: 1,580/60 = 26.33
   e. Standard deviation from the ungrouped distribution is 5.13. Rationale: $\sqrt{26.33}$
   f. It is skewed to the right. Rationale: See definition of skewed curves.

CHAPTER 12 Organizing Data for Analysis

1. Construct a qualitative frequency distribution and include a frequency column, relative frequency column, and frequency percentage column. Rationale: See frequency distribution for qualitative data.

Relative Frequency and Percentage Frequency
Surgical Technology Student Survey

Rating	Relative Frequency	Frequency Percentage
Very	8/20 = 0.40	0.40 (100) = 40%
Moderately	6/20 = 0.30	0.30 (100) = 30%
Slightly	4/20 = 0.20	0.20 (100) = 20%
Not at all	2/20 = 0.10	0.10 (100) = 10%

3. a. (85 − 20)/5 = 30. Rationale: Divide the range by the class size provided.
   b. (50 − 8)/3 = 14. Rationale: Divide the range by the class size provided.
   c. (113 − 43)/7 = 10. Rationale: Divide the range by the class size provided.
   d. (160 − 131)/2 = 14.5. Rationale: Divide the range by the class size provided.

5. a.

Number of Tests	Frequency	Cumulative Frequency
0–2	3	100
3–5	9	91
6–8	8	83
9–11	8	75
12–14	6	69
15–17	5	64
18–20	2	62
21–23	2	60
24–26	1	59
27–29	1	58
30–32	1	57
33–35	0	57
36–38	1	56
39–41	0	56
42–44	1	55

b. 12.02. Rationale: See definition of average.

7. Rationale: Range is 442 − 58 = 384. 384/25 = 15.36 or 16 scores per interval.

Blood Glucose Levels	Blood Glucose Levels
58–73	266–281
74–89	282–297
90–105	298–313
106–121	314–329
122–137	330–345
138–153	346–361
154–169	362–377
170–185	378–393
186–201	394–409
202–217	410–425
218–233	426–441
234–249	442–457
250–265	

9. a. Range is 133. Rationale: 291 − 158 = 133
   b. 14. Rationale: 133/10 = 13.3
   c.

Serum Cholesterol	Frequency
150–159	1
160–169	1
170–179	2
180–189	2
190–199	2
200–209	3
210–219	4
220–229	8
230–239	10
240–249	6
250–259	4
260–269	3
270–279	2
280–289	2

d.

Serum Cholesterol	Frequency	Cumulative Frequency
150–159	1	100
160–169	1	99
170–179	2	98
180–189	2	96
190–199	2	94
200–209	3	91
210–219	4	87
220–229	8	79
230–239	10	69

Serum Cholesterol	Frequency	Cumulative Frequency
240–249	6	63
250–259	4	59
260–269	3	56
270–279	2	54
280–289	2	52

11. a. N = 75. Rationale: See definition of N.
    b.

Days of Hospitalization	Frequency	Cumulative Frequency
1–2	16	100
3–4	13	87
5–6	15	72
7–8	8	64
9–10	6	58
11–12	3	55
13–14	5	50
15–16	2	48
17–18	5	43
19–20	2	41

   c. 1) 68% of scores are greater than 7–8 days.
      2) 12% of scores are greater than 15–16 days.
   d. 1) 71st percentile. Rationale: $52 + 0.5(2)/75 \times 100 = 71$st percentile
      2) 25th percentile Rationale: $16 + 0.5(6)/75 \times 100 = 25$th percentile
13. The difference in the rankings is due to the varying numbers/segments that a distribution is broken into; percentiles have 100 segments, deciles have 10 segments, and quartiles have 4 segments.

CHAPTER 13 Displaying Data for Analysis

1. d. Histogram
3. d. Frequency polygon
5. a. The x-axis usually represents the primary variable (independent variable). Rationale: See anatomy of a chart/graph.
   b. Along the y-axis are the values used to measure the primary variable (frequency, number of cases, cost, or other quantitative measure). Rationale: See anatomy of a chart/graph.

7.

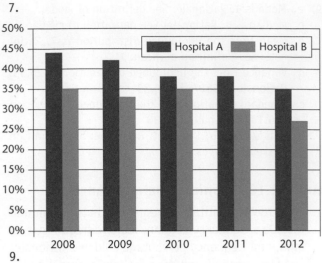

9.

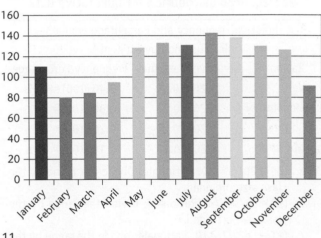

11.

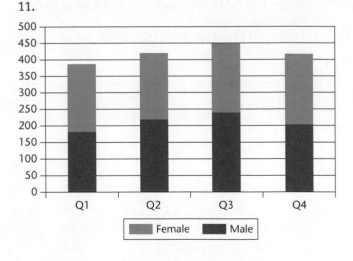

13.

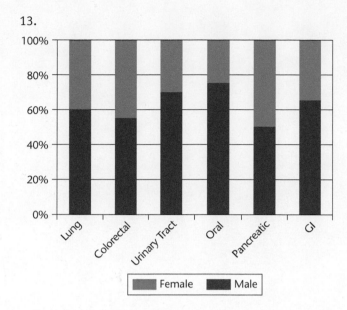

Female   Male

CHAPTER 14 Fundamentals of Research

1. a. Basic and applied
3. b. Inductive
5. d. Longitudinal
7. b. Hypothesis
9. c. Evaluation
11. e. Experimental
13. b. Systematic
15. b. Reliability
17. a. 0.05
19. e. Alternative
21. d. −1 to +1
23. Follow-up reminders
25. b

INDEX